Cubase S$_X$ & S$_L$ Complete

the musicians' guide and reference

Marc Cooper

Published by
Auxbuss Publications

Auxbuss Publications
Loweswater
Cumbria CA13 0RR
UK

Phone: +44 (0)1900 85430

email:info@auxbuss.com
http://www.auxbuss.com

First Published 2002
Cubase Sx v1.03
Copyright © Marc Cooper 2002

ISBN 1-932133-28-3

Printed in Great Britain by Antony Rowe Ltd., Chippenham, Wiltshire

This book is dedicated to everyone who makes music.

꓅ ꖐ ꖐ θ

...especially my old mate, Tim.

Preface

The seemingly ceaseless increase in power of desktop computers has lead to an ever-increasing ability for composers and songwriters, musicians, mixers and mastering engineers to perform more and more of their work inside of their computers. Indeed, it is feasible, with today's hardware and software, to wholly produce a track for release whose only tangible, touchable entity is the final CD. And truth be told, even the CD is unnecessary. Whether this is progress is moot; but it is certainly a lot of fun.

Hardware power, however, can only be harnessed by software; the gateway that enables us to exploit the number crunching, digital machinery in those whirring boxes.

Music software comes in many flavors, including: dedicated audio manipulation software; sound generation software (among its number many fine emulations of classic hardware); and sequencers. There is so much more; an almost inexhaustible supply.

Cubase Sx is a sequencer (a piece of software dedicated to the production of audio), but it takes the genre a step further, a step further even than the sequencer from which it was born: Nuendo. Cubase Sx's ability to edit and combine both audio, MIDI, video and virtual instrument, is second to none (at the time of writing). Indeed, one wonders whether its arrival prompted the withdrawal (from the PC platform) of a major competitor; Sx really is *that* good. Certainly anyone serious about music, audio-visual and multimedia production should be taking a long, hard look at Cubase Sx.

Cubase Sx Complete is written for those folk looking to exploit the wealth of features to be found in Cubase Sx for creating music. It takes you all the way from song writing, composition and arrangement, through recording and editing, to the production of a 2-Track master. (Cubase Sx is also Surround Sound enabled, and this is covered briefly in the text.) The book describes the techniques for using Cubase Sx in a studio production environment. A basic familiarity with sequencers and their fundamental operations is assumed. My hope is that *Cubase Sx Complete* can be used as a reference, as well as a guide. To this end, it has a generous index, special indexes based on Sx's commands and a huge amount of cross-referencing within the text.

There are many definitions required to complete a book such as this, and I felt that putting these directly inline with the text would, for the most part, be inappropriate. Equally, I understand, from my own experience, how difficult it can be to grasp the various concepts and, in particular, how they interrelate.

Cubase Sx Complete   v

So, as well as a glossary, I have endeavored to cover the essentials of digital, audio and MIDI recording theory and technique in the text. There are many specialist books on any one sub-topic of these fields, so much of the text is concise, and further investigation might be necessary to fully explore a point of specific interest. I hope, however, that someone coming cold to Cubase Sx, and audio software, will find enough here to enable them to grasp the fundamentals of digital audio. However, I felt that those who chose to own Cubase Sx would be familiar with much of this content, and would rather just get right down to it. I know I would!

All errors and omissions are mine. Please be liberal with comments and suggestions (and any mistakes you find), and send them to me via the email given below. Support questions regarding Cubase Sx should be posted to the Steinberg support boards at

`http://forum.cubase.net`

I'll see you there.

Enjoy.
Marc
`marc@sxcomplete.com`

Contents

1 Overview

Cubase Sx is a Windows and Mac OSX computer software program for the recording, editing and play back of audio, video, MIDI and VSTi's. This type of program is generally called a sequencer. The technology has advanced to such a degree, however, that what we in fact have in Cubase Sx is a virtual recording studio. Cubase Sx also has integrated surround sound features, and it can import and playback video.

A large array of file and project formats can be imported into and exported from Cubase Sx, including REX and REX 2 files, and the popular MP3 and Real Audio formats.

One of Cubase Sx's significant features is the ability to be able to perform almost all tasks from the main Project window. This, combined with an audio editing approach that enables totally non-destructive audio editing with unlimited undos, provides a truly flexible and creative environment for music production. Furthermore, full automation can be applied to almost every function, both in visual and list formats. It is possible to have multiple Cubase Sx projects open at the same time, and items can be dragged from one to the other.

Audio processing of any plug-in effect (both VST and DirectX) or the in-built Cubase Sx processes can be applied immediately to any audio event. Not only that, but one is able to preview the result in real-time while adjusting to taste. The supplied processes include fully integrated audio time stretching (see page 95 and 229).

Almost all functions have keystroke equivalents, and these are fully user configurable. (See appendix B for a complete list of available functions.)

Cubase Sx provides the user with, theoretically, unlimited audio and MIDI Tracks. In reality these will be limited by the processing power of the computer in use, since the CPU of the computer performs all audio processing (so-called *native processing*). However, external effects processors, such as Universal Audio's UAD-1, allow you to off-load the processing of plug-in effects, not only freeing the host processor, but also providing extremely high quality processing.

Each audio Track (which can be mono or stereo) has the following features, all of which operate in real-time:

- Volume, Pan, Mute and Solo
- 8 Aux (or Send) effects buses (that can also be routed to groups). Sends can be pre or post fader, and are provided with individual and Track bypass switches.
- 4-band parametric EQ with user-definable presets

Fig. 1.1: Channel Settings – Available for each track

- 8 Insert buses with individual and Track bypass switches.
- Full automation of all Track items
- Monitoring

Cubase Sx supports VST and DirectX plug-in architectures for effects and audio processing; a number of VST plug-ins are supplied with the package (see appendix A, page 315). Cubase Sx also comes supplied with a number of in-built processes. These include time stretching, phase-reversal, audio stamping, and more (see chapter 16, page 219). VST plug-ins can be controlled via automation (see chapter 18, page 257)

VST instruments (VSTi) are fully supported, allowing automation of all parameters that a VSTi makes available. A number of VSTi's are supplied with Cubase Sx (see appendix A, page 315)

Audio mixdown can be performed to produce many common file types, using a variety of encoding methods (see chapter 17, page 231). Audio file resolutions from 16-bit, 24-bit and 32-bit float are available, as are sample rates of 11kHz to 48kHz. UV22 HR dither is supplied as standard (as a plug-in).

MIDI input and output is available on all installed MIDI ports. Cubase Sx introduces MIDI insert and send plug-ins, and fourteen such effects are provided as standard (see appendix A, page 315).

S_L *SL Info*

S_L is supplied with UV22 dithering plug-in instead of UV22 HR. UV22 can only produce 16-bit output.

Basic Requirements

Cubase Sx is supported on:

○ Windows 2000 and XP, and Apple Mac OSX.
From version 1.02 onward, Cubase Sx is available on Windows 98. However, the Windows 98 version of Cubase Sx is currently unsupported by Steinberg.

♪   **Note**

A USB port must be available for use by the Cubase Sₓ dongle. Cubase Sₓ will
not run without the dongle installed at all times.

Cubase Sₓ versions, and OS support, will change at intervals, and the latest
information can be found at `http://www.steinberg.net/`

Steinberg's recommended *minimum* PC specification is:

▷ 500MHz Pentium III (or AMD equivalent)
   Recommended: 1Gb Dual Pentium III (or AMD equivalent)
▷ 256Mb RAM
   Recommended: 512 Mb RAM
▷ Hard disk (the bigger and faster the better)
▷ A wheel mouse (this is an important item for moving around the Project Win-
   dow, see page 11) and the fine adjustment of many on-screen values (see
   page 9).
▷ A appropriate computer soundcard (see below)
▷ A MIDI computer interface (see below)
   (MIDI use is optional, but will be a requirement for almost every user.)

To be able to use Cubase Sₓ, you will require an audio soundcard. There are
many suitable soundcards on the market, and these are being added to all the
time. You should investigate the one that is most appropriate to you based on
your studio set-up and particular computer. Nevertheless, your soundcard must
meet the following minimum specification.

○ Stereo record and playback
○ 16-bit
○ 44.1kHz sample rate
○ ASIO (Audio Stream Input Output), DirectSound or Windows MME driver
   (many cards have all three types of driver). See the following section for
   a discussion on software drivers.

ASIO drivers will provide the best performance and should be regarded essential when using Cubase Sₓ.
   Furthermore, it is highly recommended that your soundcard should provide
ASIO Direct Monitoring. This becomes important, in particular, when you wish
to perform overdubs (punch-ins) in real-time. See chapter 14, page 171 for an
example of using ASIO Direct Monitoring.
   If you wish to record and playback MIDI then you will need a MIDI enabled
keyboard (or another MIDI input device, such as a wind controller), and a MIDI
interface for your computer. MIDI playback can be routed to VST instruments
(VSTi) within Cubase Sₓ or through Cubase Sₓ to an external MIDI enabled
device, such as a synthesizer.
   To complete your studio set-up you will also need appropriate audio reproduction equipment including:

○ Speakers
○ Amplification (possibly via a hardware mixer)
○ Appropriate cables

Quick 101 on Audio Hardware and Drivers

It is not vitally important that you read this section, nor understand it. It might be useful background to some, and of assistance should you run into a soundcard related problem. For others it will probably be a great cure for insomnia. It's a bit of a geeky section, and the simple message is to pair up Cubase Sx with a soundcard with native ASIO drivers.

For an audio program to be able to communicate with an item of audio hardware, a special piece of software is required. This software is called a driver. The manufacturer writes the drivers for each piece of hardware.

These drivers are *specific* to the external device that they are written for (e.g. a soundcard), but *general* for the programs that can use them. In other words, a particular soundcard will not have one driver for Cubase Sx, another for Sonar, another for Logic, and so on. There will be just the one driver. Also, because of the "low-level" nature of a driver, they will frequently be operating system dependent; certainly a different driver will be required for a Mac than for Windows, for example. It may also be the case that a particular version of one of these operating systems requires a specific driver. So, when purchasing a new soundcard, it is imperative that you ensure that a driver exists to allow you to use it with the target system.

Since many different programs will want to use the driver to communicate with the soundcard, a further requirement is that the interface to the driver must be well-defined and published, so that the software developers of an audio program can use it.

To further complicate matters, there are a number of different ways in which the driver can communicate with the hardware. A hardware manufacturer may not provide drivers that support all of these formats. You need to be aware of these different formats because they will often provide different levels of functionality and, most importantly, the latency (delay) associated with different drivers can vary dramatically.

In the case of Cubase Sx you will, almost certainly, want to use an ASIO driver. Furthermore, always ensure that you are using the latest available drivers.

Figure 1.2 shows Cubase Sx's Device Set-up dialogue with the ASIO Driver dropdown showing. This machine has an RME Hammerfall soundcard installed. The top entry is for the "native" ASIO driver provided by the card's manufacturer. The other two entries are Cubase Sx's drivers for accessing the manufacturers' drivers, supplied for both DirectX and Windows Multimedia.

When you make your driver selection, you should be aiming for the top of the list and choose the native ASIO driver.

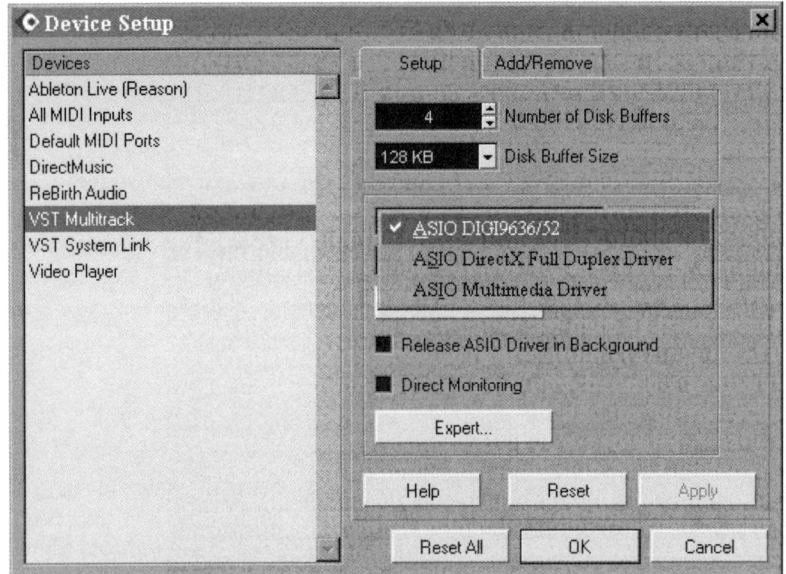

Fig. 1.2: Device Set-up dialog showing the available soundcard drivers

Drivers for audio hardware come in three major flavors, all of which are supported by Cubase Sχ. They are described in the following sections.

ASIO

This is Steinberg's own soundcard driver format, and most hardware manufacturers support it on their soundcards. There are also many non-Steinberg software applications that support ASIO. It would be most unusual, nowadays, for a soundcard to be released without an ASIO driver being available for it. An ASIO driver allows direct communication between Cubase Sχ and the audio card, with minimal intervention from the operating system. As a result, these drivers can provide lower latency (see chapter 20, page 281). The ASIO specification also provides facilities for hardware manufacturers to exploit other functionality that can be useful in an audio environment (e.g. ASIO Direct Monitoring and sample accurate synchronization).

DirectX

DirectX is a complex software environment developed by Microsoft that provides flexible use of a vast range of functions with Multimedia under Windows. DirectX is divided into a number of different areas of functionality, such as DirectDraw and DirectPlay, but the part that Cubase Sχ supports is called DirectSound. DirectSound is used for the playback and recording of audio.

When using DirectX with Cubase Sχ, Steinberg have provided a further "layer" of software that is dedicated to interfacing with DirectSound. This is called the *ASIO DirectX Full Duplex driver* and it is installed along with Cubase Sχ. So, to use DirectX (DirectSound) you will need a DirectX driver for the audio card to be provided by the soundcard manufacturer. Be aware that not all soundcards support DirectX.

The difference between the ASIO DirectX Driver and the ASIO DirectX Full Duplex Driver is simply that the former does not support the recording of audio. To be able to take full advantage of the DirectX Full Duplex mode, your soundcard must support the Microsoft Windows Driver Model (WDM) and DirectX version 6.1 or higher. In all other cases, the audio inputs will be emulated by DirectX. Emulated inputs result in much higher latency, since the emulation takes place in software. These drivers also use a lot more CPU. This is a highly undesirable state of affairs all around, so it's best to use an alternative driver; preferably ASIO. You get the picture.

Windows Multimedia system
When using this driver, the soundcard will communicate with the Windows Multimedia system and this will, in turn, communicate with Cubase Sx. As with DirectX, this option requires two types of drivers: the driver installed along with Cubase Sx, and one provided by the soundcard manufacturer. On selecting the ASIO Multimedia Driver for the first time, you will be asked whether you want the configuration to self-test. You should do this, and act on any failures reported. Changes to the ASIO Multimedia set-up are performed from the Control Panel found on the Devices/ Devices Set-up/ VST Multitrack tab.

2 Introduction

The support forums, hosted by the Steinberg team, are highly recommended as a source of support information. These can be found at:

`http://forum.cubase.net/`

Conversations can get pretty esoteric, but there's almost always a helping hand ready to solve your seemingly impenetrable, unfathomable problem. And if not, well you can just nose around and pick up a few tips and ideas.

The Cubase Sx manuals and Cubase Sx's Help system (both of which can be accessed from the Cubase Sx Help menu) are useful A-Z and context sensitive references to Cubase Sx. The Help system can be useful for quick explanations on the meaning of options to many of the parameters to Cubase Sx's functions. The manuals can be usefully put to work in their electronic format in collaboration with the find functions in your PDF reader.

Conventions used in this book

References to Cubase Sx's Menu items are made in the following way: *File/ New Project*, where each division represents another level in the menu hierarchy.

References to chapter and sections are made with page numbers to assist navigating and cross-referencing within the text. For searching by topic, you can use one of the following methods:

- ○ the index at the back of the book
- ○ the *Key Commands* appendix B, page 321
- ○ the contents list at the front of the book
- ○ the glossary (page 309) for some technical definitions

Throughout the book the Cubase Sx Key Commands (shortcuts) are referenced in the following manner: *Transport Panel* [F2)] or *Browser* [CTRL+B]. These refer to the Cubase Sx default key commands (which can be changed as you wish, or by using the templates provided for Logic, Sonar and older versions of Cubase). Where a key command is available, but has no default value, the notation [No default] is used.

The *Key Commands* [No default] function can be found here *File/Key Commands*. It is advisable to set this window to a Key Command itself right way. *K* is free to be assigned, and it is the recommended option. How to do this is explained right at the start of chapter 5, page 31.

Installation Notes

Installation of Cubase Sx is covered in detail in *Cubase Sx: Getting Started Manual* in the chapters *Installation Requirements* and *Setting up Your System*. Note that the supplied dongle must only be fitted onto the computer, in the appropriate USB port, *after* installation of Cubase Sx. Audio hardware and MIDI interfaces, and all soundcard and external device drivers, should be fitted, and preferably tested, before installing Cubase Sx.

If you are unsure of how to set-up your audio and MIDI equipment, then chapter *3: Setting up your system* in *Cubase Sx: Getting Started Manual* is the place to start. Providing you are getting sound out of system, then you can proceed with the *Quick-start* chapter 3, page 13.

VST plug-ins can be accessed by Cubase Sx from two places; a dedicated folder named `Vstplugins`, directly under the Cubase Sx installation folder, and a shared folder, of the same name, that can be placed wherever you wish.

It is advisable that you keep your Cubase Sx plug-ins in the dedicated Cubase Sx plug-ins folder. This is because many of the plug-ins supplied with Cubase Sx will only work with Cubase Sx. You can then use the shared plug-ins folder for VST plug-ins that you wish to use with Cubase Sx *and* other applications. Some applications may crash if they try to use Cubase Sx's plug-ins.

There are, however, a number of VST plug-ins supplied with Cubase Sx that *will* work with other audio software, and you may wish to move these to the shared VST plug-ins folder after installation. A list of Cubase Sx plug-ins that can and cannot be shared is given in appendix A, page 315.

Please ensure that you de-fragment the disk to which you will be recording audio files, before commencing recording audio. Before installation, it is suggested that you also de-fragment the disk onto which you are going to install Cubase Sx itself.

After installing Cubase Sx, make sure that you re-boot your computer, and attach the dongle, before trying to run Cubase Sx.

Basic User Interface Features

There are many common display and interaction features between Cubase Sx's various windows. Most of these are described below.

Menus and on-screen information

Main Menus

Standard menus are always visible (e.g. File, Edit, Help). Menu items that are not relevant in the current context will be unavailable for use (grayed-out in the menu list). For example, the Score menu items will be unavailable unless you are using Score.

Dropdown Lists

Available on many screens (as shown).   Used for selecting a field value from the available options.

A dropdown list

Quick Menus

Right-click almost anywhere to obtain a quick menu of available functions and processes. The menus are context sensitive, so the Ruler quick menu will differ from the Event List quick menu, etc.

Tool Tips

Available for most screen items when you hover the mouse for a second or two. (Tool-tips can be switched off in *Preferences/ User Interface*.)

A tool-tip

Help

Hit [F1] to bring up Cubase Sχ's context-sensitive Help system. Thus, when you are in, say, the Sample Editor, the help page for the Sample Editor will be displayed. There are also Help buttons on most dialogues. This is an excellent feature providing access to most information contained in the *Cubase Sχ: Operations Manual*.

Editing and entering Values into Fields

The way that fields can be edited is influenced by *Files/Preferences/User Interface Controls* tab *Value Box/Time Control Mode*, see page 41.

There are many editing methods for fields, some of which will only apply to certain field types. For example:

○ Click a field and over-type (or edit) the entry. Press [Return] or click away from the control to complete the action. This can be useful for making rapid changes in the *Info Line*.
○ Use the mouse-wheel. Try this on the tempo field in the *Transport* [F2]. Switch off *Master* first, by the way.
○ Point at the upper or lower edge of a numerical field value (or one of the segments within it) and click the small + (increment) or − (decrement) icons that appear. This is a bit fiddly, but can be a rapid way of accurately changing a value.
○ Click on a numeric field then drag the mouse to change the value. You will need to click away from that field, or perform a keyboard operation, to complete the operation.
○ Similar to above, but hover the mouse pointer over a field then use the mouse wheel to adjust the value.

Note that if Snap is switched on, then this will be applied to most editing operations.

Notes on editing fields

There is some inconsistency in the way these functions operate, so experiment and find the best method that works for you. Most folk seem to prefer a mixture of using the mouse-wheel and entering directly from the keyboard. This section is simply to make you aware of the options and explain what might sometimes appear to be confusing behavior.

You can move through the segments (e.g. Hours, Minutes, Seconds, Frames, etc.) when editing a field by using the cursor keys, period or colon.

Format field editing varies depending on the format being edited. This is determined by the Ruler display type being used (see page 59). Note that some fields must be right-clicked to allow free-format data entry, while others must be double-clicked.

Bars + Beats (1/16th notes and ticks)

Numeric field

If you enter a value with less than four segments, then the least significant segments will be set to their lowest values. E.g. "4.2" becomes "4.2.1.0".

Frame-based (i.e. "24 fps" or "30 dfps" types)

If you enter a value with less than four segments, then the most significant segments will be set to their lowest values. E.g. "7:5" becomes "0:0:7:05".

Slider

Seconds

This is the same as Frame-based, except that the milliseconds segment is treated as if you were using a calculator. E.g. "2:50" becomes "0:0:2:500" and not "0:0:2:050"

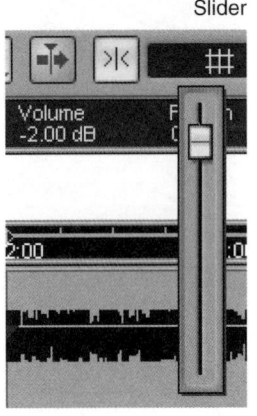

Editing Numeric Fields

For numeric values other than positions (e.g volume), you can right-click, or double-click and edit. For some values, a slider is available via ALT+Click Sliders are also available for many values in the Inspector. For these fields, a right click will usually open the field for text editing.

Knobs and Faders/Sliders

You've never seen a fader, right? Or twiddled a knob? And you've been into music for how long? The thing to know is that the behavior of knobs and sliders can be changed in *File/ Preferences/ User Interface/ Controls* tab.

Knobs have three settings: Circular, Relative Circular, and Linear. Whichever you choose to use will be very much a matter of personal preference. The Circular options are those that require a circular movement of the mouse, whereas Linear allows you to go left/right or up/down.

Sliders/Faders also have three settings (in all three cases you can grab the handle and move it): Jump, which causes the handle to move to that spot immediately; Touch, where the handle will only move when you click and drag it; Ramp, where the handle will move slowly to a spot clicked on the control.

These two options affect Cubase Sx's controls, VST plug-ins (but not DirectX plug-ins) and VSTi's, although some plug-ins and instruments may override this setting and implement their own control over knobs and faders.

Scrolling the Views

There are, of course, the standard slider controls alongside the edge of every window for horizontal and vertical scrolling. However, there are also these additional methods if you have a mouse-wheel:

Sample Editor
The mouse-wheel scrolls the audio image left to right.

Event Display, MIDI Editors and Audio Part Editor

○ If the data in the editor does *not* extend off the bottom of the display, then the mouse-wheel will scroll the Event List left to right (along the timeline).
○ If the data in the editor *does* extend off the bottom of the display, then the mouse-wheel will scroll the data items up and down. However, if you want to scroll left to right, then simultaneously hold [Shift].

Zooming

Typical Zoom Sliders

Basic horizontal and vertical zooming in and out can be performed with the zoom sliders at bottom-right of most display windows, or with the *Zoom Tool*. The default key commands for horizontal zooming are **G** and **H**. There are no defaults key commands for vertical zooming, but these can be set from the key commands editor. For more on zoom controls see chapter 6, page 57.

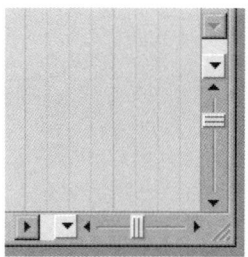

Launching Programs

The Cubase Sx installation process adds a number of shortcut items to the start menu enabling you to launch Cubase Sx and other utility programs. These are:
○ *Documentation:* Giving access to the *Cubase Sx: Getting Started Manual*, the *Cubase Sx: Operations Manual* and *Cubase Sx: Score Layout and Printing Manual*.
○ *ASIO DirectX Full Duplex Set-up:* Utility for adjusting the ASIO DirectX settings for a soundcard for audio playback and recording.
○ *ASIO Multimedia Set-up:* Utility for adjusting the ASIO Multimedia settings for a soundcard for audio recording and playback.
○ *Cubase Sx:* Gateway to infinite wealth, beauty, and sleepless nights for all the *wrong* reasons.
○ *LCC:* Not very interesting, but if you ever need it, it'll be here.

Note that the soundcard driver utilities noted above can also be launched from *Devices/ Device Set-up/ VST Multi-Track* tab then pressing the Control Panel button.

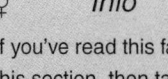 *Info*

If you've read this far in this section, then take heart, it really does get a lot more interesting from here.

3 Quick-start

For those of you who are new to Cubase S×, but familiar with other music software, this chapter is a hand-holding exercise to get you through creating your first Cubase S× Project with both audio and MIDI. It will also allow you to determine whether your equipment set-up is operating as expected.

Cubase S× is probably the easiest of the commercial sequencers with which you can get immediate results. Providing your audio and MIDI interfaces, instruments and sound reproduction gear are operating and interconnected correctly, then you can be producing sound as soon as Cubase S× loads. Well, after a few mouse-clicks.

You are going to need to switch on some sound making equipment for this chapter. And, if you are going to be using MIDI equipment, then that will be needed too. It is assumed that your gear is working and properly interconnected.

We will start with audio and move on to MIDI.

Your first Project: Audio first

Make sure that all the gear that you want to use is switched on, plugged in and correctly connected. Now let's load her up, and go and make beautiful music.

The first thing that you will see when you load Cubase S× for the first time is a big blank work-surface and the Cubase S× *Transport Panel* [F2]. Select *File/New Project* [CTRL+N] and you will be presented with a list of Templates kindly supplied during the Cubase S× installation.

We will ignore the more complex template options and select the *Empty* Template.

Cubase S× will then prompt you to select a directory for the Project Folder. For now, create a folder in a convenient location (there's a handy *Create* button to facilitate this), then highlight the folder and press OK. (For more detail on Project Folders see chapter 4, page 27.

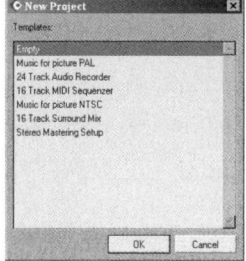

Templates choices

> ✗ **Tip**
>
> It can be useful to keep a "dummy" folder on your Desktop for unimportant experimental Projects, such as learning Cubase S×.

Fig. 3.1: The Project Window

Houston, we have a Project.

In front of you is the Project Window. We will examine the Project Window in detail in chapter 4, page 27 and you are welcome to take a quick read through the introduction of that chapter now if you wish to familiarize yourself with what is on display. For now, simply ensure that you can identify the two main work areas: the Track List to the left, and the Event Display to the right.

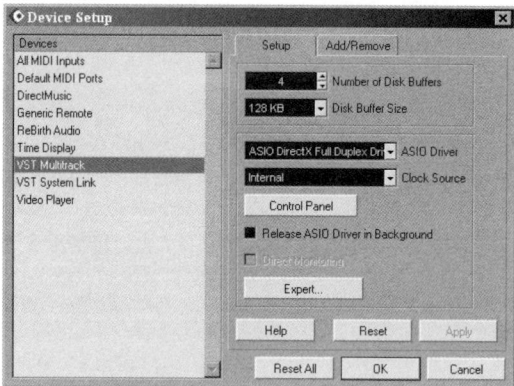

Fig. 3.2: Selecting a soundcard driver

Select an audio device

Before we do anything else it is very important that we establish that your sound-card is set-up correctly and that Cubase Sx is set to use the driver that you want to use (presuming that your soundcard has different driver types).

Go to *Devices/Device Set-up* [No Default] and select VST Multi-Track. From the ASIO Driver dropdown list select the soundcard you wish to use. You can configure the soundcard from this dialogue, should you wish, by pressing the Control Panel button.

It is very strongly recommended that you select the ASIO driver written by your hardware manufacturer and supplied with your soundcard. It is also recommended that you regularly check for the availability of updated drivers on your manufacturer's Web-site.

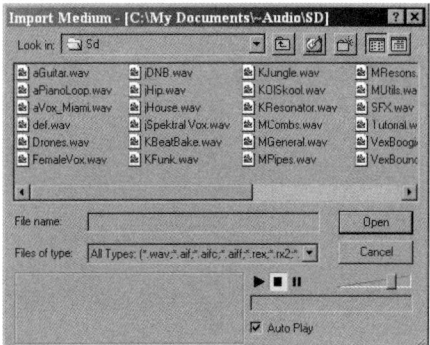
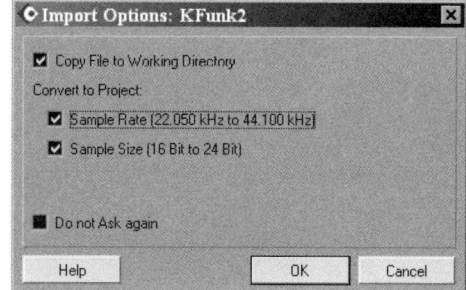

Fig. 3.3: Importing audio

Importing some audio into the Pool

Let's not get ahead of ourselves. First, let's check playback before trying to record. For this you will need to have access to an audio file on one of your disks. (If you don't have anything to hand, there are usually audio files in one of the operating system's folders. Alternatively, grab some from the Cubase SX demo projects). Open the *Pool* [CTRL+P] and press the *Import* button. Now navigate to your audio file, make sure it is highlighted, then press OK.

You will be presented with the Import Options window. Check the *Copy File to Working Directory* box and the Sample Rate and Sample Size boxes and then press OK. (The Sample Rate and Sample Size check boxes will be greyed-out if the values for the audio file match the corresponding values for the Project (see *Project Set-up Box* [SHIFT+S]). Voila, the audio file appears in the Pool.

(*Important*: If you mistakenly checked the *Do Not Ask Again* box on the Import Options window, then you should immediately reset the option by going to *Preferences/Audio* [No default] and set *On Import Audio Files* to *Open Options Dialog*. This setting is not specific to a particular Project and so you are at risk of importing audio in the wrong format if you do not make this change.)

It's actually a Clip

Of course, the audio file is not really in the Pool. Eh? What we actually have is a reference to the audio file; something that "points" to the audio file. In

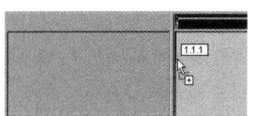

Dragging a Clip over the Event Display

After dropping the Clip

   Info

If you are feeling up too it, then you can get the detail on Clips and Events (and a few more objects) in chapter 9, page 83.

Cubase Sx this is called a *Clip*. It's important to begin to understand Cubase Sx's terminology early on, as things start to get a little more complex than this.

There are many ways of inserting our newly imported Clip into the Project. Let's start by using Cubase Sx's graphical interface and drag the Clip on to the Project Window.

Grab the Clip from the Pool and drag it over the Event Display in the Project Window. Don't worry about the marker jumping around, or the box of numbers, as you do this; just place the Clip at the left-hand edge of the Event Display.

Now it's a Track *and* an Event

As you drop the Clip onto the Event Display a new Track is created. The newly created Track will be either mono or stereo, depending on the original audio file. Cubase Sx cannot mix mono and stereo audio on the same Track, so you will have to convert any audio that is not of the correct format should you wish to include it in a Track. This can be done by right-clicking on a Clip in the Pool and choosing the *Convert files...* [No default] function (see 214).

The representation of the audio file in the Event Display is called an Event (hence Event Display). You should be able to see a visual representation of the audio waveform in the Event. If you can't, then you might have imported an empty (or very low-level) audio file. This is not much use to us right now, so make sure that the audio file has some playable content before proceeding.

You can double-click on the Event to get a close up view of your audio in the Sample Editor, if you wish. Then use *Zoom In* [H] and *Zoom Out* [G]. You can also try *Zoom/Zoom Full* [SHIFT+F] to zoom all the way out.

You might want to save the Project *File/Save* [CTRL+S] at this point.

A quick Undo and Redo

Cubase Sx's Undo feature is very powerful; one of the most powerful features in Sx. Gone are the one level undos of the past (that still exist, unfortunately, in some other sequencers). In Cubase Sx, the number of levels of undo is unlimited. It is actually bigger than that, in a sense, since Undo is contextual. In other words it is possible to Undo operations at an object level (e.g. for an Event or a Part). For example, say you printed reverb to a vocal section last week, but now you want to remove it; in Cubase Sx this is not a problem.

You will learn how to do all this later, that was just to whet your appetite. Right now press *Undo* [CTRL+Z]. The Event will disappear. Now press *Redo* [CTRL+SHIFT+Z]; the Event reappears. That is all there is to perform a simple Undo and Redo. Marvelous.

As mentioned, there is a great deal more power under the Undo hood. But we'll get to it later. (See chapter 16, page 219.)

Time to play

Make sure the Project Cursor is to the left of the Event that you wish to hear. Since our Event is at the start of the Project, then we can set the Cursor to the start position by using *Return to Start* [Pad '.' (point) or ',' (comma)]. Now *Start the Transport* [ENTER] and you should hear your audio. Rock and R-o-l-l.

When Cubase Sx is playing back audio on a Track, the Output Activity Indicators will show green level meters. These indicators are found on the right-hand edge of the Track List for each Track.

Green level indicator shows that Cubase Sx is outputting audio

Sigh...No sound!

If you don't hear anything, then it's basic diagnostic time.

There are many reasons that could be the cause of why you aren't getting any sound. And right now that is the foremost thing on your mind, so it's a big deal. First things first: chill. Cubase Sx does work, trust me, so the problem is sitting right in front of you and we need to find it. It's not possible to provide a list of all of the possible causes here (that would be another book), but below is a guide to help with the diagnostics.

The most probable sources of the problem are:

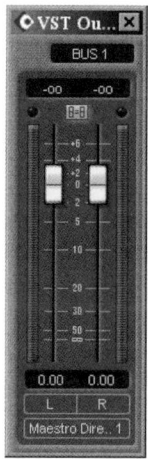

A VST Output fader

- Audio file
- Cubase Sx audio chain incorrectly set
- Wrong soundcard driver selected
- Soundcard driver corrupt/inoperative
- Soundcard audio chain incorrectly set
- Post soundcard audio incorrectly routed

Start by ensuing that the Output Activity Indicators are showing active - jumping green bars when audio is playing. If they aren't, then check that the Track is not muted. A Track is muted when the **X** button for the Track is active, when it will be yellow; when off it is gray. Next check that the Track level is not fully attenuated by opening the *Track Mixer* [F3]. If this still doesn't work, then create another Track by dragging the Clip across from the Pool again. Make sure you create another Track when doing this. If the meters are still not registering when you hit Play, then check that the audio file is not empty. (It is possible that the file contains sub or ultrasonic audio and for the Output Activity Indicators to light, but let's ignore this eventuality.)

If the Output Activity Indicators are showing green, then the problem is a routing problem. Check that you have not selected the wrong soundcard driver, and that you've wired and routed your external audio correctly. Check your soundcard output by using it with another audio application. If it works using another ASIO audio application, then it will work with Cubase Sx.

Show Master Button from the Track Mixer

Next check that the *VST Outputs* [F4] are set to 0dB ([CTRL+Click] on the fader to reset it). Also check that the *Master* section on the *Track Mixer* [F3] is set to 0dB (you will need to switch this on by pressing the Show Master button found bottom left of the VST mixer). There is no reason for this to happen, but it's worth a check.

If you're still not going, you will need more help. A cup of coffee and a ten minute break usually does the trick.

The Sound of Music

Presuming all is well, then congratulations. You can wear your Cubase S$_X$ User's Badge with pride. Maybe even a bumper sticker. Perhaps both. Coz there ain't no stopping you now.

Performance, performance, performance

Just as a quick aside, press [F12]. This is the Performance monitor. It gives you approximate readings on the current disk and CPU usage. If the meters ever move across to the right-hand side and light the red "over" indicators, you will need to reduce the stress levels on you computer. Usually when this happens you hear it as audio glitches. Suggestions on how to reduce CPU an disk usage are littered through this book, but obvious causes are: the use of processor intensive plug-ins or VSTi's; a large Track count; a large number of plug-ins or, perhaps, recording to or playing back audio from the same physical disk on which Cubase S$_X$ is loaded.

If you [right-click] on the meters you will find an *Always on Top option*. Keep this in mind, as many 'floating' windows in Cubase S$_X$ have this option available, and it might come in handy when organizing your window layouts.

Basic Audio Recording

We'll now go through the outline procedure for recording a mono signal coming into Cubase S$_X$ from a soundcard. It is assumed that the audio connections to the soundcard are operational and correctly configured. Please test this with another program before trying Cubase S$_X$. Or be brave and fearless, and try it in Cubase S$_X$.

Making the connection

Decide what it is that you are going to record and make the appropriate attachments to the soundcard. Now open the *VST Inputs* [F5]. This window shows a list of all the available input ports for the soundcard that you selected on the *Device Set-up/VST Multitrack* screen. Make sure that the button is lit for the input port that you wish to use. The routing to this port will vary depending on the soundcard you have. Please refer to the soundcard's documentation if input signal routing is not obvious.

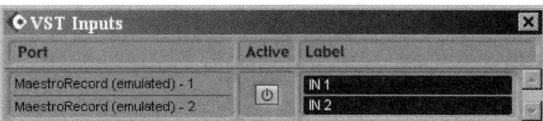

Fig. 3.4: A VST Input

Select an Input Port

Create a new Audio Track by right-clicking in the Track List and selecting *Add Audio Track*. (You can set a key command for this action if you are feeling adventurous. ALT+A is free.) By default a mono Track is created, we'll change this in a second should you require a stereo Track.

There are quite a few ways to select an input port for a Track, but let's do it by way of one of Sx's great innovations, the *Inspector* [ALT+I]. Once open, when you select a Track in the Track List (but not an Event), the Inspector will provide a wealth of information on the selected Track and a veritable host of editing options (more later).

Before selecting the input source, you need to select whether you wish the Track to be stereo or mono. Audio Tracks are created in mono by default. If you want to change the Track to stereo then hit the Stereo/Mono button for the Track in the Inspector. For mono the button is 'off' and shows a small circle; for stereo it's 'on' and shows two interlocking circles.

Now locate the dropdown labeled *in :* in the Inspector and click the downward pointing arrow. A dropdown will appear from which you can select the input you wish to use. This action routes the soundcard's physical input port (or ports) to an audio Channel (either stereo or mono) that can then be recorded on an Audio Track. (There is nothing to stop you assigning the same audio input to multiple channels, if you wish.)

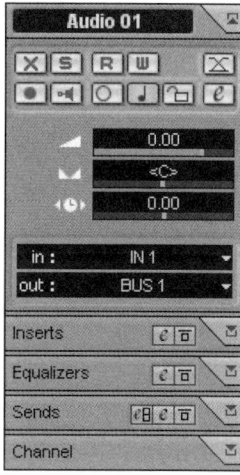

The Inspector

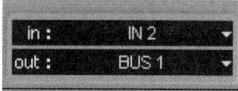

Input selector

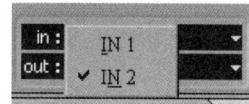

Available input ports

Checking the input level

We are now in a position to monitor the incoming level of the audio. This is often necessary to ensure that the level of the incoming signal is neither too low, nor too high. Click the button that looks a bit like a loudspeaker. You can find it both in the Inspector and on the Track (where it's immediately below the Track name). This switches the visual level indicator from showing the output level, to showing the input level.

Make some noise. By sending your audio source to the appropriate sound-card input port, you should see the level indicator show a reading.

We can now adjust the level of the incoming source signal to an appropriate level for recording. If you click the Channel tab on the Inspector, then the main audio page will close and the Channel tab will open. The channel fader does not alter the level of the incoming signal, however; this must be done outside of Cubase Sx. It is important that the signal does not clip; this is shown when the channel meter turns red. This can be checked visually by reading the numerical

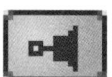

Monitor button

value above the channel strip fader. If it ever reads zero, then lower the level of your input source in some way.

Arm a Track for recording

To arm the Track click on the *Record Enable* [R] button marked • in the Track list or Inspector. The button will turn red.

Recording audio

Let's get down to it. Display the *Transport* [F2]. Make sure the Cursor is in the position that you wish to start recording. Moving the Cursor can be achieved in a variety of ways, but for now just click in the Ruler, which is just above the Event Display. This will move the Cursor to the spot that you clicked.

The Ruler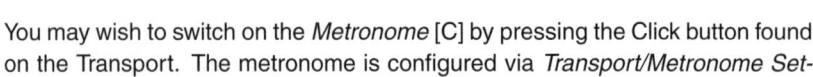

You may wish to switch on the *Metronome* [C] by pressing the Click button found on the Transport. The metronome is configured via *Transport/Metronome Set-up* [No Default] (see page 71).

Make sure that the buttons on the left-hand side of the Transport (Punch-in, Cycle and Punch-out) are all switched off. Also ensure that the Sync button on the Transport is off.

> ♫   *Note*
>
> When a Track is selected (indicated by a bright color in the Track List), then you can use *Arm for recording* [R], *Solo* [S] and *Mute* [M].

When you are ready, press the Record button on the Transport [Pad *]. If you switched on the metronome then you might get a pre-count with appropriate beeps. The Cursor will then start to move across the Event Display and an ever-enlarging rectangle will appear on the Track that represents the recording in progress. Make some more noise. When you are finished, press *Stop* [Pad 0]. You can now playback your masterpiece, and the world will tremble...with anticipation, of course.

If you have the *Preferences/Transport* entry *Return to Start Position on Stop* checked, then the Cursor will have automatically returned to the start of the Project. If you have switched this option off, then the easiest way to get back to the start of the Audio Event you have just recorded is to select the Event by clicking on it (with the default Select Tool), and press L (Locate Selection key command). If you just want to go back to the start of the Project then *Return to Zero* [, (comma) or Pad . (point)] will do the job.

To start playback, simply press [Space] or ENTER.

Audio recording and playback: Summary

At this point you should be happily recording and importing audio into Cubase Sx for playback. In going through this process you have been exposed to a large number of Cubase Sx's features. You will also have noted that there is a lot more to explore and experiment within this tool.

Depending on your specific requirements you are free to leap off and explore at your leisure. But before you go, be advised to investigate Cubase Sx's key commands at the earliest opportunity. There is a brief list of the basic key commands at the end of this chapter.

An aside on resizing Tracks

At this point, I think that it's worth exploring how Tracks can be resized in the Project Window.

The most basic way is to grab the bottom edge of the Track in the Track List and drag it in the required direction. If you do this to the audio and MIDI Tracks that we have created you will discover a bunch of buttons and dropdowns. All of these are duplicated in the *Inspector* [ALT+I], but to save screen real estate you may wish to work with the Inspector closed and use these buttons and hopefully, in time, Key Commands.

If you take a look at Appendix B *Key Commands* (page 321), in the *Zoom* section you will find some useful commands. For much more on zooming see page 57.

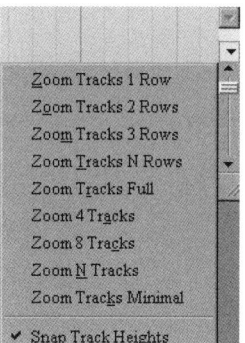

To zoom selected Tracks without affecting the other Tracks use *Zoom In and Out Tracks* [ALT+Up] and [ALT+Down]

To zoom selected Tracks and 'minimize' *all* of the other Tracks use *Zoom Tracks Exclusive* [Z] or [CTRL+Down].

To zoom *all* Tracks together use the zoom sliders at the bottom right of the Event Display. This method will retain the Tracks' relative height. You can also [CTRL+Drag] a Track border, which will resize all Tracks. Finally you can use *Zoom In Vertical* [No Default] and *Zoom In Horizontal* [No Default] to do this, but you will first have to assign key commands to them.

Also try out the Track Scale popup options. This is hidden away as a downward pointing arrow down by the Zoom sliders at bottom right. The *Snap Track Heights* option hidden away here is useful to keep Track heights to workable sizes.

Notice that you can zoom the contents of Parts and Events with the slider at the top right hand corner of the Event display. This affects all Tracks at the same time.

I'm not particularly keen on the keystrokes assigned to the zoom functions. In part this is because there is no *Undo Zoom* command. It is all too easy to, say, hit the **Z** key and upset a carefully laid out Project Window. Further more, unlike Nuendo, track height and timeline positions settings cannot be stored with a Window Layout (see page 43), so you cannot set-up preferred Track height zoom settings for instant recall.

For those superstar Sxers interested in MIDI, here we go...

MIDI input and recording

I'm sure that you are dying to start fiddling with all the audio options that you have stumbled across, but we have work to do.

You'll need a MIDI keyboard (or another type of MIDI note generator) and a MIDI sound module (e.g. synth) for this section, so make sure that they're set-up correctly. Check that you are getting sound from the module by plugging the keyboard directly into the sound module's MIDI In port before you begin with Cubase Sx.

Track List add options

Now trundle over to the Track List and right-click in the space below the audio Track created above. You'll see a whole bunch of 'Add' options. Select *Add MIDI Track* [No Default] and gaze in wonder as a MIDI Track is created before your eyes. There are plenty more where that came from.

If you've not discovered Cubase Sx's right-click options until now, then spend a few moments right-clicking on things...plenty to explore, huh?

You might feel like renaming the MIDI Track. To do this either click on the current name (it should be MIDI 01) in the Inspector (or double-click in the Track List), then edit or retype the name.

Don't forget to *Save* [CTRL+S] your Project periodically, by the way.

Back to MIDI input

By default, Cubase Sx creates new MIDI Tracks with the input set to *All MIDI Inputs*. Rather than using the *All MIDI Inputs* option here, click the Input dropdown list in the Inspector and select the MIDI port that your keyboard is attached to. (Note that you don't need to click directly on the tiny little arrow to see the dropdown list, you can click anywhere in the box. This applies generally in Cubase Sx, so try not to get in the habit of forcing yourself to click the arrows.) Most importantly, arm the Track by clicking on the *Record Enable* [R] button marked ● in the Track list or Inspector. The button will turn red.

In the same way as an audio Track, when a MIDI Track is selected, then you can press R on the keyboard to arm a Track for recording. Similarly, you can use S for Solo and M for Mute.

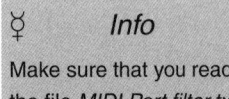

Activity indicator

Now play a few notes on your MIDI input device. If Cubase Sx is receiving MIDI then the *Output Activity Indicators* will respond by lighting. The indicators respond to MIDI velocity, so the harder you hit the keys, the higher the bars will jump.

If you are not getting activity on the indicator then there is a connection problem somewhere, or a problem with your MIDI interface set-up. You will need to diagnose this before you can use your keyboard with Cubase Sx.

Switch on MIDI Thru

By default MIDI Thru will be switched on, but before we continue let's just check. Open the *Preferences* MIDI tab and ensure that the second entry *MIDI Thru Active* is checked.

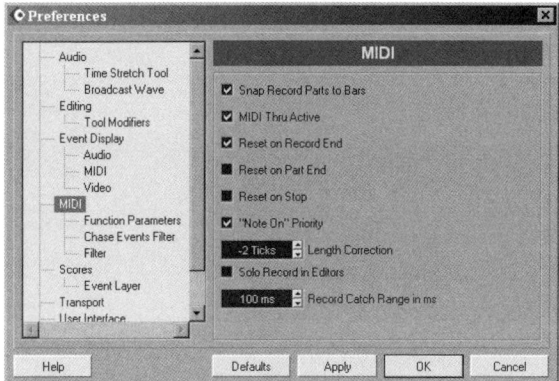

MIDI Preferences

When *MIDI Thru* is active, any incoming MIDI data on a Track will be routed to the Track's output, provided it is either *Record Enabled* or the Monitor button is active.

Set the output MIDI Port

Unless you have earlier amended the default MIDI output port via *Devices/Device Set-up/Default MIDI Ports*, then the MIDI output field will show *Not Connected*. In the same way that you did for the MIDI input port, click on the MIDI output dropdown and make your selection. The list of available ports will depend on your set-up. Also select the appropriate MIDI channel from the numbered drop-down just below. Note that this is the *output* MIDI channel that you wish to use, and not the input MIDI channel. The channel setting will default to 1 for the first MIDI Track created, 2 for the second, 3 for the third and so on.

Getting sound via MIDI

Now play a few notes on your keyboard and, presuming everything is switched on and correctly routed, you will hear your synth module burst into glorious life.

If you hear nothing, then check the following:

○ The MIDI Track is armed (the *Record Enable* button is red or the *Monitoring* button is orange)
○ The activity indicators are lighting up when you play
○ MIDI Thru is checked in *Preferences/MIDI tab*
○ The correct channel number is selected on the Track.

  If you have selected the Any option, then the MIDI channel used will be that produced by the keyboard.

Finally, check that only the SYSEX options are checked for both Record and Thru on the *Preferences/MIDI Filter* tab. See below.

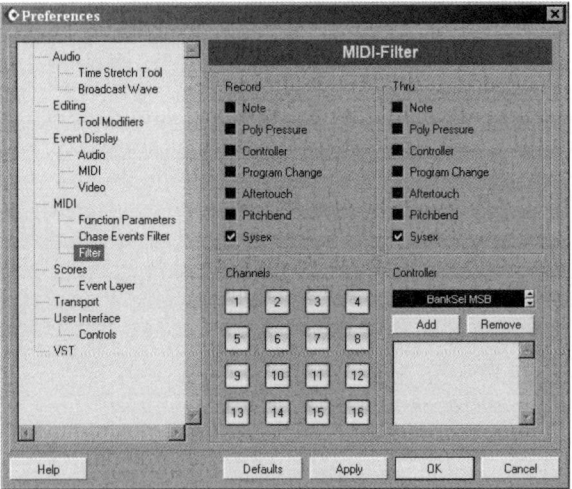

MIDI Filter

Recording MIDI

To record, first display the *Transport* [F2] and position the Cursor where you wish to start recording. You may wish to switch on the metronome by pressing the Click button in the Transport, or enable a pre-count. See the above section on recording audio for more on the metronome (or see page 71).

When you are ready, press the *Record* [Pad *] button on the Transport. The Cursor will move across the Event Display, identically to recording audio, and a similar ever-enlarging rectangle will appear on the Track representing the recording in progress. Play your heart out. And when you are about to expire from creative exhaustion, press *Stop* [Pad 0].

For MIDI recordings, Cubase S$_X$ adds the MIDI Events to the Tracks as it records, so you will already see a smattering of MIDI Events displayed in the MIDI Part.

Playback your masterpiece and revel in your genius. See the above section on recording audio for more on rewinding and playback.

Basic Default Key Commands

Key Command	Function
Ctrl + N	Create a new Project
Ctrl + O	Open an existing Project
Ctrl + W	Close the active Project
Ctrl + S	Save the active Project
Ctrl + Shift + S	Save the active Project as...
Ctrl + Alt + S	Save a new version of the Project
Shift + S	Project Set-up
1	Select Tool
3	Split Tool
5	Delete Tool
7	Mute Tool
8	Draw Tool
Ctrl + P	Open the Audio Pool
Ctrl + B	Open the Browser
Ctrl + G	Open the List Editor
Ctrl + M	Open the Markers
Ctrl + T	Open the Master/Tempo Track
Return	Open/Close Event/Part/Drum Editor
Alt + I	Show/Hide the Inspector
Ctrl + I	Show/Hide the Info Line
Alt + O	Show/Hide the Overview
Ctrl + Z	Undo
Ctrl + Shift + Z	Redo
Ctrl + X	Cut
Ctrl + C	Copy
Ctrl + V	Paste
Ctrl + D	Duplicate
Alt + X	Split at Cursor
F2	Open Transport
F3	Open VST Mixer
F4	Open VST Outputs
F5	Open VST Inputs
F6	Open Sends
F9	Previous Tool
F10	Next Tool
F11	VST Instruments
F12	System performance indicators

Key Command	Function
L	Cursor to start of selection
Pad 1 or Shift + 1	Cursor to Left Locator
Pad 2 or Shift + 2	Cursor to Right Locator
N	Cursor to next Event
B	Cursor to previous Event
Pad . (point) or , (comma)	Cursor to Project start
P	Locators to selection
Ctrl + Pad 1 or 2	Set Left/Right Locator
Space	Play
Alt + Space	Play Selection
Space or Pad 0	Stop
Pad *	Record
Pad +	Forward
Pad -	Rewind
/	Cycle/Loop toggle
C	Metronome togle
H	Zoom In
G	Zoom Out
Alt + S	Zoom to Selection
Shift + E	Zoom to Event
Shift + F	Zoom Full
Alt + Up or Down	Zoom Track In/Out
Z or Ctrl + Down	Zoom Track Exclusive
S	Solo
M	Mute
R	Record Enable
I	Punch in toggle
O	Punch out toggle

See Appendix B, page 321 for a full list of the available keyboard commands and their defaults.

4 What is a Project?

It is important to understand the way in which Cubase Sx stores a Project; that is, the directory structure it creates and uses, and where it places Project files. When you come to back-up and archive a Project (see chapter 22, page 303), or you simply want to move a Project to a new location (perhaps another disk or another computer, say via *File/Save Project to New Folder* [No Default]), you will want to ensure that nothing is misplaced. Cubase Sx makes this process straightforward. However, understanding from the outset where data is going and why, will ensure that the essential back-up processes are in order should you need to restore the Project at a later date.

Saving Projects

We have all lost work on a computer. Losing a Project is, almost without exception, a disaster. The old adage of "save, and save often" is good advice, and a highly recommended practice, but Cubase Sx does make life easy in this department.

As well as *Save* [CTRL+S] and *Save As* [CTRL+SHIFT+S], there is also the extremely useful *Save As New Version* [CTRL+ALT+S].

As you are working on a project you will probably want to save your work at various points, not only for security, but so that you might return to it later. Clearly, you do not want to overwrite a previously saved project, so the *Save As New Version* is the way to go. (Note that this does not exist as a menu option.) The result of *Save As New Version* is that Cubase Sx saves the current project as a new Project file by adding the suffix "-01" to the file name. Each subsequent Save As New Version will add 1 to the suffix. I.e. "-02", "-03", etc.

If you want to go back to the position at which the Project was last saved, then you can use *File/Revert* [No Default] to achieve this. It has the same effect as closing and re-opening the Project (without a Save).

> **S$_L$ SL Info**
>
> S$_L$ can open an S$_X$ Project, and vice versa. Conflicts due to S$_X$'s extra features are reported on loading into S$_L$.

Default.cpr

If you create, and save, a Project called `default.cpr` to the S$_X$ folder, then S$_X$ will load this automatically at startup providing you set *Preferences/User Interface* tab *On Startup* to *Open Default Project*.

The Project Folder

Project Folder structure

The Project Folder is the top-level folder for a Cubase Sx Project. It is recommended that you create a new Project Folder for each Project/Song. In fact, not doing so can make life unnecessarily difficult for you later when you want to separate a Project's audio files. It is also highly advisable to place the Project Folder on a different physical disk to that on which Cubase Sx is installed, and to that which the operating system is installed. Ensure that a different physical, and not just a different logical, disk is chosen.

It pays to be organized with your Project Folders. Many folk dedicate a entire disk to them. Another method is to create a folder called, say *Songs*, and place all your Project Folders directly under that folder. However you decide to proceed, it is easy to change later. All the files that constitute your project are stored within the Project Folder and its sub-folder (all those, that is, unless you specifically tell Cubase Sx to reference files from elsewhere).

The Project on disk

A Cubase Sx Project is contained within the Project Folder. This is the top of Cubase Sx's hierarchy of folders. You choose the location of the Project Folder when you create a *New Project* [CTRL+N].

When you create a new Project in an empty Project Folder, the only thing Cubase Sx does is create a sub-folder within it called *Audio*.

If you now *Save* [CTRL+S] the Project, then the Cubase Sx Project file is created in the Project Folder. You will have been prompted for the name of this file and the suffix .cpr will be added.

You may choose to share the same Project Folder for several Projects, but you need to take great care with file management and archiving if you do so. It is not recommended that you do this unless you are absolutely clear about the implication of any file management functions you may apply. In other words, it is very easy to mistakenly delete something in use by another Project.

Where do my audio files go?

If we import an audio file then the file will be placed in the Project's *Audio* folder. In fact, there is an option available on the Import Options screen to leave the audio file in its current location and for Cubase Sx to reference it from there. If this is done, then care must be taken that the Audio File remains in a suitable state for all the Projects that make use of it.

By keeping all of the Project's audio files in one place, in the Project's Audio folder, we are guaranteed to keep all of our audio in sync across this, and other Projects. As well as this, it makes moving and replicating the Project straightforward, and also permits easy archiving of the Project.

When the first audio file is added to the Project, a folder named *Images* is created in the Project Folder. Thereafter, whenever an audio file is imported, or

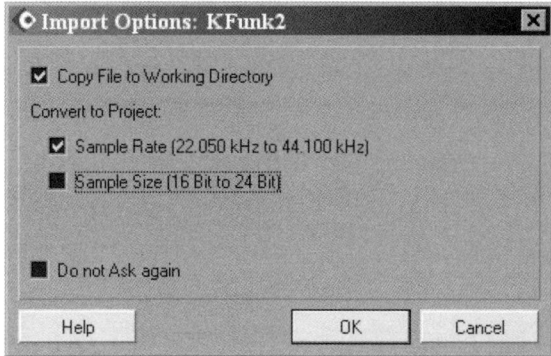

a recording is made, an image of the audio is created by Cubase Sx and placed in the *Images* folder. You will see these images in the Event Display and the Pool, for example.

Fade and edit files

When you apply a fade to an audio Event using the Fade Handles, the fade is created as a new audio file and placed in the *Fades* folder within the Project Folder. Only that part of the audio file that has the fade applied to it is copied, but this can still be of significant size. It might be worth considering an automation fade as an alternative, depending on requirements. If the fade is removed, then so is the fade's audio file.

Note, however, that the original audio file is left unchanged in the *Audio* folder. This is the key to understanding Cubase Sx's highly creative *Undo* feature.

A similar chain of events occurs when you Edit audio. The edit is created in a new audio file and placed in the `Edits` folder within the Project Folder, but only that part that has been edited is copied (with the edit applied to it).

Wrapping up

From the above, it should be clear that the *Audio* and *Edits* folders are the key storage areas for your Projects' valuable audio files. Messing with these folders can be extremely hazardous to your Project, and therefore your health. Be very careful when manually fiddling with these folders and their contents.

The best way to manage the *Audio* and *Edits* folders is via the *Pool* [CTRL+P]; this tells you what is available and what is being used. If you need to trash files, then do it from the Pool (see chapter 15, page 201).

The *Fades* and *Images* folders can be deleted and Cubase Sx will recreate the folders and files.

Cubase Sx can, under certain conditions, recreate files deleted or otherwise "lost" from the Edits folder. If this is possible, the file will be marked as "Reconstructable" in the Pool's Status column. To rebuild the file use *Pool/Reconstruct* [No Default]. You got lucky.

The cubasesx.log file

Cubase Sx records any errors that it detects during its processing in the file
cubasesx.log. This file is created at the top level of the Project Folder. The
file contains technical information about the error. A warning is placed on the
screen to inform you that an error has been detected and that the file has
been created or updated. If the file already exists then subsequent errors are
added to the file. Sometimes you are able to save your work before Cubase
Sx crashes. If you do attempt to save the current Project, then it is suggested
that you give the Project a new name rather than overwriting the latest version
of the current save (i.e. avoid using *Save* [CTRL+S] and instead use *Save As*
[CTRL+ShiftS]).

5 Important Set-up Issues

Before you start to use Cubase Sx in fury, you will probably want to set-up a few of the configurable items to work the way that you are used to working in other tools. This section doesn't cover everything, of course, but is a quick run through the things that you might want to get to early on, but don't particularly want to trawl through the manuals to find.

Basic Key Commands

Key commands are either a single keystroke, or sequences of keystrokes (e.g. CTRL+ALT+A), that can be assigned to functions within Cubase Sx. A whole bunch of these are predefined, but you are free to change these. Many functions are available for which a key command has not been defined. If you wish, you can assign a key command to these as you see fit. Key commands are essential to being able to use Cubase Sx effectively and efficiently. However, there is no default key command to open the *Key Commands* editor itself; so, go to *File/Key Commands* and open it. Now resize the Key Command editor's window. This resizing is remembered globally, so you will only have to do this once.

♪ *Note*

You can have multiple key commands for the same function.

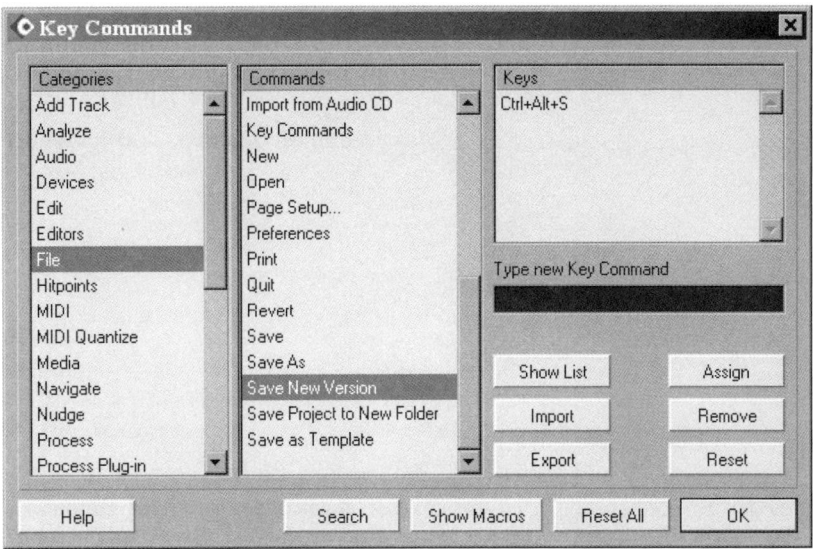

Select *File* in the Categories column and *Key Commands* from the *Commands* list. In the dark-colored *Type new Key Command* box insert *K*, then press *Assign*. Click on the OK button to close the Key Command editor. Now press [K]. You do not yet realize the amount of time that this action has saved you.

Now that you know how to assign a Key Command, it might be worth your while making yourself familiar with the assignable functions available in Cubase Sx. Almost everything is available as a Key Command, but most folk find something that is unavailable. Some functions can only be used once they have been assigned a Key Command, so do make sure you explore appendix B, page 321 at some point.

It is well worth reviewing the Key Commands available in the editor every month or so. It is easy to forget that a useful command is available. In particular, as you use Cubase Sx and develop a style of working, certain commands that might not have appeared useful at an early stage, become useful later on. Just write them down and leave them next to the keyboard; you'll use them if they are truly useful.

This is a list of Key Commands the author finds invaluable, and so creates on any new installation of Cubase Sx. In doing so, most of the Cubase Sx's default key commands are left undisturbed; this ensures that movement from one installation to another is straightforward. This list is, naturally, an individual list, since everyone will, inevitably, work in a different manner.

<table>
<tr><td>Add Track: Audio</td><td>ALT+A</td></tr>
<tr><td>Add Track: MIDI</td><td>ALT+D</td></tr>
<tr><td>Add Track: Group</td><td>ALT+G</td></tr>
<tr><td>Add Track: Folder</td><td>ALT+F</td></tr>
<tr><td>Audio: Events to Part</td><td>CTRL+ALT+P</td></tr>
<tr><td>Audio: Open Process History</td><td>ALT+H</td></tr>
<tr><td>Devices: Set-up</td><td>ALT+Z</td></tr>
<tr><td>Edit: Split at Cursor</td><td>/ (not Pad /, which is Cycle/Loop)</td></tr>
<tr><td>Edit: Zoom in Vertical</td><td>CTRL+H</td></tr>
<tr><td>Edit: Zoom out Vertical</td><td>CTRL+G</td></tr>
<tr><td colspan="2">(replacing Edit: Open List Editor which becomes ALT+L)</td></tr>
<tr><td>File: Export Audio Mixdown</td><td>ALT+B</td></tr>
<tr><td>File: Preferences</td><td>ALT+P</td></tr>
<tr><td>Nudge: Left</td><td>CTRL+SHIFT+left cursor</td></tr>
<tr><td>Nudge: Right</td><td>CTRL+SHIFT+right cursor</td></tr>
<tr><td>Transport: Restart</td><td>; (semicolon)</td></tr>
<tr><td>Transport: Sync Set-up</td><td>SHIFT+Z</td></tr>
</table>

Options are available on the Key Commands dialogue to Export, Import and Reset the Key Commands. There are also some Key Command templates provided with Cubase Sx that replicate (as close as possible) the key commands of other DAWs. You can use the *Show List* function to search for a free *Key*

Tip

When searching for a free keystroke sequence to use (or to evict), simply type into the *Type new Key Command* field. You can go through the whole alphabet very quickly.

Tip

Export your Key Commands periodically and keep them as a backup.

Command, but a better method is to type commands into the *Type new Key Command* area. When a Key Command has been used, its assigned command will be shown just below. You can type commands repeatedly, thus finding a free command through trial and error. It's a shame that the *Show List* can't sort by its columns.

Macros
Down at the bottom of the *Key Command* dialog is a button that reads: *Show Macros*. When you click it, you will, disappointingly, find nothing inside. The cupboard is bare. So, let's put a single morsel on the shelf.

♩   *Note*

The *Alt Gr* key is the same as CTRL+ALT.

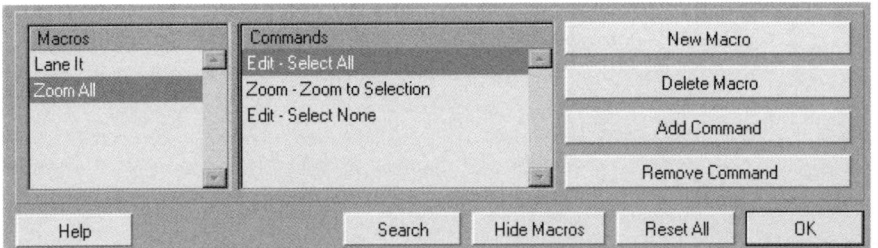

Macros are sequences of S𝗑 operations that, once created, appear in *Edit/ Macros*. Macros can themselves be assigned a Key Command. The dialog shown is probably self-explanatory but, briefly, the idea is, after clicking *New Macro*, to select commands in the Key Command dialog, then click *Add Command* for each command. In this way, you build up a sequence in the *Command* list that will be carried out when the *Macro* is run.

✗   *Tip*

Can't quite remember that key command? Use the *Search* function in the *Key Commands* dialog. Also, note that key commands are displayed in the menus.

   Try adding the *Zoom All* macro shown. When you are done adding commands, assign *Macro/Zoom All* a Key Command of your choice, then try it out in the Project Window.

   One word of caution: *Macro* commands do not necessarily wait for the previous command to complete. This can cause unexpected behavior.

Adding Some Color

It is remarkable how adding a sprinkling of color to a Project can improve its readability on screen. If you develop a consistent color scheme across you Projects, it can significantly speed up your understanding of the Project's structure when you return to it after some time.

   Tracks and Parts can be colored via the *Color Selector* shown. Automation Events cannot be colored (which is a great shame). There are seventeen colors to choose from, plus a "default" option that removes any previous color assigned.

Color selector

   You can change any of the seventeen default colors and rename them (e.g. to Drums, Bass, etc.) by clicking *Select Colors...* in the *Color Selector*. The sequence required to change a color is to select a default color box to overwrite (in the lower section), create a mind-bending color in the top section, then click *Apply*. To change a name, simply over-type one of the existing names.

If you apply color to a Track in the *Track List*, then all existing, and future, Events and Parts on that Track will take the chosen color. However, if you apply a color to a Part/Event, then it will retain that color even when moved to a Track that has been assigned a different color.

Note that *Preferences/Event Display Tab/Colorize Event Background* option can be used to swap whether the background, or the waveforms, of Events are colored.

In the *MIDI Part Editor*, it is possible to color the display by either velocity, pitch, channel, or for Events to take the Part's color. The colors can be customized for each type (except for Part, which is done as explained above). Unfortunately, the MIDI colorings are applied to the editor and not the Parts. But you can't have everything.

Templates

↗   *Tip*

Create your own *My Empty* Template with your common new Project settings.

A Template is a starter Cubase Sx Project. Every new Sx Project is created from a Template, whether you use one of the supplied Templates or the *Empty* Template.

A Template can, in fact, be a completed Cubase Sx Project. There is nothing to stop you saving audio or MIDI in a Template, although do remember that the Template will try to reference the audio files from their location at the time the Template was created. If you are organized enough to manage this then things will work just fine.

♪   *Note*

If you wish to load a default Project each time you load Cubase Sx, then see page 27.

Templates are stored as separate files in the *Templates* folder that resides beneath the Cubase Sx folder, by using *File/Save As Template* [No Default]. The files are named the same as the names that appear on the *New Project* list (with a suffix .cpr, the same as a Cubase Sx Project). There is no Template management available in Cubase Sx, so to remove a Template you must go to the folder and delete it manually. If you wish to amend a Template, then the simplest way is to load it, amend it, and then overwrite it.

Basic Preferences

☿   *Info*

If you use, say, F3 to open a window, then you can close it with F3, providing it has the focus. ESC and RETURN will close a lot of dialogs too.

Earlier, I suggested setting-up a Key Command of [ALT+P] to open the *File/Preferences* [No Default] window. You will find yourself in Preferences fairly frequently, especially in your early days with Cubase Sx, so it is recommended that you assign a Key Command of your choice.

Most of the installation defaults are fine for starters, and these are noted in the text in the appropriate place. For a reference to where preferences are noted in the text see appendix C, page 335. It is important to understand that the *Preferences* you set are global. In other words they apply from the point that you make a change, both to the current Project, and then to all Projects that you subsequently open or create. Preferences are not saved with a Project. This can be quite confusing, since some of the options could be better placed at Project level.

Audio, Timestretch and Broadcast Wave tab

On the first tab, *Audio*, it is recommended that both *On Processing Shared Clips* and *On Import Audio File* are set to *Open Options Dialog*. By keeping to these options, you will be required to make a conscious decision on each audio file import, and audio processing action, regarding precisely what you want Cubase S_X to do with the result. It is recommended that you only change these settings for bulk file operations, and then change them back immediately. Once you are settled in with Cubase S_X then you may well decided on an another setting.

Create Images During Record determines whether Cubase S_X calculates and displays the waveform images during recording. This incurs a processing overhead during recording and may affect the performance of the recording operation. Whether you check *Create Images during Record* is a personal choice. It will be dictated by the way that you work (i.e. you can't wait for images to be created after recording) or by real-time image creation eating up too much processing power during recording a particular Project. It's easy to leave this option unchecked until you find that you require it.

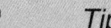

Tip

Switch off Create Images During Record to save those important CPU cycles when recording.

Snap to Zero Crossing [Not available] ensures that all audio editing is performed at 0dB points in the waveform. This will reduce clicks due to amplitude differences between two audio segments. Best to leave it on. More on this topic when discussing *Crossfades* (see page 194).

Cycle Record Mode is discussed on page 178. Leave this set to *Create Events + Regions* for now. Leave the *Use additional level scan for Hit-point detection* option checked also. This last item is a bit of a mystery. It does indeed cause an extra scan to take place during hit-point detection, but to what end? Presumably it should give better results, but I couldn't spot the difference.

Time Stretch tab

For an explanation of the *Timestretch* options see pages 95 and 229. These settings allow you to configure the time-stretch *tool* available from the Project Window. There is also a time-stretch process that these options do not affect. Put simplistically, if you believe that you are going to use time-stretch mainly for drums loops, then set *algorithm* to Drums, if you think that you'll be using it for melodic audio then set it to the MPEX algorithm. Once you start using time-stretch you'll probably want to revisit these settings. They are explained later.

Broadcast Wave tab

The settings on the Broadcast Wave tab allow you to write personal data to Broadcast Wave audio files, should you choose to use them. The type of files that you create when working with a Project are determined by the *Record File Type* in *Project Set-up* [SHIFT+S]. See page 176 for more detail.

Editing tab

These options (in the main) influence the way that the Project Window responds to some basic user actions, so it is mainly a matter of personal taste how you set them. Detailed explanations are available in Cubase Sχ *Help.*

The default options are generally fine for most folk, with perhaps a change to one or two options. If the dragging and dropping of Events seems either too fast or too slow for you, then adjust the *Drag Delay* in the appropriate direction.

For folk who like to micro-manage their automation, set the *Automation Reduction Level* to *min.* Even at this level, some Events can be automatically removed by Cubase Sχ. While this automatic reduction in automation Events feature can be useful, there have been occasions where it failed to recreate what was intended. In the absence of an *Off* switch for it, you'll have to make do with *min.*

Delete Overlap is not as dramatic as it sounds; nothing is deleted. As you will discover later, Events on the Event Display are "pointers" to the audio, so the deletion or adjustment of length to an Event is completely non destructive to any associated audio. If *Delete Overlaps* is checked, then when you drag and drop an Event so that it overlaps with another, the static Event will be shortened so that it doesn't overlap the dropped Event. If you later decide that you want to lengthen the Event, then that can be done.

Link Editors is worth a quick look. What linking editors boils down to is whether you have one *separate* editor window for every MIDI Part, Audio Part or Sample Editor, or one *shared* editor for all MIDI Parts, one for all Audio Parts and one shared Sample Editor. When using the shared editors you select an Event/Part on the Event Display to view the item in the open editor. Where this can come in very useful, other than for reducing screen clutter, is if you create a separate Window Layout for one or more of these editors. In this way you have your editor immediately available in another window, perhaps with other useful display items to hand.

Tools Modifier tab

The *Tools Modifiers* can be left as is. Indeed, you may never need to change them at all. These option affect how some Tools change behavior when another key is simultaneously held. They are explained in the *Cubase Sχ: Operations Manual* and noted in the appropriate sections.

Event Display Tab

These options concern how items on the Event Display appear. Changing some of these items can have a impact on screen refresh rates, often getting worse as the Project size grows, so take heed of the warnings below.

Ensure that Quick Zoom is switched on, since this will have a positive impact on zooming (and other screen movements) as the Project grows. *Quick zoom* switches off waveform displays when zooming at low zoom ratios (zoomed out). The effect is to stop redraws of the waveforms while zooming, thus making zooming in and out faster. As you zoom in, the waveforms will reappear and this switch has no effect. However, it is best left checked as it does improve zoom speeds overall.

Colorize Event Background determines whether Tracks that have been colored (see below) appear with a colored background or a colored waveform (or Events for MIDI and automation).

You can also make Events transparent (in their upper section), by setting *Preferences/Event Display Tab/Transparent Events*.

Show data on small track heights only affects Track sizes of one row or less, and does what it says.

For more on coloring Events and Parts, see the following section *Adding Some Color* on page 33.

Audio: Event Display tab

Interpolate Audio Images
This option applies to all editors. When the zoom level shows one sample per pixel or less, the appearance of the samples is determined by this setting.

○ No interpolation.

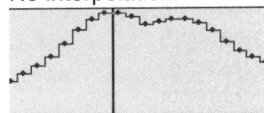

○ Interpolation

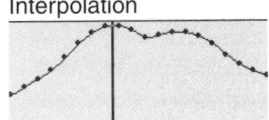

Wave Image Style (Default = Solid)
This option changes the way in which audio waveforms are displayed on the Event Display. The Choices are:

○ Solid image (default)

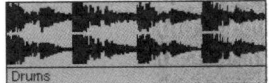

○ Frame (only the waveform outline is shown)

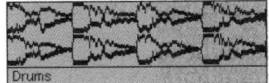

○ Inverted Image (i.e. solid and framed)

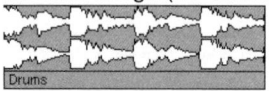

Both the Framed and Inverted Image display styles are more CPU intensive and might slowdown your system.

Show Event Volume Curves Always (Default = On)
Determines whether Event volume curves are shown for all Events or only for Events when selected. These are the blue curves displayed on the Events themselves. (You can adjust fades and volumes for unselected Events when the curves are off, but since the handles are invisible, this can be tricky. The handles are only ever shown for selected Events.)

MIDI: Event Display tab

The *Default Edit Action* determines which editor will be opened when you edit a MIDI Part (i.e. double-click, RETURN, CTRL+E). For Drum Parts, this can be overridden with the *Edit as drum when drum map assigned* option, so that the Drum Editor is always opened for Drum Parts.

Part Data Mode and *Show Controllers* are display options. The former lets you choose score notes, lines or drum notation, the latter whether MIDI control data is shown in the Part.

Note Name Style gives you various options for displaying the note information in the Info Line of the *Key Editor* [No Default], or in the *Browser* [CTRL+B], for example. *MIDI and Value* is a good start point, but if *DoReMi* is your thing, who am I to stop you.

Video: Event Display tab

Not much to say... If *Show Video Thumbnails* is checked, then thumbnail frames of a video's content are shown on the Video Track. *Video Cache Size* determines how much memory is made available for video thumbnails.

MIDI Tab

First off, *Snap Record Parts to Bars* does exactly that for both start and end points. It's best to leave this checked initially, since one tends to work with MIDI Parts in bars, making this option a logical choice.

Leave *MIDI Thru Active* checked unless you are sure you won't need it. Cubase Sx only passes thru MIDI messages on record enabled (or monitoring enabled) channels, so this is unlikely to cause any problems.

The three MIDI Reset options (on Record End, on Part End, and on Stop), will cause MIDI Reset messages to be sent on all channels. The Reset is sent to every non-muted MIDI Track. See page 114 for more.

You might want to check *"Note On" Priority.* The timing of notes is about as important as it gets in music, so by checking this option they get to ride up front. Be aware that this might impact the tonality of a patch due to a controller, or MIDI Clock, being delayed. Let your ears be the guide.

You may or may not want *Length Correction.* Consider two notes of the same pitch and on the same MIDI channel, the value of this spin control adjusts the length of the first note so that there is always a short time between the end of the first note and the start of second. A patch might have its sound affected by this parameter, so use it wisely. Be aware that it is there, and use it if you need it.

Solo Record in Editors is quite neat, and you might want to use it. If set, then when you open a MIDI Part, the corresponding Track will be record enabled exclusively (although audio Tracks will be unaffected). When you close the MIDI Part (or it loses focus), then record enable settings are returned as they were. Note that if other MIDI Tracks have monitoring active, then they will still playback any incoming MIDI data. Also note that the MIDI Track opened will still only receive incoming MIDI on its selected input port and channel.

Leave the next two tabs *Chase Events Filter* (page 148) and *Filter* (page 149) as they are for now.

Scores tabs

Best to leave these as they are until you get into *Score*.

Transport Tab

These options are described in detail in *Transport Preferences* on page 76. The default options are generally fine. However, consider checking *Locate When Clicked in Empty Space* and unchecking *Return to Start Position on Stop.* The former is useful for quickly locating the Cursor to a general area in the Project. This can often be sufficient in many cases, either on its own or quickly followed by another Transport key command. The latter is almost redundant, since the key command *Restart* [No Default] is available to perform a similar function that is sufficient in most instances.

User Interface Tab

You can run Cubase Sx in English, French, German and Spanish; select from *Language.* Switching off *Tooltips* might give you a small performance improvement, but is best left on until you are familiar with Cubase Sx's many graphic buttons that are not always as intuitive as the designer probably hoped. Leave *Maximum Undo* at ∞.

Auto Save seems like a commendable feature, but the trade-off is an unscheduled interrupt to operations periodically. This might occur in the middle of a great vocal take or similar, so you must consider the risk involved. Securing good Project backups is extremely important, but it is perhaps better to control these by using *Save New Version* [CTRL+ALT+S].

When the *Auto Save* checkbox is activated, Cubase S$_X$ will automatically save backup copies of all open Projects with unsaved changes every n minutes, where n is the value in *Auto Save Interval*. The backup files are named `<Project Name>.bak`, and are saved in the Project folder.

The same is true for Projects that have not yet been saved. In this case the backup copies are named `#UntitledX.bak` where X is an incremental number, allowing for multiple backup copies in the same Project folder.

Also on this tab is the option that determines the Project to be opened when you start-up Cubase S$_X$.

The options available in *On Start-up* are:

o *Do Nothing*: This will leave you having to make a selection from the Cubase S$_X$ menus.
o *Open Last Project*: This will cause the last saved Project to be opened
o *Open Default Project*: Open the Project file `default.npr` from the Cubase S$_X$ application folder.
o *Show Open Dialog*: Displays the *Open* [CTRL+O] dialog from which you can locate, select and open a Project.
o *Show Template Dialog (Default)*: Opens the template dialog from which you can select a dialog to create a new Project.
o *Show Open Options Dialog (Recommended)*: This option is the most flexible. This dialog will also open if you press and hold down [Ctrl] while launching Cubase S$_X$. The dialog lists the most recently used Cubase S$_X$ Projects. You can open one of these by selecting it and clicking Open Selection. To open a project not listed, click *Open Other*, when the Open dialog will be shown. Finally you can choose to create a new project from a template by clicking *New Project*.

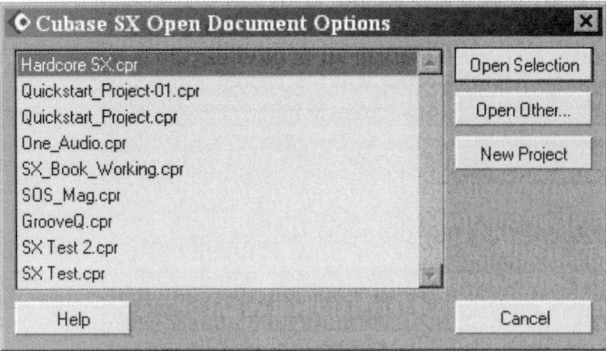

Open Options Dialog

Controls Tab (for knobs and sliders)

In many windows, most parameters are shown as knobs, sliders and buttons. For knobs and sliders, you can select the various ways in which these can be adjusted.

Knob Mode can be set to the following:

- ○ *Circular (Default)*: To move a knob, you click on it and drag it in a circular motion. You can get a finer controller of the knob by continuing to hold down the mouse-button and moving the mouse pointer away from the knob. From a distance it is easier to make small adjustments to the control. When you click inside the knob's edge, the knob will move to that position.
- ○ *Relative Circular*: Similar to Circular, but clicking inside the knob does not change the setting to that point.
- ○ *Linear*: To move a knob, click on it, hold the mouse-button down, then drag it up and down.

Slider Mode can be set to the following:

- ○ *Jump (Default)*: Clicking on a slider makes it instantly jump to that position. Be careful, since a right-click also causes the slider to move.
- ○ *Touch (Recommended)*: Here you must click on the slider handle to adjust the parameter. This significantly reduces the risk of accidentally moving a slider. Since there is no undo on the sliders in the *Track Mixer* [F3], this setting is highly recommended once you are mixing. It is far too easy to accidentally move a fader without realizing in Jump mode.
- ○ *Ramp*: By clicking on a slider, but not on the slider handle, the handle will move smoothly up or down to the position of the mouse cursor.

The options for *Value Box/Time Control Mode* deserve some experimentation to determine what method you are most comfortable with. The easiest way to try out these options is to drop an audio Event on the Event Display and select it. Make sure the Event is placed three or four bars into the Project, to allow room for manoeuvre. Switch on the *Info Line* [CTRL+I]. You can now try out the three options. Note that different field types often behave in different ways (e.g. compare *Volume* with *Start* or *Length*).

- ○ *Text input on left-click*
  When you click on a value field it will drop straight into text edit mode. Note that you can ALT+right-click on *Volume* to obtain a slider. Furthermore, you can point at the upper or lower edge of a numerical field value (or one of the segments within it) and click the small + (increment) or − (decrement) icons that appear. This is a bit fiddly, but can be a rapid way of accurately changing a value.
- ○ *Increment/Decrement on Left/Right Click*
  First, you can double-click to enter a value in text mode. Take care with the double-click, as it is easy to adjust the value by mistake with slightly incorrect timing of the clicks. A left-click will decrease a value, and a right-click will increase a value. Note that different fields behave in different ways. For example: *Volume* changes in units of ±1dB; *Length* will change in different units that depend on whether *Snap* is active and which *Display Mode* is being

used; *Start* can have each segment individually adjusted by clicking on the appropriate segment. Got all that?

o *Increment/Decrement on Left Click and Drag*
Oh boy, what a mouthful. This is, perhaps, the most useful of the modes. Here you can double-click to gain text entry. A single-click will highlight a field and then allow the value to be increased or decreased by moving the mouse up or down with the button held. As above, *Length* is affected by *Snap* and *Display Mode* settings.

VST Tab

The VST Tab provides the following options:

Scrub Response (Speed)
Sets the responsiveness of the *Scrub* function in the Project Window, Sample and Part editors.

Auto Monitoring
Monitoring is the process of listening to the incoming audio during recording. This item provides a number of different choices of how this will operate. See more about this in chapter 14, page 171.

These *Auto Monitoring* options only apply when monitoring through Cubase S$_X$, or when using ASIO Direct Monitoring. When monitoring externally through a mixer, it is best to select the *Manual* option, and ensure that the Monitor buttons for all Tracks are turned off.

The following options are available:

o *Manual:* With this option you determine which Tracks are to be monitored thru Cubase S$_X$ by switching on the Track List monitor button for each Track individually.
o *While Record Enabled:* Input monitoring only occurs for Tracks enabled for recording.
o *While Record Running:* Input monitoring only occurs for Tracks enabled for recording while recording is taking place.
o *Tape Machine Style:* Input monitoring occurs in stop mode and during recording, but does not take place during playback. This is similar in operation to how many tape machines operate.

VU-Meter Peak's Hold Time
This item allows you to vary the Peak Hold Time for the meters in the *Track Mixer* [F3]. This is only of use if the *Meter Hold* option is also switched on in the *Track Mixer*. Right-click in the *Track Mixer* to switch *Meter Hold* on and off. A value can be set between 500 and 30000 ms.

Pre-load Waves Plug-ins on Start-up
For those lucky enough to be using the Waves plug-ins, this option loads the `waveshell.dll` when Cubase S$_X$ starts. The effect is to load the names of the

Waves plug-ins into Cubase Sx so that they appear as VST plug-ins (the Waves plug-ins being DirectX). The cost for this is a small delay in the start-up time of Cubase Sx.

Window Layouts

It is quite possible to work within Cubase Sx using a single view, or *Window Layout* as they are called in Cubase Sx. Working in this way, you can simply open and close the windows you require (e.g. Pool, Browser, Track Mixer, and so on) as you need them and as you finish with them. You can also leave windows open and use CTRL+TAB to move between the open windows.

However, the availability of multiple views, a single key command away, is a useful feature. A *Window Layout* is simply a snapshot of the open windows at any particular time. Cubase Sx is always operating in a *Window Layout*.

While each *Window Layout* is numbered, unfortunately this numbering is not shown on the screen. Note that when you move to another layout, then return to the original, that it is the snapshot that you will see and not the layout of the screen as you left it. There is no way around this. So, if you wish to quickly check something on another layout without disturbing your work, you are forced to open the appropriate windows or dialogs on the current layout. This seems a bizarre state of affairs, since *Window Layouts* should be a labor-saving feature.

The easiest way to demonstrate their use is to create one. So create a new Project, close all open windows and minimize the *Project Window*. It is not possible to close the *Project Window* in any Window Layout, but it can be minimized to get it out of the way. Now open the *Track Mixer* [F3] and edit to taste. Next do *Window Layout/New* [CTRL+Pad 0]. Name the layout *Track Mixer* and click *Ok*. Congrats, you've just created a *Window Layout*.

You can take a look at your shiny new creation, in context, with *Window Layout/Organize* [W]. This lists all layouts and provides options to create, delete and activate all layouts. Select #1 and click *Activate*. You are back at your original layout.

You can create as many *Window Layouts* as you wish, but there are only key commands for the first nine, *Window Layout/Layout 1* [ALT+Pad 1] (and similarly for 2 to 9).

A layout is not completely cast in stone, however. By way of demonstration, ALT+2 to your *Track Mixer* layout, and open, say, the *Browser* [CTRL+B]. Arrange it in the layout with the Track Mixer, then hit *Window Layout/Recapture* [ALT+Pad 0]. There is little point in renaming the layout on the dialog that appears, but you must hit RETURN twice to save the layout. .

Window Layout operations are not included in the Edit History, so you can't accidentally remove a Window Layout, or other layout action, when applying Undo.

The Windows' Dialog

Opened from *Window/Windows...*, the *Windows' Dialog* provides a method of managing Cubase Sχ's open windows from one place. It's of very limited use, simply because it retains focus, it can't be resized, and you can't assign it a key command).

6 The Project Window and Tools

Each and every Cubase S$_X$ Project has one, and only one, Project Window. You can't miss it. You can also open more than one Project at a time (but things can get a little sluggish when you do). To assist you in applying the million and one functions that are available in Cubase S$_X$ en route to producing yet another international smash, there are, arranged neatly at the top of the Project Window, the Tools. (You can also get to the Tools with a right-click on the Event Display. The choice is yours.) Right here, right now, we are going to take a closer look by zooming into...

Overview

Back in the Quick-start chapter you were directed here for a quick tour of Main Street, Cubase S$_X$ville. At the time we didn't want to get bogged down in the trivia of detail when there was the smell of fresh shrink-wrap in the air, but times are different now, so let's take a flying trip around the Project Window, and then take a closer look at the individual items.

As you open more and more windows in Cubase S$_X$, you might want to assign *Project/Bring To Front* [No Default], which brings the *Project Window* to the front of the pile.

A new Project is created with *File/New Project* [CTRL+N]. One then selects the desired Template, sets the Project Folder and the Project is created. Existing Projects are opened with *File/Open* [CTRL+O]. You can have more than one Project open at the same time. The main bulk of the Project Window is divided horizontally, by a moveable bar, into the Track List on the left, and the Event Display on the right.

The Template selected on creation of a new Project determines the contents of the Track List and the Event Display. It is worth taking a trip around each of the provided Templates. There are plenty of ideas for alternative set-ups.

The Track List can contain any number of the available Track Types. If you right-click on the background of the Track List the list of available types is shown. To the left of the Track List is the *Inspector* [ALT+I].

The bulk of the Project Window is taken over by the Event Display. The *Event Display* greedily gets the whole of chapter 11, page 101. That's the place to look for more detail on editing in the *Event Display*. As its name suggests, this area displays the Project's Events. However, it also displays items known as Parts. Parts are a means of gathering together Events. Indeed, each MIDI note

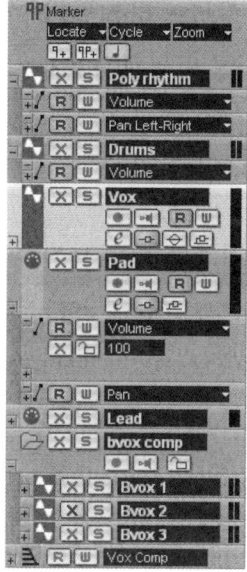

Track List

Available Track types

is an Event, so a collection of MIDI notes can only exist within a MIDI Part. A MIDI Track might contain one single Part, or many.

Open views buttons

An audio Track may contain audio Events and audio Parts. An audio Part is a collection of audio Events. There are times when it is useful to manipulate a number of audio Events as one; this is one use for an audio Part.

Some of the Tracks shown are displaying automation data. Automation is discussed in detail in chapter 18, page 257.

The Tool Bar

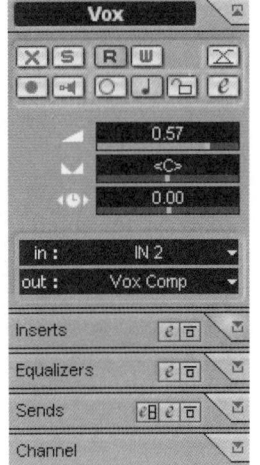

The Inspector

At the top of the screen, below the menus, is the *Toolbar*. The red light (*Activate*) in the left-top corner shows that the Project is active. When you have multiple Projects open, then only one of these will be lit; that of the active Project. It can be clicked to perform a VST reset, which is sometimes useful if you are experiencing strange behavior on playback.

The buttons to the right of the *Activate button* allow you quick access to:

Automation mode

- The Inspector [ALT+I] (see page 51)
- The Info Line [CTRL+I] (see below)
- The Overview [ALT+O] (see below)
- The Pool [CTRL+P] (see chapter 15, page 201)
- The Track Mixer [F3] (see chapter 17, page 234)

The Inspector, Info Line and Overview are all shown in the above picture.

Next along is the *Automation Mode Selector* (see page 265). This affects the way in which Cubase S$_X$ responds when recording automation data. Following

Stop and go

on are the Stop, Play, Record and Cycle buttons that are duplicates of those on the *Transport* [F2].

The *Tools* [1 thru 8] available in the Project Window are also shown (*Scrub is not assign a key command*). Each is selected by clicking the appropriate button. The rightward facing arrow button is for switching *Autoscroll* [F] on and off. The *Tools* can be assigned to Key Commands in different ways. By default you have:

Tip

ALT+1 the ALT+9 are available for assigning to Tool1 to Tools9, if you wish.

Key	Tool	Key	Tool
1	Select tool	9	Play tool
2	Range tool	F9	Previous tool
3	Split tool	F10	Next tool
4	Glue tool		
5	Delete tool	Not assigned	Scrub tool
6	Zoom tool	Not assigned	Drumstick tool
7	Mute tool	Not assigned	Hit-point tool
8	Draw tool		

However, you can also assign Key Commands to Tool1 thru Tool10, where the number represents the left–right position of the Tool for any window. If you assign Tool3 to, say ALT+3, then ALT+3 will select the *Split Tool* in the Project Window, but the *Zoom Tool* in the Sample Editor.

Moving across we reach some tools that affect the alignment of Events and Parts when they are moved around on the Event Display. These are the *Snap Settings*. When *Snap* is *inactive*, objects can be moved freely around the Event Display. When active the objects will be aligned according to the *Grid Setting* and *Snap Mode*. (For the lowdown on *Snap* see page 108.)

Snap

The Info Line, Overview and the Ruler

Moving down we find the *Info Line* [CTRL+I]. The Info Line can be toggled on/off by the second button from the left at the left-end of the Toolbar, so it may not be immediately visible. The Info Line shows information on a *single* selected Event or Part.

Info Line

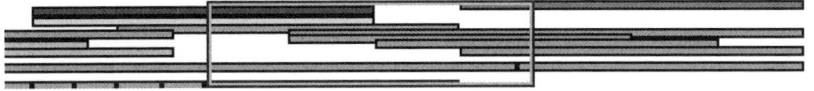

File	Description	Start	End	Length
See me	Heal me	0002.01.01.000	0003.02.03.075	1.1.2.75

Immediately below the Toolbar and Info Line is the *Overview* [ALT+O], which presents a large scale view of the Project. It can be used to select the area shown in the Event Display.

Overview

Next down (but above the Event Display) is the Ruler.

Bars+Beats mode

A right-click on the Ruler will bring up the available Ruler options, and allow you to select your desired format. It is worth noting that each of the editors (e.g. Sample, Part, MIDI) have their own format context. So you can easily work with, say, the Samples format in the Sample Editor, Bars+Beats in the MIDI editor and Seconds in the audio Part Editor without changing the formats of other editors.

The remaining items scattered around the edge of the Project Window are the various Zoom tools.

Zoom controls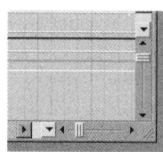

The Track List

♫ *Note*

You can add multiple Tracks of the same type via the *Add Multiple Tracks* quick-menu option.

The Track List is the set-up and admin area for all Tracks in a Project. You add a Track by right-clicking on the Track List and selecting the required Track Type (or via *Project/Add Track*, or right-clicking on the Event Display and choosing Add Track).

Project/Remove Tracks [No Default] is performed from the same menus. Track Duplication is also performed from these menus. A duplicate Track has identical content and settings to the original. Track order is changed by dragging a Track (or Tracks) up or down in the Track List.

Track types

♫ *Note*

Right at the bottom of the *Track List* is a small are that shows the *Sample Rate, Record format* and amount of space left on the disk containing the *Project Folder* in hours and minutes.

The eight *Add Track* options (including *Multiple*) are available as key commands, but none are set-up by default. The following Track Types are available:

○ Audio
○ Folder
○ Group
○ MIDI
○ Marker Track
○ Master Automation
○ Video Track

Automation Tracks can be added (as well as shown or hidden) to the following Track types:

- Audio
- MIDI
- Group
- VST Instrument Automation
- Master Automation
- Effect Automation

The automation Track for a VSTi instrument is added by pressing one of the Write Automation (W) buttons for the VSTi.

When you do this for the first VSTi in a Project a Track called *VST Instrument Automation* is created. This Track is a bit like a Folder Track in that it will contain all automation data for all VSTi's.

An important point to note is that there are separate sub-Tracks for VSTi S_X Channel Events and for VST control Events (e.g. filter cut-off, LFO rate). The former is created by clicking the Write Automation button in the Track Mixer (for the required channel if the VSTi has multiple output channels), and the latter by doing so on the VSTi interface itself (top-left corner of the display panel).

Once the first type of each has been created for the VSTi, you can add sub-Tracks for whichever parameters require automation.

The *Effect Automation* Track is created in a similar way, but by activating Write Automation for a Send Effect. Similarly, the *Master Automation* Track is created by activating Write Automation for a Master Effect.

Automation is covered in detail in chapter 18, page 257; The Marker Track is covered in chapter 7, page 73; and Groups are covered in chapter 17, page 231.

> ↗ **Tip**
>
> Consider using the following key commands: ALT+A for Add Audio Track; ALT+F for Add Folder; ALT+G for Add Group; ALT+D for Add MIDI Track.

Track Controls

If we look at both Audio and MIDI Tracks, we notice a number of common controls.

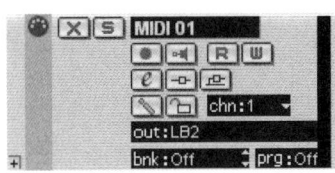

Audio and MIDI Tracks

The Track name at the top can be changed by double-clicking and editing. (For more detail on setting up a MIDI Track see chapter 12 *MIDI: Recording and Editing*.)

The buttons to the left of the Track Name are the Track *Mute* and *Solo* buttons. Most of the rest of the buttons move around if you change the size of the Track List, so images are shown with labels to indicate their purpose (page 50).

The time-base toggle button switches a Track between being time or tempo based. Audio, MIDI and Marker Tracks are all created as tempo-based. (The time-base toggle for MIDI tracks is on the *Inspector*, in case you were wondering where it had gone.) Groups also have this toggle available, but this was

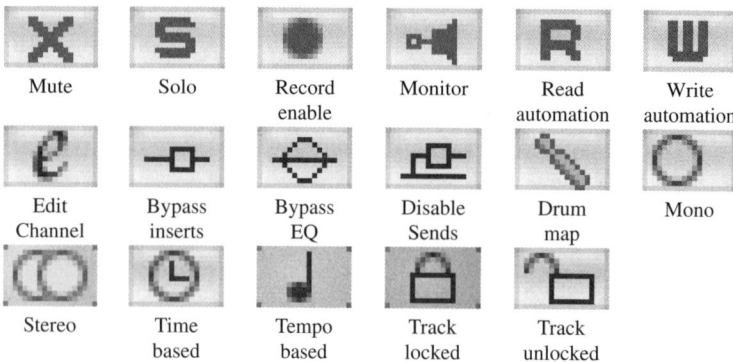

Fig. 6.1: Buttons from the Track List and the Inspector

not operating in Cubase Sx v1.03; Groups remained tempo-based even when switched. In general, for song-writing, you will want all Tracks to be tempo-based.

All audio and MIDI Tracks are either time-based or tempo-based. The chosen state will determine what happens to Events on a Track when the tempo (bpm) changes during playback.

On a time-based Track, Events are anchored to their start time (every Event has a start time associated with it) so changing tempo has no effect on their absolute position in a Project. In a 120bpm Project, an Event starting 10sec into the Project will still start at 10sec when the tempo is changed to 150bpm.

On a tempo-based Track, Events are anchored to their meter position (i.e. bar, beat, 1/16 note and tick (where 1/16 note = 120 ticks). So, increasing the tempo will move Events forward in time, and reducing the tempo will make them play later. Using the above example: In a 120bpm Project, an Event starting after 10sec will now start at 8sec when the tempo is changed to 150bpm

Steinberg warns that there is a potential timing issue when a Track is repeatedly changed from one base to the other; though it's unclear why someone might want to do this. Any change that might occur would be minimal at worst, though this might be sufficient to cause phasing issues with audio.

The Read and Write automation buttons are explained in chapter 18, page 257. The padlock-shaped Lock/Unlock toggle button will disable all editing of all Events on a Track.

On an audio Track, the *e* button will display the Channel Settings window, which is a full mixer channel allowing the set-up of inserts, sends, EQ, fader settings, etc. On a MIDI Track, the *e* button will display the MIDI Channel Settings window, which is similar in concept to an audio channel, but any inserts and sends will operate on the MIDI messages and *not* the audio. This is an important point to grasp when working with VSTi's, in particular.

The send, insert and EQ bypass buttons will light to show whether their respective process is active, and orange when bypassed. When there is nothing available to activate then the bypass buttons are unlit.

♪   *Note*

When a VSTi has been assigned to a MIDI Track, the *e* button in the *Inspector* will open the VSTi's interface and not the MIDI channel settings.

♪   *Note*

Audio channel settings are available for VSTi's, but the window can only be opened from the *Track Mixer* [F3]. See the Tip on page 258 for obtaining this from the Inspector.

Audio monitoring is discussed in chapter 14, page 171. Having this button lit will enable monitoring of an input signal, including any effects on the signal path (unless ASIO Direct Monitoring is in use). The precise monitoring behavior can be adjusted by way of the Auto monitoring options that are found on the VST page of *Preferences*.

For MIDI Tracks, the Monitor button allows you to route MIDI messages thru to the attached output device without having to enable record.

The stereo/mono toggle determines the status of an audio Track. This is usually only set once, since stereo and mono Clips cannot be mixed on an audio Track. If you need to include a stereo Event on a mono Track (or vice versa), then you will need convert the underlying Clip to the appropriate format and recreate any Events manually (see page 214).

The *Drum Map* button on MIDI tracks allows you to select a *Drum Map* or open the *Drum Map Editor*, see page 120 for more.

The Inspector

The *Inspector* [ALT+I] is one region of the Project Window that can be used to adjust almost every setting relating to a Track. The view in the Inspector changes depending on the Track-type selected in the Track list. Most of the features provided in the Inspector are the same as provided elsewhere, so there is almost always more than one way (and often three of fours ways) of achieving the same objective.

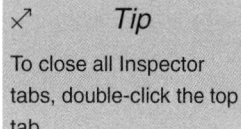

> ✗ *Tip*
>
> To close all Inspector tabs, double-click the top tab.

Once you have the *Inspector* [ALT+I] open, you can select various tabs by clicking the top righthand corner of each tab. Multiple tabs can be opened simultaneously by CTRL+click. All tabs can be opened with ALT+click. Each tab has a specific set of functions.

The type of *Inspector* window (e.g. Insert or Sends) is remembered for each different Track type.

Don't miss the sliders for controlling, say, volume and pan. Click under the numeric value and a slider appears. This can be controlled further by holding SHIFT. You can, of course, enter values directly into the fields. CTRL+click will reset the value to its default.

Inspector slider

Each Inspector Track-type is described in the section relating to that Track-type. The features of each are, briefly:

Audio

Tabs: Inserts, EQ, Sends, Channel strip.

Main Tab extras: Being able to control the volume and pan from here is very convenient, since it removes the need to continually go to the *Track Mixer* [F3]. Similarly, it is easy to establish, and change, input and output routing.

The *Delay* is worthy of note. Ranging from −2000 to +2000ms, this can be used to adjust for latency created by some plug-ins. Positive values delay the Track, while negative values play the Track early. It can also be used creatively, of course. It can be useful for establishing a track in the groove, though not too late in a Project. Another way of achieving this, but by selected Events, is to *Nudge left/right* [No Default] when in an appropriate Display Format.

♪	Note

It's worth testing the *Delay* function by performing an *Audio Mixdown* [No Default] on an Event. This gives you faith that even 0.1ms delays are accurately available (to the nearest sample). Nice one.

Auto Fades

The only other thing of note is that the Track Auto-fades editor is available here. See page 196 for more on Auto-Fades.

MIDI

Tabs: Track parameters, Inserts, Sends, Channel strip.
Notes: See chapter 13, page 151 for the meat and potatoes on *MIDI Processing.*

Input Transformer

Note that the MIDI *Input Transformer* (see page 130) can be accessed on the main tab. Also note that when a VSTi has been assigned to a MIDI Track, the *e* button in the *Inspector* will open the VSTi's interface and not the MIDI channel settings.

You also have access to the powerful Program and Bank selection mechanism from the main MIDI tab. From here a VSTi can make its currently loaded patches available so that they can be selected from a dropdown list. Similarly, patch lists can be managed for outboard equipment via the *Devices/MIDI Device Manager* [No Default]. A large number of patch lists are provided with Cubase Sx for many popular synths.

There is a great deal of control afforded over MIDI here, hence the above mentioned chapter devoted to it.

Folders

See section below.

Groups

Groups are not dissimilar to *Audio Tracks*, and so many of the features are the same. One *big* difference is that delay compensation is not available on Group Tracks. It is worth noting here that *plug-in delay compensation* is not available on Groups either. The result of this is that if you route your audio though a Group that contains a plug-in that delays the audio, then this cannot be adjusted for automatically. The only way to do this is by bouncing the audio and adjusting by hand. See chapter 20, page 281 for more on this topic.

Groups are always stereo (which is why they make great Send buses (see page 233).

Markers

Markers in all their glory are on page 73.

Folders

For organizing your Tracks and making your Project easier to work with, Folders are an essential part of an Sχer's armory. Got drums? Keep each part on a separate Track and manage them in a Folder. Got multi-tracks of vox? Put 'em in a Folder. Audio, MIDI, Groups, even other Folders, can go in a Folder.

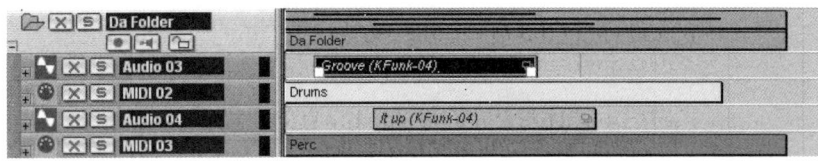

Tracks in a Folder

You populate a Folder by dragging Tracks into it, and remove them by dragging them out. A green horizontal arrow indicates where the dropped Track will be placed. You can 'collapse' the Folder, once populated, by clicking the open Folder icon left of its mute button. Click again to open the Folder.

A Folder Track can be muted and solo'd. These actions affect all Tracks in the Folder. Note that if you have some Tracks in a Folder that are muted or solo'd, then the result of muting or soloing the Folder may not behave as you expect. If you have Tracks muted in a Folder, then soloing the Folder will solo all Folder Tracks including the muted Tracks. When you deactivate solo for the Folder, then the mutes will return. If you have Tracks muted in a Folder, then muting the Folder will mute all Folder Tracks. However, when you deactivate mute for the Folder, then the original mutes will be lost. This is destructive behavior and is a 'feature' for which change would be welcome.

An interesting feature of using Folder Tracks is provided by the *Inspector*. When you select a Folder, the Inspector displays a tree-view of its Tracks. (If you have nested Folders, then these will shown collapsed.) By selecting a Track in the Inspector tree-view, the Inspector for that Track will be displayed. In this way, a Track can be edited without having to open the Folder, select the Track, etc.

> ♪   **Note**
>
> Tracks are created *below* the last selected Track. If the Track is in a Folder, the new Track will be created in that Folder. Selecting a Folder will not place new Tracks in that Folder.

Folder Parts

In the above diagram you can see that there is, what appears to be, an overview of the Folder's contents in the Folder Track (it even shows the colors of the Folders Parts); this is a *Folder Part* . This Part behaves much like an audio or MIDI Part: you can reposition it on the Event Display; create copies; cut; resize; and so on.

You can double-click a Folder Part to open editors for its component parts. This can be useful when the Folder contains MIDI as all Events are shown. By choosing the *As colors* option, you can identify the Parts more easily.

Resizing a Folder Part is relative, and influenced by the *Select Tool* type, see page 55 (you cannot *Timestretch* a Folder Part, however). So, to shorten a Folder Part in length (i.e. chop an end off), you will need to resort to cutting the Part. Cutting a Folder Part will result in all Folder Tracks being cut at the cut point.

♪   **Note**

Folder Parts cannot be shared. That said, when a copy is made of a Folder Track, any audio Events are created as shared. However, MIDI and audio Parts are not created as shared (although audio Events within the Parts are shared). You might think to try and create a Folder Part using shared MIDI and audio Parts. You can do this (and it works as you'd expect), but subsequent copies of the Folder Part will create non-shared versions of the shared Parts. Shame.

As you drag audio and MIDI Parts around in a Folder, they may become detached from the original Folder. The *Cubase Sx: Operations Manual* describes the rules. However, note that a Part can just as easily be "reabsorbed" in a Folder.

✗   **Tip**

If the way in which resizing Folder Parts works is not quite to your taste, then consider creating an audio Track containing a single empty Part. By resizing the empty audio Part, you can resize the Folder Part.

The Tools

Let's take a quick drive-thru the Tools. Here they are:

If you look closely at the bottom right corner of the icons, you will notice a small downward pointing arrow on some of the tools' icons. This indicates that the Tool has multiple functions. To swap functions, make the button active then click on it once more; a popup selection menu will appear. For the Project Window, the available *Tools* default key commands are as follows:

Key	Tool	Key	Tool
1	Select tool	9	Play tool
2	Range tool	F9	Previous tool
3	Split tool	F10	Next tool
4	Glue tool		
5	Delete tool	Not assigned	Scrub tool
6	Zoom tool	Not assigned	Drumstick tool
7	Mute tool	Not assigned	Hit-point tool
8	Draw tool		

Tools are also numbered by their position, 1 to *n* (left to right) in every window. You can also assign Key Commands to Tool1 thru Tool10, where the number represents the left–right position of the Tool for any window. If you assign Tool3 to, say ALT+3, then ALT+3 will select the *Split Tool* in the Project Window, but the *Zoom Tool* in the Sample Editor. Since the Project Windows has 9 tools, then key commands 1, 2,.., 9 will work here. By way of comparison, the Sample Editor on has 5 Tools for key command, so 1 thru 5 will be used.

> ♫   *Note*
>
> For tools with multiple functions, repeatedly pressing its key command will cycle through the options.

> ♫   **Note**
>
> You can cycle through the Tools with the F9 and F10 keys. Tool selection can also be made by right-clicking on the Event Display and selecting from the quick menu.

Object Selection Tool (or Arrow Tool)
- *Normal Sizing:* This is the default, general-purpose selection tool. It is used for dragging Events and Parts, resizing, Event fades and other general manipulation. Used in combination with keystrokes (like ALT, SHIFT and CTRL) this is the most commonly used Tool.

- *Sizing Moves Contents:* See *Resizing Events and Parts* in chapter 11, page 105. Basically, if you move a resize handle on an Event/Part then the Clip content will move. So, if you move the left resize handle, you will be moving the Event start-point and shortening the Event, while moving the right one moves the Event end-point and shortens the Event. Compare this with *slipping* audio (see page 105).

- *Sizing Applies Timestretch:* With this tool you can compress or expand audio Events/Parts and MIDI Parts to a desired size, with respect to its start-point or end-point. Used in conjunction with *Snap*, you can quickly scale loops to fit the current tempo. MIDI Parts are scaled relatively, so that spacing is preserved (useful for rapidly creating double-speed parts, or other multiples). For audio, ensure that the *Preferences/Audio/Time Stretch Tool* algorithm is set as you require. (See also the *Timestretch* Process on page 95.)

Range Selection Tool The Range Tool lets you select ranges across Event/Part and Track boundaries to facilitate Range Editing (see chapter 11, page 110). Range editing has its own submenu of commands: *Edit/Range*, as well as options in *Edit/Select*. Some of these options only become available once a selection has been made on the Event Display. Note that double-clicking an Event will select it (or multiple Events); you can then enlarge the boundary by dragging its edges.

Split Tool Used for splitting Events and Parts. Note that any Snap setting will affect the split point. Also note that if *Snap to Zero Crossing* is switched on (see *Preferences/Audio*) then this will additionally adjust the split point to the nearest zero crossing in the audio.

By holding ALT, you can apply the split throughout the selected Event. The size of the splits are from the the start of the Event to the split point. This only works on a single selected Event. When multiple Events are selected the spit occurs vertically along the timeline.

Glue Tool The reverse of Split? Pretty much, but not quite. Gluing two Events will create a Part containing the two Events. However, if you Split an Event and then Glue the two together again, the original Event will be restored. In fact if the two Events are arranged to play a continuous section of the same Clip, then gluing them should create a single Event.

Erase Tool You guessed it. You can drag the Erase tool around with the mouse-button held to delete multiple Events. On the Project Window it can often be quicker to select an Event, or Events (use lasso), and hit the Delete or Backspace key.

Hold ALT to erase a Part, and all subsequent Parts on a Track. (This also works for notes in the MIDI editor within the Parts being edited, in the Marker Track and, interestingly, in the Tempo Editor.) The ALT key can be changed to another in *Preferences/Editing/Tool Modifiers*.

Zoom Tool See the following section on zooming (page 57) for key command zooming methods. This tool is *almost* redundant given the key command and screen options.

That said SHIFT+click with this tool if useful (and frustratingly there is no key command for it). This will fit the whole Project, both horizontally and vertically, into the available screen area. This effectively does a *Zoom Full* [SHIFT+F] plus a similar operation vertically (whuch is available from the Track Scale pop-up).

                                Tip

Here's a alternative *Zoom Full* macro that you might find useful. Don't forget that you can assign macros a Key Command. The macro commands are:
o Edit/Select All
o Zoom/Zoom to Selection
o Edit/Select None

There is a noticeable delay when when clicking to zoom-in (presumably be-cause S𝑥 is "waiting" to find out whether you intend a double-click, which causes a zoom-out). You can overcome this shortcoming by holding CTRL+ALT.

If you persist in using the *Zoom Tool* then click to zoom-in one step, and ALT+click (or double-click) to zoom-out horizontally one step. CTRL+click halves both the vertical and horizontal size of the Project. (Do SHIFT+click then CTRL+click to see the effect.) You can also zoom-in horizontally to an area by dragging a rectangle around the area of interest. (The zoom key commands are often quicker and more precise.)

Mute Tool Mutes [SHIFT+M] and *unmutes* [SHIFT+U] Events and Parts. There is also *Mute Toggle* [ALT+M]. You can lasso the Parts to be muted/unmuted. It is also possible to click on a Part with this Tool then, holding the mouse-button down, "touch" other Parts that will then be muted. Muted Events are greyed-out on the display, but can still be edited.

Draw Tool
○ *Draw:* On the Project Window the Draw tool will create a Part. It is also used for drawing freeform automation curves on Automation Tracks.
○ *Line, Parabola, Sine, Triangle, Square:* These are used for drawing lines on Automation Tracks. (See chapter 18, page 263)

Scrub/Play Tool
Playback in both cases is routed to Bus 1 and bypasses all Channel Settings.

○ *Scrub:* Audio Only. Allows the location of audio position by moving the mouse over a single audio Track and hear it playback - either backwards or forwards. The speed of playback is dictated by the speed with which you move the mouse. The Scrub Response Speed can be adjusted in *Preferences* VST tab. An Event/Part is selected during this action and this permits resizing.

○ *Play:* Audio only. Play will simply play the audio Track under the mouse from the point that you click, until you release the mouse-button. Since only one Part is playing, this can be an extremely useful tool. The Part is not selected when using the *Play* tool.

Zoom Controls

While zooming can be achieved by using the graphical Zoom sliders (shown), and Zoom Tool (see above section), the key commands are generally a lot quicker, and more accurate, to work with. These key commands work in the Event Display and the other editors. Take care when zooming as you cannot undo a Zoom function.

Zoom Commands
Horizontal zooming will center on the Cursor, providing it is visible. This is very useful, especially when zooming into one of the editors from the Event Display, since hitting, say, Zoom In will immediately center the the editor on the Cursor. If the Cursor is not visible, then zooming will center around the center of the current view.

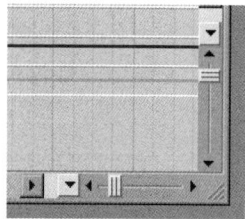

Zoom controls

List of zoom key commands (also found on the Zoom submenu):

○ *Zoom Full* [SHIFT+F] – horizontal
○ *Zoom In* [H] – horizontal
○ *Zoom Out* [G] – horizontal
○ *Zoom In Vertical* [No Default] – all Tracks
○ *Zoom Out Vertical* [No Default] – all Tracks
○ *Zoom to Selection* [ALT+S] – horizontal and vertical, all selected Parts

○ *Zoom Tracks Exclusive* [Z] and [CTRL+down] – vertical, all selected
○ *Zoom In Tracks* [ALT+down] – vertical, all selected
○ *Zoom Out Tracks* [ALT+up] and [CTRL+up] – vertical, all selected

○ *Zoom Presets* 2/3/4/5 [No Default] – horizontal only
○ *Zoom to Event* [SHIFT+E] (Sample Editor only) – horizontal

Since horizontal zooming is sensibly centered on the Project Cursor and relative Track heights are maintained. In can often be quicker to use the Key Commands [G] followed by [H] to center the Cursor in the Event Display, instead of shifting the view with the scroll controls.

Zoom Tracks Exclusive [Z] "minimizes" all Tracks except those selected. Remember: no undo. You can hit [Z] again and it will deepen the Track(s) further. You can then use *Zoom In Tracks* and *Zoom Out Tracks* to to fine-tune the height.

Note that vertical zoom commands are affected by the *Snap Track Heights* option in the Track Scale pop-up (see below).

Unfortunately, *Zoom Full* [SHIFT+F] does not display the whole Project (which is from zero to Project length, as defined in *Project Set-up* [SHIFT+S]), but rather it zooms to show all content. The same is true in MIDI and audio Part editors, which can be a nuisance. It would be good to have both options.

It is possible to increase the Track height for selected Tracks by dragging one of their borders in the Track List. To resize all Tracks, hold CTRL before dragging. This latter function is not a relative operation however; so all Tracks heights will become the same once the mouse-button is released.

Don't miss the *Waveform Zoom*; a slider found top-right of the Event Display. It has occasional use for inspecting waveforms.

Another handy Zoom feature is provided when you have the option *Zoom While Locating in Timescale* switched on. (Perhaps 'Mouse Zoom' might have been a better name.) It is found in the *Preferences* Transport tab. Once set, you can zoom in and out around a specific point, by clicking in the Ruler and dragging the mouse up and down. This will cause the Project Cursor to move to where you clicked, but this can be averted by pressing the SHIFT key.

Track Scale pop-up
This pop-up is hidden away in a dropdown activated by clicking the downward pointing arrow above the horizontal zoom slider. The options are self-

Tip

You might find it useful to reassign *Zoom to Selection* to SHIFT+S and move the Project Set-up key command to ALT+S.

Waveform zoom

descriptive.

The *Snap Track Heights* setting is very useful if you want to enforce horizontal zooming in "one line" units. You can usefully combine this setting with *Zoom In Vertical* [No Default] and *Zoom Out Vertical* [No Default] after assigning them suitable key commands.

The Overview

The *Overview* [ALT+O] can also be used for zooming, as well as navigating, around the Project. The idea is a common one, but it can be slow compared to using key commands.

The box in the Overview corresponds to the section of the Project being shown in the Event Display; change one and the other follows. There are only three operations available to the Overview: lasso, resize and drag. Lasso an area to create a box in the Overview. You must start the lasso operation in the top half of the Overview display. To resize, either grab an edge and drag, or click *outside* the box in the lower half of the display and the nearest edge will be positioned where you click. To drag, grab the current box with the 'hand' tool that appears.

Zoom Presets (Horizontal)

There's even more Zooming functionality to play with. Phew! Horizontal Zoom settings can be stored by using the wee *Zoom Preset* selector at bottom-left of the Project Window. The *Add* and *Organize* options give you the familiar CRUD functions (create, rename, update, delete). Once a zoom setting has been stored, then it appears in the list and can be selected to apply the zoom.

> ♫ **Note**
>
> Zoom Presets are global; they apply to all Projects. Cycle Markers apply to the current Project only.

Guess what? Zoom Presets don't remember their position in the Project, nor can position be set. Opportunity missed? Cycle markers (see page 73) are also listed here and do provided positional and zoom scaling information.

You'll hear no "I'm tired out after all that zooming around" quips from this author. So, moving swiftly on...

The Ruler

You'd never believe it by looking at it, but there is fair bit of power under the hood of the Ruler. We're not talking "forces of nature" power, but some speedy little functions that will help nudge a Project along.

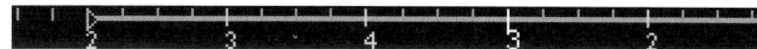

Track scaling options

> ↗ *Tip*
>
> Consider setting up *Zoom In Vertical* [CTRL+H] and *Zoom Out Vertical* [CTRL+G], and moving *Open List Editor* [CTRL+G] to, say, [ALT+L].

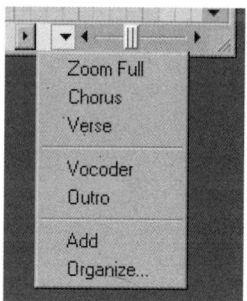

Zoom Presets

The Ruler

The Ruler sits at the top of the Event Display. It shows the Project timeline. When a Project is created from the Empty template, the format of the timeline, along with all other position related fields and functions, is determined by the *Display Format* set in the *Project Set-up* [SHIFT+S]. Other templates may specify different formats.

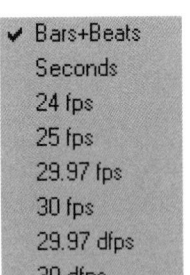

✔ Bars+Beats
Seconds
24 fps
25 fps
29.97 fps
30 fps
29.97 dfps
30 dfps
Samples

Display formats

To change the Ruler format, right-click on it and select from the dropdown list (shown). There are no options to assign Key Commands to these settings. This would be very useful, since many folk will work with two or three of these only, and swapping between formats is a regular event for many.

Changes to the Ruler format affect:

○ Timeline
○ Info Line
○ Nudge/Snap setting
○ Tool tip values shown when dragging Events on the Event Display

The Project Browser and the Pool take the value that is set on the *Transport* [F2], which sets the Project global format. This can also be achieved by changing the Ruler format while holding down CTRL.

There are Rulers in the Sample, Part and MIDI editors. The format for each can be set independently. The format for each will be retained. However, if you change the format in the Transport when an editor window is open then that window will take on the new format selected in the Transport.

The Ruler: Features and Functions

Positioning the Project Cursor
Wherever you click on the Ruler, the Project Cursor will follow. If you continue to hold the mouse-button, then you can drag the Cursor around. It is also possible to position the Cursor by clicking in the Event Display. To do this you need to activate the *Locate When Clicked in Empty Space* option in *Preferences/Transport* tab.

Set Left and right Locators
The *Left Locator* [CTRL+1] and [CTRL+Pad1] can be set by holding CTRL and clicking in the Ruler. The *Right Locator* [CTRL+2] and [CTRL+Pad2] can be set by holding ALT and clicking in the Ruler. In both cases the Snap value is applied when active.

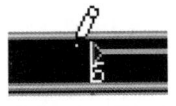

Draw both locators (loop)

You can "draw" a line from left to right Locator in the very top of the Ruler. The mouse icon will turn into a pencil to indicate that drawing can commence. Similarly, you can drag the locators. The mouse icon will turn into a hand in this case. Snap applies in both cases when active.

Drag locators

Transport Play and Stop
By double-clicking in the Ruler you can *Start* [Enter] or *Stop* [Pad0] the Transport. The Project Cursor will move to the nearest Snap point to where you double-click. You can also click on a new location while the Project is playing

	Audio Event	MIDI Part	Audio Part	Automation Event	Marker	Cycle Marker
File	X					
Name/Desc	X	X	X		X	X
Type				X		
Start	X	X	X	X	X	X
End	X	X	X			X
Length	X	X	X			X
Offset	X	X	X			
Snap	X					
Volume	X					
Value				X		
ID					X	X
Fade In	X					
Fade Out	X					
Mute	X	X	X			
Lock	X	X	X			
Transpose		X				

Table 6.1: Cubase Sx object attributes

and the Cursor will jump to this point. SPACE will also start and stop the Transport.

Zooming
As described above in Zoom Controls, you can zoom-in and out around a specific point, by clicking in the Ruler and dragging the mouse up and down. Check the section above for the details.

The Info Line

The *Info Line* [CTRL+I] shows all the details of a single Event or Part that is selected in the Project Window.

File	Description	Start	End	Length
See me	Heal me	0002.01.01.000	0003.02.03.075	1.1.2.75

Info Line

The contents of the Info Line change depending on the type of object that is selected in the Event Display. The values shown in the Info Line will be in the format of the current format of the Ruler. If multiple objects are selected then a message to that effect is displayed in the Info Line. Almost all of the information displayed can be edited.

Table 6.1 shows the attributes available for the various objects (Video Events may also be present).

For detailed descriptions of these values, see the *Cubase Sx: Operations Manual* section *The Project Browser*. Note that *Offset* is the equivalent of *sliding* an Event/Part, and that *Snap* is the absolute position of an Event's Snap

♫   *Note*

The Info Line also appears in the Audio Part and MIDI Part editors.

Point and not the offset of the Snap Point from the start of an Event. Thus, changing Snap will move the Event and not the Snap Point within the Event.

Much of that which can be edited here can also be edited in the *Project Browser* [CTRL+B]. For single items, and quick fixes, the Info Line is a lot quicker. It also encourages the naming of Events and Parts. This is recommended for easy comprehension of a Project as a it grows, and especially when you return to it after some time. Whether you change the Description field, the Name field (which also changes the associated file name), or both, is your call.

⚡   **Warning**

If you change the File item for an Audio Event, then the physical file name on disk will also be changed. (The name reference is also changed in the Pool, of course.) This change is made without warning.

Most items are edited simply by over-typing the current contents, but the general way in which these fields can be changed will be determined by the *Preferences* User Interface/Control tab entry *Value Box/Time Control Mode*.

Some items have a slider available. To see this, press and hold the [Alt] key while hovering the cursor over the field.

↗   **Tip**

Adjusting automation Events in the Project Window can be a delicate and tricky operation. An alternative editing method is to select an Event and use the [Alt] operation on the value field in the Ruler.

Unfortunately, there is no Key Command to place the cursor in the Info Line. This would be useful, since once within the Info Line it is possible to TAB through the fields (then use the left and right cursor keys to move through sub-fields) and use the cursor up and down buttons to adjust values.

There is a trick to circumvent this, though. However, it may well be an "unsupported" feature, and might not work in all cases, so apologies if it doesn't work for you. If you have an Event selected then hit TAB, the focus will move, but where it goes depends on the type of Track currently selected. If you tab somewhere between one and three times then the cursor will move to the first Info Line field.

The behavior in the Info Line changes depending on the setting of the *Preferences* [No Default] *User Interface* tab option *Value Box/Time Control Mode*; the *Text Input* selection giving access to the most fields.

The Project Set-up Info Box

The *Project Set-up Info Box* [SHIFT+S] allows you to adjust the core Project details. The following settings are available:

Start
The Project start time. This will affect the values shown in the timeline (for all but *Bars+Beats*). It is most useful when used to set the Sync Start Position when synchronizing Cubase S$_X$ to external devices (see chapter 19, page 267). If you are sync'ing to SMPTE (or MTC) then this field is the familiar start location.

Length
This determines the length of the Project. Its value will affect the scaling of the *Overview* [ALT+O]. If you usually work on 3 to 4 minute songs, then set this to 4 minutes for convenience.

Frame Rate
If you need this, then you will know which value you require. Frame rate is used to sync Cubase S$_X$ with external equipment. If you have an external master clock, and Cubase S$_X$ is slaving to it, then the Cubase S$_X$ frame rate is ignored and Cubase S$_X$ will adopt the frame rate of the master clock. If Cubase S$_X$ is the master, and other equipment is slaving to it, then this value will determine the frame rate of the sync signal that is sent. Cubase S$_X$ only recognizes MTC and Steinberg's own ASIO Positioning Protocol.

Display Format
This performs a change of the global display format. It is identical to changing the display format on the Transport (see page 69).

Display Offset
Offsets the Project time position displays, allowing you to compensate for the Start setting.

Sample Rate
The Project Sample Rate. Not only does Cubase S$_X$ record and playback audio files at this sample rate, but it will also prompt for conversion to it, where it differs, when importing files to the Pool.

Record Format
The Project bit-depth. As for Sample Rate, not only does Cubase S$_X$ record and playback audio files at this sample rate, but it will also prompt for conversion to it, where it differs, when importing files to the Pool.

Record File
Three options: Broadcast Wave, Wave and AIFF.

Stereo Pan Law
The *Stereo Pan Law* setting can dramatically alter the mixed sound produced by Cubase S$_X$. There has been much debate over how this value, more generally, subtly affects our perception of the quality of sound coming from not only Cubase S$_X$, but also other sequencers and DAW's. So let's start by examining what Pan or Panning Law is and does.

Early in the history of stereo audio, a relationship was established between the proportion of left and right audio levels and the apparent position of a sound source. By adjusting the left and right levels following this relationship, the sum of the two levels is constant. In other words, as a sound moves from the left speaker, through the center, and across to the right speaker, then the volume of the signal sounds the same throughout.

What this relationship shows is that a 3dB loss is required, on both acoustic signals, for the signal to appear dead center.

However, if we think of summing the signals in the above example to mono, the result is a signal that is 3dB higher when dead center than at either of the two sides. For example, as may occur when played back on a radio.

To circumvent this loss, one could engineer a 6dB loss dead center. This removes the above summing effect, but results in a level drop at dead center when playing back in stereo. A compromise level drop of 4.5dB is yet another approach.

Cubase Sχ provides us with three Pan laws:

○ -6dB
○ -3dB (default)
○ 0dB

Unfortunately, we are not provided with a -4.5dB setting, indeed a continuously variable pan law might be the most desirable. However, unlike many DAW's, at least we have a choice. The setting you use is wholly dependent on your application and the use of your ears; use them wisely. For most uses, the default -3dB setting should be fine.

Other Tools

The Performance Monitor (F12)

The F12 Perf Mon

The *Devices/VST Performance monitor* [F12] shows the current CPU and disk load. It poses no real overhead to Cubase Sχ and is worth keeping open in the Project Window so that you have a quick visual check on your machines stress levels. It is not always apparent that you are approaching the maximum load on your computer, and it's better to be forewarned, than lose a great take through a glitch brought about by over-stretching your machine.

If the meters are approaching the right-hand side, then start to take action. If the red indicators light, then you are treading very dangerously (although the hard disk indicator might light very briefly from time to time).

Reduce CPU levels by switching off plug-ins (Master, Send, Insert), EQ, or simply reducing the number of Tracks playing, or disable Tracks that you are no longer using. Since it is so easy to bounce Tracks in Cubase Sχ, then consider doing this where possible, and then switching off the effects.

You can reduce disk and CPU usage by disabling Tracks (from the Track List quick menu); simply muting them will not have any effect on performance. If you have a serious disk performance problem, then a new, faster disk might be the only answer.

Disabling Tracks

Disabling a Track will stop Cubase Sχ from retrieving any audio for the Track from disk. Only audio Tracks can be disabled. The benefit is less disk activity and a saving in processing. Note that muting a Track does not have the same effect. Muting is simply attenuating the audio signal and all disk activity for a muted Track is carried out regardless. Cubase Sχ must do this since an unmute could occur at any instant, requiring Sχ to start playback. The Disable and Enable Track functions are available from the Track List quick-menu for a Track.

Time Display

The *Time Display* [No Default] is a resizable clock that displays the Cursor position in any of the Display Formats; simply right-click and select the required format. You can open multiple *Time Display* windows, but each one must first be created via the *Add/Remove* tab in *Devices/Device Set-up* [No Default]. Once created, each will appear in the *Devices* menu and the *Key Commands Editor*.

Time reflexes like a...

The Device Panel

Cubase Sχ's audio windows can be managed from the *Devices/Show Panel* [No Default]. Each entry toggles the respective window on or off. Unfortunately you can't configure the contents of the list.

Notepad

You'll work it out. Each is saved with a Project, so make notes.

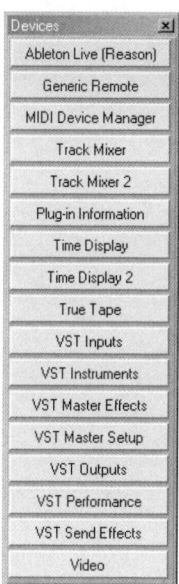

So much choice.

7 The Transport, Markers and Movin' Around

Stop, start, record: all good, essential stuff, and all available, plus much more, from the *Transport Panel* [F2]. Most of the functions provided by the Transport are so frequently used, that it is very likely that you will use the key commands for them.

Note that most Transport functions will move the Project Cursor, and doing so may move it outside the viewable area. If you wish the Cursor to remain in view, then ensure that the *Auto-Scroll* [F] is switched on; it's to the right of the Tools icons. It appears in the Sample, Part and MIDI editors, as well as the Project Window, and it is independent for each window; so you can switch it on in the Project Window and off in the Sample Editor, for example.

Auto-Scroll

Another mechanism for moving around the Project is provided by *Markers*. Key commands are available for setting and locating to markers, as well as locating to the next and previous marker. A section of a Project can also be marked by a *Cycle Marker*. You can locate to, zoom and cycle around Cycle Markers.

More details on using the Transport functions as part of the recording process (and other processes) are given in the appropriate chapters.

Since we are focussing on the Transport, it seems a good time to detail the many items that appear on the Transport menu list, most of which relate to navigating around a Project, and most of which have key commands well worth learning.

However, first, let's take a quick look at the [F2] item itself. Ladies and gentlemen I give you...

↗ *Tip*

The way you configure the Transport is saved with a Windows Layout, so you can have differently formatted Transports on different screens.

The Transport

The Transport can be grabbed and moved, but it isn't resizable. However, if you right-click on it, you will be presented with a range of configuration options.

The Transport

It's never safe to assume anything, but in this case the Stop, Start and Record buttons are going to go without explanation. Note that Tracks must be armed

---

Cubase Sx Complete   67

(record enabled) in the Track List to be affected by pressing Record. You can also drop into Record while playing the Project – it is a useful alternative to using punch points. These functions, plus Cycle (see below) are included in a *mini*-Transport in the Toolbar.

Mini-transport

Note that if the *Preferences/Transport* tab option *Return to Start Position on Stop* is checked, then the Cursor will automatically return to the the last stopped point when you hit Stop. If you would rather the Cursor stayed put on Stop, but would also like the option to Play from the last stopped position, then you can use *Transport/Restart* [No Default].

You can Start and Stop a Project by double-clicking on the Ruler/Timeline. The Cursor will move to the nearest snap point to where you double click. If you click in the Ruler when the Transport is running, then the Cursor will jump to that position (or its nearest snap point) and playback will continue.

The *Fast Forward* [Pad +] and *Rewind* [Pad −] buttons are obvious; the two buttons either side of these take the Cursor either to the start or the end of the Project. It is left as an exercise for the reader to determine which is which.

Note that there are a number of Transport operations that are available from the Transport menu, and as key commands, that cannot be performed from the Transport. These are shown in a table later in this chapter.

Above the Transport Buttons are the *Position Slider*, the *Nudge Buttons* and the *Position Display*.

Function	Key Command
Transport Panel Show/Hide	F2
Play/Start	[Enter] or [Space]
Stop	Pad 0 or [Space]
Restart	No default (suggestion: ';' (semicolon))
Record	Pad *
Fast Forward	Pad +
Rewind	Pad −
Return to Zero/Start	Pad . (point) and , (comma)
Go to End of Project	No default (suggestion: '.' (point))
Nudge (Transport) Up/Right	CTRL+Pad +
Nudge (Transport) Down/Left	CTRL+Pad −

Fig. 7.1: Basic Transport Key Commands

The Position Slider can be used to move the Cursor to a new position very quickly; simply click and you're there, or use the mouse-wheel to scroll. Note that the Slider does not follow any Snap setting that might be active.

Above the Position Slider and to the left of the Position Display are two tiny + and − buttons; the *Transport/Nudge up* [CTRL+Pad +] and *Transport/Nudge down* [CTRL+Pad −] buttons. These nudge the Cursor left or right by an amount determined by the display format as follows:

○ *Bars + Beats:* One Tick (1/16 note = 120 ticks)
○ *Seconds:* One second
○ *Frame-based:* One Frame
○ *Samples:* One Sample

The key to navigation is setting the Project Cursor to a desired location, although often you can locate and do something in one command.

The Project Cursor can be moved in the following ways:

○ Clicking in the Ruler
○ Dragging the Cursor in the Ruler
○ Clicking on the Event Display when *Locate When Clicked in Empty Space* is ticked in *Preferences* Transport tab
○ Click the Position Slider
○ Edit the Transport Position Display [SHIFT+P]
○ With key commands

Tip

Lost the cursor? A neat trick is to toggle *Auto scroll* [F] on (or off and on again). This will move the Project window to be aligned with the Project Cursor. This works in the editors too.

Scrolling with the mouse

Standard windows scroll bars are available to move the viewing area, but the easiest way to scroll the Project Window is by using the mouse-wheel. Rolling the mouse-wheel will scroll the Project Windows vertically bringing different Tracks into view.

If SHIFT is held while rolling the mouse-wheel, then the view will scroll horizontally on the time axis.

However, if vertical scrolling is not possible (because all the Track are visible), then both these actions scroll along the timeline, although in different directions!

Position Display

The Position Display displays the Project Cursor's position in the Project. There is also a dropdown selector that determines the display format for the items in the Transport, and also permanently changes the display formats of any open editors and the Ruler. When the display format is changed here, all open windows in the current Window Layout will take the format chosen. Thus, when making a change of format in the Position Display, the Ruler in the Project Window will also be changed.

Thereafter, all editor windows of the affected type will also take the new layout, irrespective of which Window Layout they happen to be in.

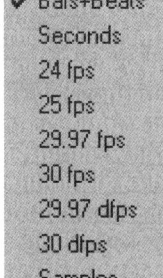

Display formats

This sounds a little confusing, and indeed it can be tricky to follow. If you find yourself frequently opening an editor and finding that it is not in the format that you most frequently use, then this is the likely cause.

Rec and Cycle Rec modes

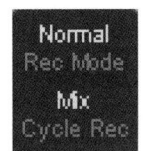

MIDI record modes

These two options only affect MIDI recording and are described in chapter 12, page 129.

Auto-quantize, Punch-in, Punch-Out and Cycle (Loop)

The four buttons on the far left of the Transport are, from left to right:

o *Auto-Quantize* [No Default]
o *Punch-in* [I]
o *Cycle* [Pad /]
o *Punch-out* [O]

If *Auto-Quantize* [No Default] is active, then any MIDI recording is quantized to the setting in *Quantize Set-up* [No Default]

The *Punch-in* [I] and *Punch-out* [O] buttons are only relevant during recording. For a full explanation of punching in and punching out see: For MIDI, see chapter 12, page 129, and for audio see chapter 14, page 177. Be aware, however, that activating the Punch-in button will start recording, on any armed Tracks, should the Cursor be in Play mode and cross the Left Locator.

Activating *Cycle* [Pad /] puts Cubase Sx playback and recording (cycle recording) into a loop. The Left and Right Locators determine the start and end points of the loop.

In Play, with Cycle activated, the Project will cycle around the loop until stopped, or Cycle is deactivated. There is a small break in the continuity of play when activating and deactivating cycle; continuously looping playback is, however, seamless.

Pre and Post Roll

Pre and post roll

These fields are used mostly for recording. Note that *Transport/ Use Pre/ Post-Roll* [No Default] must be switched on for the values in these fields to be active. There is a tick in the Transport menu to indicate when it is switched on.

When Pre Roll is active, then the Cursor will be moved back by this amount, from its current position, each time you start to play or record. This can be useful when you want to record (or cycle record) from the Left Locator and need a lead-in.

Post Roll is only effective after an automatic punch-out has occurred. In this instance the Transport (and playback) will continue for this amount of time before stopping. Note also that *Preferences/Transport* tab *Stop after Automatic Punch-out* must also be active for this to occur.

During cycle record, pre-roll only applies to the first cycle. Each subsequent cycle will commence from the left locator (in an identical way to playback with Cycle switched on). Also, any post-roll setting is ignored.

Master, Click and Online (Sync) Buttons

Click
Turns the *Metronome/Click* [C] on and off.

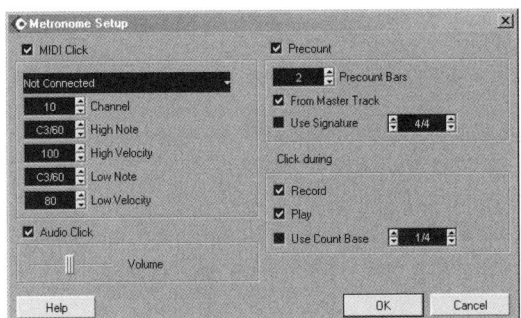

Metronome set-up

Customizing the Click is performed via *Transport/Metronome Set-up* [No Default] (which can also be accessed by CTRL+click on the Transport's *Click* button). Both MIDI and Audio clicks are available, as is an option for a pre-count when recording, and whether the Click should sound in record and/or play modes.

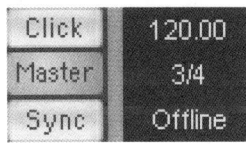

Click button

The metronome pre-count only sounds when Punch-in is on and you start recording from Stop mode. However, you can use pre-roll to achieve a lead-in in all other cases. Any pre-roll setting is ignored when using pre-count.

♪ **Note**

You can change the Key Signature here on the Transport. The effect is to change the most recent Time Signature Event (it does not create a new Time signature Event at the Cursor position). Warning: The mouse-wheel can quickly change the Time Signature into something quite bizarre; and this can easily be done unintentionally.

Sync

This button switches external synchronization on and off (*Transport/Sync Online* [T]). CTRL+click on the Transport's *Sync* button will open the *Synchronization Set-up* window. See chapter 19, page 267.

Function	Key Command
Set L and R Locators to selection	P
Set left Locator	CTRL+Pad 1 or CTRL+1
Set right Locator	CTRL+Pad 2 or CTRL+2
Locate selection	L
Locate next Event	N
Locate previous Event	B
Play selection then stop	ALT+Space
Loop selection	SHIFT+G
Loop/Cycle toggle	Pad /
Play from selection start	
Play to selection start	
Play from selection end	
Play to selection end	
Start record at left Locator	
Master Track toggle	
Auto punch-in	I
Auto punch-out	O
Use pre/post roll	
Auto-quantize toggle	
Metronome set-up	
Metronome toggle	C
Sync set-up	
Sync toggle	
Input Transport position	SHIFT+P
Input left Locator	SHIFT+L
Input right Locator	SHIFT+R

Fig. 7.2: Not-so-basic Transport Key Commands

Master

Transport/Master Track toggle [No Default] switches tempo modes between Rehearsal and Master Tempo Track modes. CTRL+click on the Transport's *Master* button will open the *Tempo Track*.

o *Rehearsal Mode (unlit):* This simply means that the tempo displayed to the right of the Master button is fixed across the whole Project. To edit this field either highlight it and type or use the nifty mouse-wheel in the usual Cubase Sx fashion.

o *Master Tempo Mode (lit):* tempo will follow the Events in the *Tempo Track* [CTRL+T]. These can also be viewed in the Browser. Tempo only affects Tempo-based Tracks; it does not affect Time-based Tracks. (See chapter 10, page 89.)

The Locators

The Left and Right Locators (LL and RL) are central to many operations in Cubase Sx. For example, they are used to determine the range of the Cycle loop; as the start and end points for punching in and punching out; for setting the range for an *Audio Mixdown*; as well as being useful easily movable navigation points. They are, however, just two examples of markers, albeit with a number of special functions assigned to them.

Locator positions

The Locator fields on the Transport allow you to edit the LL and RL. See below (page 75) for a full exposition on the subject.

 ✗⁊   Tip

When looping a section, it is very easy to get into the habit of selecting a number of Events, then hitting P, then L, then Play. All of which can be done in under a second admittedly. However, SHIFT+G does the same thing.

Markers in detail

The easiest way to identify the location of Markers is on the Marker Track in the Event Display, and in the Inspector for the Marker Track. It is recommended that a Marker Track is created in every Project. The Markers can also be viewed and edited in the Browser and from the *Marker List* [CTRL+M].

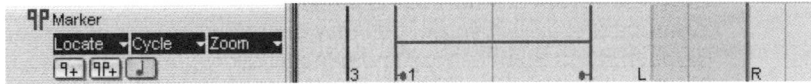

Marker Track

There are two forms of markers:

o *Standard:* that simply mark a position (or point) on the time-line within the Project.
o *Cycle:* that define a time range in the Project. Cycle Markers can overlap one another.

The primary function of Standard Markers is to aid the rapid positioning of the Cursor, and hence the Project Window view, to a chosen location in the Project. The primary function of Cycle Markers, however, is to identify a section of the Project, so that the section can be selected, zoomed in to, or looped around.

Each marker can be labeled with text, allowing verses, choruses, key changes to be labeled, as required.

♫   **Note**

Once you have created a Marker Track it is a good idea to decide immediately whether you need it to be time or tempo-based. By default it is created as tempo-based (the same as audio and MIDI Tracks), but there might be circumstances where you wish to change this.

Creating Markers

A *standard marker* can be created in the following ways (Snap applies):

- ○ Position the Cursor at the desired location and press [Insert]
- ○ Use the Draw Tool on the Marker Track
- ○ Use [Alt] + click with the Selection tool on the Marker Track
- ○ Use the *Set Markers (n = 1 thru 9)* key commands CTRL+Pad *n* and CTRL+*n* (when the marker doesn't exist)
- ○ Use Add in the *Marker List* [CTRL+M]
- ○ Use Add on the Marker Track in the Browser
- ○ Use the Add Marker button in the Track List

You can also create markers while the Transport is running by pressing [Insert], the *Add Marker* button in the Track List, or the Add button in the Marker List. In these cases, snap is not applied.

A *cycle maker* can be created by:

- ○ Use the Select Tool or Draw on the Marker Track while pressing CTRL (This only works left-to-right, and can be problematic if you try to start drawing within Snap distance of an existing marker.)
- ○ Use Add in the *Marker List* [CTRL+M] while its dropdown called *Show* has Cycle Markers selected
- ○ Use Add on the Marker Track in the Browser
- ○ Use the Add Cycle Marker button in the Track List

In the last two cases the Cycle Marker is created between the left and right locators.

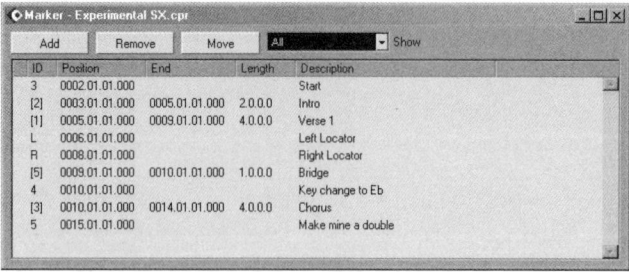

The Marker List

Moving Markers

A marker can be repositioned by:

- ○ Dragging it in the Marker Track to another location (Snap applies)
- ○ Changing values in the Info Line, Inspector or Browser
- ○ Use of Move and editing in the Marker List
- ○ Use the Set Marker key commands, which default to CTRL+*n* (and CTRL+Pad *n*) for markers 1 to 9 (with 1 representing the Left Locator and 2 the Right Locator). When this last command is used, and the marker doesn't exist, then a new marker will be created in that position.

You can drag either endpoint of a Cycle Marker to resize it.

Editing and Deleting Markers

To edit a marker's text you can select it on the Marker Track, either in the Event Display or the Inspector, then edit the text in the Info Line. Markers can also be edited from the Marker List, Inspector and Browser.

A Cycle Marker can be cut with the Scissors Tool (Snap is adhered to). If ALT is held while cutting, then the Cycle Marker is cut into segments the size of the first.

It is quite legitimate to edit a Marker's ID. If the ID is changed to a marker that already exists then the Ids will be swapped. The ID corresponds to the number used in the Set and Locate To key commands. (Remember that Ids 1 and 2 are reserved for the left and right locators.)

Similar to all the above, Markers can be deleted from the Marker List, Browser and by using the DEL key on a selected marker in the Marker Track. Obviously, using the Erase tool works and, in addition, if the ALT key is held, then all subsequent markers will also be deleted.

Setting the Left and Right Locators

The Left Locator can be set by holding CTRL and left-clicking in the Ruler (if active, Snap is applied), or to the current Cursor position by either CTRL+1 or CTRL+Pad 1. The Right Locator can be set by holding ALT and left-clicking in the Ruler (if active, Snap is applied), or to the current Cursor position by CTRL+2 and CTRL+Pad 2.

The simplest way to set both Locators quickly is to select a number of Events in the Event Display and use *Transport/Locators to Selection* [P].

The Left and Right Locators can also be set by manipulation of the Locator fields on the Transport. You can either edit these directly or use the *Input Left Locator* [SHIFT+L] and *Input Right Locator* [SHIFT+R] commands.

There are a number of ways these fields can be edited:

- ○ Typing numbers directly into the fields
- ○ Using the up and down cursor keys
- ○ Highlighting a field and using the mouse-wheel to scroll the values
- ○ Clicking above a field, when the cursor is shown as a plus sign, to increase its value, and below when the cursor is shown as a minus sign to decrease the value.

♪   *Note*

The minimum permissable *time* between the left and right locators is 500ms. Sx will allow you to set the locators below 500ms, but will automatically move the left locator to a distance of 500ms from the right locator when the Cursor is moved.

Function	Key Command
Insert Marker (at Cursor)	[Insert]
Set Markers (*n* = 1 thru 9)	CTRL+Pad *n* and CTRL+*n*
Locate Cursor to Markers (*n* = 1 thru 9)	Pad *n* and SHIFT+*n*
Locate Next Marker	SHIFT+N
Locate Previous Marker	SHIFT+B
Play to Next Marker	No default
Return to Zero/Start	Pad . (point) and , (comma)
Go to End of Project	No default
Locate Next Event	N
Locate Previous Event	B

Fig. 7.3: Marker Key Commands

Navigating, Selecting and Zooming with Markers

Once created, you can begin to use the various marker navigation functions. Remember that Standard Markers are related to Cursor position whereas Cycle Markers are related to identifying ranges.

For Standard Markers you have the following that relocate the Cursor. The Project Window will follow providing *Auto-scroll* [F] is active:

○ Set Marker key commands (markers 1 to 9 only)
○ Locate directly to markers using the keypad numbers 1 thru 9.
○ Click the unnamed field to the left of the Marker List or Inspector.
○ Use the *Locate* dropdown in the Track List

You can select the range that a Cycle Marker represents by double-clicking it or by clicking in the unnamed field to the left of the Marker List or Inspector. You can also use the Cycle dropdown in the Track List.

The Range Selection tool can be used in conjunction with the Marker Track. See chapter 11, page 110.

To zoom to a Cycle Marker's range either use the Zoom dropdown in the Track List or ALT+double click the Cycle Marker. You can, of course, use *Zoom to Selection* [ALT+S] after selecting the Cycle Marker's range.

Transport Preferences

The Transport has a dedicated tab in *Preferences*. The options do the following:

Stationary Cursors
○ *Ticked:* When *Auto-scroll* [F] is switched on, the Cursor will remain in the middle of the screen and the Project will scroll around it. This setting might cause performance problems on your machine.

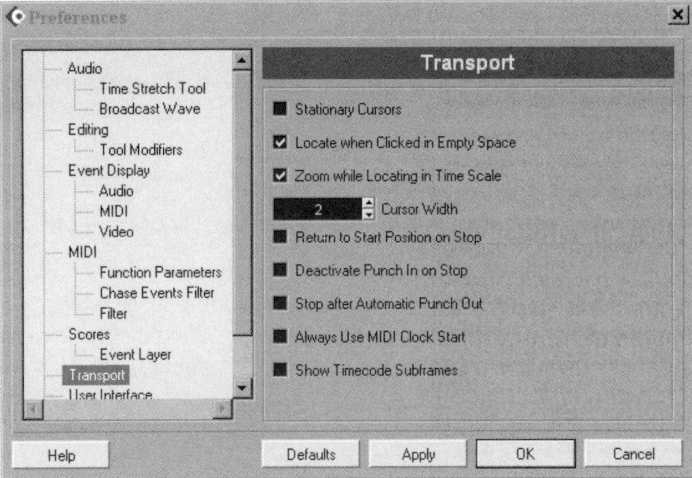

Fig. 7.4: Transport Preferences

○ *Clear:* The Cursor will move across the Project. When Auto-scroll is on, the next "page" of the Project will be displayed when the Cursor approaches the right hand edge of the Event Display.

Locate When Clicked in Empty Space
○ *Ticked:* Allows positioning of the Cursor by clicking in the Event Display.
○ *Clear:* No movement of Cursor when clicking in the Event Display.

Zoom While Locating in Time Scale
○ *Ticked:* Permits you to zoom in and out around a specific point, by clicking in the Ruler and dragging the mouse up and down. This will cause the Project Cursor to move to where you clicked. Movement of the Cursor can be avoided by pressing the SHIFT key while performing this operation.
○ *Clear:* This zoom feature is switched off.

Cursor Width
Settings of 1, 2 (default), 3 and 4 are available.

Return to Start Position on Stop
○ *Ticked:* The Cursor will return to the last position where it was stationary when the Project is stopped.
○ *Clear:* Cursor remains at its stopped position when Stop is applied.

Deactivate Punch In on Stop
Does what it says.

Stop After Automatic Punch Out
Does what it says, but note that any post-roll value set will be followed.

Always Use MIDI Clock Start
This option only affects MIDI Clock output. All MIDI messages are sent to all

MIDI ports selected to send MIDI Clock in *Transport/Sync Set-up* [No Default] (see page 267).

○ *Ticked:* When Cubase Sx is started, a MIDI Start message is sent, followed by the MIDI Clock messages. When stopped, a MIDI Stop message is sent. When the Cursor is repositioned in the Project Window, a MIDI Stop message is sent.

MIDI messages sent when in this mode are: Start, Clock and Stop.

○ *Clear:* When Cubase Sx is started, a MIDI Continue message is sent, followed by the MIDI Clock messages. When stopped, a MIDI Stop message is sent followed by a MIDI Song Position Pointer. When the Cursor is repositioned in the Project Window, a Song Position Pointer is sent.

MIDI messages sent when in this mode are: Continue, Clock, Stop and Song Position Pointer.

Show Timecode Sub-frames
○ *Ticked:* Timecode sub-frames (80 per frame) are shown in all appropriate displays and edit fields when a Timecode format is selected.
○ *Clear:* Sub-frames are not shown.

8 The Project Browser

The *Project/Browser* [CTRL+B] is a list-based, rather than a visual, representation of a Project. From the Browser you can edit and view all Events and Parts on all Tracks (including Markers, Tempo and Time Signature).

Editing is performed by typing values directly into the fields in the Browser window. Changes made in either the Browser, or the Project Window, are reflected in the other.

By right-clicking on the Browser background, a number of basic editing facilities are available (essentially the *Project* menu), including adding Tracks.

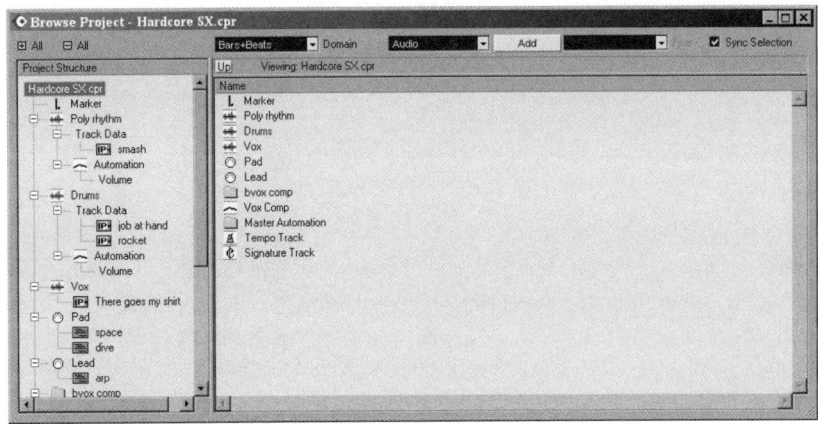

The Project Browser

As list editors go, it is quite basic, but all the essential tools are here. There are no global editing functions, nor are there any logical editing functions. For MIDI editing, the Key, Score Drum and List editors are generally a better option.

Basic Features

The Browser is divided vertically into two discrete sections:

○ *The Structure List:* left-hand side, showing all Tracks in the Project
○ *The Event Display:* right-hand side, shows the item selected in the Structure list.

Above the Structure List are two buttons: one to expand the list fully, the other to collapse it fully. Above the Event display are three dropdowns and a checkbox:

○ *Domain* dropdown (allowing the display format to be changed to Samples, Seconds, 30fps, etc.)
○ *Add* button with its associated Event type selector to its *left*. You can add audio Parts, a variety of MIDI Events, tempo and time signature changes
○ *Filter* dropdown selector for filtering MIDI Parts and Markers
○ The *Sync Selection* checkbox (see below)

To view the contents of an item in the Event display, select it in the Structure List. Click the plus boxes to expand any further content. To delete any item in the Browser, simply select it, in either window, then press DEL or BACKSPACE.

♪	**Note**

You can edit the name of many objects in the Structure List. To do so, select the object then click again (or press RETURN) to activate editing.

The Event display can be can be formatted in the following ways:

○ Sort the Events by clicking on a column heading. An arrow appears on the column showing the current sort order. If you click on this column again the sort order will be reversed (as will the indicator arrow).
○ Change the display format in the Domain field (in the same way as the Ruler (e.g. Bars+Beats, Samples, etc.))
○ Move columns – by dragging their title boxes to new positions.
○ Change column widths – by dragging the column dividers.

Sync Selection

Checking the *Sync Selection* checkbox (at the top-right corner of the Browser) will apply some *selection* synchronization between the Project Window and the Browser. Some inconsistency has been observed when using *Sync Selection*. You sometimes find that when you select an Event in the Project Window, that the Event has not been selected in the Browser. When selecting items in the Browser, selection sync seems to work correctly, with Tracks and Events being highlighted.

♪	*Note*

There is only one Browser and that, when open, will appear in every Window Layout. You cannot save an open Browser in a Window Layout.

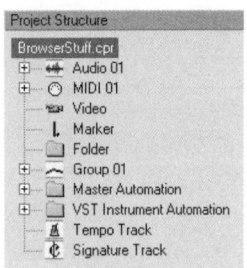

Browser Project structure

Editing in the Browser

The Browser shows the following Tracks types at its top level: Tempo; Time Signature; and all Tracks in the Track List (Audio, MIDI, Video, Marker, Folder, Group (automation), Master Automation, and VSTi Automation).

Different icons are used to represent the various Track types. It's worth assigning these to memory since, as the Project grows, these icons make navigating the list much faster.

(Time) Signature
The only function available here is adding a new Time Signature. Place the Cursor at the appropriate position in the Project Window, click the Add button,

and then adjust the Time Signature to the one you want. Double-clicking the Time Signature Track in the Browser will open the visual *Tempo Track* [CTRL+T], see chapter 10, page 89.

Tempo

Tempo behaves much the same as Time Signature in the Browser: add then season to taste. As above, double-clicking the Tempo Signature Track in the Browser will open the visual *Tempo Track* [CTRL+T].

Markers

The Marker Track will only exist in the Browser if a Marker Track exists in the Project Window. The easiest way to create a Marker is to position the Cursor at the required spot and then press [Insert]. There is no shortcut for creating Cycle Markers. In the Browser, you can either add a Marker (at the Project Cursor position) or add a Cycle Marker (from the Left Locator to the Right Locator). Editing is the same as described in *Markers in Detail* on page 73.

Automation Events

It is only possible to edit and delete automation Events in the Browser. Each existing automation sub-Track is a separate entry in the Structure List, thus each is easy to locate.

Audio

Each Browser Audio Track consists of:

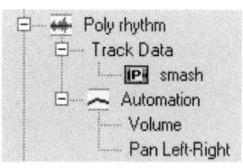

○ Track data (Events and Parts)
○ Automation data

When you select the former, then all Events and Parts in the Track will be displayed in the Event display.

Typical Browser Track

To edit Events in a Part, expand the Structure List for the Part and select. The data available for editing are the same as those available in the Info Line in the Project Window (see page 61). The only exception to this is Lock information, which can only be changed from the Project Window. Note that Clips, and thus Regions, are not shown.

Empty Audio Parts can be created when the Audio entry is selected in the Structure list by using the Add button. This will create an empty Part between the Left and Right Locators.

MIDI

The MIDI Editor in the Browser is not dissimilar to a cutdown MIDI *List Editor* [CTRL+G]. In the Browser you can perform the essential create, delete and update functions, but that is all; there are no creative aspects to have fun with.

As with Audio, the MIDI data is separated into Track data and Automation data. In this case the former is the MIDI Parts and associated MIDI Events, and the latter automation data to control items associated with the MIDI Track (such as toggling MIDI Inserts, adjusting Track Parameters, etc.).

MIDI Parts have their Start, End, Length, Offset and Mute available for editing. An empty MIDI Part can be created in the Browser by using the Add button (the Track must be selected). This will create an empty Part between the Left and Right Locators.

MIDI Events that can be added in the Browser are:

Note	Aftertouch	SMF
Controller	Pitch Bend	Text
Program Change	SYSEX	

The data available for editing MIDI Events are the same as those available in the Info Line of the Key Editor. The only exception to this is *Off Velocity*.

Use of filtering simplifies the MIDI Events being displayed. The filter options are:

None	Program Change	Pitch Bend
Note	Poly Pressure	SYSEX
Controller	Aftertouch	

Notes:

○ Note Off Events are implied by Note On Length.
○ Controllers cannot be further filtered to a particular controller in the Browser display; it's all or nothing.

SYSEX Editor

SYSEX data are an integral part of a Project's archive material for many musicians. Equally, some instruments use SYSEX for real-time control and so recording these data is a requirement. The Cubase Sx SYSEX editor is opened by double-clicking on the comments field for a SYSEX Event in the Browser. You can adjust the SYSEX Event's *Start* position in the Browser. For more on SYSEX editing see page 132.

For reference, shown below is a table that lists the MIDI data values for MIDI Events that can be edited:

Event Type	Data 1	Data 2
Note	Note Number (Pitch)	Velocity
Pitch Bend	Fine adjustment	Coarse adjustment
Poly Pressure	Note Number (Pitch)	Coarse pitch adjustment
Controllers	Controller Name*	Value
Other Events	Value	Not used

*The Controller name can be edited by inserting the corresponding MIDI CC number in this field. A full list of MIDI CC's is supplied in appendix D, page 339.

9 Audio: Understanding Audio Objects

This section is dedicated to Cubase Sx objects in the Event Display, and to audio rather than to MIDI (although much of the Part Editing described here applies equally to MIDI Parts).

A clear understanding of the various audio objects is fundamental to using Cubase Sx effectively. It's not essential that you understand what follows, but a clear understanding will make creative use of Cubase Sx much easier.

What are Cubase Sx's Audio Objects?

Here we are talking about:
○ Audio Files
○ Clips
○ Events
○ Parts
○ Regions

Audio Files, Clips and Events

Whether we record the audio in Cubase Sx ourselves, or whether we import audio, the audio itself resides in an Audio File on the hard disk. Easy. In general, this Audio File will either be created in or copied to the Audio folder in the Project Folder.

A reference (or pointer) in the Pool to an Audio File is called a *Clip*. That was easy. Now I'd like you to re-read that statement. And now I'll repeat it: A reference (or pointer) in the Pool to an Audio File is called a *Clip*. It is very important to grasp the distinction between an audio file and the Clip that points to it. You'll see in a moment that a Clip is in fact a sequence of pointers. But for now just consider that it's pointing to a single audio file.

When audio is inserted onto the Event Display then an *Audio Event* is created. There are other types of Events, namely: MIDI Events, Automation Events and Video Events, but we will only be concerned with Audio Events here.

Each Event is associated with a single Clip. Again that is worth repeating. An Event is associated with a single Clip. (Events can be created in many different ways see chapter 11, page 101 for more details.)

Note that an Event has a start time. It has other properties, most notably the length of time that it plays, but its start time in the Project is very important.

So, if we have two copies of the same Event (say, chorus background vox), then we can use them at different start times in the Project (and, perhaps, on different Tracks) and get the expected result.

As alluded to above, an Event not only has length and a start position in the Project, but it also has a start-time in the Clip.

For example, you record a vocal take that includes a frank and open discussion about the merits of different guitar strings. This fascinating discussion at the start of the take is probably best left off the final master of you Track. Thus, in Cubase Sx terms, the Event of that take will need to be adjusted to reference a useful start-point of the Clip; somewhere after the above guitar string discussion and just before the vocal starts.

This Clip start-point for an Event (if you like "play from here"-point), that is present with every Event, is called the Event *offset*. The offset for an Event can be viewed in the *Browser* [CTRL+B] or on the Info line provided that the Event is selected.

So an Event is a window on part of a Clip (though it could be a window on the whole Clip). And throughout all of this, note that the Clip remains unchanged.

Clips: The Plot Thickens

So that's that then? Well, no. A Clip may point to more than just the originally referenced Audio File.

When a section of a Clip is processed in some way (usually by processing an Event), say a fade applied or a plug-in applied, then a new audio file is created for that section of the Clip, but with the changes applied to it. (These files are placed in the *Fades* or the *Edits* folder, as appropriate.) Note that the original audio file is left unchanged. The Clip is then updated to take account of these changes and will "point" to the correct audio file at the appropriate places. When the Project is played, Cubase Sx will select the appropriate audio files to play during each Event automatically.

Since it is seamless, then I can forget about it?

Not quite. Say, you have used an Event twice in a Project. In the second Event you decide that you want to apply a fade out. If you do this by dragging the blue Fade Handles on the Event, then indeed, the change will be seamless. In this case, the fade will be applied to the second Event and the first will remain unchanged.

But say you wish to process the second Event by applying a filter sweep, over the whole Event. To do this you preview the Event with you filter plug-in (select the Event, right-click, and choose the plug-in), tweak as necessary, then press Process. The following window appears

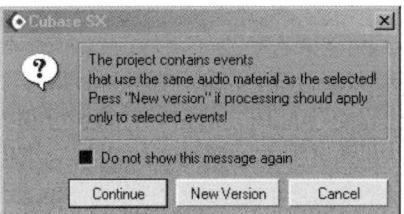

In this case, you want the filter effect on the selected Event, and the original left unprocessed, and so you press *New Version*. If you wish to apply the effect to all Events that use that part of the Clip, then you press *Continue*.

What happens when you press *New Version* is that a *new* Clip is created, as you can see by taking a look in the Pool. So we now have two Clips pointing to the same audio file.

As you can imagine, this process gives us a great deal of flexibility over how different Events, referencing the same audio, can be utilized. Add to this the fact that Undos can be applied to individual Events (and the processing applied to them) and we have a very powerful creative tool.

Audio Files, Clips and Events: A summary

On first encountering the relationships between audio files, Clips and Events, it can be a little confusing. The central themes are:

○ the underlying original audio files remain unchanged in the Audio folder
○ a Clip is a reference to the original audio plus newly created audio files where processing has been applied
○ an Event is a cue to playback part of a Clip at a chosen time during a song (Project).

You soon get used to it.

Parts

Parts are yet another powerful part of Cubase Sx's armory. Reality is deceptive, since a Part is simply a container in which one places Events. To create a Part from Events, select one or more Events on a Track and choose *Audio/Events to Part* [No Default]. The Part appears on the Track "surrounding" the selected the Events. The Part can now be manipulated in the Project Window in essentially the same ways as an Event. The reverse function is *Audio/Dissolve Part* [No Default].

There are two major advantages of using Parts over using Events:

○ *The Part Editor* (see chapter 14, page 181) which is extremely useful for comp'ing
○ Easy manipulation of multiple related Events

Many users find that aligning audio is more easily achieved in the audio Part Editor than directly from Events on the Project Window. For example, in the Part Editor it becomes unnecessary to continually zoom in and zoom out to view the Events. There is also an Undo history associated with the Part, in addition to those for the Events, and this can prove to be very useful.

Note that offset for Audio Parts has a different meaning to offset for an Audio Event. In the case of Audio Parts, the offset value determines the start positions of the Events within the Part. In effect, this is like sliding the Events backwards or forwards in the Part.

Regions

Regions in the Pool

A Region is a section of a Clip. You will find them shown in the Pool and in the Sample Editor. They can be manipulated in the same way as a Clip; they are essentially sub-Clips. Regions are most often created and edited in the Sample Editor or via *Audio/Event as Region* [No Default].

They are useful for creating reminders and reference points/areas within a Clip. Also, since Events can be created from the Regions in a Clip (*Audio/Events From Region* [No Default]), they can also be used to identify useable areas in a Clip for later conversion to Events.

A Region can be exported as an audio file (via *Audio/Bounce Selection* [No Default]). When you do this a new Clip is created that references the new audio file.

The distinct difference between Events and Regions is that an Event must exist on the Event display while a Region does not (it "exists" in the Pool). Keeping this in mind, you can see that you can reference many Regions without cluttering the Event display. An Event can be created from a Region at any time simply

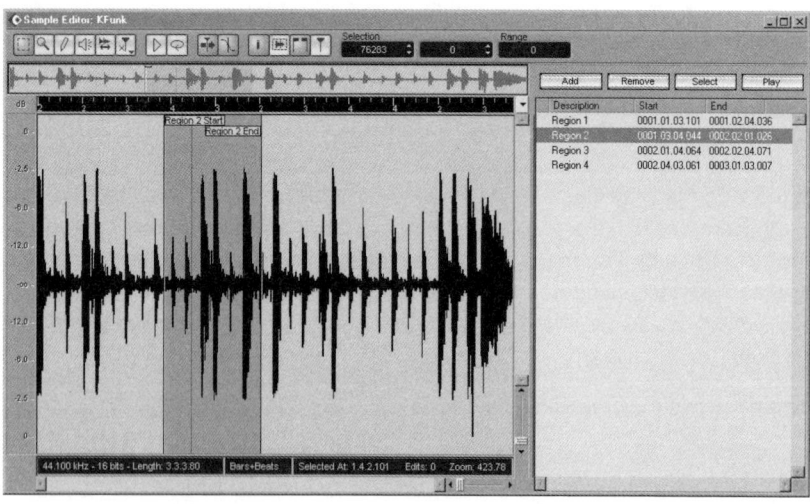

Fig. 9.1: Regions in the Sample Editor

by dragging it from the Pool into the Event Display.

When an Event references a Clip that contains Regions, the Region that the Event references in the Clip can be changed very rapidly via the Event's quick menu (*Set to Region*). This feature can be exploited in many ways, but is most useful when a Clip contains multiple version of the same (or a similar) source. For example, when auditioning the takes after recording in Cycle mode. See chapter 14, page 178 for the details.

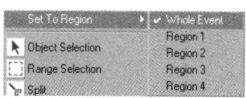

Changing Regions quickly

A few uses for Regions

It's not immediately apparent, to many folk, how useful Regions can be, so here are a couple of ideas to get you started.

Say that you want to apply an effect to a section of an Event or Clip. Select the area in the Sample Editor and create a Region for that area and name it appropriately. After applying the effect, you will later be able to identify the area in the Pool or Sample Editor (or, indeed, the Event Display using the technique mentioned above).

A common use is to create Regions for useful sections of a Clip; almost like a notepad. They are also handy if, say, you receive audio in long sections (perhaps for every Track you receive the audio the length of the song, which is a common occurrence). You can then identify the used sections of each Track as Regions and create Events from these, as required. This also facilitates removing unnecessarily long Clips from the Project, which might be useful for speeding up Processing, reducing machine load, and simplifying archiving.

When processing an Event, and selecting the *New Version* option that creates a new Clip, the Off-line Process History (OPH) does not get copied to the new Clip, but Regions do. In this way, you can retain reminders of processing previously applied to the original Clip.

You can use the commands *Audio/Events from Regions* and *Audio/Event as Region* to both create Regions rapidly, and to create Events from Regions (see page 107). You can also create Regions from hit-points (page 100).

The work-flow, quite often, is not to create Regions and then create Events, but more to work with Events until you're satisfied that you have something permanent (or semi-permanent), then create Regions from these Events. (You can do select all, or multiple Events, for this.) In a sense, this provides a kind of backup of your useful audio.

There are a lot of ways to use Regions and, once you are in the habit, it's hard to imagine life without them.

Exporting Regions to Files

A Region can be exported from the Pool to a destination outside of the Project. To do this select the Region in the Pool then do Audio/Bounce Selection. A dialogue will appear from which you can select the destination on disk.

10 Tempo and Time Signature

Tempo and Time Signature settings apply across the whole Project, although both can be varied throughout the length of a Project. Only one tempo and one time signature can be active at any one time. The Events that represent these changes can be made in both the *Browser* [CTRL+B] and the *Tempo Track Editor* [CTRL+T]. In the Browser, Tempo Events and Signature Events are given their own Tracks and are managed in list form. In the Tempo Track Editor, the tempo Events are managed in a graphical manner, and the signature Events along a timeline.

Tempo Button

Whether an individual Track, and its Events, are affected by Tempo and Time Signature changes is dependent on its Time/Tempo Base Button.

Time Sig Button

While MIDI Tracks (almost invariably tempo-based) can be freely abused with tempo changes, the same is not the case for audio. As you will see, high quality time stretching is available in Cubase Sx (a mathematical process where the length, and hence tempo of audio is changed without altering pitch), but it is best avoided, if at all possible. It can, of course, have many creative uses. For tempo-based audio Tracks, the start position of audio Events is dependent on the tempo setting, but the audio itself will playback precisely as it sounded when it was recorded. In other words, audio Events do not get automatically adjusted in length when the tempo changes.

However, Cubase Sx offers *Recycle*-like deconstruction of loops, (in fact any audio, should you wish). This technique allows you to identify so-called *hit-points* in the audio. These hit-points are then, effectively, locked to tempo, and the audio loop or segment lengthened or shortened automatically as tempo changes.

Tempo in Cubase Sx

All audio and MIDI Tracks in Cubase Sx are either time-based or tempo-based. The Events on time-based Track are independent of any tempo changes that occur in a Project. That is to say that their start time in the Project will remain unchanged despite tempo changes occurring. Tempo-based Tracks are, natu-rally, affected by tempo changes.

For most MIDI Tracks it makes sense for a Track to be tempo-based, and this is the default setting. For audio Tracks it is more common for them to be time-based (the default is tempo-based). Automation Events for a Track will share the Track's state.

The Marker Track is created as tempo-based. Your circumstances will dictate the appropriate setting.

On a time based Track, Events/Parts will play according to their Start positions. On a change of playback tempo, their start position will not change.

On a tempo based Track, the positions of Events are represented as meter values (Bars, Beats, 1/16th notes and ticks, where 1/16th note = 120 ticks). On a change of playback tempo, the Events will either play earlier in time (on an increase in tempo), or later (on a decrease in tempo).

Steinberg warns that there is a potential timing issue when a Track is repeatedly changed from one base to the other; though it's unclear why someone might want to do this. Any change that might occur would be minimal at worst, though this might be sufficient to cause phasing issues for audio.

There are two Tempo modes in Cubase Sx:

○ *Rehearsal* (Master button unlit)
  The tempo, displayed to the right of the Master button, is fixed across the whole Project.
○ *Master Tempo* (Master button lit)
  Tempo will follow the Events in the Tempo Track. These Events can also be viewed in the Browser.

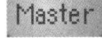

The Master button (*Transport/Master Track toggle* [No Default]) on the Transport switches between these two modes.

External Tempo Sync

Cubase Sx does not accept MIDI Clock input, so cannot be tempo synchronized externally. It can, however, send MIDI Clock, so that other devices can be tempo synch'd to it. Cubase Sx can, however, sync to MIDI Time Code (MTC) (see chapter 19, page 269).

Time Signatures in Cubase Sx

Time Signatures can be added, deleted and edited in the *Browser* [CTRL+B] and the *Tempo Track Editor* [CTRL+T]. In the Browser, the Signature Events are collected in a dedicated Signature Track and can be edited in the usual list-editing manner. In the Tempo Track Editor, they are displayed on a timeline above the Tempo display and below the Ruler. Signature Events can be created by double-clicking in the timeline (or by ALT+click), edited by dragging (to a measure), and deleted by selecting then pressing the DEL key.

Irrespective of the Master button on the Transport being active or inactive, Time Signature changes are always active, and their impact displayed in the Event Display.

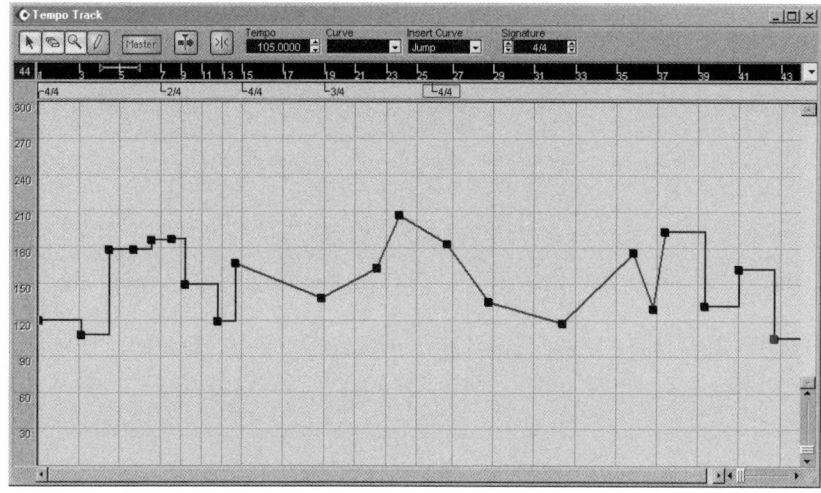

Fig. 10.1: The Tempo Track - Master Tempo Mode

The Tempo Track Editor

The *Project/Tempo Track* [CTRL+T] can be used for inserting and editing tempo and time signatures in a Project. The alternative is to use the Browser. Whichever method you use, it can be useful to note the tempo and time signature changes in markers, and display them on a marker Track in the Project Window as an aide-memoire

Figure 10.1 shows the Tempo Track from a well-known James Brown Track. Well, okay, even James Brown doesn't move the groove that much (thankfully), but as an indication of what is available and what can be done, this shows it. In particular, note the stepped and ramped tempo curves, and the liberal use of signature changes.

> ♪   *Note*
>
> CTRL+click on the Transport's *Master* button will open the *Tempo Track*.

Tempo Track Ruler

The Tempo Track Editor has its own Ruler, the format of which can be changed in the usual way. However, it has two additional modes available for selection: Time Linear; and Bars+Beats Linear, one of which is always active.

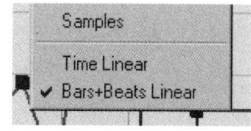

Tempo Track modes

○ *Time Linear*
  In this mode, time is the constant for the display. So, if the Bars+Beats format is on display, the distance between the bar lines will vary with tempo changes.
○ *Bars+Beats Linear*
  In this mode, the constant for the display is a bar. So, if a time format is on display, the distance between, say, two ten-second time-slices will vary with tempo changes.

The Toolbar has Snap and Auto-scroll buttons available. The Master switch is also replicated here to allow switching between rehearsal and master tempo modes.

Next to the tools are four separate information and edit boxes. They show:

○ Tempo – 1–300bpm
○ Curve – Jump or Ramp
○ Insert Curve – Jump or Ramp
○ Signature – $1/2$ to $64/16$

The last of these shows the value of the currently selected Signature Event. You can edit this value by first selecting it and then either using the spin buttons, or typing directly into the field. Note that time signatures can only take the form n/2, n/4, n/8, and n/16, where n is an integer value from 1 to 64.

When you open the editor, the first tempo and time signature Events are selected in the editor (highlighted in red), therefore the Tempo field will contain the Project start tempo. The Tempo field will only contain a value if a single Tempo Event is selected. This field can be edited in the usual ways (determined by Preferences), or by way of the spin buttons.

Tempo Track Editor: Main display

The main display shows all tempo changes. Each blob represents a Tempo Event. Zooming is performed in the usual ways, and Events can be added and deleted here.

Note that in Rehearsal mode, since tempo is forced to be constant through-out the Project, there are no tempo Event blobs in the display. Instead, the Rehearsal tempo is displayed as a horizontal line. Be very careful here, as any changes made in Rehearsal mode cannot be undone.

In Master Tempo mode the Events can be selected and edited, either by using the fields in the tool bar, or by dragging the Event on the display. When dragging, you can use the CTRL key to either maintain the tempo or the time value of the Event. When multiple Events are selected then only the Ramp Type can be edited. Ramp type cannot be edited in the Browser.

Tempo Events only have three attributes:

○ Position
○ Tempo
○ Ramp Type – Jump or Ramp

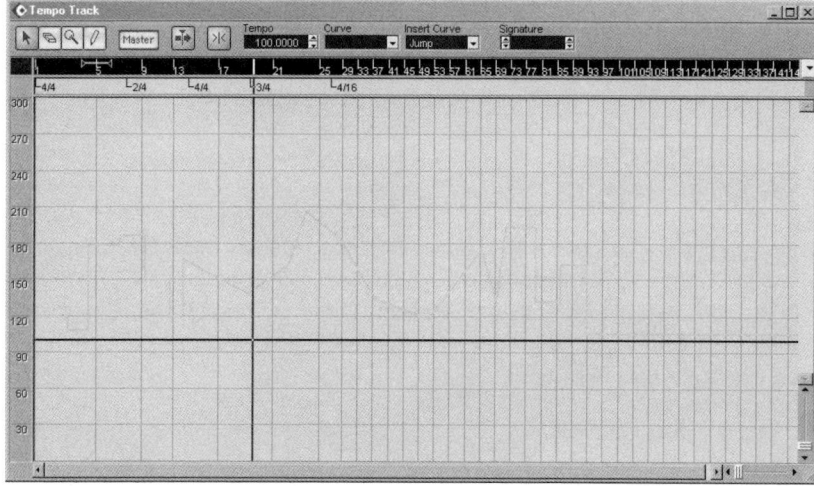

Fig. 10.2: The Tempo Track - Rehearsal Mode

The Ramp type applies to the way in which the tempo will change from the preceding tempo Event. It can only take two values: ramp and jump.

If you use the pencil tool to create Tempo Events, then a tempo "curve" will be drawn. The way it works is a little bizarre.

You can create a Tempo Event with the *Select* tool by holding ALT. Now select the ramp type you require leading up to the Event, and click and hold in the display. Note that snap can be activated, if required. You can now position the Event as needed using the visual and numerical cues. The Event is created when you click, and another may be created on release of the mouse-button depending on the actions you have taken.

You can also create a Tempo Event with the *Project/Beat Calculator* [No Default] (see below).

VSTi and VST Plug-in Tempo Sync

The VST Plug-in specification now makes it possible for plug-ins to receive MIDI messages from the host application. The most useful applications for this are automation (see chapter 18, page 257), and for MIDI Clock to be passed to a VSTi or VST plug-in. Note that neither of these are available for DirectX plug-ins. MIDI Clock is very useful in the case of temporal effects such as delays, and also for the LFOs of VSTi's. Many such plug-ins and VSTi's exist that make use of this feature, including a number of the plug-in supplied with Cubase Sx (e.g. Double Delay). There are many older VST plug-ins that will not respond automatically to tempo, so check with your plug-in documentation if things are not working out as you expect. (You will also find details of plug-ins via *Devices/Plug-in Information* [No Default].)

In Cubase Sχ, MIDI Timing information is automatically provided to any VST 2.0 plug-in that requests it. No action is required on the part of the user to make use of this feature.

The Beat Calculator

The *Project/Beat Calculator* [No Default] helps to identify the tempo of a piece of audio. It can also calculate tempo by you manually tapping SPACE. The results can then be placed directly into the Project. There are great pieces of software out there that do this a lot more accurately, but if you don't have one of those, then this is the next best thing.

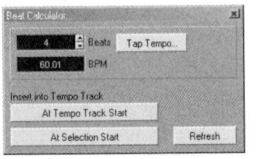

The Beat Calculator

For audio it works like this:

o Select the relevant audio Event/Part. This either needs to be accurately trimmed or, alternatively, you can use the Region tool to make a selection.
o Enter the number of beats in the selected audio in the Beats field of the Beat Calculator (you can type into this field)
o The tempo is displayed in the BPM field

For tapping it goes like this...2...3...4:

o If you want to tap along to some imported audio (and why not, it's harmless fun), then set it playing before you...
o Click the Tap Tempo button
o Now either click the mouse (on the Tap Tempo window) or bash away on the space bar. This is the stuff computers were made for. You can use both mouse and space bar for added pleasure.
o When you're done. The final tempo will be shown a few seconds after the final tap.
o Press ESC to close the window.

You can, if you wish, insert the displayed tempo into the Tempo Track. In Rehearsal mode, pressing either of the two buttons described below will replace the current rehearsal tempo. Warning: this cannot be undone. Pressing *At Tempo Track Start* will create a new Tempo Event with the displayed BPM as the first Tempo Event of the Project. Warning: this cannot be undone. Pressing *At Selection Start* will insert a Tempo Event at the current selection start point. This will overwrite any Event that currently exists there. Another warning: The Beat Calculator doesn't remember the selection start point when you calculated the tempo, it simply uses the current selection. Oh and this action can't be undone either.

It's hard to get excited about the *Beat Calculator*, however the tap tempo feature can be used when writing, to get an approximation of the tempo that you think you might want a song to go. And, daft as it sounds, the mouse + SPACE method does have its merits. Let's leave it at that.

Changing the Tempo of Audio – Time-Stretch

With the best will in the world, and all the pre-production you can muster, there will come a time when a tempo change is required after the audio has been recorded, and it is just not possible to go back and re-record. At these times we have to get creative. Steinberg, and their buddies at Prosoniq, to the rescue: Cubase S$_X$ comes supplied with a very useable time-stretch process that can be used in these situations, *Audio/Process/Time Stretch* [No Default].

As well as this S$_X$ Process, it is also possible to time-stretch audio with the Time-stretch tool, see page 55.

The Time-Stretch window is a little confusing, but it does contain a lot of functionality. The left-hand side shows the information for the selected Event/Part. The adjustable fields in the Input section will often reflect the details of the selected audio, but should they be different (for example, if you have imported a drum loop of a different tempo to the Project tempo), then adjust these to their correct value to assist the time-stretch algorithm in giving the best results (or mess them up completely in pursuit of creative madness).

Next adjust the Time-Stretch slider, or the Output fields, to the desired values. Note that the Effect box allows you to extend the time-stretch range significantly; though you can expect to hear significant artifacts when stretching beyond the non-Effect limits.

The *Algorithm* dropdown provides a selection of sound quality modes. Since this is an off-line process you will, almost without exception, use the highest setting: the MPEX Algorithm. For Preview purposes, however, this option is not available.

Probably the most useful technique is to use the *Set to Locators Range* option. Providing you know the precise location and length of where you want your audio to go, you can set the locators in the Project Window, press the above but-

♫　　*Note*

The sliders can be moved with greater precision by holding down SHIFT.

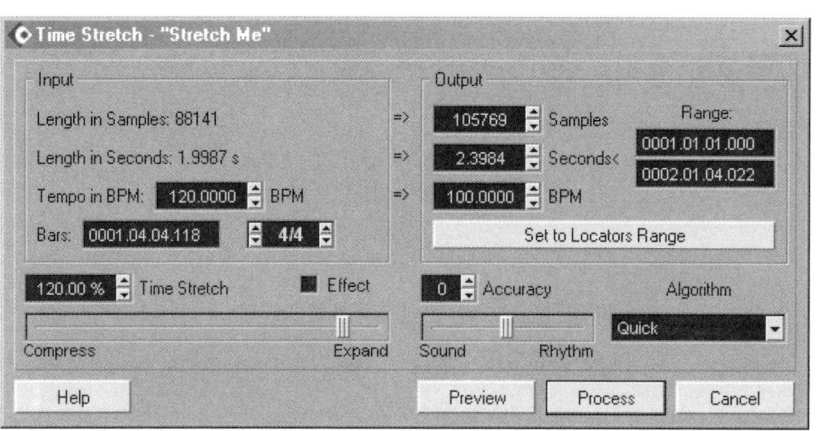

Fig. 10.3: Time Stretch

ton in Time Stretch and it will perform the necessary calculations. All you have to do is press Process and you are done.

> ♪   **Note**
>
> Time-Stretch "remembers" its previous stretch settings from the last time it was used. This can be useful when stretching a number of audio Events affected by a single tempo change within a Project.

When changing the tempo of an audio Event, there are a number of ways to proceed. The obvious way is to use the *Output BPM* field. Another way is to set the locators to the required size after you have adjusted the tempo of the Project. In this case, you need to ensure that the start position of the audio is in the right place after the tempo change (a problem that might occur if the Track is in time-mode). It is worth considering ensuring that the audio Track is tempo-based prior to the tempo change, if that makes sense in your Project. Certainly, if you were working with a lot of audio that is aligned to bars, then this would be the case.

Where you have many audio Parts, don't forget that Time-Stretch "remembers" its setting. So rather than having to continually reset the conversion parameters, you simply open Time Stretch for each Event and press Process. (It would be very neat if there were a "batch" process when you have multiple Events selected, but you can't have everything.)

Also, be careful of how audio Parts are affected when changing tempo. It might be worthwhile dissolving the Parts before apply the *tempo* change.

The choices you make very much depend on what you are trying to achieve. Don't forget that you can undo any off-line processing, so there are no worries about losing your audio. You can freely experiment until you achieve the desired result...or a happy accident.

Changing the Tempo of Audio – Hit-points

> ♪   *Note*
>
> Hit-points are not the exclusive domain of drum loops. Guitar, piano, and many other sources can respond equally well to hit-point processing.

Cubase Sx provides another method for changing the tempo of audio, via a feature called *hit-points*. Using this method, the audio itself is not mathematically changed, as it is with time-stretch, but instead it is 'chopped-up' into a number of smaller Events (that are then wrapped up in a Part). Each of these Events can then follow any tempo changes made to the Project (providing the resulting Events remain on a tempo-based Track). These Events are called "slices". Each slice will usually start with an identifiable tempo-related attack (such as a drum hit). Because the slices usually start with a rapid attack, it is computationally simple to automatically identify them; these attacks are used as the basis of hit-point creation.

By manipulating audio in this was, a surprisingly broad range of tempi can be accommodated before either noticeable gaps appear, or individual slices start to merge into a blur. And even in these cases, effects can often be used to stretch a few more bpm out of the audio. For example, try using a short reverb with a little pre-delay.

As well as responding to tempo changes, the resulting Events produced by this process can, of course, be replaced. In this way it is easy to swap a loop's kick drum (or whatever) for a preferred sound.

As you can imagine (or may be aware from similar processing in other products, such as *Recycle* or the excellent *BeatCreator* – www.beatcreator.com), this is an ideal process for loops, and drum loops, in particular.

Before showing how hit-points work in practice, it is worth noting that the hit-points can be used to create a *Groove Quantize* template, which can be used to quantize other MIDI or audio Parts. By using this technique, you can extract the "feel" of any audio and superimpose it on target material of your choosing. Very useful indeed. See chapter 13, page 161 for more.

At the time of writing (Cubase SX v1.03) there were a lot of shortcomings in this function (and, indeed, a number of bugs). I have not covered all of these here, as I hope they will be rectified in subsequent versions.

Creating Slices

The process starts with an audio Event and ends with an audio Part containing slices; the start point of each slice is determined by a hit-point.

As you know, an Event is simply a window onto a Clip. It is at this point that you must be warned of the way that hit-point processing operates. Hit-point processing does not operate on the Event, it operates on the whole Clip. This is fine if you are working with an Event that represents the whole Clip, but it is potentially disastrous if not.

> ♩ **Note**
>
> Once you have created your slices, it is easy to replace or process individual slices in the Part Editor

♮ **Warning**

If you use *Create Audio Slices* [No Default] on an Event, then *all* existing Events that reference that Clip are destroyed.

Because of the way that hit-point processing has been implemented, it is strongly recommend that you do not create other Events that reference the same Clip that will be used for hit-point processing. If you wish to use the same underlying audio file, then make sure that you create a new Clip via *Pool/New Version*. I will return to this issue later.

The following run-through on using hit-points assumes that you are using a Clip that is a known number of bars and beats in length.

○ Start with an Event representing the whole Clip and place it on a tempo-based Track. The easiest way to do this is to drag it from the Pool.

○ Perform *Locators to Selection* [P] for convenience, if you wish, and then open the Event in the Sample Editor. Figure 10.4 shows a typical single-bar drum loop in the *Sample Editor*. Note that the *Event Flags* are switched off to avoid them obscuring a hit-point.

> ↗ **Tip**
>
> One generally creates a single hit-point (and slice) per beat.

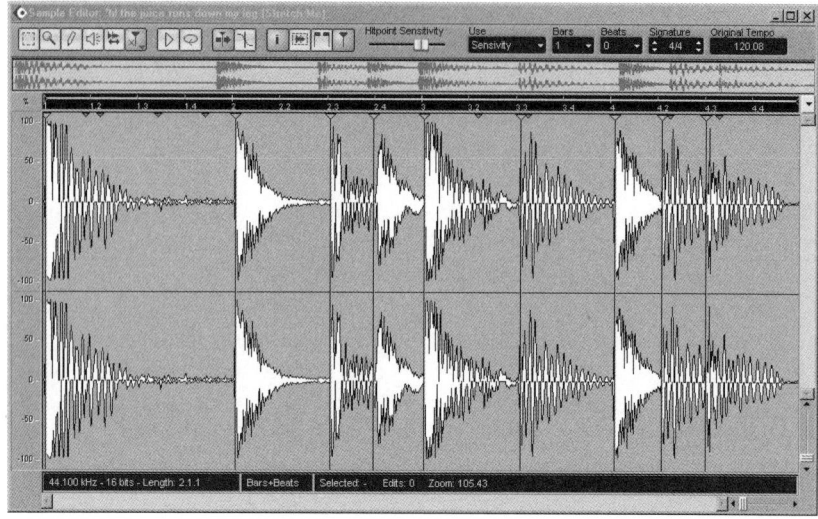

Fig. 10.4: Typical single-bar loop with hit-points.

Hit-point toggle

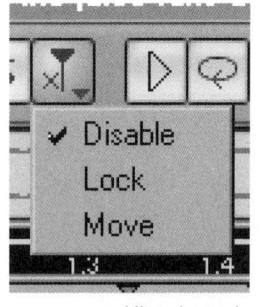

Hit-point tools

○ Create the hit-points by pressing the hit-point button. (*Audio/ Hit-Points/ Calculate* [No Default]) Once you have created hit-points on a Clip for the first time, this button will switch you in and out of *Hit-point Mode*. When you need to recalculate the hit-points, for whatever reason, you will need to use the menu command *Calculate*. Also, the icon for the Clip changes in *The Pool*.

○ Note the yellow line in the Ruler that indicates the range of audio that will be use when you later create the slices.

○ Check that the *Use* dropdown has *Sensitivity* selected, then adjust the *Sensitivity* slider to create more or less hit-points. Hold SHIFT if you need fine control of the slider.

As an alternative to the 'Sensitivity' *Use* option, there are the options 1/4, 1/8, 1/16 and 1/32. These do not create hit-points on the precise locations, but instruct the hit-point algorithm to locate beats near these locations.

○ Create hit-points manually by using the *Draw* tool. It is recommended that *Snap to Zero-crossing* is active when manually adding hit-points. This minimizes the likelihood of audio glitches, at these points, on playback.

○ It's often easier to create more hit-points than you will need with the slider, since disabling them is easy.

○ Slices can be auditioned by using the Play tool.

○ Now edit the hit-points, as required. The tools available, which all operate on the small hit-point marker, are:

○ *Disable:* the vertical line disappears to confirm. Use the same tool to re-enable.

○ *Lock:* a tiny padlock appears next to a locked marker. Use the same tool to unlock.

○ *Move:* simply click and drag. If *Snap to Zero Crossing* is active, then this will be followed.

You might want to set-up *Tool/Hit-Point tool* [No Default] to make cycling round the tools more rapid.

○ Once you are satisfied with the positions of your hit-points, ensure that the *Bars, Beats* and *Time Signature* in the dropdowns top-right are set correctly. Cubase Sx needs these to be correct in order to create the slices correctly. Providing these are set correctly, then the tempo is calculated and shown in the *Original Tempo* display box.

○ Create the slices with *Audio/Hit-points/Create audio slices* [No Default]

> ♫ **Note**
>
> The *Bars* and *Beats* dropdowns dictate the length of the Part created by *Create audio slices*

Cubase Sx now converts the Clip to a Part containing one Event for each hit-point.

> ☿ **Info**
>
> A bug in v1.03 means that the actual length of the created Part is not always shown correctly. Instead, the length of the Part is rounded down to complete bars. Correct the length via dragging, nudge or the Info Line.

The Events in the newly created Part will reflect the number of bars and beats that you provided in the Sample Editor. The Events are shifted, within the Part, to reflect the current tempo, and maintain their relative distance from each other. In other words, the Part is now sync'd to the Project's tempo. Nice.

If you followed the above example, you can now hit play and let your loop loop.

The Part can now be used like any other audio: You can swap Events, replace Events, flange a kick and reverse a snare, mute Events. Just remember, to maintain its ability to follow tempo, then it must be on a tempo-based Track.

Slowing tempo cause gaps

When lowering tempo, the slices within a sliced Part move apart and, possibly, gaps will appear between the Events. Gaps in audio are silence. And silence can be a problem. To assist with this problem, Cubase Sx provides a command, *Audio/Close Gaps* [No Default], that performs time-stretch on each Event to close the gaps.

> ↗ **Tip**
>
> Slice-up a loop and save or use individual sounds

The time-stretch algorithm used by *Close Gaps* is the same as that for the *Time Stretch* tool, which is set on the *Preferences/Audio/Time Stretch Tool* tab. However, you can override this setting and force *Close Gaps* to use the *Drum* algorithm by checking *Always use Drum mode for Close Gaps* on the same tab.

Other programs, such as *Recycle* and *BeatCreator*, offer similar options, often with more flexibility and creative options. *BeatCreator*, for example gives the option of adding a tail, rather than simply stretching the slices, which might give better results.

A few more details

If you have an Event that is a section of a larger Clip, then you can create hit-points for just that Event. Open the Sample Editor and do *Select/Select Event*

[No Default], then do *Hit-points/Calculate.* You can, in fact, select any range for this to work.

You can use a range selection to isolate an area of the audio in which you wish to create hit-points. You can then move the end-points of the yellow ruler line to mark the area to be created in the Part. The length of the Part is still dictated by the *Bars* and *Beats* settings. The same trick will work when creating groove templates, or when using *Divide Audio Events.*

Replacing Slices

To replace a slice with another Event, open the Part Editor and place the required Event in the required spot in the Lane below. The simple way to line up one Event with another is to select the source Event, then *Locate Selection* [L]. Now select the target Events and *Edit/Cursor* [CTRL+L], the two Events will now be aligned precisely. You might want to mute the original Event if it is longer than the replacement.

Other hit-point functions

As well as *Create audio slices* [No Default], you can also use hit-points to slice an Event where the hit-points are placed. In this case, *Divide Audio Events* [No Default] will perform cut operation where the hit-points occur, so there will be no overlapping nor gaps between Events on completion. Note, however, that these Events will be affected by tempo changes if they are on a tempo-based Track.

As mentioned above, the hit-points can also be used to create a Groove Quantize template that can be used to quantize other MIDI or audio Parts. This is discussed in chapter 13, page 161.

Retrieving the Clip

Having performed *Create audio slices* on a Clip, when you subsequently drag the Clip onto the Event Display you will obtain the sliced version. This is probably what you will require most of the time. To obtain the un-sliced Clip, hold CTRL when placing the Event.

Regions from Hit-points

One final trick. You can create Regions from hit-points. First create your hit-points as above, then do *Audio/Create Regions* [No Default]. A Region will be created for each range between two hit-points. Note that the last range does not have a hit-point, so you will have to manually insert one, if needed. Furthermore, Regions will not be created when hit-points are less than approximately 100ms apart.

Once you have created Regions, you can start to manipulate them by using effects and processes. This is particularly useful when you have a loop, where you want to process the individual sounds, but don't necessarily need to go the whole way with *Create Slices.* This is a very useful feature. Note that *Audio/Detect Silence* [No Default] (page 230) can also create Regions.

11 The Event Display

The Event Display is the heart of Cubase Sx. It is where Cubase Sx's objects are manipulated and processed in a graphical manner. There are often multiple ways to achieve the same action, and knowing when and where to apply the appropriate technique will allow you to become very efficient at moving and processing Parts and Events around the Project. The by-product of being able to manipulate the Project at speed is that it aids creativity; it becomes very natural to try something speculatively, or respond to a client's whim without any pre-planning. By making use of incremental saves and Cubase Sx's Undo, you can just "go there" immediately, confident that you can return to a chosen spot.

As well as covering all of the ground of Event and Part editing, this chapter covers Range Editing, one of Cubase Sx's most powerful tools.

Auto Scroll

Auto-scroll [F] is a viewing option. When switched on, the Event Display will scroll horizontally, in pages, as the Cursor reaches the edge of the viewing area. The Cursor is always visible. When *Preferences/Transport* tab *Stationary Cursors* is checked, the Cursor will settle in the middle of the viewing area and the Event Display will move "behind" it. Stationary Cursors is quite a processor intensive task, and should only be used on sufficiently powerful hardware.

Auto-scroll

Auto-scroll is present in all editors and is individually switchable in each.

Snap to Zero Crossing

Snap to Zero Crossing [Not available] ensures that all audio editing is performed at 0dB points in the waveform. This will reduce the likelihood of clicks due to amplitude differences between two audio segments. Nevertheless, it is wise to examine these areas and apply a cross-fade if necessary, especially with stereo audio. *Snap to Zero Crossing* is a *Preferences/ Audio* tab option.

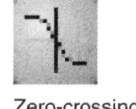

Zero-crossing

Snap to Zero Crossing is also available in the Sample Editor, where the global setting can be overridden temporarily.

Basic Manipulation of Events

Selecting Events/Parts

When you select an Event it obtains a red border, and red handles appear. The red handles are used for moving the edges of the Event. Audio Events, in

---

addition, have blue handles; these are used for creating and editing fades and changing the audio Event's volume.

Events are selected by clicking on them with the Object Select tool. To select multiple Events, hold SHIFT while clicking; alternatively you can lasso them.

You can navigate around Events with the cursor keys. Holding SHIFT will select multiple Events. The up and down cursor keys will move between Tracks. If you left cursor to the Track List, you can select a new Track without an Event being selected, then move up and down the Tracks.

There are Event/Part selection options in *Edit/Select* (menu, key commands and quick menu):

o *All* [CTRL+A]: Select all Events in the Project.
o *None* [CTRL+SHIFT+A]: Deselect all Events.
o *In Loop:* Select all Events between the Left and Right Locators (including those partially inside the loop, but not those touching it).
o *From Start to Cursor:* Select all Events that start left of the Project Cursor.
o *From Cursor to End:* Select all Events that end right of the Project Cursor.
o *All on Selected Tracks:* Select all Events on selected Tracks.

You can opt to automatically select all Events on all Tracks under the Project Cursor. For this you must check *Preferences/User Interface/Editing* tab *Auto Select Events under Cursor.* This option can come in handy when moving sections of a Project around. This very much depends on the way that you arrange and organize Parts and Events, so it is best to plan the use of this option, should you intend to use it.

Renaming an Event/Part

It is good discipline to name Events as you create them. While it is often apparent from the Event Display what an Event's function might be, the same cannot be said when using the Browser. In the Bowser there are no visual clues, so naming becomes the main guide to function (the same is true for Track names). It is surprising how quickly you can end up with many Events on the same, and different, Tracks sharing the same name, so think carefully about how you will manage these.

Every Event initially takes the name of its associated Clip. You rename an Event by editing the *Description* entry in the Info Line, or from the Browser. Be careful not to change the File entry in the Info Line, since this will rename the audio file on disk.

Event and Part *Names* and *Descriptions* are displayed on the objects themselves in the Event Display providing *Preferences/Eent Display* tab *Show Event Names* is checked.

Renaming all Events/Parts on a Track

This can be done by holding SHIFT, CTRL or ALT and renaming the Track. All the Events on that Track will take the same name as the Track.

Tip

If you want to rename all Events on a Track, but want to keep the Track name, then start by copying the Track name to the Clipboard. After renaming the Events, simply paste the Track name back.

Adding and Removing Events/Parts to a Track

Events can be added in a variety of ways. Most commonly, for Audio, this will be by recording, or by importing an audio file into the Pool and then inserting an Event representing it onto a Track, either by drag and drop, or by using the *Insert into Project* options. For a MIDI Part, recording is the most likely technique, or by drawing a Part and then inserting Events via the MIDI Editor. Automation Events, similar to MIDI, can be recorded or drawn. In all cases, Copy and Paste are available.

Events are deleted by selecting and pressing DEL or BACKSPACE, or using the *Erase* tool.

Other functions, such as *File/Import/Audio File* [No Default] and *File/Export/ Audio Mixdown* [No Default] may also create Events, sometimes as an option. These are described in the appropriate sections.

Info

If you have more than one Project open, then you can drag Parts and Events from one Project to another.

Moving Events

Cubase Sx has a number of methods for manipulating Events and Parts. All selected Events and Parts are affected by these actions.

Dragging
CubaseSx provides a safety feature that avoids accidentally moving Events with the mouse. It is a slight delay that only allows movement after the delay period has been exceeded. The delay time is variable and is set in *Preferences/Editing* tab *Drag Delay*. Note that the delay doesn't apply to the handles and it is quite easy to accidentally move one of these without noticing.

Note

If you hold down CTRL while dragging an Event or Part, then the movement of the Event/Part is restricted to the same Track (horizontally), or precisely the same time position on another Tracks (vertically). This key can be changed in *Preferences/Editing/Tool Modifiers*.

Info Line

Don't overlook the ease with which Events can be moved by simply editing the Start position in the Info Line. This only works for single Events, but is nevertheless fast and accurate in many cases.

Nudging

An Event can be nudged by setting-up the Key Commands: *Nudge/Left* [No Default] and *Nudge/Right* [No Default]. (CTRL+SHIFT+Left/Right Cursor are natural extensions to those already used.) Nudging will move the Event by the amount shown in the Snap dropdown (see page 108).

Edit/Move To

The very useful *Move to Cursor* [CTRL+L] aligns an Event/Part to the Cursor position. *Audio/To Origin* [No Default] (also Edit/Move to Origin) will move an Event according to the underlying Clip's *Origin Time*. Any offset in the Event is adhered to, so the absolute Origin Time of the Event is maintained with respect to the Clip.

Cycling through overlapping or stacked Events

Overlapping audio Events will often have a crossfade applied to minimize the risk of an audio glitch at the crossover point. However, it might be that you wish to leave them as is, or stack them one on top of the other for a variety of reasons. When MIDI Parts are stacked, or overlapped, the stacked Parts playback everything in all Parts (unlike audio Events/Parts).

☿	Info

For the overlapping part of two or more audio Events, only the topmost Event will sound (unless a cross-fade is applied); for MIDI Parts all will sound.

To change the order of overlapping Events use *Edit/Front (Move to)* [No Default] and *Edit/Back (Move to)* [No Default].

Duplicating an Event/Part

The two most common way of duplicating an Event are to hold ALT and drag, and *Edit/Duplicate* [CTRL+D]. Cut and Paste can also be used. Paste will create the Event with its Snap Point aligned to the Cursor.

The ALT key, used above, can be changed to an alternative in *Preferences/ Editing/ Tool Modifiers.*

The standard *Copy* [CTRL+C] and *Paste* [CTRL+V] can, of course be used. This will copy the Event at the Cursor position. There is also *Paste at Origin* [ALT+V], which will paste the copied Event at the location from which it was copied.

Audio Events are always created as shared Events (indicated by the icon shown in the bottom-right corner of the Event). However, for audio and MIDI

Parts you must hold SHIFT+ALT to create a shared Part. Editing a shared Part will change all of the other shared copies. Try it on both MIDI and audio Parts.

The SHIFT+ALT key-combination can be changed to an alternative in *Preferences/Editing/Tool Modifiers*.

Edit/Duplicate [CTRL+D] also works on multiple items, and can be handy for duplicating sections of MIDI Events, within a Part, to create echo and arpeggiator-type effects. *Edit/Repeat* [CTRL+K] is similar, but you can input the number of duplicates and whether or not these should be shared. Finally, you can set the Locators and fill it with the selection by using *Edit/Fill Loop* [No Default]. Note that these functions ignore Snap Points.

Shared icon

Resizing Events and Parts

Events and Parts are usually resized by dragging their red resize handles (this works with the Scrub tool as well as with the Select tool), although you can use Info Line fields. Multiple Events can be resized at the same time.

In fact, it isn't necessary to select an Event to resize it. The handles are available regardless. The same is the case for the fade and volume handles, so take care that you moving the right one if they are close together.

The left and right ends can also be adjusted by grid setting increments by the four *Nudge* commands *Nudge/Start Left* [CTRL+Left], *Nudge/Start Right* [CTRL+Right], *Nudge/End Left* [ALT+Left] and *Nudge/End Right* [ALT+Right].

If you have *Sizing Moves Contents* selected for the Select tool, then the content of the Event/Part (audio or MIDI) will move with the edge being resized. Snap is followed if active.

You can also resize an audio or MIDI Event/Part with the *Sizing Applies Time-Stretch* tool. See pages 55 and 95. Note that any automation associated with Events resized with Time-Stretch will not be affected by the resize.

♪ *Note*

Hold CTRL to temporarily disable *Snap* while resizing an Event or Part.

↗ *Tip*

If you convert an Event to a Part, then you can slide it past its Clip endpoints.

Slipping – Sliding the contents of an Event or Part

If you hold CTRL+ALT (or *Alt Gr*) and drag the contents of an Event/Part (it doesn't have to be selected and this works with MIDI too), then the content will move and the Event/Part's position will remain unchanged. In the case of an audio Event, you cannot slide past the start or end of its Clip.

♪ *Note*

The Slip Event tool-modifier CTRL+ALT can be changed in *Preferences/ Editing/ Tool Modifiers*.

Splitting and joining (gluing) Events/Parts

There are three options for splitting an Event or Part:

Split tool

o *Scissors tool:* Follows Snap, if active. Hold ALT to repeat the Split throughout the Event/Part. This key can be changed in *Preferences/Editing/Tool Modifiers*.

o *Edit/Split at Cursor* [ALT+X]: Splits all selected Events at the Cursor. If none are selected then splits all.

○ *Edit/Split Loop* [No Default]: Splits all selected Events at the Left and Right Locators. If none are selected then splits all.

The result of splitting a MIDI Part during a MIDI Event (e.g. a note) is determined by *Preferences/MIDI/Function Parameters* tab *Split MIDI Events*. When unchecked, the split note(s) will remain in the Part in which it starts and its duration will not change (even though it now extends beyond the Part boundary). When checked a new note is created. The original note will end at the split point, and the new note will commence at the start of the new Part, and extend until the endpoint of the original note.

Glue tool

You can join one audio Event with the next by clicking it with the Glue tool. This will create a Part containing the two Events. Further Events and Parts can be glued thereafter.

Muting Events/Parts and Tracks

Each Track has a *mute* [M] button; that does this job for a whole Track. Events and Parts can be muted in a number of ways:

Mute tool

○ *Mute tool*
   ○ Click a single Event or lasso multiple Events. This will reverse the mute status of the Events.
   ○ Lasso Events while holding SHIFT will mute all unmuted Events. This key can be changed in *Preferences/Editing/Tool Modifiers*.
   ○ Lasso Events while holding CTRL will unmute all muted Events. This key can be changed in *Preferences/Editing/Tool Modifiers*.
   ○ Click on an Event and drag the mouse over other Events; all will take the state of the first changed Event.
○ *Edit/Mute* [SHIFT+M], *Edit/Unmute* [SHIFT+U] and *Edit/Mute toggle* [ALT+M]
○ Info Line for a single selected Event/Part

Muted Events/Parts change to a lighter shade to indicate their status. A muted audio Event in a Part will be shown, but in its lighter form. A muted MIDI Event will not be visible when viewed from the Event Display; it will be shown in the MIDI Editor.

Locking Events and Tracks

Locking Events and Tracks is a safety measure. Locking a Track is simply a matter of activating its Lock (padlock) icon in the Track List or Inspector. This will disable all editing for the Track.

The Lock options for a Part or Event can be viewed in the Info Line. The dropdown allows a selection to be made. Items that can be locked are:

○ Position
○ Size
○ Other (which means all editing)

The *Editing/Lock* [CTRL+SHIFT+L] function will apply the lock settings specified in *Preferences/Editing* tab *Lock Event Attributes* to the selected items. If you perform *Editing/Lock* on a locked object, then a window will open with checkboxes for each lock option. Unlock an object via *Edit/Unlock* [CTRL+SHIFT+U] or by selecting the blank entry in the Info Line.

Creating Regions from Events and vice versa

A Region is a section of a Clip (see chapter 9). Regions are most easily viewed in the Pool. On the Event Display we have two Region manipulation functions available to us, both found on the Audio menu.

○ *Event as Region:* Creates a Region (or Regions) in the Clip(s) that mirrors the size and position in the Clips(s) of the corresponding Event(s). This also works on multiple Events (even if the Events refer to different Clips).

○ *Events from Regions:* Replaces an Event with new Event(s), positioned and sized, to match the Region(s) in the underlying Clip that are within the original Event's boundaries.

An example will hopefully make these two functions clearer. Consider the following Clip (in the Pool) and its associate Events.

 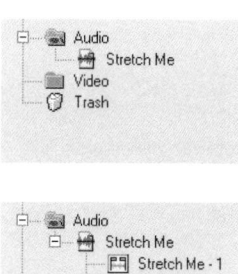

Now let's shorten both Events; taking the start from the first, and the end from the second. If we now select the two altered Events and perform *Audio/Event as Region*, then the result in the Pool is two Regions representing the altered Events.

 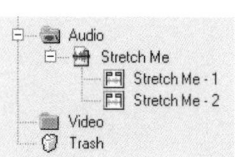

The reverse process should now be apparent. Let's create a new Track and place one Event corresponding to the whole Clip on it.

If we now perform *Audio/Events from Regions* on the Event, the Event is altered to

Snap Points

The purpose of *Snap* [J] and *Snap Points* are to make editing fast and accurate. Every Event Display object has a Snap Point; for Parts it is fixed at the left-hand edge, while for an audio Event the Snap Point can be graphically moved in the Sample Editor and adjusted in the Info Line.

Snap settings

The Snap value and type forces Events and Parts to be aligned in a particular, pre-defined way when being moved in the Event Display. A Snap Point is a marker within an audio Event that is used by Snap to align the Event when moved. A large number of other operations are affected by Snap (e.g. Project Cursor, split, range selection, sizing, etc.).

When editing music you will most likely find yourself aligning audio Events to a bar or a beat (though smaller segments will, no doubt, be used). The procedure for aligning audio Events is to identify an appropriate Snap Point in the audio (perhaps a downbeat), and position the Snap Point at that point within the Sample Editor. Next select the appropriate Event display format from the Ruler (in the Project Window), and select the Snap value (e.g. bar, beat, or second, etc.). Now drag the Event to its location.

The Snap Point is visible in the Sample Editor as a vertical line marked with the letter '**S**. It is also visible on the Event in the Event Display as a blue vertical line, providing the Snap Point is not at the start of the Event (its default).

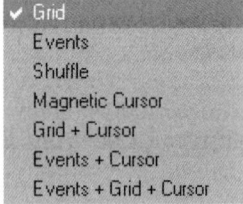

♪   *Note*

Hold CTRL to temporarily disable *Snap* while resizing an Event or Part.

Snap when moving Events and Parts

Snap assists in the precise location of Parts and Events when moving them in the Event Display. The Snap setting defines an invisible grid to which Events are aligned by restricting their placement to these points

Snap can be turned on and off by way of the toolbar button shown. When switched off, Events can be placed in an unrestricted fashion.

The Snap grid is determined by the display format selected from the Ruler together with the Snap value (selected from the dropdown in the Toolbar). For example, if the display format is Bars + Beats then the following Snap values are available: Bar, Beat, or Use Quantize (when the Quantize dropdown determines the grid). If the display format is Seconds, then the Snap values are: 1000ms, 100ms, 10ms, 1ms.

The grid is only one part of Snap, the other factor that determines the outcome is the Snap mode:

Snap

Grid

This is the default mode for most folk. Events will be positioned along the grid defined by the display format and Snap value. (e.g. Bars+Beats and Use Quantize at $1/8$ Note)

✓ Grid
  Events
  Shuffle
  Magnetic Cursor
  Grid + Cursor
  Events + Cursor
  Events + Grid + Cursor

Snap modes

Events

The effect of this mode can appear quite confusing when you drag an Event along a Track of a populated Project. What happens is that the start, end and Snap Points of other Events become the snap points for the Event being positioned (and the dragged Event will be positioned around its Snap Point). Do examine this option, it makes sync'ing two or more Events very easy. Markers are affected by Snap, so the Events mode can be used to rapidly position them.

Shuffle

The effect of shuffle depends on which direction you move the Event, and the spacing between the Events. It is useful for swapping two adjacent Events, especially when there is little or no space between the Events. The dragged Event will always end up touching its associated Event. If an Event is dragged from left to right, and over other Events, then the Events will be shifted left to fill the vacated space.

> ♪   **Note**
>
> A Clip also has a Snap Point. This can be adjusted by opening the Sample Editor for the Clip from the Pool. It is used (providing Snap is active) when dragging the Clip onto the Event Display to create a new Event.

Magnetic Cursor

The Project Cursor becomes the snap point. The same function can be achieved via *Edit/Cursor (Move to)* [CTRL+L] .

Grid + Cursor, Events + Cursor, Events + Grid + Cursor

These three modes are simple combinations of the above.

Snap Points

When an Event is created, its Snap Point is positioned at the start of the Event. To adjust the Snap Point in the Sample Editor, open it by double-clicking the Event and locate the Event (SHIFT+E will Zoom to the Event, and it will be clearer if you have the Event markers showing).

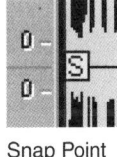

Snap Point

The Snap Point is shown by the letter **S** in a box at the start of the Event (unless it has already been moved). This box can now be dragged to position the Snap Point.

The Snap Point can be set in the Project Window. This is extremely useful. For example, say you have carefully nudged an audio Event into a very precise position in the Event Display. If you want to use the same Event elsewhere, you will want to preserve this positioning. In this case you will need to use the following method to accurately set the Snap Point.

To set the Snap Point from the Event Display, first select the Event and position the Cursor where you want the Snap Point. Now select *Audio/Snap Point to Cursor* [No Default]. The Snap Point is moved to the position of the Cursor; indicated by a blue line in the Event (you will need to move the Cursor to see this).

> ♪   **Note**
>
> Every Event has its own unique Snap Point.

One word of caution: When you move an Event's Snap Point in the Sample Editor, the Event is not automatically realigned to the Snap setting; you must return to the Event Display and reposition the Event for Snap to take effect.

Range Editing

The Range Selection tool allows you to draw a rectangle over the Event Display and then select the contents of that area for processing. The main difference between Range Editing and Event/Part Editing is that a selected range ignores Event and Part boundaries. You can, therefore, select any rectangular portion of a Project and simply copy it to another part of the Project. This is a very powerful feature. It is also possible to remove Tracks from a selection.

Range tool

Range Selection

o *Range Selecting an Event:* To select an Event double-click on it with the Range tool. Multiple Events can be selected by holding SHIFT, when the range will enlarge to encompass the Events and everything in between.

o *Range Selecting a Track:* When in Range Edit mode, it is possible to use the Track List quick-menu function *Select All Events*. This will create a Range Edit area that covers the Track from the start of the Project until the end of the last Event.

o *Range Selecting using the Marker Track:* When you double-click between two Markers with the Range tool, then a range selection is made across all Tracks between the two Markers.

o *Range Selection Menu Options:* There are a number of predefined *Edit/ Select* options including All, None, In Loop, From Start to Cursor, From Cursor to End, and Left and Right Selection Side to Cursor.

o *Resizing a Range Selection:* Once you have selected a Range you can resize it in the following ways:
  o Dragging its horizontal and vertical edges.
  o Adjusting values on the Info Line.

o *Adding and Removing a Track from a Ranges Selection:* Once a Range Selection has been made a Track can be added or removed by CTRL+clicking the Track.

×⁷   *Tip*

When using *Select All Events* on a Track in Range Edit mode, automation Events are selected as a Range.

Range: Move and Copy
This is identical to moving Events, except that the Events/Parts will split at the edge of the Range Selection. Note that *Edit/Duplicate* [CTRL+D] and *Edit/Repeat* [CTRL+K] also work.

☿   Info
When performing a Range Selection *Repeat*, you might get unexpected results if you have both time and tempo based Tracks in the selection. In this case, the time base Tracks will always take precedence.

Range: Cut and Paste
Regular Edit/Copy, Cut and Paste work as expected, but there are two additional functions:

○ *Cut Time:* As an Edit/Cut, but Events to the right are shifted to fill the space left by the Cut selection.

○ *Paste Time:* Inserts the Clipboard content at the Cursor position, shifting existing Events to the right to make way for the inserted Events.

Other Range editing functions

For completeness here are the other Range Edit functions:

○ *Delete Time:* As Cut Time, but the selection is not moved to the Clipboard.

○ *Paste Time at Origin:* As Paste Time, but the Paste occurs at the original position of the selection and not at the Cursor.

○ *Split:* Splits all Events and Parts along the edges of the selection.

○ *Crop:* Easily explained with a couple of diagrams:

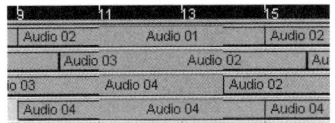 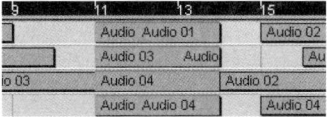

A very neat way of tidying up Events in the Project. Events and Parts partially within the selection range are split, and the reminder, outside the selection, discarded.

○ *Insert Silence:* The Range Selection is replaced by silence. Events are moved to the right to make way for it.

♫   **Note**

Delete Time and *Insert Silence* are also available when the *Range Tool* is not in use. In this case, the range is indicated by the *locators*. Both of these functions will move automation Events with their Events/Parts, even when the automation Tracks are closed.

12 MIDI: Recording and Editing

MIDI functionality has been broken-down into two chapters. This chapter focusses on recording and editing (of the cut and paste, and drag and drop variety). The next chapter (page 151) concentrates on processing MIDI Parts and Tracks with operations such as quantize and MIDI effects. There is, of course, some overlap, but references are provided where appropriate, and small sections are duplicated to make life easier for everybody.

Cubase Sx's implementation of MIDI functions and operations is comprehensive. Editing facilities are provided via four types of graphical editors (Key, Drum, List and Score) and one static editor (Logical Editor). All editors operate on the MIDI Tracks themselves, so changes in one apply to the others. So you have total freedom to work as you please.

VST instruments (VSTi's) are, of course, fully supported, but configuration of external MIDI devices is simplified with the *MIDI Device Manager*, which allows you to configure and customize Bank and Patch settings, then access them from the Tracks on which the instrument is assigned.

Extending this idea, the *Drum Map Editor* allows drum machines and patches to be configured and customized; the chosen names (e.g. kick, snare, crushed melon) then being available in the Drum Editor.

There are many predefined MIDI processes (e.g. transpose, delete controllers, etc.), most of which can be configured when used. The quantize functions are highly configurable, with presets being extensible manually and via groove quantize maps created from audio.

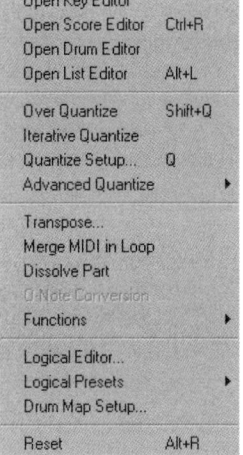

The MIDI menu

Each MIDI Track has a number of real-time configuration options associated with it, allowing you do such things as set ranges for notes and velocities, or randomize pitch, length, velocity and start position by variable amounts. There is an enormous amount of freedom to experiment creatively.

The icing on the cake, however, is the inclusion of MIDI effects (both insert and send). A number of MIDI plug-ins are provided (including an arpeggiator, auto-pan, echo, etc.). As well as Cubase Sx MIDI plug-ins, *Cakewalk* MFX-compatible MIDI plug-ins can be used by installing a small 'wrapper'.

There are a number *Preferences* that can be set in Cubase Sx that relate to MIDI; these are described in detail at the end of this chapter. So that's the place to go and look when these are referenced in the text.

But before we start messing with MIDI, let's take a little precaution...

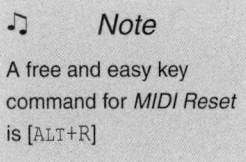

Note

A free and easy key command for *MIDI Reset* is [ALT+R]

MIDI Reset

Let's start with a most useful MIDI function : *MIDI/Reset* [No Default]. This will cause MIDI Reset messages to be sent to all channels on every non-muted MIDI Track. The following is the comprehensive set of MIDI messages and values sent:

CC1: Modulation	0
CC2: Breath	0
CC64: Pedal (sustain)	0
CC121: Reset All Controllers	0
CC123: All Notes Off	0
Channel After-touch	0
Pitch-bend	64

Some equipment will not respond well to these messages. Unfortunately, the resets cannot be filtered by port or channel, so it's all or nothing. All active ports receive resets on all channels.

♪   **Note**

Channels assigned in the *MIDI Device Manager* are opened by Cubase S$_X$ on start-up, so these ports will be active and will receive reset messages.

✗   *Tip*

MIDI Reset does not appear to be sent to VSTi's. Indeed I have had occasions where unloading the VSTi doesn't stop the audio. In these cases, saving the Project can often stop the noise.

MIDI Reset is most usefully deployed when something goes cranky in MIDI-land. This is not so common in these days of multi MIDI inputs and outputs, but should you need it, you are now informed.

Note that Cubase S$_X$ can optionally perform a reset on Stop, Part End and Record End. These are set in the *Preferences/MIDI* tab. *On Stop* sends a global reset (i.e to all ports and channels even if muted). *On Part End* sends a reset at the end of each Part, but only on the Part's channel and only if the Part and its Track are unmuted. *On Record End* didn't appear to be working in Cubase S$_X$ v1.03.

Basic MIDI Set-up Info

Naming Input and Output MIDI Ports

The default names associated with MIDI ports are rarely descriptive; and in these days of multiple port devices, it can make life a lot easier by renaming your MIDI ports to reflect their use. This is a global change that will be valid across all Projects. You rename the MIDI Ports from *Devices/Device Set-up/DirectMusic* tab. The names can be changed by retyping in the Device field.

MIDI Thru

When MIDI Thru is active (when *Preferences/MIDI* tab *MIDI Thru Active* is checked) then all MIDI received on a MIDI In port, for a record or monitor enabled Track, will be echoed on the selected MIDI Out (and MIDI Channel) selected for that Track. That is how you play a MIDI device. If MIDI Thru is inactive then you will not be able to play connected instruments or VSTi's.

However, incoming MIDI messages can still be recorded; it is just that they are not passed to (or echoed at) the output.

In all but a very small number of cases, having MIDI Thru active is the most common setting. If you are using a keyboard that is also being used as a MIDI sound source, then you will, most likely, want to switch it to Local Off mode (see the manual for your keyboard, if you don't know how to do this). Note that the MIDI messages are not strictly being passed "thru", as the channel embedded in the MIDI messages might be changed by Cubase Sx as it passes through (a process called *re-channelization*).

For example, say your keyboard is sending MIDI messages on Channel 1, but the Cubase Sx Track you wish to play is set to Channel 3. Set-up as above (MIDI Thru Active checked and Record/Monitor Enable the Track) and this will work due to Cubase Sx re-channelizing the MIDI messages from your keyboard.

> ↗   *Tip*
>
> Since you will be frequently creating Audio, MIDI, Folder and Group Tracks it is a good idea to assign key commands for these functions. One idea is: ALT+A, ALT+D, ALT+F and ALT+G, respectively.

Creating and setting up a MIDI Track

A MIDI Track is created via *Project/Add Track/MIDI* [No Default]. This function appears on many quick menus, including everywhere on the Project Window.

Once a MIDI Track is created you will want to assign its input and output ports, MIDI Channel and the patch you require. These are selected from the *in* and *out* dropdown lists, either in the Track List or the Inspector. The input port is only available in the *Inspector* [ALT+I]. VSTi's only appear in the output list once they have been loaded from the *VST Instruments* [F11] panel (see page 124).

You can set-up the default MIDI in and out ports that Cubase Sx uses when a new MIDI Track is created. These can be changed via *Devices/Device Set-up/ Default MIDI Ports* tab. If you have a keyboard that you generally use, then making it your default input will save you having to make the change every time you create a MIDI Track.

For VSTi's, all patches for the currently loaded bank are available for selection in the *prg* dropdown. How cool is that?

For external synths patch/bank set-ups might be available from the *MIDI Device Manager* [No Default] (see page 117). If a default has not be provided for your instrument, then you might consider creating one yourself. If a default is not available, and you are not in the mood to create a script for the Device Manager, then you can set these manually in the *bnk* and *prg* boxes. Patch/Bank selection can be a little problematic for some devices, and this is covered below.

You can, of course, send MIDI Program and Bank Change Events from a MIDI Part, if you prefer.

As with audio Tracks, *Delay* is available with a range of ±2000ms. This is useful to compensate for MIDI propagation delays, and any delay other timing difficulties in the chain to, and from, your MIDI instrument. Positive values delay the Track, while negative values play the Track early. It can also be used creatively, of course.

To test whether the connections are working as expected, or to audition patches, make sure you have set the *in* port then activate either *Monitoring* or *Record Enable*. When you hit a key on your keyboard (or provide MIDI input) attached to the selected port, then the green level meters will indicate whether MIDI Input is being received. Providing that MIDI Thru is active, then the incoming MIDI messages will be routed to the output port (or VSTi) and you will hear the output. MIDI messages are rechannelized to the selected channel, except when *Any* is selected from the Channel dropdown. In this case, the Channel embedded in the incoming message is retained.

Patch/Bank Selection, and MIDI Device Manager

Adjusting the Bank and Program fields will send MIDI *Bank Select* and *Program Change* messages to the selected output port. These messages are also sent when the Project is loaded, and every time the Transport is stopped and every time it is started from the beginning of the Project. Nothing is sent when either Bank or Program is set to Off.

Program values are: Off, 1 thru 128. Bank values are: Off, 1 thru 16,383. This gives access to $128 * 16384 = 2$ million+ patches. Enough?

However, Cubase Sx has a trick up its sleave called the *MIDI Device Manager* [No Default] (see below). But first, here's a little more information on the task at hand. You might still need it.

Changing Banks: The extended picture

♪   *Note*

MSB = most significant byte and *LSB* = least significant byte.

Devices differ in the way that they respond to Bank Select, and it is sometimes necessary to unearth the details from the device's manual, or by experimentation. Cubase Sx's MIDI Bank Change feature is basic, but functional, providing you know how your device responds to Bank Change messages.

MIDI Bank Select messages have two components: the MSB and the LSB. Many hardware devices work using MSB and LSB as a basis for Bank selection. We can translate Cubase Sx's Bank number into MSB and LSB by dividing the Bank number by 128. For example:

Cubase Sx Bank Value	LSB	MSB
0	0	0
127	127	0
128	0	1
1073	49	8

How your hardware instrument translates these values should be descried in your instrument's user manual, but can also often be found on a display on the device itself.

A good example to use, to explain how this might be useful, is by considering the EMU Proteus 2000. This device is supplied with the Composer ROM (8 banks of 128 voices plus 4 banks of User voices), but has space for three expansion ROMs. To ensure consistency when using the expansion ROMs, each ROM has been assigned a different MSB for its patches. The Composer ROM, for example, has MSB 4 assigned to it. The four User banks have been assigned MSB 0 (zero). Other ROMs include the Orchestral 1 ROM MSB = 10; the World ROM MSB = 9; and so on.

In Cubase Sx, we access the four EMU User Banks by entering Bank 0,1,2 or 3. To access the 8 Composer ROM Banks we would enter 512 through 519. That is, $4 * 128 = 512$. To access the 4 Orchestra 1 ROM Banks we would enter 1280 through 1283. That is, $10 * 128 = 1280$.

MIDI Device Manager

Enough of the sums. There is another way to gain access to the patches in your outboard gear. Don't get your hopes up yet, however, since a script is required to gain access to those sounds, and if your synth is not in the list, then there could be work ahead (or a search on the Internet).

Cubase Sx provides an interface called the *MIDI Device Manager* [No Default] to help make access to your synths' bank and patch libraries as easy as falling off a log. If a script already exists for your synth, all you have to do is select it from the *Install Device* list, then assign it a MIDI output port. You can then select your synth from the *out* dropdown in a similar way as with a VSTi. Whatever patches are defined in the active script will appear in the *prg* drop down. Usefully, patches can be subdivided into *Folders* within each bank, so you can group, say, leads, basses, drums, etc. together, if you wish. Folders can also contain folders.

If you are out of luck with the supplied scripts, but your device conforms to either GM (General MIDI) or XG (Yamaha) standards, then you can select the *GM Device* or *XG Device* scripts. These will at least get you started.

If a script does not exist (and you can't hunt one down from other sources) then you will have to define your own (see below).

♫ *Note*

The *MIDI Device Manager* will be blank if there isn't an installed device.

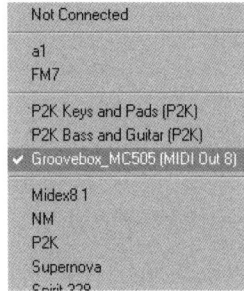

Selecting the new device

♪   Note

The banks in the *MIDI Device Manager* do not have to have a one-to-one cor-
respondence with the banks in your synth. The selection of a patch in the
MIDI Device Manager is usually associated with a Bank Select and a Program
Change message in the script. The corollary is that your *MIDI Device Manager*
banks can contain whatever patches you choose, from any bank, provided they
are loaded into the instrument at the same time.

Figure 12.1 shows three active scripts in the *MIDI Device Manager*. Note that
two of them apply to the same devices (*EMU Proteus 2000*). For simplicity I
have created my own scripts with selections of patches that I commonly work
with. At bottom-left you can see the *Preset Patches* and *Rhythm Set* banks
associated with the MC505. The *Preset* folder has been opened in the *Rhythm
Set* bank to show the available patches, and the TR-909 patch has been selected to show the Bank Change and Program Change MIDI messages that will
be sent by Cubase Sx when that patch is selected from the *prg* dropdown. Also
note that the MC505 has been linked to the *MIDI Out 8* port.

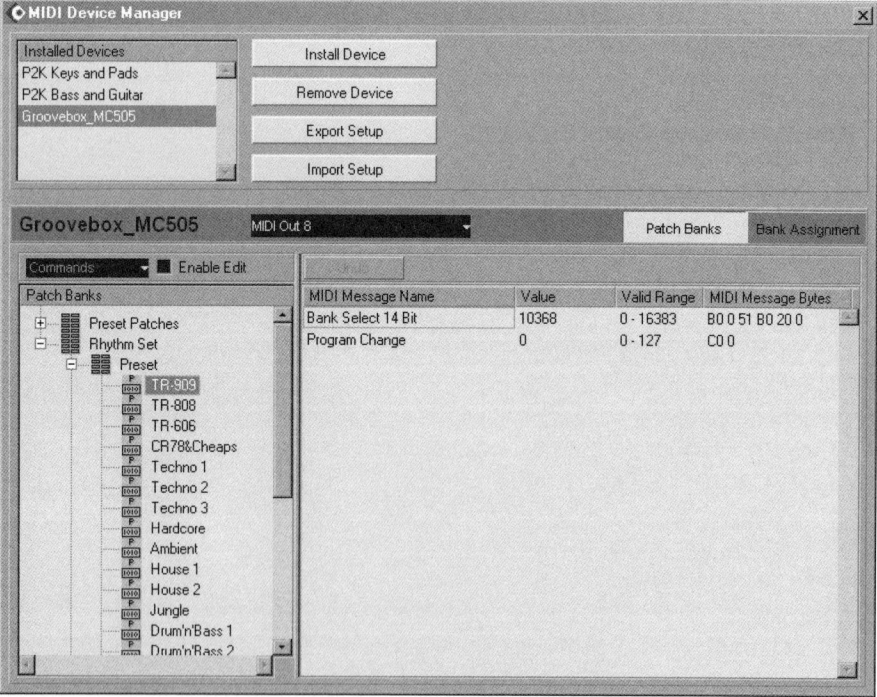

Fig. 12.1: MIDI Device Manager

> ⚡ **Warning**
>
> *MIDI Device Manager* devices that have a MIDI port assigned are opened when Cubase Sx loads, since *MIDI Device Manager* devices are global and not associated with a specific project. This means that these MIDI ports are always active when Cubase Sx is loaded. Furthermore, since the *active devices* are global, any changes made to them could cause difficulties when later opening an old Project. As a precaution, it is advisable to save *MIDI Device Manager* scripts with you Project archive by using the *Export Set-up* function.

Finally, note the *Bank Assignment* button. This button only appears for scripts that contain two or more banks. When pressed it presents you with the option of selecting a bank for each MIDI channel (1 thru 16). When you select the device in the Project Window, only the bank associated with a particular channel is available.

Bank Assignment

Creating and Editing devices in the *MIDI Device Manager*

To install a device from scratch, click *Install Device* and select the *Define New...* option. Next, name the device, and proceed to add banks, folders and presets. There is an *Add Multiple Presets* command that is very useful should you be setting up even a small device from scratch. Make sure that you include all necessary MIDI messages before clicking *Ok*.

If you want to save a script permanently for use in the *Install Device* dialogue, then you must manually create and edit the script outside of Cubase Sx.

The scripts are found in the *Scripts* folder under the main Cubase Sx program folder. Here you should find a text file call *script documentation.txt* that contains details of the file structure. By using this file, and a script from a device with which you are familiar, you can easily (but a little laboriously) create scripts to meet your needs.

> 🎵 **Note**
>
> New event lines are added to patch (and add multiple) scripts by clicking just below the last entry. To delete press DEL

There is a workaround for the inability to save scripts to the Device dialogue within Cubase Sx. When you *Export Set-up*, then all the currently installed Devices are saved to a single file on disk. When you import the same file, you will be presented with a dialogue that allows you to select the Devices you wish to install. The selection you make will be added to any Devices currently installed. In this way, you can manage all of your customized Device scripts.

Editing a device requires that *Enable Edit* is checked. After that, renaming is accomplished by over-typing a selected field. New banks, folders and presets (patches) are created by selecting the function after clicking the *Commands* dropdown. Banks, folders and presets can be re-arranged by drag and drop. Note that items are always placed at the bottom of the tree into which they are dropped, so you might have to play one of those Christmas-cracker type games to organize things at times.

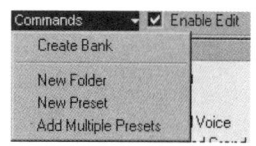

Commands dropdown

A *MIDI Device Manager* script can be configured to send any MIDI message (or sequence of MIDI messages) when a *prg* selection is made. SYSEX cannot be sent. By digging deep, and providing your device supports MIDI controllers,

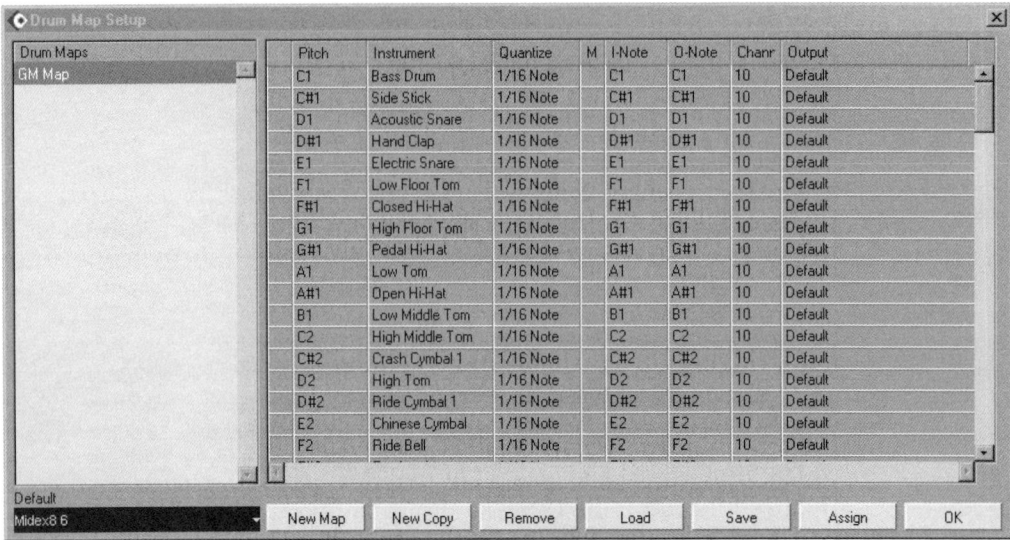

Fig. 12.2: Drum Map Set-up

it is possible to create banks of unique patches for, say, a reverb unit, or banks for changing the effects unit only of you synth. In my case I have used presets to configure a digital mixer. Another favorite is to store presets for patches on a Nord Modular, a device that doesn't have its own preset system. Experiment, why don't ya?

♪   *Note*

Changes can be made to a Drum Map in both *Drum Map Set-up* and the *Drum Editor.*

Creating Drum Tracks and Drum Maps

When creating a MIDI Track that will be used for drums, you may well wish to set-up up a *Drum Map* via *MIDI/Drum Map Set-up* [No Default] for the drum kit(s) that you are using.

We'll look at the *Drum Track Editor* later in this chapter. It is not necessary, however, to use the Drum Editor for editing drums (nor is it necessary to *only* use the Drum Editor for editing drums).

♪   *Note*

A *Drum Map* is also required for the specialized drum functions in the *Score Editor.*

A *Drum Map* performs three basic functions:

1. it builds a single drum kit from different sound sources
2. it maps each incoming MIDI note (say, C1) to an instrument in the kit (say, kick drum) and then re-maps it on the way out to the kick drum (in this case) in one of your external synths (or VSTi's)
3. it provide working data for the *Drum Editor*, such as instrument name.

So, if you simply want to set-up a Drum Map for a single drum patch (for use in the editor), then the process is simply one of naming the instruments to those you wish to see in the Drum Editor (although you might want to adjust the default note length used when inserting Events in the Drum Editor). However, you can also set-up a series of drum maps that map the same MIDI notes to the same sounds for all the drum kit patches you use. Taking it one step further, you can build kits that use sounds from a variety of sources, and still retain your preferred key/MIDI note mappings.

An example

The easiest way to understand this process is to get down and dirty with it. So let's create a new drum kit from scratch and see what comes up.

Create a new MIDI Track and assign a device for output with a drum kit patch. Select an appropriate input device too. Also create a Part of a couple of bars, as something to work with. Don't create any Events yet, just leave the Part empty. Now open the *Drum Map Set-up* by either clicking the *Drum* icon in the Track List or from the *map* dropdown in the *Inspector* [ALT+I], then select *Drum Map Set-up*.

If you've never been here before then you will be presented with the default drum map called *GM Map* (as shown in figure 12.2). Now click *Assign*. You've guessed it, *map* now shows *GM Map*, and if you open the MIDI Part in the *MIDI/Drum Editor* [No Default] then you will see the effect of the Drum Map in the editor. If the drum kit that you are working with is a GM kit then you are done.

You might hit a problem here because of the default MIDI channel. Note that the default MIDI channel for all instruments in the *GM Map* is channel 10. This will override the channel selected in the Project Window. You can change the channel for each instrument individually, via the dropdowns, or for all instruments in one-shot by holding CTRL and selecting the desired channel.

Go back to *Drum Map Set-up* by selecting it from the *map* dropdown bottom-left. (Just leave the Drum Editor open behind the set-up screen.)

It might be that one of the Drum Maps supplied with Cubase Sx matches your drum sound-source. Click *Load* and navigate to the *DrumMaps* folder under the main Cubase Sx folder. If a map seems appropriate, then try it out.

We could work with this map (or take a *New Copy* and edit), but let's get hardcore and start with a clean slate by pressing *New Map*. Again, press *Assign* and note that the changes are replicated in the Drum Editor. Audition a few drum sounds by clicking in the left-hand of the *Drum Editor* (it is not necessary to activate *monitoring* or *record enable*) to ensure that everything is working as it should.

At this point you should have a fair idea of how the editor and set-up interact, and also the basic function of a Drum Map. Let's now build a kit from two sources (extrapolating this to more than two is an identical process).

Go back to set-up once again with our *New Map*. First, note that all 128 MIDI notes are present and cannot be removed. This means that the Drum Map routes every incoming MIDI note. We saw above that the MIDI channel can be changed for an instrument so, if you have a multi-timbral synth, then you can, say, load drum kit patches to receive on channels 1 and 2 and use both in the same kit by changing the channel entry for an instrument as follows:

Pitch	Instrument	Quantize	M	I-Note	O-Note	Chanr	Output
C1	Kick	1/16 Note		C1	C1	1	Default
C#1	Woodblock	1/16 Note		C#1	C#1	2	Default
D1	Snare	1/16 Note		D1	D1	1	Default

Similarly, if you wish to use another device (e.g. a VSTi) for an instrument, then select a different *Output*.

Pitch	Instrument	Quantize	M	I-Note	O-Note	Chanr	Output
C1	Kick	1/16 Note		C1	C1	1	Default
C#1	Woodblock	1/16 Note		C#1	C#1	1	Attack 2
D1	Snare	1/16 Note		D1	D1	1	Default

It's worth pointing out that the default output can be overridden for *all* instruments (in the same way as all channels can be overridden, by holding CTRL). In this case, the output selected in the Project Window no longer has any significance on the triggered sounds.

Pitch	Instrument	Quantize	M	I-Note	O-Note	Chanr	Output
C1	Kick	1/16 Note		C1	C1	1	Attack
C#1	Woodblock	1/16 Note		C#1	C#1	1	Attack 2
D1	Snare	1/16 Note		D1	D1	1	Attack

Re-mapping with I-notes and O-notes

The above is all well and good, but when mixing and matching, the chances are that you will want to use a sound from two drum kit patches that share the same MIDI note. Either that, or you will want to keep C1 as the kick, but assign another sound to it, say C2.

> ♪ **Note**
>
> This I/O-note stuff is a little heavy going, but once you've grasped it, its application during a Project can save a lot of editing and aid creativity.

These problems are solved using the entries in the *I-Note* and *O-Note* columns. These two columns introduce two separate mappings. *I-Note* provides a keyboard mapping to the *Drum Map* Pitch, and *O-Note* provides a mapping from the *Drum Map* Pitch to pitch/channel/device.

Let's say you have a great kick drum on E4, but your preferred kick drum key is C1. All you have to do is enter C1 in the *I-Note* entry for *Pitch* E4. When you record your Part, your C1 keystrokes will be mapped to E4 and you will hear the E4 sound as you play. But the good news is that the Events recorded in the Part will be for E4, so that on playback you hear E4.

I-Note is only applicable to MIDI notes coming into the Drum Map via the input device selected in the Project Window. It performs no function during Cubase Sx playback with Events from MIDI Parts.

In the above example, when you enter C1 in the *I-Note* entry for E4, note that E4 gets entered, automatically, in the *I-Note* entry for C1. This always happens, as there is a one-to-one mapping of *I-Note* to *Drum Map* Pitch. This is worth noting in case you start thinking that you're hearing strange things when playing your keyboard.

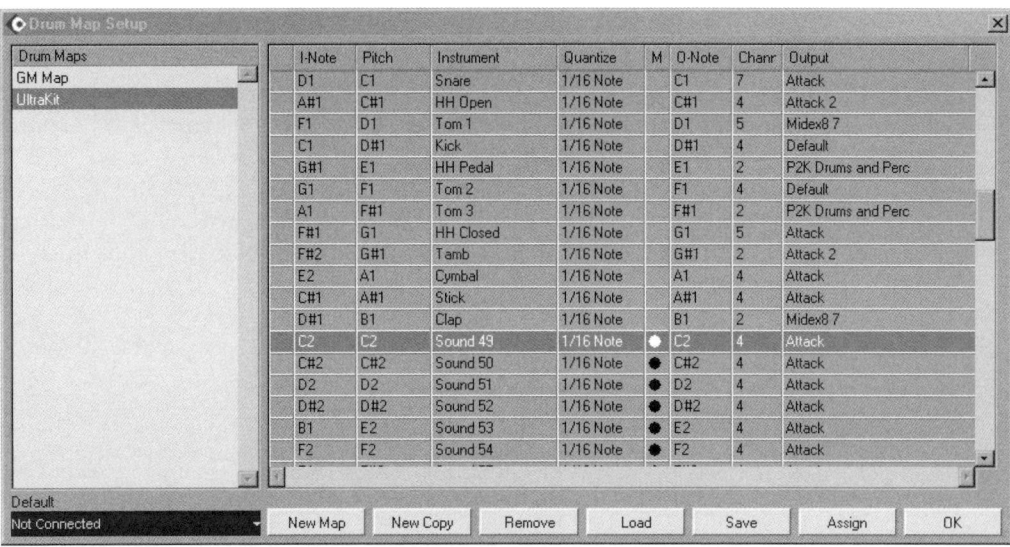

Fig. 12.3: Populated Drum Map

The bigger picture with *I-Note* is that you can re-map as many drum kits as you like, to play the same type of sounds from the same keystrokes.

O-notes

O-Notes perform an entirely different function. Using the same example as above, if you later decide that instead of using the E4 kick, that you want to use the one on D3, then all you need to do is change *O-Note* to D3 for *Pitch* E4. Note, that in this case, both C1 and D3 keys will play the D3 sound (while the E4 key will still be playing the C1 sound).

Incoming MIDI notes (*Pitch* column) are mapped to the notes in the *O-Note* column. This mapping is applied to both incoming playback Events and to MIDI Thru notes. Note that changing an *O-Note* entry does not change any other *O-Note* entries. So you can map as many incoming notes to a single sound as you wish.

Therefore, if you are playing back a song, and want to change the sound of a drum sound to another in the same patch throughout the Track, then you can re-map it by changing the *O-Note* entry. Making this change will also affect the sound heard from a MIDI Thru note. You can, of course, change channel and/or output settings to map the note to an alternative destination.

Back to our Drum Kit

We now have all the tools needed to create the ultimate drum kit. Figure 12.3 shows an example of a rather over-complicated, but nevertheless working, Drum Map.

The *I-Note* column has been dragged over to the left to make the mapping clearer (although it would be clearer still if the set-up could be sorted by this

♪   **Note**

No need to restrict Drum Maps for use with drums and percussion. You can use them to create unusual patches by mixing sounds from different sources without having to layer.

♪   **Note**

Drum Maps can be saved to disk individually for use in other Projects, but they are also stored with a Project.

column). The instruments have been renamed to make referencing them easier in the *Drum Editor*. (Click on the label and edit to do this.) Some of the Quantize fields have been changed. This value is used when adding notes in the *Drum Editor*. Also, notes outside the kit have been muted as a precaution. And last but not least, the incoming MIDI has been mapped to a variety of output devices and channels.

As a final note, *MIDI/O-Note Conversion* [No Default] will convert the pitch of each MIDI Event, in the selected MIDI Parts, to the *O-Note* values of the Track's Drum Map.

MIDI Track Tricks

When selecting the MIDI Input, or MIDI Output, for a Track, you can change *all* MIDI Tracks to the same selection by holding CTRL. Note that all MIDI Tracks are changed, not only selected Tracks.

You can name all the Events/Parts on a Track by holding CTRL when renaming a Track. Neither of these operations can be reversed with [Undo].

Using VST Instruments (VSTi's)

☿   *Info*

Both Cubase S$_X$ and S$_L$ come with a few VSTi's out of the box. See page 319

A VSTi is a software synth or sampler. VSTi's are loaded for use via *VST Instruments* [F11]. They are almost always played via MIDI (a very small number are played via their on-screen interface – theremin anyone?), but the audio output is controlled and routed within Cubase S$_X$ in the same way as an audio Track. So it is possible to process the VSTi output with the full range of audio tools available in S$_X$. You can, of course, route the output directly to your soundcard, if you wish.

When played in real-time, there will be latency (or delay) associated with audio produced by a VSTi, but playback is sample accurate when triggered by MIDI Events during playback. The total delay between striking a key and hearing the sound from a VSTi will be dependent on your available computer power and the buffer size of your soundcard's driver. (See chapter 20, page 281 for a discussion on latency issues.)

S$_L$ *SL Info*

Cubase S$_X$ has 32 VSTi slots whereas S$_L$ has 16

VSTi's can be automated and they can accept tempo sync – providing these have been implemented by the developers of the instrument, of course. These are extremely powerful features and should be explored thoroughly. Loads of fun.

Despite real-time latency issues, VSTi audio can be bounced down within Cubase S$_X$ to sample accuracy (the highest degree of accuracy available in digital audio), so for the purposes of the final mix, things couldn't really be much better.

VSTi's are loaded for use via *VST Instruments* [F11]. The dropdown, when selected, will show all VSTi's available to Cubase S$_X$. Depending on the number of instruments you have, you may wish to move them into folders identifying their function (e.g. Drums, Lead, FX, etc.). Most VSTi's can be moved quite easily within the *VSTPlugins* folder hierarchy, but some may require that certain files, or sub-folders, remain in the same relative position to the main VSTi file.

♪ **Note**

The number of VSTi's that you can run at one time will vary greatly depending on the power of your computer, the processor usage of the VSTi, and the general load on your machine. Keep an eye on the CPU meter *Devices/Performance Monitor* [F12] for an indication on the reserve processing power available to you.

Once loaded, an instrument is switched on and ready for use. The VSTi's name will then be available in the *out* dropdown list for all MIDI Tracks, and simply selecting it will enable you to use it as if it were any other MIDI instrument.

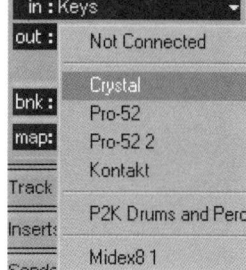

Assigning a VSTi

Note that there will be one entry in the dropdown list for each instance of the VSTi. It is usually possible to load multiple versions of a particular VSTi, and these will be listed individually with a numeric suffix.

You can open the editor for the VSTi by clicking the Edit button on the VST Instrument window. Refer to the VSTi's documentation to configure the instrument.

✗ **Tip**

Having been selected as output for a MIDI Track the VSTi interface can also be opened by clicking on the 'e' button in the Track's Inspector and on the 'e' button at the bottom of each of the VSTi's channel strips in the *Track Mixer* [F3].

Most VSTi's will provide a default bank of patches when loaded. These are then accessed from the *prg* dropdowns for the Track or from the patch dropdown underneath the loaded VSTi's name in the VST Instrument window. If a default bank is not loaded, then loading a patch bank can be achieved (and later saving, if required) via the Load/Save Bank/ Instrument functions found at the top of every VST editor (and also by clicking the File field on the VST Instrument window).

Fig. 12.4: Loading VST Instruments

> ☿
> ♀
> **Info**
>
> MIDI Program Change messages can be embedded in a MIDI Part. A VSTi will respond to these (providing that it supports VST v2.1, or better). By doing this you might be able to save processing power by reducing the number of instances of a VSTi.

If the instrument is multi-timbral (can play more than one patch at one time), you will have to assign the appropriate MIDI Channel to the Track for the patch in the VSTi that you wish to use. For example, it is usual for a sampler VSTi to require that a patch be assigned a MIDI channel (or to receive on all channels (omni mode)) and for output channels to also be selected for each patch. The documentation for the VSTi will detail how this is achieved for a VSTi.

☿
♀   *Info*

Why not create a Window Layout just for VSTi's?

You must, of course, Record or Monitor Enable a MIDI Track for it to accept incoming MIDI messages. Also ensure that MIDI Thru is not switched off in *Preferences/MIDI/Filter* tab when using an external keyboard to trigger sounds.

A VSTi will be represented by a number of Channels in the Track Mixer. The number of Channels can be fixed, or configurable; it depends on the VSTi (check the VSTi's documentation for details). If the VSTi has multiple Channels available, then you will want to route your patch to the appropriate Channel.

Using Rewire

Rewire is a Steinberg and Propellerhead Software innovation that allows an audio program to transfer sample-accurate audio to another without any intermediary device. The program receiving the audio also gains control of the transport of the sending device. In this case, Cubase Sx will be receiving audio, and will be able to control playback of the sending program (including tempo changes). *Rewire2* allows Cubase Sx to pass MIDI data to the audio supplying program. The two best-known *Rewire* enabled applications are Rebirth and Reason, although I'm a fan of *Ableton Live!*

♩   *Note*

Up to 256 audio channels are available in *Rewire2*. That should keep you busy.

A *Rewire* enabled application makes itself known to Cubase Sx behind the scenes, and a control panel that enables routing audio to the *Track Mixer* will automatically appear in Cubase Sx's *Device* menu list. Ensure that you load Cubase Sx first, then the *Rewire* application. Thereafter, you can activate whichever channels you wish to use from the *control panel*, and they will appear in the *Track Mixer*. Playback is initiated from Cubase Sx.

Providing an application supports *Rewire2*, then any MIDI channels it makes available will automatically appear in Cubase Sx's MIDI output's list.

Note that Rewire channels are available during *Audio Mixdown*, so it is simple to convert the *Rewire* output to audio files for further processing, if you wish. Very nice.

MIDI Part Editing

Creating MIDI Parts

MIDI Events are placed within MIDI Parts. This is similar to the way that Audio Events can be placed in Audio Parts; the difference being that MIDI Events are *always* placed in a MIDI Part.

When you record a sequence of MIDI Events, a MIDI Part is created. However, it is possible to create an empty MIDI Part in which you can enter Events manually. To create a MIDI Part either:

○ Draw the Part directly onto the Track with the Draw tool, or
○ Double-click on the appropriate MIDI Track between the left and right locators with the Select tool.

To create, edit or delete Events in a MIDI Part, you can use one of the four MIDI Editor's at your disposal (see below) or the Browser.

Moving MIDI Parts

Other than dragging the Part, you can change the *Start* value in the *Info Line*. This moves the whole Part, so length is preserved. *Nudge/Left* [No Default] and *Nudge/Right* are very fast for this operation. The *Grid Value* is used regardless of Snap being active. And don't forget *Move to Cursor* [CTRL+L].

The above options, all move the Part and Events, and retain the length of the Part. For many musicians, it is imperative to be able to shift the Events by small amounts, yet retain the other Part properties intact. This is even more important when *shared* Parts are being used (see below) when you may well want to shift the Events of one Part, but not others. To do this you adjust the *Offset* value in the *Info Line*. Use a negative value to shift Events later in the Timeline.

Shared MIDI Parts

MIDI Parts can be shared. That is, one Part can be represented on the Event Display in more than one place. To create a shared MIDI Part, drag the Part to the desired location while holding ALT+SHIFT. The resulting Parts will have a small symbol place in their bottom-right corner, as shown, to indicate that they are shared.

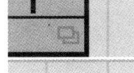

Shared Part symbol

Note that the same process applies to Audio Parts. However, Audio Events are created as shared copies and need to have *Edit/(Convert) To Real Copy* [No Default] applied to be freed from sharing. (An Audio Event created by *(Convert) To Real Copy* still points to the same Clip as the original audio Event.)

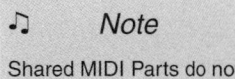

♫   *Note*

Shared MIDI Parts do not share their *Offset*.

Dissolving a MIDI Part

There are two discrete *MIDI/Dissolve Part* [No Default] functions:

○ Dissolve into separate channels
○ Dissolve into separate pitches

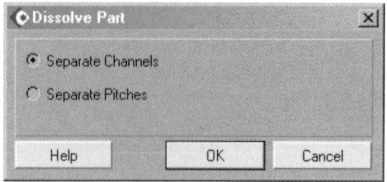

Dissolve Part

Dissolving into separate channels

The need for this function generally arises when importing a Type 0 MIDI Track (which contains all MIDI data on one Track), or when Events have been recorded onto a single Track from multiple sources. Depending on how you route your MIDI data, and to which Channel you have the Tracks set, will determine the playback results. By separating the data by Channel, you can then manipulate the Parts and Tracks individually, giving you a lot more flexibility.

This function will result in one new Track for each channel present in the selected Parts. The new Tracks are set-up identically to the original except that the appropriate channel number is set. The original Parts being dissolved are muted.

Dissolving into separate pitches

This function is commonly used to separate a drum part into its constituent sounds. It is also useful as a "scan" function when searching for errant notes in complex parts. The benefits are the same as before; added flexibility.

The result this time is one new Track for each pitch present in the selected Parts. The new Tracks are set-up identically to the original. The original Parts being dissolved are muted.

Stacked and overlapping MIDI Parts and MIDI merge

Unlike Audio Parts, *all* Events in overlapping MIDI Parts will playback. This means that you are able to stack MIDI Parts on top of each other to preserve screen real estate. This does, however, make editing more difficult. You can, of course, put such Parts into a Folder Track and us the *Edit/ (Move to) Front/Back* [No Default] commands.

Another method for simplifying a build-up of MIDI Parts (that can accumulate during editing) is provided by *MIDI/Merge MIDI in Loop* [No Default].

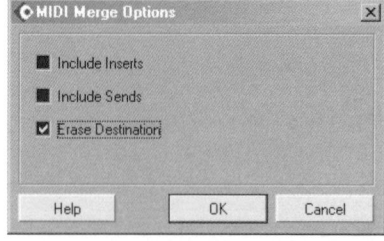

MIDI Merge

> ↗   *Tip*
>
> To bounce a single MIDI Part: (1) Select and *Solo* [S] the Track, (2) Select the Part and do *Locators to selection* [P], (3) Do *MIDI/Merge MIDI in Loop* [No Default] with you chosen options, (4) Turn off the unwanted effects

This function merges all MIDI Events (that *start* between the locators), for all non-muted Tracks, into a single Part. The new Part is created on the selected Track (which could be one created especially to receive it). You can optionally chose to "bounce" any MIDI Insert of Send effects into the new Part. (Track Parameters are considered to be Insert effects for this function.)

Recording MIDI

MIDI recording in Cubase Sx is much more straightforward than audio recording, primarily due to the fact that levels are less critical and routing is much easier. The result of recoding MIDI is a MIDI Part on a Track. The Part contains MIDI Events (e.g. MIDI Notes and controllers).

A MIDI Part

Presuming that you have tested your input and output devices, as described elsewhere, then recording MIDI is simply a matter of record enabling the required Tracks, positioning the Cursor at the appropriate start position, pressing *Record* [Pad *], and playing your masterpiece. (For a more detailed explanation of the basics of setting-up and recording MIDI see the *Quick-start* chapter, page 22.)

Auto Quantize

If you have switched on *Auto Quantize* [No Default] (the 'AQ' button) on the Transport, then your recording will be quantized automatically to the current *Quantize Set-up* [Q] settings. You can also merge a MIDI recording into an existing Part by switching from *Normal* to *Merge* in the *Rec Mode* toggle on the Transport (see below).

You will only be able to hear what you are playing if *MIDI Thru Active* is checked on *Preferences/MIDI* tab.

Rec Mode

This option is set on the Transport. It affects how the resulting MIDI Part is created when a recording is made that overlaps another MIDI Part.

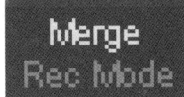

o *Normal:* This will result in a MIDI Part being created that overlaps the existing Part(s). The original notes remain unchanged in their existing Part(s).
o *Merge:* This merges the new notes into the existing MIDI Part(s). The original notes remain unaffected.

Punching in and out

A punch in, together with its opposite punch out, is the process of dropping in and out of record mode. When recording MIDI, the automated punch process is done in the same way as for audio (see page 177). To punch in and out manually, set the Transport running with Play or Record, then switch in and out of record mode by hitting *Record* [Pad *].

You may also want to consider using Cycle Recording with Merge, as an alternative in some cases. Take care when recording into Parts with existing

> ↗ *Tip*
>
> If your recording will only start from the left locator, then *Transport/Stat Record at Left Locator* [No Default] is switched on.

MIDI Control data, as these can cause problems. Remember *MIDI Reset* [No Default].

Cycle Recording

Cycle Recording is simply recording with loop active. There are two MIDI Cycle Record Modes, selected from the Transport toggle *Cycle Rec*:

○ *Mix:* Each completed cycle is added to the Part.
○ *Overwrite:* Each completed cycle replaces the existing Part.

The Input Transformer

The *Input Transformer* allows you to transform and filter incoming MIDI messages in realtime and record the results. It works in a very similar way to the *MIDI/Logical Editor* [No Default] transform function (see page 164), but instead of being a static edit of the MIDI messages (after recording them), it operates dynamically, as you play. Furthermore, you get four transformer modules instead of only one in the *Logical Editor*, so you can make some quite significant transformations to you MIDI input, if you wish. The modules are processed sequentially, in numerical order, with the output from each piped into the next. Each module can be set as either a *filter* or a *transform*.

Input Transformer

Open the *Input Transformer* by clicking the button top-right in the *Inspector* for the Track. The button will only light when a module is checked as active.

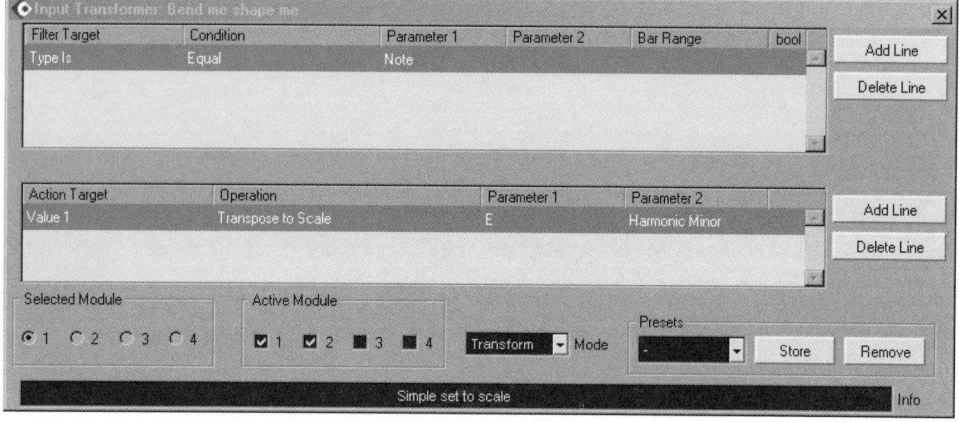

As with the *Logical Editor*, the idea is to identify the messages to be modified in the top section, and provide the actions to be performed in the the lower section. *Filters* are defined completely in the upper section (anything in the lower section is ignored), *Transform* uses both.

When you store a preset, it only stores the currently selected module. Similarly, when you select a preset, it is only applied to the currently selected module.

Uses for the *Input Transformer* are based around real-time control. Simple functions are the filtering of a continuous controller, such as after-touch

♪ **Note**

Modules only work when switched on (i.e. checked in *Active Module*).

(Mode: Filter, TypeIs/Equal/Aftertouch)), or using the Mod Wheel for one-way pitch-bend (Mode: Transform, TypeIs/Equal/Controller, Type/Set to fixed value/ Pitchbend).

When trying examples, make sure that you periodically check that you haven't changed the pitch of the incoming MIDI notes, accidentally taking them out of scale, or out of context (unless that is what you want, of course). It's easy to do this when messing with controllers.

There are certainly many creative possibilities for use with both pitched and unpitched instruments. The *Transpose to Scale*, for example, can be used for inspiration (or to cover a limited ability to play a keyboard in different keys). If, for example, you set (Mode: Transform, TypeIs/Equal/Note, Value 1/Transpose to scale/C/Oriental) then run your finger from C-to-C over a couple of octaves with a piano (or steel guitar) type patch, you immediately get that suspenseful oriental effect. Simple key transpositions are easy and effective.

One thing worth trying, if you have the appropriate routing, is routing MIDI sequences into an Sx MIDI input on a Track, activating the *Input Transformer* and playing around with the transforms and output devices (or VSTi's).

The possibilities are endless, and well-worth exploring for inspiration, if for no other reason than they can easily lead you out of familiar territory and into considering new sequences of sound. Thumbs up.

Recording and editing SYSEX

First, a bit of MIDI background info. There are two types of MIDI message:

○ *Channel messages* are Events that contain a MIDI *channel*. There are five of these: Note on/off; Pitch-bend; After-touch; Control Change (including continuous controllers (CC's)); and Program Change.
○ *System messages* do not contain a channel and so pertain to the whole MIDI System. There are three types of *System messages*:
  – *System Exclusive (SYSEX)* are aimed at being accepted by a single device type (e.g. a specific make and type of synth).
  – *System Common* are aimed at any device in the system that can accept it. These are: MIDI Time Code (MTC); Song Select; Song Position Pointer; and Tune Select.
  – *System Real Time* are MIDI Clock, Stop/Start/Continue, System Reset, Active Sensing

So, a SYSEX message will, in general, be unique for a particular make and model of MIDI device. Why "in general"? Well, there are 128 manufacturers' IDs available, but some of these are used for *Universal SYSEX* messages. Theses include: master volume; master pan; time signature; MIDI Machine Control (MMC); MIDI Show Control; Turn on GM (or GM Reset); and Turn off GM.

Many devices use SYSEX to change patch settings and, similarly, these transmit movements of their controls as out-going SYSEX. SYSEX is often used

♫ **Note**

The activity meter will only indicate MIDI activity if the message exits the *Input Transformer*

✗ **Tip**

You only know C major but you wanna play the Blues? Try the Input Transformer's *Transpose to Scale* operation. Then get into some RagaTodi.

♫ **Note**

Cubase Sx will chase SYSEX Events (see *Preferences*)

✗ **Tip**

Put SYSEX set-up dumps in the run-in to a Project, but avoid sending more than one SYSEX dump at a time.

by manufacturers to supply OS upgrades and new patch banks for customers to install themselves. This has become particularly common with the advent of the Internet. In the same way, facilities are often provided for users to save (or *dump*) patch banks, and other archivable material from their MIDI devices. Hence the need to record and playback SYSEX.

Some folk are hardcore enough to edit SYSEX by hand. You can do this in Cubase Sₓ, but it's not for the fainthearted and the detail is far beyond the scope of this book.

Recording and transmitting SYSEX

SYSEX is recorded to a Track in real-time. Refer to the documentation for your MIDI device on how to configure your device to send SYSEX from your device. If your device needs to receive a *Dump Request* to initiate a *SYSEX dump*, then you will have to create one of these in a MIDI Part by-hand, then send it to the device as part of the *SYSEX dump* recording process. See the *SYSEX Editing* section below on how to do this.

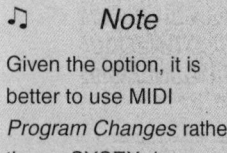

SYSEX in Key Editor

One thing you must do when dealing with SYSEX is ensure that the *File/ Preferences/ MIDI/ Filter* tab *SYSEX* options are correctly set. To record, clear the *Record SYSEX* option (on the left) and check the *Thru SYSEX* option.

If you are recording parameter changes, then record as you would normally. If you are recording a *SYSEX dump*, then ensure that *Cycle* [Pad /] is off, start recording, and initiate the SYSEX dump from your device. Watch the activity indicators to double-check that something is being sent.

To view the SYSEX Events, stop record, and open the Part in Key, Drum or List editors, or the Browser. (If you use the Key or Drum editor, then you will need to select the SYSEX Controller Lane to see the SYSEX Event.) You may see one or more SYSEX messages, depending on what your device sent.

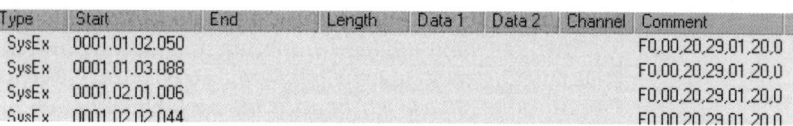

Type	Start	End	Length	Data 1	Data 2	Channel	Comment
SysEx	0001.01.02.050						F0,00,20,29,01,20,0
SysEx	0001.01.03.088						F0,00,20,29,01,20,0
SysEx	0001.02.01.006						F0,00,20,29,01,20,0
SysEx	0001.02.02.044						F0,00,20,29,01,20,0

A few SYSEX messages

To transmit a SYSEX dump simply play it back to the receiving device. The device may need to be set to receive SYSEX. Check the docs for details.

SYSEX Editing

♪   *Note*

Given the option, it is better to use MIDI *Program Changes* rather than a SYSEX dump.

Cubase Sₓ's SYSEX Editor can be accessed through the Key, Drum or List editors, or the Browser. We'll use the *Browser* [CTRL+B] here since, if you are starting without a Part, it is easy to do everything from this interface.

If you are creating a SYSEX Event from scratch, then create a Part for it in the appropriate spot and ensure that the Cursor is at the location that you you want to place the SYSEX Event. Now, select the Part in the Browser. Select *SysEx* from the *Add* dropdown.

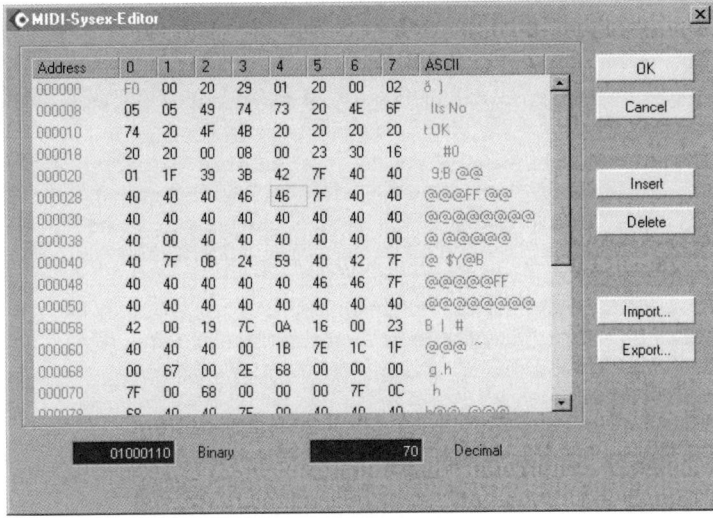

Fig. 12.5: SYSEX Editor

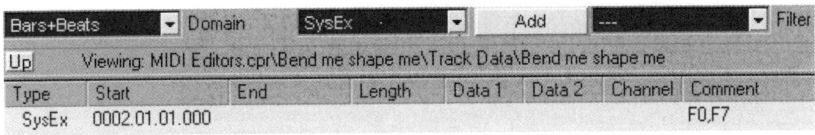

Adding SYSEX

The SYSEX editor is opened by clicking on the *Comment* entry for the required SYSEX Event (see figure 12.5).

Editing is intuitive: click on an entry to overwrite, *Add* inserts a character before the one selected. If you are a SYSEX hacker then this will be easy stuff.

Finally, notice that you can import and export SYSEX files via the SYSEX Editor. When you import a SYSEX file the current Event is overwritten, so you'll need to create an empty SYSEX Event (as described above) if you want to add a saved SYSEX dump. SYSEX Exports are saved as *Raw SYSEX* format and will be compatible with other software.

The MIDI Editors

Overview

The basic function of the MIDI editors is to edit MIDI *Events*. Cubase S_X has four MIDI distinct editors:

- o *Key Editor* [No Default] – typical piano roll editor
- o *List Editor* [CTRL+G] – numerical Event editor; single part only
- o *Drum Editor* [No Default] – specialized editor designed for drums and percussion; can use *Drum Maps* (see page 120)
- o *Score Editor* [CTRL+R] – (See chapter 21, page 289.)

○ *Browser* [CTRL+B] – (See chapter 8, page 79.)

Browser

The *Browser* is included for completeness. It provides a similar view on Events to the text display in the *List Editor*, but can be quicker to use in many circumstances. In particular, it allows you to move between Parts and Tracks very easily, and to view automation Events. The *Browser* columns can be sorted and also provides Event filtering. (See chapter 8, page 79.)

S_L   *SL Info*

S_L has a much reduced version of *Score* than S_X.

Score Editor

The *Score Editor* is distinct from the other MIDI editors in the way that it manipulates Events. Its main function is as a presentation layer for creating type-set printed musical scores, and as a composition tool for musical notation. As such, for those familiar with 'dots', *Score Editor* can be used as an intuitive editor for notes. It is not, however, the editor for manipulating control messages or automation data. (See chapter 21, page 289.)

Common Features

From here on we examine, a little more closely, the three MIDI editors (*Key Editor*, *List Editor* and *Drum Editor*). If we take a look at the toolbars of each of these editors we can spot many common items.

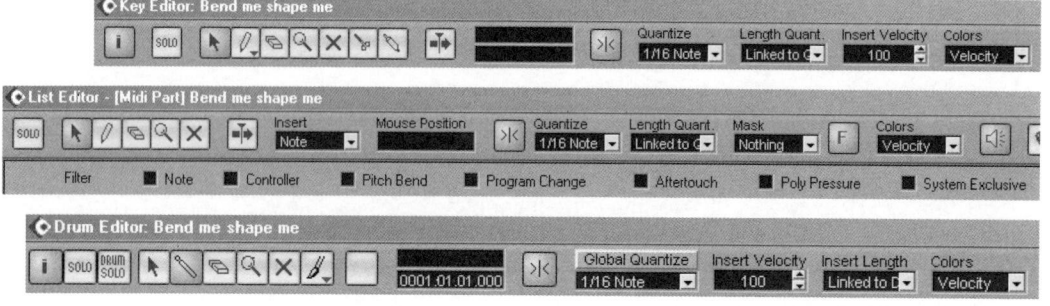

Familiar common function buttons are: *Info Line*, *Snap (page 108)* and *Auto-scroll (page 101)*. The editors each have their own *Auto-scroll* setting, and this is independent from the *Project Window*. Familiar common tool buttons are: *Select, Draw, Erase, Zoom, Mute, Split, Glue* (see page 54). The *Drum Editor* has the *Drumstick* [No Default] tool, instead of the *Draw* tool. Each editor also has a Part *Solo* button that will solo the MIDI Track during playback.

✔ Velocity
  Pitch
  Channel
  Part

  Setup...

         Colors

Length

The editors either have *Length*, *Length Quantize* or *Insert Length*. In the Key Editor (*Length Quantize*) and Score Editor (*Length*), these settings can be adjusted with the *Set Insert Length* [No Default] key commands.

Colors

All the editors have a *Colors* dropdown allowing coloring of Events by Velocity,

---

Cubase S_X Complete

Pitch, Channel or by Part. Coloring by Part is useful to show which Part and Event belongs to when simultaneously editing multiple Parts.

There is also a *Set-up* option on the dropdown that allows you to customize the color settings for Velocity, Pitch and Channel selections.

Audition
The *Audition* button will cause the appropriate MIDI note message to be sent whenever an Event is created, moved or selected (this does not work for *Nudge/ Left & Right* [No Default], however).

Audition

Working with the MIDI Editors

The default MIDI Editor is opened either by double-clicking a selected MIDI Part (or Parts) in the Event Display, or by selecting the Part and pressing RETURN. The default MIDI Editor can be changed via *Preferences/Event Display/MIDI* tab *Default Edit Action*. However, if the Track has been assigned a *Drum Map* (see page 120) and *Preferences/Event Display/MIDI* tab *Edit as Drum when Drum Map is assigned* is checked, then the *Drum Editor* will be used. An alternative editor can be opened via *MIDI/Open... Editor*.

Multiple MIDI Editors can be opened at one time depending on the setting of *Preferences/Editing* tab *Link Editors*. If this option is checked, then all selected Parts are shown in the open editor (with the usual exception of *List Editor*). You can open multiple editors for the same Part, but not of the same type.

When you open a single MIDI Part in an editor, the Track is automatically *Record Enabled* (this will be deactivated if you minimize the Editor). When multiple Parts are opened, only one Track is *Record Enabled*. Other MIDI Tracks that are *Record Enabled* may or may not have *Record Enabled* switched while the editor is open depending on *Preferences/MIDI* tab *Solo Record in Editors* (see page 148).

> ↗   *Tip*
>
> Don't forget that you can cycle through the open windows using CTRL+TAB

The Key Editor

The main area of the *Key Editor* [No Default] is the Note Display, which is a traditional sequencer grid with note pitch on the vertical axis. (Once a MIDI device is associated with a MIDI Track, the keyboard can be used to play notes on the device.) Notes are represented on the grid by blocks whose width represents the notes' length.

Each note has the following associated information (which is visible in the *Info Line* only when a single Event is selected):

- ○ Start position (usually in *Bars+Beats*)
- ○ End position
- ○ Length
- ○ Pitch (range C-2 to G8)
  (See *Preferences/Event Display/MIDI/Note Name Style*, page 38)

Fig. 12.6: The Key Editor

- Velocity (range: 0 to 127)
- MIDI Channel (range: 1 to 16)
- Off Velocity (range: 0 to 127)

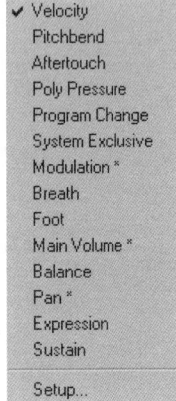

CC Select and Set-up

The lower section of the Event Editor display is used to edit MIDI Continuous Control (CC) data (the default display is Velocity). The dropdown list to the left shows the available CCs. There is a set-up option at the bottom of this list that allows you to add any of the 128 MIDI CCs available. A list of MIDI CCs has been provided in Appendix D (page 339) for reference.

The Ruler is the standard Cubase S$_X$ Ruler with its variety of display options. However, there is a display options that affects whether the vertical spacing of the editor will be affected by Tempo changes:

- *Time Linear:* As Tempo increases the vertical grid lines will be closer together. As Tempo deceases the vertical grid lines will be further apart.
- *Bars+Beats Linear:* The vertical lines will always remain equally spaced.

The right-hand side on the Toolbar contains a range of functions:

Key Editor

The first two boxes contain the pitch and position of the tool in the matrix (it works for all the available tools).

Next to this is the *Snap* button. When *Snap* is on then both *Quantize* and *Length Quantize* values affect the results when creating, resizing and moving

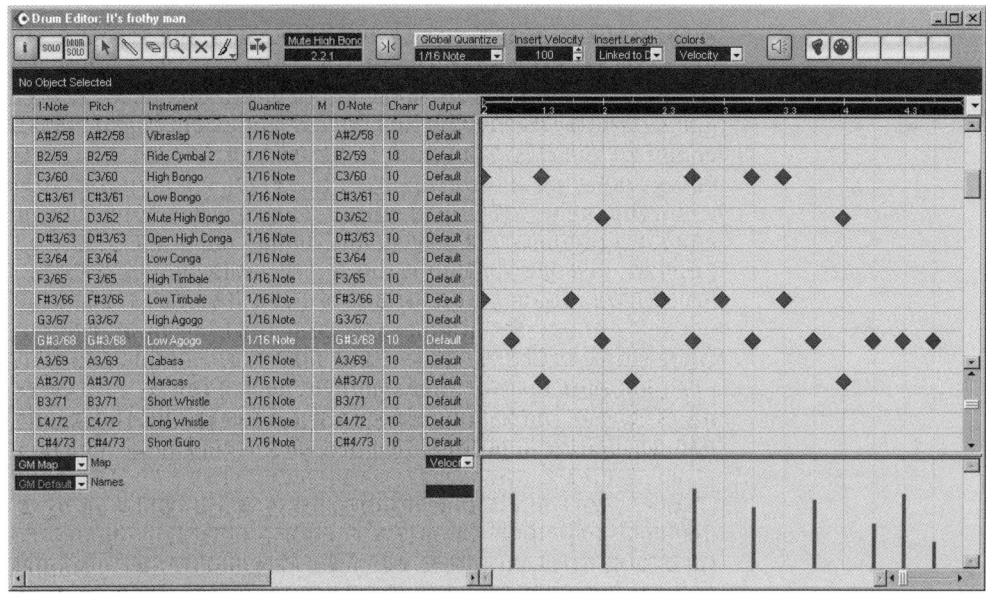

Fig. 12.7: The Drum Editor

Events on the matrix. They do not affect *Info Line* editing. When Snap is off, *Length Quantize* remains in operation for newly created notes, until you move the tool. So you can create a note of length precisely '*Length Quantize*'. *Insert Velocity* is the velocity given to notes created in the Editor. (They are created with the MIDI Channel of their Track.)

The six buttons to the right of the *Audition* button are described below in *Editing MIDI notes from a keyboard*, page 144.

The Drum Editor

The *Drum Editor* [No Default] is very much a specialized tool for drum and percussion programming and editing, although it can be used for general MIDI editing if desired. The main differences between the *Drum Editor* and the *Key Editor* are the lack of a graphical representation of note length; that each pitch is given an instrument name; and the ability to edit a *Drum Map* assigned to the Track. *Drum Maps* are discussed in detail on page 120. We will only look at the differences to the *Key Editor* here.

There are five main areas of the *Drum Editor* display: Toolbar, Instrument list, Pop-ups, Note display, Controllers.

The *Drum Solo* button will solo the selected instrument. Unfortunately, when you select another instrument the instrument solo doesn't follow. Since note lengths are not shown there is no need for *Split* and *Glue* tools. However, we gain a *Drumstick* tool, but lose the *Draw* tool.

Each instrument can be assigned a *Quantize* value in a Drum Map. By

♫   *Note*

If you open Parts from multiple Tracks in the Drum Editor, and at least *one* Track is assigned a *Drum Map*, then only the Tracks assigned to the *Drum Map* will be displayed. If no *Drum Map* has been assigned, then all Parts will be shown.

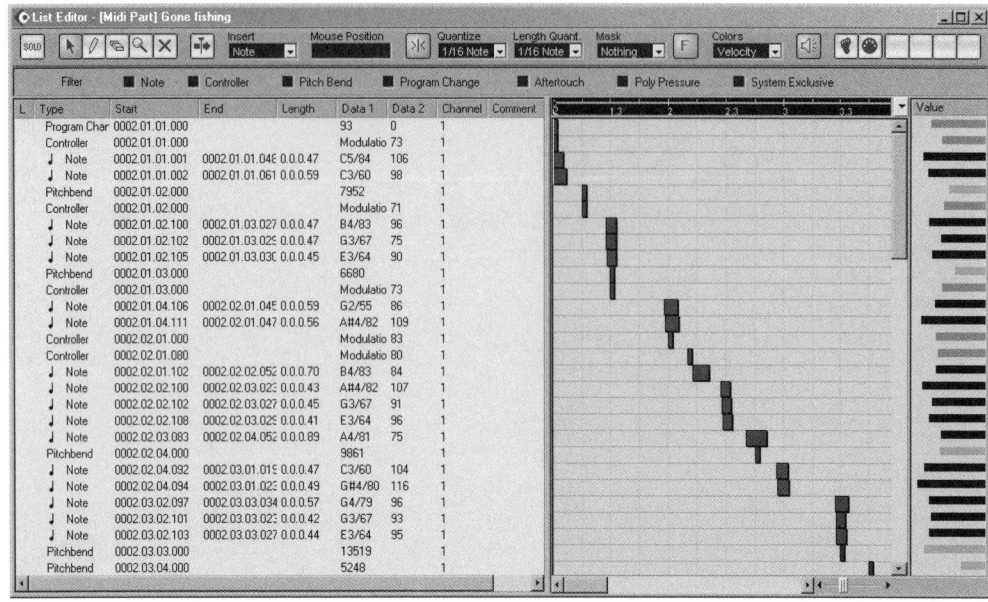

Fig. 12.8: The List Editor

switching the *Global Quantize* button, you can switch between following the Project quantize of the individual quantize values. Finally, *Insert Length* performs a very similar function to *Insert Quantize*.

The *pop-up* area allows selection of a Drum Map or, when no Drum Map is selected, a *Names List*. A Names List is derived from a Drum Map, plus the default "GM Default"; those shown in the dropdown are for the Drum Maps currently loaded. You lose the following columns and related functions when no Drum Map is assigned: I-Note, O-Note, Mute, Channel and Output.

The Instrument list contains an entry for all of the 128 MIDI note values. Clicking the left-hand column will audition the instrument. The rest of the columns should be self-explanatory, except for the *I-Note* and *O-Note* entries. All will become clear by reading the section on *Drum Maps* on page 120.

The Note display is a simple pitch vs. start position matrix. As noted above, note length is not shown, but it can be edited in the *Info Line*.

The Controller display is identical to the *Key Editor*.

The List Editor

The *List Editor* [CTRL+G] is restricted to showing a single Part. Much of what can be done with it can be also be done in the *Browser* [CTRL+B]. At heart, the *List Editor* is an low-level Event editor.

The layout is composed of the toolbar, the *Event list* (on the left), the *Event display* and the *Value display* (on the far right). The central bar can be moved to expose more of the *Event list*, if necessary. You can also move and resize

> ♫   **Note**
>
> The *Drumstick* has its own key command. Nope, you can't use the same one as you do for *Draw*.

the columns.

The *Event list* is an ordered list of all MIDI Events. Events are edited by entering text into the selected field. Notes will sound when the row is selected when *Audition*is active. The *Event display* displays Events graphically. Here Events can be inserted, dragged horizontally in the timeline, notes lengthened, etc. The *Value display* (on the far right) is a graphical representation of either *Data 1* or *Data 2*. The *Draw* tool will always appear when the mouse is in this area and can be used to change the values. The *Filter View toggle*, in the toolbar, will display a row of checkboxes allowing the Events in the Event display to be filtered, as required.

The *Mask* dropdown is another filter. It hides Events based on data from the selected Event. It provides four filters/masks:

☿ *Info*

MIDI Controllers must be entered by number. See chapter D, page 339 for a complete list.

○ *Nothing:* Three guesses?
○ *Event Types:* only displays Event-types of the selected Event's *type*
○ *Controller and Event types:* used to isolate a specific controller (e.g. pitch-bend) rather than all controllers, which is what the *Event Types* mask displays
○ *Event Channels:* only displays Event-types of the selected Event's *channel*

The Event display shows the following associated information for Events. Events will not have an entry in every column:

○ Type (the Event-type e.g. Note, Pitch-bend, Controller, etc.)
○ Start position of Event
○ End positions of Notes only
○ Length (Note only)
○ Data 1 (Event data – see below)
○ Data 2 (Event data – see below)
○ MIDI Channel (range: 1 to 16)
○ Comments (not available to all Event-types)

The following table shows the entry in the *Value display* and the meaning of *Data 1* and *Data 2* for each Event-type. The values for *Data 1* and *Data 2* vary by Event-type.

Event-type	Data 1	Data 2	Value
Note	Note number/Pitch	Velocity	Velocity
Controller	Controller type	Amount	Amount
Program Change	Program number	n/a	Program number
After-touch	Amount	n/a	Amount
Pitch-bend	Amount	n/a	Amount
SYSEX	n/a	n/a	n/a

– The format of Note number/Pitch can be altered with *Preferences/Event Display/MIDI* tab *Note Name Style*.
– Controller type must be entered by number. See appendix D, page 339.

The SYSEX editor can be opened by clicking in the *Comment* entry for the Event. For more on SYSEX editing see page 132.

Useful key commands in the MIDI editors
As well as the standard *Zoom in* [H] and *Zoom out* [G], consider setting-up *Zoom in vertical* [No Default] and *Zoom out vertical* [No Default]. I like to use CTRL+H and CTRL+G, respectively, but this does mean changing the assignment for *Open List Editor* [CTRL+G]. Also useful are *Zoom full* [SHIFT+F], *Zoom to selection* [ALT+S] and *Zoom to Locators* [No Default].

MIDI Editing

Editing of Event parameters in the Key and Drum Editors can always be performed by editing the data in the *Info Line*. See *Selecting Events* below for more on this.

Creating and Deleting MIDI notes

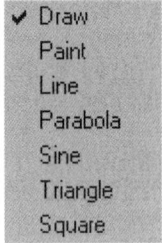

Draw tools options

Key Editor

To create Notes, select the drawing tool that you want to use from the dropdown selection via the *Draw tool* button. The Drawing Tools, and their modifiers, are described in detail on page 146. Note how the pitch is shown on the keyboard (and in the display box on the Toolbar) as you move the pointer over the matrix. When you click on the matrix with the *Draw* tool, a MIDI Note is created. Its start position will be dictated by where you click and the state of *Snap*; length will be determined by *Length Quantize*; and velocity will be governed by *Insert Velocity*. A longer note can be created by holding the mouse-button and dragging it. Deletion is achieved either with the Erase tool, or by selecting an Event and pressing DELor [Backspace].

> ♩   Note
>
> Modifiers can be applied one after the other. For example it is quite possible to, say, draw a triangle wave, then shift its phase (CTRL), then increase its period (SHIFT), then move the whole curve (ALT+CTRL), then skew the curve into a saw wave (CTRL+SHIFT).

Draw Tool
The *Draw tool* creates individual Events that are aligned with the *Snap* setting, if active. You draw the length of each note.

Paint tool
Snap on: Creates Events aligned with *Quantize* step with a length of *Length Quantize*.

Snap off: It paints notes freely.
Modifiers:
CTRL: Horizontal movement only.

Line and Parabola

Snap on: Creates Events every *Length Quantize* step on the curve with a length of *Length Quantize*.
Snap off: Creates Events every along the curve with the start of the next being aligned with the end of the previous.
Modifiers:

○ CTRL (Parabola only): Inverts the curve (you have to move the cursor around a bit to force this to occur). You can achieve the same thing by drawing the parabola from right-to-left.
○ ALT+CTRL: Moves a drawn curve.
  Draw the required curve. Press ALT+CTRL. Drag the curve to the required spot. Release ALT+CTRL, then release the mouse-button. You can invert the curve before doing this. Snap for this operation is $1/4$ of *Quantize*.
  Note that you can use this to move a curve vertically, as well as horizontally.
○ SHIFT: Alters the exponent (steepness) of the parabola.
  Draw the required curve length. Press SHIFT. Pull the curve-end back to the left. Release SHIFT. Return the curve-end to its intended endpoint. Release the mouse-button. The curve will have steepened. The further back you take the curve when holding SHIFT, the steeper the curve.

Sine, Triangle, Square

Snap on: Creates Events every *Length Quantize* step and of length *Length Quantize*. Period of curve determined by *Quantize*.
Snap off: Creates a sequence of Events with start and end points as drawn. The notes do not overlap. The period of the curve is 2 seconds.
Modifiers:

○ CTRL: Changes the phase of the curve.
  Draw the curve and, while still holding the mouse-button, press CTRL and drag the curve until the phase is as you require. Release CTRL and draw the required number of phases.
○ SHIFT: Increases or decreases the period of the curve.
  Draw the curve and, while still holding the mouse-button, press SHIFT and drag the curve until you have the period length that you require. Release SHIFT and draw the required number of phases.
○ ALT+CTRL: Moves a drawn curve (see above for explanation).
○ CTRL+SHIFT: (Triangle and Square only.) Allows Triangle waves to be skewed toward a Saw shape in steps of $1/4$ of *Quantize*. Square waves can have their pulse width varied.

Drum Editor

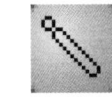

Drumstick tool

The *Drumstick* has been specially crafted for this editor, and works just fine. Click and create. Click and delete. Snap works as expected with the exception that an instrument's *Quantize* will be used if *Global Quantize* is off. *Insert Velocity* and *Insert Length* are used. When *Linked to Drum Map* is selected for *Insert Length* then the instruments' *Quantize* values are used.

When Snap is on, you can drag the *Drumstick* horizontally to create a note every *Quantize* step. This is very useful for quickly creating repeating drum and percussion sounds, or for filling a loop in preparation for editing by removing hits.

List Editor

MIDI Events can be added by selecting from the *Insert* dropdown in the toolbar and then clicking with the *Draw* tool in required location in the *Event Display*. The following Events are available:

Note	Aftertouch	SMF
Controller	Pitch Bend	Text
Program Change	SYSEX	

Selecting Events

As well as the *Edit/Select* command the *Select* tool provides the following

- To select a single Event, click on it, or navigate to it using the left and right cursor keys.
- To select multiple Events hold SHIFT+click or lasso them. You can also hold SHIFT and make a selection with the cursor keys.
- To select a note and all following of the same pitch, select the note and then double-click it.
- To select all notes of a single pitch, click the appropriate key on the keyboard while holding CTRL.
- To select all notes of a single pitch starting from a selected note, double-click the note while holding SHIFT.

When multiple Events are selected in the *Key Editor* or *Drum Editor* the entry in the *Info Line* turns yellow. These Events can then be edited as a group. The edit will be relative, except for *channel*. So, if you select three Events with velocities 10, 35 and 52, then editing an Info Line entry of 10 to 15 will result in velocities of 15, 40 and 57, an addition of 5. If you perform the same operation, but this time hold CTRL, then the all Events will take the same value. In the given example the result would be 15, 15, 15.

Moving and Transposing Events

When dragging Events, Snap will apply, if activated. You can maintain the current start position of the Events being moved (vertical movement), or the pitches (value for CC's) of the Events (horizontal movement) by simultaneously holding CTRL when dragging the Events. Vertical movement is simple transposition. You can transpose the selection in octave steps by using SHIFT+up and SHIFT+down.

○ To move a single Event, click on the Event and drag it, or edit its start position on the Info Line.

○ To move more than one Event, select and drag. Relative positions are maintained.

○ Use *Nudge left* [No Default] and *Nudge right* [No Default] on single or multiple Events (not CC's). These commands nudge selected Events by the *Quantize* setting, but do not apply any additional quantizing.

○ Use *Edit/Move to Cursor* [CTRL+L] to move a selection. When multiple Events are selected relative positions are maintained. The same thing can be achieved by doing a *Cut* [CTRL+X] and *Paste* [CTRL+V].

> ♫ **Note**
>
> To transpose notes by an octave, select the note(s) and use SHIFT+up and SHIFT+down

If you want to move all Events in a Part, perhaps by a few ticks, but leave the Part where it is, you can, of course, move the Events in the MIDI Editor. However, if this is a shared Part, you might not want all the shared Parts to be affected. If this is the case, see the section on *Offset* in *Moving MIDI Parts* on page 127.

> ↗ **Tip**
>
> It is often useful to precisely align (or create) a MIDI Event at an audio Event of some kind. To do this, position the Cursor at the precise point that you require the MIDI Event, either in the Project Window or in the Sample Editor. Now open the MIDI Editor. You can now either select a MIDI Event or create a new one. With the MIDI Event selected, do *Edit/Move to Cursor* [CTRL+L].

Creating copies of notes

The usual technique of holding ALT and dragging can be used, as can *Edit/Duplicate* [CTRL+D] and *Edit/Repeat* [CTRL+K].

Also very useful are the *Copy, Cut and Paste* functions. *Paste* will insert the copied notes at the Cursor. *Paste Time* [CTRL+SHIFT+V] inserts copied notes at the Cursor and moves existing notes (splitting them if required) to the right to make way for the inserted notes.

Muting, Resizing, Splitting Notes

The Mute tool can be used to select or lasso notes for both muting and unmuting. Alternatively, select the notes then use *Edit/Mute & Unmute Objects* [ALT+M] or the two separate commands *Edit/Mute Events* [SHIFT+M] and *Edit/Unmute Events* [SHIFT+U].

When in the *Drum Editor* and a Drum Map is used, then each instrument can be muted individually.

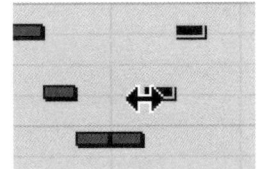

Resizing can be performed by selecting the appropriate note (or notes) with the *Draw* tool and dragging the start or end point's *Resize cursor*. Relative positions are kept. You can also resize by editing Events' lengths in the *Info Line*.

Resize cursor

Notes can be split with *Edit/Split at Cursor* [ALT+X] or *Edit/Split Loop* [No Default].

Editing MIDI notes from a keyboard

MIDI Input buttons

Keyboard edit

The keyboard can be used to edit the *Pitch, Note On* and *Note Off* velocity values of a single selected note. Simply activate the *MIDI/Toggle MIDI Input* [No Default] button and select which of the three values you wish to modify by activating the appropriate buttons. Once you've hit a key, and the edit has been applied, the next note is automatically selected in the editor.

Step input

Step input is a method of inputting MIDI notes without running the Transport. Some folk call it cheating, others a life-saver. Notes are played from a MIDI device, either singularly or as chords, with the Transport off. The created notes take the value of incoming MIDI and *Length Quantize. Note On* velocity is either taken from the incoming MIDI or *Insert Velocity* depending on the state of the *Record Note On Velocity* button.

♩   *Note*

If all three MIDI data buttons are *off*, then *Step Input* will create a single note on C3.

♩   *Note*

The step-size is set by *Quantize* when Snap is on, and defaults to 1/16ths when Snap is off.

To use *Step Input* activate the *MIDI/Toggle Step Input* [0] button. (This is shaped like a foot, either to indicate what a kickin' function it is, or as an indication that you deserve a kick up the backside for using it; depending on your point-of-view.) Click in the matrix (with the *Select* tool) and a blue line will appear (or yellow if it overlaps the Project Cursor): this is the *Step Input Position Line*. You can move it by clicking a destination in the matrix or by using the left and right cursors. You can also use *Edit/Move Insert Cursor To Part Start* [No Default], which does what you'd expect, but requires a key command to be assigned. Its position is shown numerically in the toolbar (below the note display). Set the length of the notes you wish to create and the space between them with *Length Quantize* and *Quantize* respectively, and set *Insert Velocity*, if you are not using the value from the MIDI input. Note that these values are still used even when *Snap* is off. Good to go.

Play a note or chord. When you release *all* notes, the Events are created and the *Step Line* moves on a notch. You can use the left and right cursor keys to freely move back and forth through the Part.

Turning off *Snap* allows you place the *Step Line* wherever you wish, but Events and spacing still follow *Length Quantize* and *Quantize*.

♫ **Note**

The *In* button will insert Events at the *Step Line*. All following notes are moved later in the *Part* by the step-size selected (later Parts on the Track are unaffected). Any CC's in operation at the insert-point will be applied to the new notes, and all CC's in the Part are moved later. If a CC change takes place at the same precise location as the insert-point, then the previous CC will be extended to apply to the new notes. The CC at the insert-point point will, effectively, retain its relative position. In most cases this will be okay, but you might need to move a Program Change, or suchlike.

Editing in the Controller Display

The Controller Display is positioned right underneath the MIDI edit matrix. You can resize the display by dragging the bar dividing it from the Note matrix. From here, all MIDI continuous controller (CC) messages can be created, edited and deleted. For example: Pitch Bend, Program Change, Pan, and Expression.

Note velocities shown below the MIDI note matrix

Multiple lanes can be opened (and lanes closed) by right-clicking in the editor and using the *Create new Controller Lane* and *Remove this Lane* menu items.

Only one type of CC is visible in each Lane at one time and this is selected from the dropdown on the left-hand side of the display. There is also a Set-up function available from this dropdown that allows you to add and remove any CC to the list available for editing.

Note Velocity is the default display. To change the velocity value for a note (or notes that share the same start position), drag the velocity graphic with the *Draw* tool. If more than one note starts at the same position then first select the required note in the matrix. You can also draw a velocity ramp for multiple notes by using the Line tool. Other curve shapes can be drawn using the appropriate tool (e.g. parabola, sine, etc.), see below.

All Controllers (all but Velocity) are displayed as blocks representing a constant value until the next CC Event; this is because the value applies to the whole Channel not just an individual Event. If *Any* is selected as the MIDI output then CC Events will only apply to the channel for which they were created.

♫ *Note*

For added editor real estate, you can remove all controller lanes.

The draw tools are used to create and change CC Event values. You create a new CC Event, or a number of CC Events, by dragging one of the drawing tools. The Line tool is used for creating CC Event ramps, or modifying existing Events into a ramp. If you want to restrict your editing to changing existing Events, then it is best to hold ALT while Editing. If you don't do this, and Snap is off, then you will create a large number of Events.

✗ *Tip*

It is, in general, easier to change the velocity for a single note in the Info Line.

Moving and Copying CC Events is done in the same way as for the Note matrix except that a CC of the same type, at the same position, will overwrite an existing CC Event and not create a duplicate. The same applies for Cut,

Copy and Paste, not forgetting that you can Paste into other Parts, if required. In this way, it is possible to separate the CC Events from the Note Events onto separate Tracks.

The Drawing Tools

The drawing tools are quite intricate. So here is a full explanation.

♫   Note

Modifiers (shown below) can be applied one after the other. For example it is quite possible to, say, draw a triangle wave, then shift its phase (CTRL), then increase its period (SHIFT), then move the whole curve (ALT+CTRL), then skew the curve into a saw wave (CTRL+SHIFT).

♫   *Note*

Each Controller Event retains its value until it is changed. A *MIDI Reset* (page 114) will tidy things up if you run into problems.

Draw and Paint tool

Snap on: Creates Events every *Quantize* step.
Snap off: Creates Events every 6 ticks, approximately.
Modifiers:

○ ALT: Modify existing Events *only*.
○ CTRL: Horizontal movement only.

Line and Parabola

Snap on: Creates Event every *Length Quantize* step.
Snap off: Creates Event every 6 ticks, approximately.
Modifiers:

○ ALT: Modify existing Events *only*.
○ CTRL (Parabola only): Inverts the curve (you have to move the cursor around a bit to force this to occur). You can achieve the same thing by drawing the parabola from right-to-left.

♫   *Note*

If CC Events already exist then, providing *Snap* is on, they will be modified, not replaced, when edited with a drawing tool. If *Snap* is off, then the original frequency of Events will be lost.

○ ALT+CTRL: Moves a drawn curve.
  Draw the required curve. Press ALT+CTRL. Drag the curve to the required spot. Release ALT+CTRL, then release the mouse-button. You can invert the curve before doing this. Snap for this operation is $1/4$ of *Quantize*.
  Note that you can use this to move a curve vertically, as well as horizontally.
○ SHIFT: Alters the exponent (steepness) of the parabola.
  Draw the required curve length. Press SHIFT. Pull the curve-end back to the left. Release SHIFT. Return the curve-end to its intended endpoint. Release the mouse-button. The curve will have steepened. The further back you take the curve when holding SHIFT, the steeper the curve. Combining all three of the above operations (in a meaningful way) makes you eligible for the *Sx master editor award*. Go on, impress your friends and clients.

Sine, Triangle, Square

Snap on: Creates Events every *Length Quantize* step. Period of curve determined by *Quantize*.

Snap off: Not available (requires *Quantize* for period of curve).

Modifiers:

o ALT: Modify existing Events *only*.

o CTRL: Changes the phase of the curve.

Draw the curve and, while still holding the mouse-button, press CTRL and drag the curve until the phase is as you require. Release CTRL and draw the required number of phases.

o SHIFT: Increases or decreases the period of the curve.

Draw the curve and, while still holding the mouse-button, press SHIFT and drag the curve until you have the period length that you require. Release SHIFT and draw the required number of phases.

o ALT+CTRL: Moves a drawn curve (see above for explanation).

o CTRL+SHIFT: (Triangle and Square only.) Allows Triangle waves to be skewed toward a Saw shape in steps of $1/4$ of *Quantize*. Square waves can have their pulse width varied.

♪ **Note**

To draw high definition curves, increase *Length Quantize* or turn-off *Snap*.

☿ **Info**

Poly Pressure is a unique CC in that each Event applies to a specific pitch. Ensure that you select the pitch for the notes you are editing.

MIDI Preferences

There are four tabs for MIDI in *Preferences*:

o MIDI
o Function Parameters
o Chase Events Filter
o Filter

MIDI Tab

Snap Record Parts to Bars

Forces a newly created MIDI Part to start and end on bar boundaries. Leave on for easier editing in *Bars+Beat*, especially when snap is used.

MIDI Thru Active

See earlier *Basic Set-up Info* section, page 115. When checked all Record and Monitor Enabled MIDI Tracks will thru incoming MIDI to their respective MIDI Output ports and Channels.

Reset on...

See *MIDI Reset* section, page 114.

"Note On" Priority
Gives priority to MIDI Note On messages over all other MIDI data. Checking this might impact the tonality of a patch due to a controller, or MIDI Clock, being delayed. On the other hand not checking it might delay a note when the channel is receiving other MIDI messages (e.g. pitch-bend and other controllers). Let your ears be the guide.

Length Correction
Consider two notes of the same pitch and on the same MIDI *channel*. The value of this spin control adjusts the length of the first note so that there is always a short time between the end of the first note and the start of second (from zero to -20 ticks). A patch might respond differently, in some situations, depending on the setting of this parameter.

Solo Record in Editors
When you open a MIDI Part in an editor, the Track is automatically *Record Enabled*. If this option is checked, then when you open a MIDI Part, the corresponding Track will be record enabled *exclusively* (although audio Tracks will be unaffected). When you close the MIDI Part (or it loses focus), then record enable settings are returned as they were. Note that if other MIDI Tracks have monitoring active, then they will still playback any incoming MIDI data. Also note that the MIDI Track opened will still only receive incoming MIDI on its selected input port and channel.

Record Catch Range
The idea behind this function is to set-up a buffer to catch any MIDI information ahead of a recording started automatically (see page 129). Alternatively, you could simply place your recording start point a bar or beat earlier than the expected start of play, or punch-in manually.

Function Parameters Tab
Legato Overlap (±100 ticks where 120 ticks $= 1/16$th note)
Controls how *MIDI/Functions/Legato* [No Default] operates. A positive value results in an overlap, a negative value results in a gap, and zero results in "perfect" legato.

Split MIDI Events
This affects the results when a MIDI note overlaps the cut-point when splitting a MIDI Part. When checked, two notes will be created: a new Note On at the split point, and a shortening of the original note's length. When unchecked the note will start in its current position and its length will be retained. However, you will no longer have a visual cue to the note's length (unless you resize the MIDI Part).

Chase Events Filter Tab
Chasing Events is a process whereby relocating the Project Cursor results in the appropriate MIDI Events being sent to all unmuted devices for the new Cursor position. In this way, the state of each instrument is set for the new position in the Project, as if you had played the Project from the start.

Muted Tracks do not get sent chased Events. However, chased Events are sent the instant that a muted Track is unmuted.

♪   **Note**

Checked Events in the *Chase Events Filter* are *not* chased. So, if all the options are checked, then nothing will be chased.

For example, say a Track starts out using *Honky Tonk Piano*, but changes to *Toy Piano* at verse 2. Then, providing you are chasing *Program Change* (menu item *unchecked*), when you move the Project Cursor to chorus 2, you will get *Toy Piano*. If you then move to chorus 1, you will get *Honky Tonk Piano*. In other words, it creates behavior exactly as you'd expect it.

Items available to chase are: Note, Poly pressure, Controller, Program Change, After-touch, Pitchbend, SYSEX.

MIDI Filter Tab
The MIDI Filter is used to filter incoming MIDI messages. The filter does not affect the playback of MIDI that has already been recorded. The filter is rather crude in that, like the MIDI Reset functions, it applies to all ports. However, rather bizarrely, you can select channels, but only for all ports.

By default, all SYSEX data is filtered for both recording and Playback.

The display is arranged as four segments:

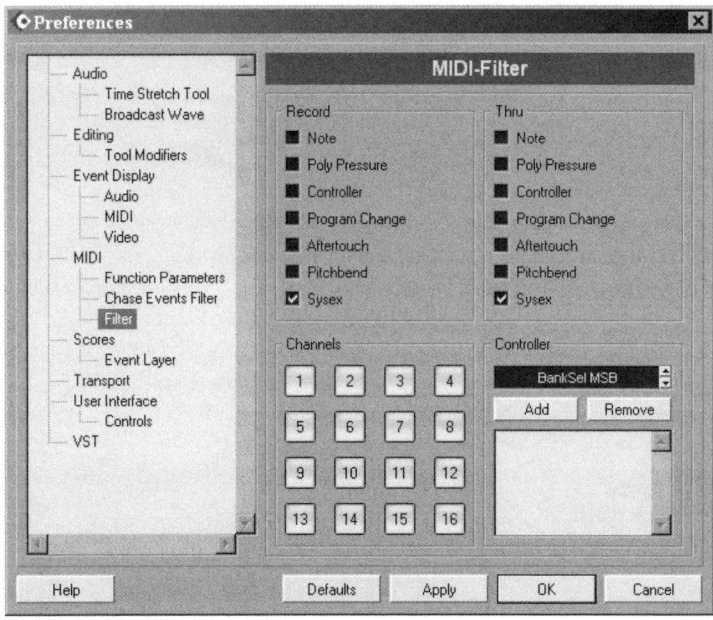

Fig. 12.9: The MIDI Filter

○ Channels
○ Controller
○ Record
○ Thru

The MIDI data passes through the filters in the above order, except that the final two are effectively performed in parallel.

For both recording and playback the Channels and Controller filters are always active. For all Channels selected, MIDI data is neither thru-put nor recorded. It is like a brick wall to those channels. Note that all ports are affected. This can be quite a big restriction to the MIDI filter's usefulness in a number of situations.

Next in line is the Controller filter. All the MIDI Controllers that have been added to the list will neither be recorded nor thru-put. This affects all ports and all channels. The Controller option in the Record and Thru sections will filter all MIDI controllers. The Controller filter allows you to be more selective. The method of selecting a controller to be added to the list can be a little tortuous, since you must click through the available controllers one-by-one until you find the one that you are looking for. This is fine if you have memorized the list of all controllers and their order. For the rest of us, the quickest way to add a controller is to click on the text field, type in the number and press return. There is a complete list of MIDI Controller messages in Appendix D, page 339.

The remaining two filters affect either the MIDI data being recorded or the messages being thru-put. The choices in the Record and Thru filter boxes are identical; it is simply their destination that is affected.

Filtering can be usefully applied during recording when, for example, the keyboard is sending unwanted controller information, such as after-touch. This type of data can be quite voluminous and affect the timing of the recorded Track. Equally, the controller information might simply not be used by the receiving device or patch, so the messages are simply wasting bandwidth.

Another typical use is to filter SYSEX data. The Cubase Sx default is for all SYSEX data to neither be recorded nor thru-put. In general, you will be aware when sending SYSEX data and only wish to switch filtering off when necessary. Equally, it is worth considering filtering after-touch for the same reason (assuming your master keyboard sends after-touch by default). Another message that can be troublesome is Program Change. Depending on how your devices are connected, this message can sometimes lead to undesirable effects. You may wish to consider filtering it for record, but allowing it thru.

13 MIDI Processing

Cubase Sx provides a rich source of creative MIDI processes that can be used in real-time (when recording and monitoring) and statically (on MIDI Parts). In this chapter we will focus on the processing of MIDI Events, both during and after recording. The dynamic functions can be found in the *Inspector* [ALT+I], while the static functions can be found in various sub-menus.

As well as these functions and processes, note that each MIDI channel can be automated, and that some MIDI effects make parameters available for automation, once they have been loaded.

Working with MIDI effects

There are two distinct ways of applying effects to MIDI Events. The first is to make adjustment to the MIDI Events as they pass through the sections that make-up the *Inspector*; namely *Track settings* (i.e. pan, volume, delay), *Track parameters*, *Inserts effects*, and *Send effects*. The other method of applying MIDI effects is to *process* the Events in a MIDI Part (e.g. quantize or reverse), which alters the stored MIDI Part.

> ♪ **Note**
>
> All *MIDI Effects* are available for use by default, but you can hide them from the dropdown lists via *Devices/Plug-in Information* [No Default] (see page 223).

The term *MIDI Effect* will be used for plug-in effects and *Track Parameters* functions, and *MIDI Process* for the menu selected processes.

All of the *Inspector* sections operate on the incoming MIDI Events in real-time. If the Events are arriving from a MIDI Part (during playback), the *stored* MIDI Part remains unaltered by these effects; the effect is applied to the MIDI Events, and passed to the device selected on the output dropdown.

Monitoring MIDI Effects

> ♪ **Note**
>
> Some MIDI effects will not work unless the Transport is running. For example, *Auto Pan* and *Step Designer*.

Basic MIDI recording is covered in the previous chapter (see page 129). Also covered in that chapter is the *Input Transformer* (page 130), which allows you to transform and filter incoming MIDI messages in realtime and *record* the transformed result.

As previously mentioned, the *Input Transformer* works in a very similar way to the *MIDI/Logical Editor* [No Default] transform function (see page 164), but instead of being a static edit of the MIDI messages (after recording them), it operates dynamically, as you play.

For all other MIDI Effects, no change takes place when the MIDI Events are recorded. So, if you play middle-C, then that is what is recorded, even if you have arpeggio and echo insert plug-ins creating a cacophony of sound. In fact,

---

if you record *thru* these effects, the incoming MIDI Events are recorded as they arrive *without* the effects being applied.

To hear the result of MIDI effect while playing a keyboard (or other MIDI device), simply active monitoring on the Track, then play. Any active effects will process the incoming MIDI Events and you will hear the result on the appropriate device *providing* the device can respond to the incoming MIDI messages. For example, not all devices will respond to volume or pan messages, so no change would be heard for effects altering these MIDI messages.

Effects during playback

As noted above, there are four parts to the MIDI effects' chain.

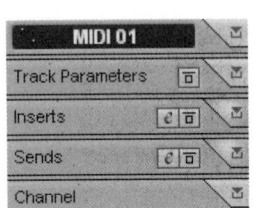

The Inspector

o Track settings (i.e. pan, volume, delay)
o Track parameters
o Inserts effects
o Send effects

All of the above appear in the *Inspector* for the MIDI Track. Insert and Send effects (along with the Channel Strip) can also be accessed from the *MIDI Channel Strip* opened via the **e** button.

Track Settings

While not *strictly* part of the effects' chain, volume, pan and delay affect playback, of course. Both *volume* and *pan* are sent as MIDI messages, so they will change the settings on the receiving device, providing that it is capable of interpreting them and the device is set to respond. These values are not sent at start of playback, so if you change the settings on the device then they will not reflect the settings in Sx. They are sent, however, when the Project is loaded and when a program change is made within Sx.

Delay instructs Cubase Sx when to send the MIDI Events, on playback, with respect to the timeline and other non delayed Events. The range is ±2000ms in 1ms steps. A negative values will cause the MIDI Events to be sent early, and positive values later.

Track Parameters

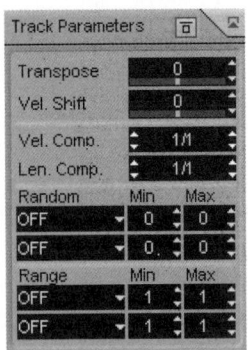

Track Parameters

The *Track Parameters* functions alter MIDI *notes* during playback and when monitoring. A bypass switch is provided in the title line allowing you to A/B your settings. The available function are:

o *Transpose (range: ±127):* Adds the value to a note's pitch. This changes the pitch of the note by the given number of semitones.
o *Velocity shift (range: ±127):* Adds the value to a note's velocity. This will usually increase or decrease the volume of the note, but may well affect the dynamics in other ways depending on the programming of the receiving patch.
o *Velocity compression:* Multiplies the value of a note's velocity. A setting of 1/2 will change an incoming velocity of 100 to play a note of velocity 50. A

setting of 2/1 will do the opposite. This function is applied after *Velocity Shift*, so if *Velocity compression* is set to 1/2, then the maximum outgoing velocity will never exceed 63, irrespective of the setting of *Velocity Shift*. This strikes me as a bug (as at v1.03), since the effect of the multiplier is to compress the velocity values but, thereafter you wish to raise or lower it by a fixed amount (as you would with an audio compressor). To quickly reset, enter 1. An alternative to using this is to use the MIDI plug-in *Compress*.

○ *Length compression:* Multiplies a note's length, thus shortening or length-ening all notes. This function doesn't work in real-time. It would be clever if it did.

○ *Random:* Two random generators that allow you to randomly adjust pitch (±100 in semitone steps), velocity(±100 in MIDI units), start position (±500 in ticks), note length (±500 in ticks). This function doesn't work in real-time.

○ *Range:* Two places in which to specify either pitch or velocity ranges. There are four options:

  – *Velocity limit:* velocities outside the range take the closer range limit value.

  – *Velocity filter:* notes with velocities outside the range do not play.

  – *Note limit:* pitches outside the range are transposed *into* the range. Notes that can't find a home, in a range of less than an octave, are given the mid-value of the range.

  – *Note filter:* notes with pitches outside the range do not play.

> ♪ **Note**
>
> All of the *Track Parameters*, with the exception of *Velocity* and *Length compression* can be fully automated in the MIDI automation Track.

Insert effects

There are four *MIDI Insert* effect slots. Each slot has a bypass and a button to display the plug-in interface. There is also a global bypass for all *Inserts*. MIDI Events arrive from the *Track Parameters* and are routed through each active effect slot in turn, where they might be transformed or deleted, or further Events might be created. Whatever emerges from the *MIDI Inserts* is passed to both the output destination selected for the Track, and the *MIDI Sends* (see below).

> ♪ **Note**
>
> Some effects have a floating window interface (e.g. Auto Pan), while other are embedded in the *Inspector* (e.g. Compress). To force the latter to *float*, hold ALT while opening the plug-in interface.

Send effects

As with inserts, there are four *MIDI Send* effect slots. Each slot has a bypass and a button to display the plug-in interface. MIDI Events arrive from both the *MIDI Inserts* and directly from the MIDI Track. Each *Send Effect* slot has a *Pre button* which, when active, will tap the MIDI Events *prior* to being routed through the *Track Parameters* and *Inserts*. When the *Pre button* is inactive, then the *Send effect* will receive the Events from the *Inserts*. Each *Send slot* can be routed, independently, to any of the available output ports.

A *Send slot* does not need a loaded effect to be able to route MIDI Events to its output port. This is an incredibly useful feature. By the time the MIDI Events have reached the Send effects, they have been fully processed. This gives us a simple way of switching to another MIDI device (whether a VSTi or device). It is also handy for trying out track-doubling, without the fuss of setting up another Track. Indeed, you could go as far as not selecting a Track output port at all, and just route via the Sends.

Bouncing MIDI Effects

MIDI/Merge MIDI in Loop [No Default] merges all MIDI Events that *start* between the locators, for all non-muted Tracks, into a single Part. The new Part is created on the selected Track (which could be one created especially to receive it). You can optionally chose to "bounce" any MIDI Insert of Send effects into the new Part. (Track Parameters are considered to be Insert effects for this function.)

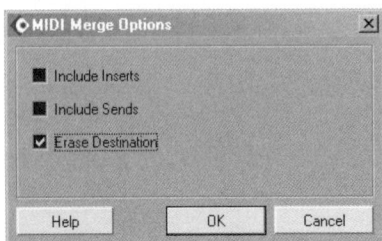

Merge MIDI

MIDI Automation

Each MIDI channel can be automated. As well as the expected volume, pan and mute, you can also toggle, individual sends and inserts, and the *Track Parameters*. All of the *Track Parameters*, with the exception of *Velocity* and *Length compression* can be fully automated in the MIDI automation Track. Some MIDI effects make parameters available for automation, once they have been loaded.

The MIDI Effects

♪   *Note*

For a complete list of MIDI Controllers for use with MIDI effects see appendix D, page 339.

The MIDI Effects are described in detail in chapter *MIDI realtime parameters and effects* of the *Cubase Sx: Operations Manual*. You can also call them up by name in *Help* [F1]. Provided here is a brief description of each (or a longer description where necessary).

Arpache

A simple and straightforward tempo-sync'd MIDI arpeggiator. As well as the usual up, down, up/down/ down/up and random modes, it is also possible to specify the order in which the held-notes are processed, up to a maximum of eight notes.

Auto Pan

Not just an automatic pan controller, but an LFO that can be routed to any MIDI controller. Various waveforms are available, and the other controls enable very detailed control of the waveform. If you have *MIDI Yoke*, or similar MIDI loopback facilities available, then try recording the output to get an understanding of what is going on. There are some very funky effects available. Try the preset: Expression/Pad Rhythm.

Do this by hand!

Chorder

Chorder allows you to either assign any chord to any single note, or to create a single chord and then the play a note to transposes the chord. It is a powerful tool (especially if you are a "limited ability" keys player) but unfortunately the interface is a little baffling.

First of all, turn off the *Thru* button in the bottom section. In most cases this will cause a duplicate MIDI Event; not something you want to happen.

There are three distinct modes: Normal, Octave and Global. The simplest is *Normal*. In this mode, each *trigger note* on the lower keyboard will play the highlighted notes in the upper keyboard. Unassigned *trigger notes* play their own note. As an example, select a C-note on the lower keyboard. It turns red. Now select a C-E-G combination in the upper keyboard. The notes turn blue. Now do the same for the adjacent D on the lower keyboard, and D-F#-A on the upper.

In *Octave* mode, the lower keyboard only shows one octave. Chords are input in the same way as in *Normal* mode. The definitions assigned to each of the lower keys are spread across the whole keyboard.

Global mode allows you to define a single chord in the upper keyboard. The chord is then automatically transposed when you play a key. So, if you select a C-E-G combination in the upper keyboard, then all keys will play their major triad base on the root. The same result would happen if you selected F-A-C; it is the intervals from the root note played that are important. The played note always sounds.

We'll go through the *Zone Set-up*, by example. Select *Octave* mode. Click the C-note and select a C-E-G combination in the upper keyboard. Increase *Use* to 2. Activate the button that looks like a pedal to me, but is probably an arrow on a key; this turns on *velocity switching*. Note that *Zone select* now has two buttons available. If you click the new *Zone select* button (marked 2), you will find that it has the same definition as zone 1. Change the E-note in the upper keyboard to Eb, thus creating a minor chord. Play a C-note at soft and hard velocities and your chord will change from major (0 thru 63) to minor (64 thru 127). As you add more zones, the velocity split is further sub-divided in equal divisions.

To explain the *Note* switching mode we'll swap across to *Global* mode. Starting from a new version of *Chorder*, switch off *Thru*. Select a C-E-G combination. Increase *Use* to 3 (three). Activate the note button in *Zone set-up*. Select zone two and change the E-note to Eb. Select zone three and add Bb as a fourth note. So, three zones with major, minor and 7th chords defined. Now hold any root note and, simultaneously, play the note a semitone above it. You should hear the major chord. Now do the same but play a note two semitones above the root. You should hear the minor chord. And similarly for the 7th.

Compress

This provides audio compressor-like control of MIDI velocities. Note velocities above *threshold* have their velocity, less the threshold value, divided by *ratio*.

The *Gain* setting simply adds or subtracts its value to the velocity after compression.

So, if the incoming velocity is 100, threshold is 80 and ratio is $8:1$ then we get: $100 - 80 = 20$ (the velocity above threshold), $20/8 = 2.5$ (the amount of compression), $80 + 2 = 82$ (the output velocity). Similarly, if the ratio is $4:1$ then we get: $100 - 80 = 20$, $20/4 = 5$, $80 + 5 = 85$.

You can also *expand* velocities in *Compress*. If the ratio is $1:2$ then we get: $100 - 80 = 20$ (velocity above threshold)), $20 * 2 = 40$ (amount of expansion), $80 + 40 = 120$ (output velocity). Sorry about the sums.

Control

This effect provides management of up to eight MIDI controllers. All controllers can be automated.

Density

Randomly reduces or adds new notes. Automation is available.

Micro Tuner

Used to create alternative tunings. It works by allowing you to detune each of the twelve semitones in cents (100th of a semitone). The information is sent to the receiving device as a SYSEX message, except in the case of a VSTi when the communication is handled internally by Cubase Sx. Tunings can be automated. There are a few presets supplied, and it is well worth exploring the subtle difference these tunings can make to a piece.

MIDI Echo

A flexible MIDI echo with pitch variation, echo quantize, note length and rate control. Echoed notes of duration *Length* are placed on a grid defined by *Quantize*. Each will sound *Repeat* times. The first repeat will sound after *Echo-Quantize*. (If *Echo-Quantize* is set to one, then the first echoed note is sent at the same time as the original.) *Velocity Decay*, *Length Decay* and *Pitch Decay* behave as expected. *Echo Decay* adjusts the delay time for each repeat; values greater than 100 increase the separation, while values less than 100 move the repeats closer together. All parameters can be automated.

Notes to CC

MIDI Controller generator from notes. Assign a CC and note pitch is converted to the controller value.

Quantizer

Does exactly what it says on the tin. It can be automated. See the following section on quantizing for details on the meaning of the parameters. Its main use is for trying quantize settings while, say, looping a part. By making adjustments, you can settle on satisfactory settings and apply these with the main quantize function. Another way to "save" the settings is to use *Merge Midi in Loop* [No Default] (see the above section on *Bouncing MIDI* 154).

Step Designer

This is a well-featured pattern sequencer with automation. The easiest way to use it is simply to create a MIDI Track and assign an output. Load *Step Designer* and press the *Rand.* (Random) button. You don't need a Part on the Track for it to work.

If you create a Part, then a MIDI note will change the *Pattern* being played, until the next change in note pitch. *Pattern* a 1 is C1 and there are 200 patterns available. Two, or more, notes can be *tied* by clicking the tie section between the step and controller windows.

Track Controls

GS and XG control panel for use with compatible instruments. There are three settings: GS Basic controls; XG Effect + Sends; XG Global. The parameters are available for automation.

Track FX

Duplicates *Track Parameters* with the addition of the *Scale Transpose* function. *Scale Transpose* transposes notes to the selected scale and scale-type. It can be automated.

Transformer

This is a real-time version of the *Logical Editor* (see page 164). Note that the *Delete* function does not *delete* the Events, but simply mutes them so that they do not sound (both when recording and on playback).

MFX Wrapper

Cubase Sx supports MFX-compatible MIDI plug-ins. This is the plug-in type originally developed for the *Cakewalk* sequencer. For MFX plug-ins to work with Sx, the file *mfxwrapper.dll* must exist in the *Components* folder beneath the main Cubase Sx folder. This file should be installed automatically with current releases of Cubase Sx.

Working with MIDI Processes

There are various MIDI processes that are sprinkled around the *MIDI, Advanced Quantize* and *Functions* menus.

The most fundamental MIDI process is quantize (up next), which aligns MIDI notes, in selected Parts, in a predictable and consistent way, under the user's control.

A powerful MIDI processing tool is provided by the *Logical Editor* [No Default] (page 164). This is a MIDI editor that operates on all MIDI Events (not just notes) within the selected Parts. The user sets up selection criteria and then chooses what to do with the Events found from a variety of actions (such as delete, insert or change (transform)). You can also create new MIDI Tracks as the output from the *Logical Editor*. A simple example of a *Logical Editor* transform

> ♪ **Note**
>
> Scripts for *Track Control* can be found in the Cubase Sx folder *Scripts/trackmixer*. The brave may wish to develop their own scripts.

> ☿ **Info**
>
> To separate a MIDI Part into separate Tracks, either by pitch or channel, is achieved via *MIDI/Dissolve Part* [No Default] (see page 127).

would be an octave transpose; where the selection criteria would be *all notes* and the transformation *add 12 to pitch*. (A similar function to the *Logical Editor* is provided, during recording, by the *Input Transformer* (see page 130) and the *Transformer* MIDI plug-in, during playback.)

Finally, there are a number of processes that perform specific functions, such as *Transpose* and *Delete doubles*. These processes are described from page 168 onward.

Quantizing and Grooves

MIDI Quantizing is the process of moving the start positions of *notes* in a controlled way; most frequently, so that they are precisely aligned with a fraction of a beat (although note lengths and note ends can be quantized). The important point to grasp is that *quantize* affects *notes*, not controllers or other MIDI Events.

♩   *Note*

You can quantize audio Events (usually in a Part), as well as MIDI Parts. This is particularly useful when used with *groove templates* (see below).

There are creative extensions of the quantize process. For example: quantize can be set-up to be selective in the notes that are moved (rejecting those within certain limits, for example), or it can move the notes in a way that imparts a particular "groove". In Cubase Sx, quantizing can only be applied to MIDI notes and to audio Events.

Advanced Quantize/Undo Quantize [No Default] will undo *all* quantizing for the Part, not only the selected notes. The usual Cubase Sx *Undo* is available for backing out changes one step at a time. The important thing to note is that the original pre-quantized Part is always available, should you wish to revert to it.

☿   Info

You can automatically quantize a Part, when recording, by switching on *Auto Quantize* [No Default] (also shown as the "AQ" button on the *Transport*). This will cause the recording to be quantized with the settings from *MIDI/Quantize Set-up* [No Default]. Therefore, swing settings, grooves, etc. can be applied. You can *Advanced Quantize/Undo Quantize* [No Default] the *Auto Quantize* after recording, should you change your mind.

Event selection for quantizing

Quantizing is possible in all of the MIDI editors. When quantizing in a MIDI editor, only selected notes will be affected by a quantize operation. *Select All* [CTRL+A] and pitch selection (CTRL+click) on a Key Editor key are useful here. When Quantizing in the Project Window, all selected Parts will be quantized.

Types of Quantizing

There are four types of quantizing available.

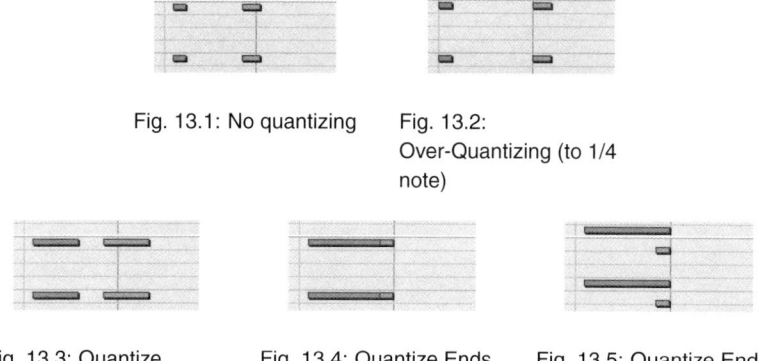

Fig. 13.1: No quantizing

Fig. 13.2:
Over-Quantizing (to 1/4 note)

Fig. 13.3: Quantize
Lengths (to 1/8 note)

Fig. 13.4: Quantize Ends
(to 1/4 note)

Fig. 13.5: Quantize Ends:
note separated

Fig. 13.6: The various quantizing functions (the grid is 1/4 note)

○ *MIDI/Over-Quantize* [Q]: uses the settings in *Quantize Set-up* (see below) to quantize the selected notes. Each time *Over-Quantize* is performed, it operates on the notes' *original positions*.

○ *MIDI/Iterative quantize* [No Default]: as with *Over-quantizing*, *Iterative Quantize* uses the settings in *Quantize Set-up* (see below) to quantize the selected notes. Instead of aligning the notes with the defined grid, however, it only moves them part way toward the grid. How far they are moved, depends on the *Quantize Set-up* setting *Iterative strength*. The result of this is that *Iterative Quantize* can be performed repeatedly, moving the notes closer to the *Over-quantize* grid each time.

○ *Advanced Quantize/Quantizing lengths* [No Default]: sets the length of all selected notes to *Length Quantize*. This operation can only be performed in the Key and List editors. If *Length Quantize* is set to *Linked to Quantize*, then the notes are resized by taking the *Quantize Set-up* settings *Swing, Tuplet* and *Magnetic Area* into account. Start positions are unchanged.

○ *Advanced Quantize/Quantizing ends* [No Default]: lengthens selected notes so that they *end* on the grid defined in *Quantize Set-up*.

Quantizing Techniques

Each MIDI note, even after being quantized (in whatever fashion), retains its original start and length data. *Advanced Quantize/Undo Quantize* [No Default] is available to revert a MIDI Part to its original state. You cannot, unfortunately, *Undo Quantize* on selected Events. You can, of course, still use the regular *Undo* function.

It is also possible to *Advanced Quantize/Freeze Quantize* [No Default], which will make the current quantized version of the MIDI Part permanent. In other words, an *Undo Quantize* will no longer revert the Part to its original state, but will instead return it to the state at which the last Freeze Quantize was

> ♫ **Note**
>
> You can quantize during playback using the *Quantizer* MIDI plug-in. This allows you to change quantize settings and hear the results immediately.

performed.

You can quantize a MIDI *recording* automatically by switching on *Auto Quantize* [No Default] (also shown as the "AQ" button on the *Transport*). The quantize applied is that of the current settings from *MIDI/Quantize Set-up* [No Default]. Therefore, swing settings, grooves, etc. can be applied.

Before taking a look at *Quantize Set-up* in detail, there is a useful method of its use that should be pointed out. It is possible to put Cubase Sx into a playback loop and make quantize adjustments from the *Quantize Set-up* window that occur in real-time. Only those notes selected in the Part will be affected. The quantize effect that is applied always relates to the original positions of the notes, rather than the effect being cumulative. To do this, simply ensure that the *Auto* box is checked on the *Quantize set-up* window.

Quantize set-up

MIDI/Quantize Set-up [No Default] can only be opened from the menu bar or by Key Command.

The simplest way to use the *Quantize set-up* window is by selecting a *Preset*. Using one of the supplied presets effectively resets the window. Note that changing the *Grid* value (which is affected by a Preset change), changes the Quantize value in the MIDI editors and Project Window.

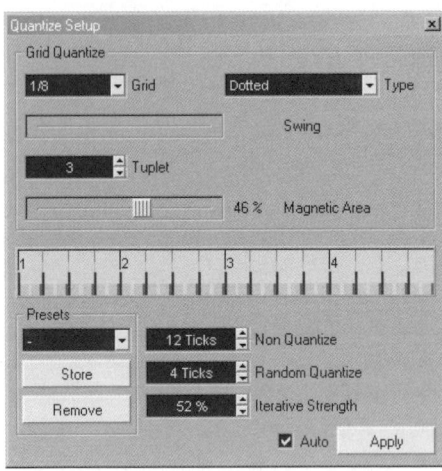

Quantize set-up

Having selected a grid of, say, 1/8 or 1/16, you will notice this spacing being reflected with blue, vertical lines in the central display (which represents one bar). These markers indicate where the notes will be placed if *Quantize* is performed. Take a little time to get a handle on the effect of making changes to the *Type* and *Tuplet* values. As you will find, it is very easy to create alternative rhythms from existing sections of music – quantizing is not just about "correction".

The *Swing* value moves every second quantize position forward by an amount determined by its value. You can see the effect on the blue grid lines, which move to reflect the swing value. Swing only operates when *Type* is set to *Straight*.

When you increase the *Magnetic Area* value a light blue area appears in the central display. This feature narrows the area in which quantize will apply. Only notes whose start time is *within* the *Magnetic Area* will be quantized.

Non Quantize and *Random Quantize* are useful for preserving feel, while "pulling in" any wayward notes. These can be used in a randomly creative way. The *Non Quantize* setting determines which notes will not be affected when quantize is applied. The value is in ticks (1 tick = 120th of a 1/16th note). Notes within the range of this value, on either side of the quantize grid, will not be quantized. The *Random Quantize* setting affects the resulting position of every quantized note. Instead of lining up each note on the quantize grid exactly, a random number of ticks (from zero to this value) is either added to or subtracted from each Events' start position after being quantized.

Iterative Strength is associated with *Iterative Quantize* as described above (page 159).

⤢   Tip

By default, Sx does not have a quantize value of 128th available in the drop-down. To create this entry, open *MIDI/Quantize Set-up* [No Default] and select 1/128 in the *Grid* dropdown. Finally, click *Store* in the *Presets*. The entry will now appear in all *Quantize* dropdowns. You can do the same for triplet and dotted versions.

Creating and using Groove Quantize templates

Back in chapter 10 (page 96), we took a look at Cubase Sx's *Hit-points* and how they could be used to *slice-up* audio so that we could change the audio's tempo, and easily replace *slices* (Events). A *Groove template* is a map created from these same hit-points that can be used by *Quantize set-up* to impart the same *groove* to MIDI Events. In other words, we can extract the groove from a section of audio and use its timing on our MIDI Events to created the same feel.

When creating a *groove template*, we only need to create hit-points for the relevant Event; there is no need to create *slices*. This is a good thing, since we can avoid the associated problems related to doing so, as covered in chapter 10. However, hit-points still get created for the whole Clip and not just for the Event, so it saves a lot of time if you create a smaller piece of audio when you wish to extract a groove from a whole track, say.

Let's go to work. Here's one way of extracting and using a groove. The basic process is described first, and then we get into the details.

○ Start by creating an audio loop of a single bar. You can do this in an audio editor outside of Sx, if you wish, or in the *Sample Editor*.

♫   *Note*

As with all quantize presets, *Groove templates* can only be one bar in length.

♫   *Note*

A *groove template* can be applied to an audio Part. This only makes sense if the Part has a number of Events.

Hit-point button

○ If the Event has been created from a Clip larger than the Event, then bounce the Event to a new Clip, and audio file, with *Audio/Bounce Selection* [No Default]. Select *Replace*, when asked.

○ Open the Event in the *Sample Editor* and calculate the hit-points by clicking the hit-point button. (Refer to chapter 10 (page 96) for details on how to fine-tune the creation of hit-points).

○ Select *Audio/Hitpoints/Create Groove Quantize* [No Default]

○ Open *MIDI/Quantize Set-up* and select your *groove* from the *Presets* drop-down. Only twelve or so characters are visible on the set-up screen, so you might want to rename it. To do this, double-click the *Preset* name. The *Groove Template* is named after the Clip (instead of the Event) and has "sliced" appended to the name (even though we haven't *sliced* the Event).

Let's look into the details of what is going on here.

You can use more than a single bar of audio to create your template (you can use as many as you like), but what gets converted to the template is the first bar in the *Sample Editor* when you perform *Create Groove Quantize*. The result will also be affected by the *Bars* and the *Beats* settings in the *Sample Editor*. Note the bar numbering in the *Ruler*.

To see this for yourself, take a four bar audio sample and create hit-points for it. Now do *Create Groove Quantize* with the *Bars* setting at 1, 2 and 4. You might want to rename the templates as you create each one, otherwise they will all be named the same.

How useful you find this method of quantize preset creation is a personal thing. A one-bar grooves is almost an oxymoron. A groove, in most folks' eyes will be something of greater length than a bar.

At this point we should tackle a couple of potential problems. The first is that Cubase Sx's hit-point detection is rather poor (at version 1.03). Here is a one bar example.

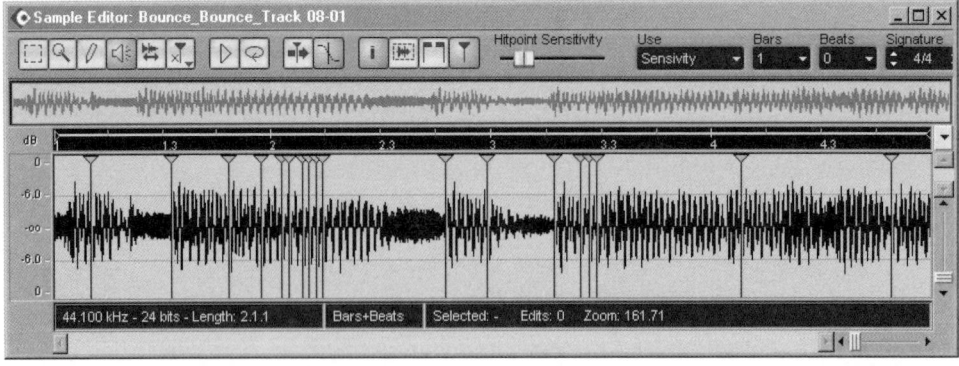

As you can see, many hit-points have congregated in areas of no interest, and some areas of interest have no hit-points. Some hit-points are simply in the wrong place. Here's what *BeatCreator* makes of the same audio.

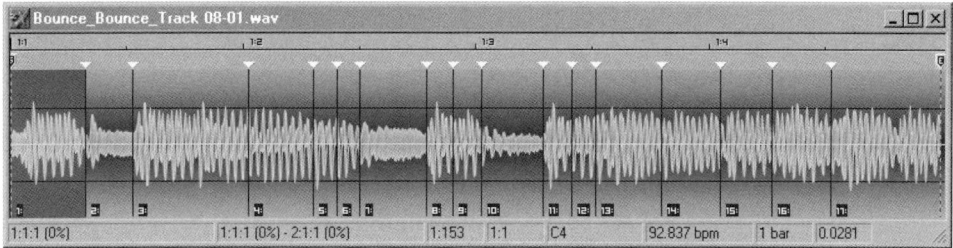

Admittedly this is not a straight drum-line, but the audio is only simple percussion with a very gentle, flute-like lead. *BeatCreator* copes with this audio with ease, and if one plays the individual slices, they are both musical and precise, for the most-part. On the other hand, the Cubase Sx *slices* are, for the most part, seemingly random.

So, how does Cubase Sx cope with a simple drum loop?

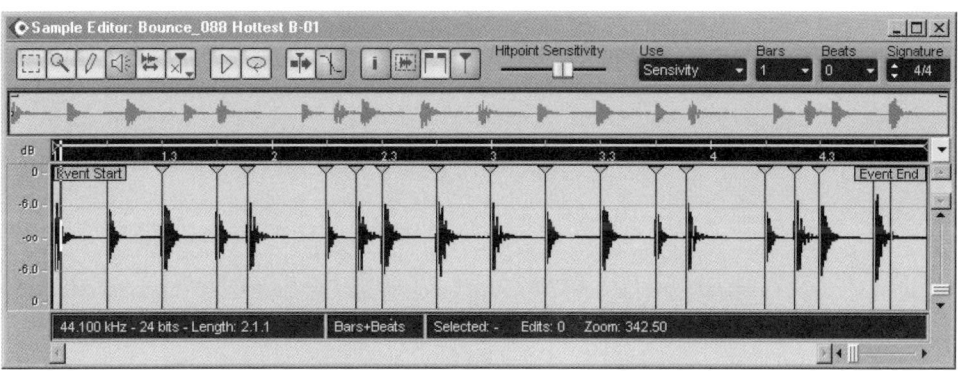

Thankfully, an awful lot better. However, some of the hit-points, when examined closely, are positioned either ahead or behind of their ideal positions. Those that are ahead are usually ahead by only a few samples. But, when the hit-point is created behind its ideal position then it is positioned at the first zero-crossing (regardless of the zero-crossing setting in *Preferences* or in the *Sample Editor*). This placement could be someway behind the start of the associated sound and, hence, not give an accurate reflection of your groove.

This inaccuracy, may or may not bother you. In general, when extracting a groove from a simple drum loop, these inaccuracies are minor and won't alter the timing of the resulting groove unduly. But for those looking for absolute accuracy from the source groove, then you have no option but to get in there and manually adjust the hit-points to the locations that you require.

Creating a *real* groove

If you need to extract a groove from audio that is longer than a bar, and more accurate in its extraction of hit-points, then you will need to do a little more work, and involve another tool. You could, of course, create hit-points in the *Sample*

Editor by-hand, but you will still be limited to a single bar (unless you create a template for each bar in the sequence, and then apply these to your MIDI Parts one bar at a time).

The common tools for this job are *Recycle* and *BeatCreator*. In my experience, *BeatCreator* is much simpler to use, and offers far more creative tools to further mangle your audio. It is also very easy to extract individual slices and to manipulate slices in a loop. *BeatCreator* will also output REX, Soundfont, LM4 Acid, Reaktor and FruityLoops file formats.

For out purposes, once we have created our multi-bar audio groove file, we are interested in creating a MIDI file of the groove. *BeatCreator* will create this file (along with the audio slices if required, which you can simply drop into a software sampler, if you wish).

Once created, import the MIDI file into Cubase Sx. You can now select a MIDI Event in the imported groove file, *Locate Selection* [L], and align other Events (whether MIDI or audio) by selecting and using *Edit/Move To/Cursor* [CTRL+L].

The Logical Editor

The *Logical Editor* [No Default] is a MIDI editor. In essence, it performs an

if these conditions are true – then do this

on each selected MIDI Event in turn (or each MIDI Event within the selected Parts). In other words, a search is made for an Event and, when found, an action is initiated. Often the action is to modify the selected Events, by changing

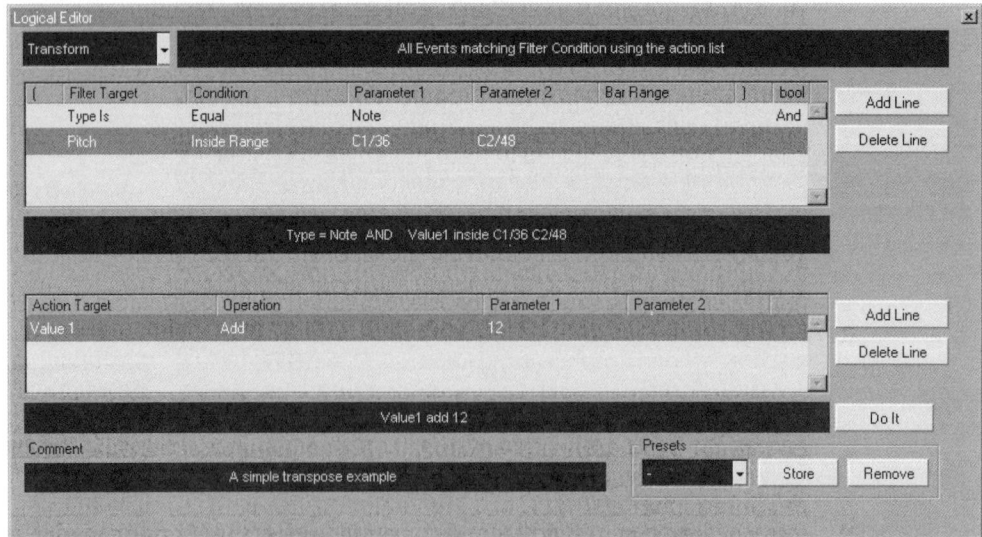

Fig. 13.7: The Logical Editor

a value, but it's possible to delete the Events, or copy (or extract) them to a new Part.

The idea is to identify the Events to be modified in the top section (e.g. all notes, or notes within a range), and provide the actions to be performed, in the lower section (e.g. delete, or transpose an octave).

There is a MIDI plug-in version of the *Logical Editor* called the *Transformer* (see page 157), and also the *Input Transformer* (page 130), which transforms *incoming* MIDI events and records the results.

A quick example

Let's get straight in and try out an example. Let's create a simple transpose of one octave. This requires that we add 12 (semitones) to the pitch of *every* note.

First, create a MIDI Part with some notes, and assign it an output. Select the Part, and open it in the *Key Editor*, then open *MIDI/Logical Editor* [No Default]. It's a good idea to leave the Part open in the editor, so that you can immediately see the editing results.

At top-left, you'll see a dropdown that contains the available functions, such as *Delete, Transform* and *Insert*. Select *Transform*, since that is the operation that we want to perform on our Part's notes.

The text to the right of the dropdown now reads:
Transform – All Events matching Filter Condition using the Action List.
So, let's do just that: create a *Filter Condition* and then create an *Action List*.

There are *Add* and *Delete* buttons for both the *Filter Conditions* and the *Action List*, so add a line to the *Filter Conditions*. It says: *Type Is – Equal – Note*. This is exactly the condition that we require. However, while we're here, make yourself familiar with the contents of the dropdowns under the fields *Type Is*, *Equal* and *Note*. Also, click in the two *brackets* entries for our condition that are both currently blank.

Now add a line to the *Action List*. We want to add twelve to the Pitch. As the chart below shows, *Pitch = Value 1* for a MIDI Note Event. So, leave *Action Target* as *Value 1*. If we were going to change all of the Notes' velocities, then we would have changed *Action Target* to *Value 2*, for example.

The *Operation* we want is *Add*, and sure enough, there it is at the top of the *Operation* dropdown (click *Not set* to see the dropdown). Finally, set *Parameter 1* to 12. You should have:

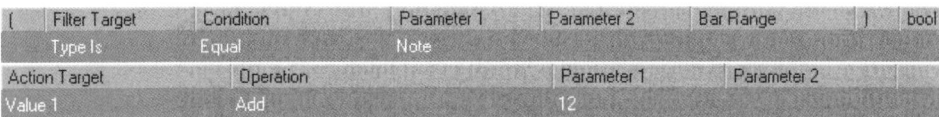

[	Filter Target	Condition	Parameter 1	Parameter 2	Bar Range	]	bool
	Type Is	Equal	Note				
Action Target		Operation		Parameter 1	Parameter 2		
Value 1		Add		12			

Now, keeping an eye on your MIDI Events in the *Key Editor* to see the effect, click *Do It*. Done job.

As mentioned above, with respect to the *Pitch* and *Velocity* of Notes, the *Value 1* and *Value 2* fields have different meaning depending in the Event-type. This chart shows what these values mean, for all Event-types that can be altered by the *Logical Editor*.

Event-type	Value 1	Value 2
Note	Note number/Pitch	Note velocity
Poly pressure	Pitch	Pressure value
Controller	Controller type or number	Amount
Program Change	Program number	n/a
After-touch	Amount	n/a
Pitch-bend	Amount	n/a
SYSEX	n/a	m/a

– Controller type is entered by number. A complete list is provided in appendix D, page 339.

Another example

By way of example, let's create a transform that adds 10 to the *Pan*. You will need to create some Pan Events for your test MIDI Part for the *Logical Editor* to work with.

♩   *Note*

Logical Editor presets can be accessed directly from the *MIDI* menu.

Pan is a controller (controller 10, in fact), so we can change the *Parameter 1* entry in the above example to *Controller*. To identify the controller we require as *Pan*, or controller 10 we must add another filter line. Note that the word *And* has appeared in the right-hand *Bool* column.

The statement we want to represent is:

*If the MIDI Event is a controller **and** the controller number = 10 then add 10 to the controller amount*

From our table, we can see that the controller type, or number, is in *Value 1*. So, select *Value 1* in *Filter Target* in the second filter line. You will see that it changes to say *MIDI Controller No.* It should be easy by now. Change *Parameter 1* to 10.

In the *Action List*, we require the entry *Value 2 – Add – 10*. We get *Value 2* from the chart again (Controller Amount). You should have:

[	Filter Target	Condition	Parameter 1	Parameter 2	Bar Range	]	bool
	Type Is	Equal	Controller				And
	MIDI Controller No.	Equal	10				

Action Target		Operation		Parameter 1	Parameter 2	
Value 2		Add		10		

You should have a good handle on the *Transform* function by now. For a few more examples have a look at the following presets: High notes to Channel 1; Low notes to Channel 2; Set notes to fixed Pitch.

Before moving on, take a look at the preset *Half tempo*.

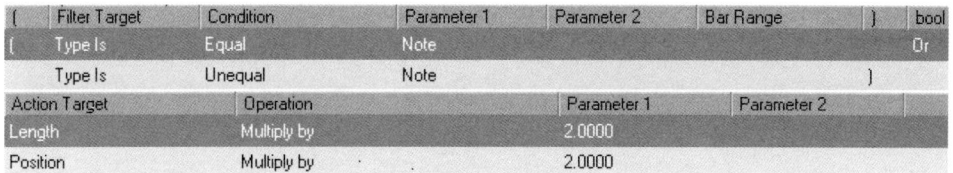

[	Filter Target	Condition	Parameter 1	Parameter 2	Bar Range	]	bool
[	Type Is	Equal	Note				Or
	Type Is	Unequal	Note			]	

Action Target	Operation		Parameter 1	Parameter 2	
Length	Multiply by		2.0000		
Position	Multiply by	·	2.0000		

There are a few interesting things to note. In the filter section, *Or* has been used to indicate that the actions will be performed should *either* of the filter conditions be true. In this case, the two conditions are exact opposites, so *all* Events will be selected. One could also use *Type Is – All Types* in this case.

The *Action Target: Position* is the Event's *Start* position (as shown in the *Info Line*). *Length* is also used; this is only available for notes. If you use this preset on a Part and observe its affect on, say, Pan Events, it appears that the Pan Events are having their length changed. This is, in fact, a side-effect of their positions being changed.

♫ **Note**

There is an initialization *Preset* for resetting the *Logical Editor*.

Logical Editor Functions

The dropdown at top-left, gives access to the *Logical Editor's* functions. We have already looked at *Transform* above.

○ *Delete:* Deletes all Events that satisfy the filter conditions. There are many presets that use *Delete*. For example: Delete patch changes; Delete notes with a velocity below a certain value; Delete muted Events; Delete black keys. One to definitely check is *Filter off-beats*, which demonstrates use of the *Inside Bar Range* condition.

○ *Transform:* See section above.

○ *Insert:* All existing Events are kept. Events are added that satisfy the filter conditions. These Events are changed by whatever actions affect them. For example, by selecting all notes, and then adding 7 to the pitch, you create perfect 5ths for each note. Similarly, by adding, say, 50 ticks to *Position* and reducing *Value 2* by, say, 75%, you can create a gentle repeat.

○ *Insert Exclusive:* Forget the name. Any Events that are not selected are deleted. Those Events that are selected are affected by the actions. You need to be careful with this function that you select all Events that you want to retain (e.g. controllers). Here's a typical example, where all notes with pitch less than C2 are deleted, and all other Events (not notes) are retained:

[	Filter Target	Condition	Parameter 1	Parameter 2	Bar Range	]	bool
[	Type Is	Equal	Note				And
	Pitch	Bigger or Equal	C2/48			]	Or
	Type Is	Unequal	Note				

○ *Copy:* This creates a new Part on a new Track. All selected Events are copied to the new Part with whatever changes are applied by the actions. The original Part is left unchanged.

○ *Extract:* This creates a new Part on a new Track. All selected Events are copied to the new Part with whatever changes are applied by the actions, but they are also *removed* from the original Part.

○ *Select:* All Events that satisfy the filter conditions are selected in the MIDI editors.

What else?

There is a chunky section on the *Logical Editor* in the *Cubase Sx: Operations Manual*. If editing in this way is something that appeals, then familiarity with the more esoteric properties and function is worthwhile. There are features for editing by bar range, and selection by mute and locked status.

Along with all the mathematical actions, also available are a random number generator, and an action that will transpose notes to a scale.

Other MIDI Transforms

There a number of functions available to manipulate either selected MIDI Events or whole Parts.

Transpose

Nothing complicated here. The Transpose value range is -127 to 127 in semi-tones. Alternatively, you can Transpose selected notes with the up and down cursor keys in the *Key Editor* (holding SHIFT will Transpose in octaves).

Legato

Extends the length of each note up to the start of the next. The gap between two notes is determined by the *Preferences/MIDI Function Parameters* tab setting *Legato Overlap*. The range of values is ±100 ticks; varying this value can produce some interesting results.

Fixed Lengths

Extends, or contracts, the lengths of all selected notes to the value in *Length Quantize*.

Delete Doubles (of a whole Part)

Notes of the same pitch and start position are deleted. Doubled notes often occur after recording in *Cycle Mode* with *Merge* active and then quantizing the Part.

Delete Controllers (of a whole Part)

Deletes all controllers (including after-touch and pitchbend) from the Part. Program Changes, SYSEX, Text, SMF and Note Events are unaffected.

Delete Notes

This function deletes either: notes whose *length* is less than that specified (in ticks); or notes whose *velocity* is less than that specified; or only when both conditions are satisfied. Namely, very short and very quiet notes.

The graphic can be used to set *Minimum Length*. Click in the graphic and drag until you have the appropriate value. The scale of the graphic can be changed between the values: Bar, 2 Bars, 4 Bars and 1/4 Bar, by clicking on the text.

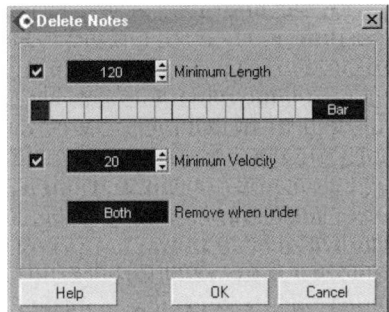

Delete Notes

The *Remove when Under* option is only available when both Length and Velocity are active. You get the choice of Both or *One of* (meaning either).

Restrict Polyphony

With a range of 1–100 voices, *Restrict Polyphony* reduces the number of simultaneously sounding voices in a Part by cutting active notes short, as new notes start. This is handy when using an existing part on an instrument with limited polyphony.

Pedals to Note Length

Converts the lengths of notes affected by sustain pedal Events, so that they match the actions of the pedal. The sustain controller events are then deleted. This can be useful for a variety of reasons. For example, some instruments don't respond to sustain, and other can leave notes hanging when playback is stopped and a sustain off has not been received (and MIDI resets are not being sent).

Delete overlaps (mono)

Affects notes of the same pitch. If a note starts, while a note of the same pitch has not ended (they overlap), then this function will adjust the Events so that the first ends before the second starts.

Delete overlaps (poly)

As soon as a new note starts, *all* sounding notes are ended, irrespective of pitch.

Velocity

This is a three-in-one function. All the functions allow the selected notes' velocities to be manipulated in different ways.

o *Add/Subtract.* Adds the supplied value to the selected notes' velocities. The range is ±127. If this operation takes the velocity out of range (0 to 127) then the Note is left with the appropriate extreme value.

○ *Compress/Expand.* This is a relative expansion, or contraction, of the selected notes velocities. The *Ratio* setting has a Range of 0% to 300%. 0% will set velocities to 0. Just keep in mind that the range of velocity is 0 to 127.
○ *Limit.* Values outside of the specified *Upper* and *Lower* limits are increased or decreased to these values.

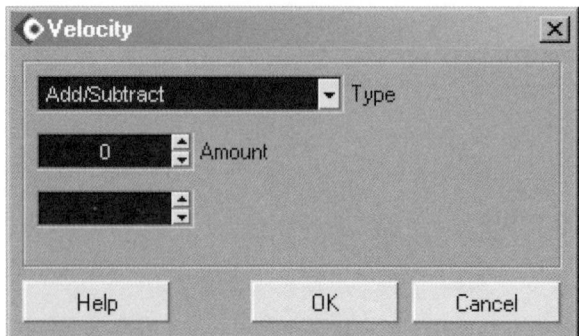

Velocity

Fixed Velocity
All selected Notes have their velocity changed to that shown in the editor's *Insert Velocity* field.

Reverse
Reverses the order of playback of all selected notes (or Parts).

14 Audio: Recording and Editing

The *Quick-start* chapter (page 13) described how to record audio, broken-down into a number of basic steps. In this chapter, we will get into the nitty-gritty details of recording in Cubase Sx. We will also look at the tools and methods available to edit audio that has been recorded or imported into Cubase Sx.

We start with a run-through of the various monitoring options, along with the auto-monitoring options that allow you to switch on monitoring automatically in a number of pre-defined ways. After this we look at recording itself, and the various ways in which you can record, including punching-in and cycle recording. Next up is audio editing in the *Part Editor* and *Sample Editor* (which can be used for editing audio Events, Clips and Regions). By way of an example of using the *Part Editor*, a section is dedicated to *Comp'ing*. Fades, Crossfades and Auto-fades round off the description of Cubase Sx functions for the chapter, which ends with an example of using manual punch-ins and monitoring in a studio environment.

So fire up the studio and let's make some noise.

Monitoring

Monitoring has a more general usage, but here we take it mean the process of listening to the audio signal that you intend to record, before and/or during recording. In general, the monitored signal is mixed with the other Tracks in the Project during recording, or when playing back in preparation for a punch-in, etc. This (*foldback*) signal is usually routed to the musicians and the studio monitors.

Track Monitoring Button

There are three modes of routing the monitoring signal when using Sx:
○ External monitoring
○ Thru Cubase Sx
○ ASIO Direct Monitoring (ADM)

♫ **Note**

When the monitoring button is switched on for a Track, then Events and Parts that currently exists on that Track will not be heard during playback.

You can pick and choose which Tracks you wish to monitor, but only one of *Thru Sx* monitoring and *ADM* can be used at one time. You can't for example, choose to monitor one Track thru *ADM* and another *Thru Sx*. However, it is possible, and extremely useful to be able to mix either one of these options with external monitoring.

There are many, many ways in which monitoring can be configured once we bring external equipment into play, and there isn't space to cover all of these. Many are personal preference, or are dictated by the equipment available and the requirements of the folk that you are working with.

If you are not using external monitoring exclusively, then Sx's monitoring can be switched on and off either manually or via the automated switching of monitoring. More below.

Let's start by taking a look at the various routing options, before examining switching.

External Monitoring

When you monitor the input audio though an external mixer, prior to it entering Cubase Sx, this is called *External Monitoring*. The signal being played back from Cubase Sx is mixed in with the incoming audio and routed, as required, for listening purposes. Nowadays, the mixer might be a physical hardware mixer (whether digital or analogue) or it could be a mixer application provided with your audio hardware.

When using external monitoring, the signal is unaffected by anything you do in Cubase Sx: level, effects and EQ must all be applied externally.

The major benefit with monitoring externally is that there will be no delay (latency) on the monitored signal. (Strictly speaking, on a digital mixer, there will be a delay due to the A/D (presuming the incoming signal is audio) and the D/A conversions that need to take place. This is a round-trip delay of approximately 2ms (using most modern converters). Note that the relative delay of playback to monitored signal will be half of this (approx. 1ms) in the case of audio, and zero for a digital input.)

> ♪   *Note*
>
> *Auto Monitoring* cannot be usefully used when monitoring externally.

Monitoring Thru Cubase Sx

Monitoring thru Cubase Sx is achieved by letting Cubase Sx manage the mixing of the incoming audio signal with the audio being played back.

The advantage of using this monitoring method is that you have full control of the input signal, and how it will be modified (by effects, etc.), before it hits the mix that you, and your performers, are listening to. So levels, pan, EQ and effects can all be applied and monitored during recording. Note that these are not actually recorded.

A big advantage of using this type of monitoring is that Cubase Sx's Auto Monitoring features can be turned on and off automatically.

The downside of this method is that the monitored signal will be delayed by the sum of all the accumulated latencies in the incoming audio's signal path. At minimum, this will be the value associated with your soundcard and the latency that applies to its current buffer size. High latency times are the biggest problem to overcome when monitoring through Cubase Sx (or any other piece of audio software). The effect of latency is most noticeable when listening to a live audio

> ♪   *Note*
>
> Effects used when monitoring are *not* applied to the audio file being recorded.

source (such as a vocalist or drummer) via Cubase Sχ that includes effects that have additional latency. (There is more on latency in chapter 20, page 281.) You can discover the delay (in samples) for VST effects via *Devices/Plug-in Information*.

It might be possible to fine-tune your soundcard to reduce your latency times. This will depend on your soundcard and its drivers.

The corollary is that monitoring thru Sχ is only practical with a soundcard that can achieve a very low latency and maintain it under whatever processing load your Project puts on your computer.

ASIO Direct Monitoring (ADM)

Many of the latest soundcards (and in any case, only those that are ASIO 2.0 compatible) support Steinberg's *ASIO Direct Monitoring (ADM)*.

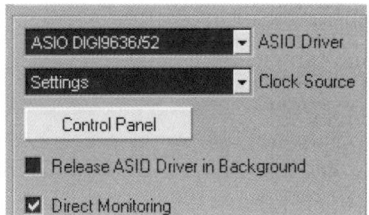

Direct monitoring switch

ASIO Direct Monitoring is activated on the *Devices/Device Set-up* [No Default] VST Multi-Track tab. Simply check the Direct Monitoring box. If the checkbox is grayed out, then you are out of luck, since either ASIO Direct Monitoring is not supported by your soundcard, or the current driver release for it does not implement it. If you believe that your card should support ADM, then check your soundcard manufacturers Web-site or support forum for assistance.

When using a soundcard that supports ADM, the monitoring is completely self-contained in the soundcard. Cubase Sχ never "sees" the audio signal used for monitoring. The major benefit of this is that there is no delay (zero latency) on the monitoring signal. This is, clearly, extremely beneficial in any recording situation, since it removes the need to manually split off a monitoring signal.

However, it also means that effects and EQ within Cubase Sχ cannot be applied to the monitored signal (as when monitoring thru Sχ). However, the monitored signal is controlled by Cubase Sχ, and so levels, pan and the return channel (although this is frequently the same as the playback channel) can all be adjusted from within Cubase Sχ. The available features will be dependent on your soundcard. Most importantly, note that Cubase Sχ's Auto Monitoring features can be turned on and off automatically when monitoring thru Sχ (see below). This provides a great deal of useful functionality for monitoring.

> ♫ **Note**
>
> ADM often routes audio inputs directly to the equivalent output. So, if your audio is coming in to ports 7/8, say, then the monitoring signal will be returned on ports 7/8.

Manual Monitoring

When using either *Monitoring Via Cubase Sχ* or *ADM*, monitoring can be switched on or off by pressing the monitor button for the appropriate Audio Track(s).

If you are using *Auto Monitoring*, then you can use the Monitoring button to override the current monitoring setting.

Auto Monitoring

♪   *Note*

Auto Monitoring only occurs on Tracks that are record enabled.

Auto Monitoring is available at any time, but is most useful when either *Monitoring thru S_X* or when using *ASIO Direct Monitoring (ADM)*. The available *Auto Monitoring* options are described below. Switching modes is done in *Preferences/VST* tab.

Whichever option is selected, the routing of the signals is determined by the setting of the *Direct Monitoring* checkbox on the *Devices/Device Set-up/VST Multi-Track* tab. If this option is unchecked then you will be *Monitoring thru S_X*.

There are three *Auto Monitoring* modes available, as well as a manual mode that is the equivalent of *Auto Monitoring* off:

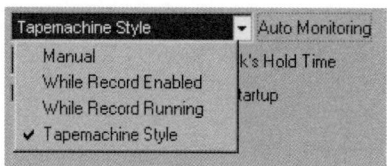

Auto Monitoring modes

○ *Manual (or Auto Monitoring Off):*
When in this mode all monitoring must be done manually by pressing the button in the Track List or Track Mixer.
○ *While Record Enabled:*
This is effectively the same as pressing the monitoring button, since every time you record enable a Track, monitoring is switched on. It is simply a time saving, and intuitive method of ensuring that monitoring gets switched on when record enabling a Track.
○ *While Record Running:*
No monitoring occurs while the transport is stopped or in play mode, but monitoring is switched on while recording. This can be usefully used when manually punching in.
○ *Tape Machine Style:*
An emulation of the way in which an analogue tape recorder operates: Input monitoring occurs when the transport is stopped and while recording. Monitoring does not occur during playback.

Below is a chart showing whether monitoring occurs on a record enabled Track with Auto Monitoring switched on. (In Manual mode monitoring is either always on, or always off depending on the setting of the Track's Monitor button.)

	Stop	Play	Record
While Record Enabled	Yes	Yes	Yes
While Record Running	No	No	Yes
Tape Machine Style	Yes	No	Yes

Recording Audio

One of the most fundamental functions of Cubase Sx is recording audio. You can record multiple Tracks at the same time in Cubase Sx with ease. To do so, simply ensure that each Track to be recorded is assigned its own input channel, record enable the Tracks, and press record. Providing the signals have been correctly routed to Cubase Sx's inputs, and that the audio levels received are sufficient to be usefully recorded, then you are done. Next chapter...

Recording in Cubase Sx is usually straightforward. Most of the work required is in the preparation of your set-up; ensuring that it is flexible enough to enable you to record what you want, when you want to without having to re-cable your studio each and every time. So, once you have nailed down the basic functions, take some time-out to consider your set-up.

Audio Set-up: Inputs

Audio inputs are activated and deactivate from the *VST Inputs* [F5] window. Inputs are routed to Tracks, and their associated Channels, via the *in :* field in the *Inspector*, or in the dropdowns at the top of the Channel Strip in the *Track Mixer* or *Channels Settings*. An audio Track is always associated with an input (there is no *Not Connected* option).

The *VST Inputs* window will mirror the ports available on the soundcard you selected on *Devices/Device Set-up/VST Multi-Track* tab *ASIO Driver*.

Be careful when switching off an input port, as Cubase Sx will need to re-map any Channels that use the port being switched off. You will be warned should you try to do this.

> ♪ **Note**
> The number of Tracks that can be recorded in one pass is wholly dependent on the power of you computer (CPU, hard disk, soundcard ports, etc.).

Levels and Inputs

Incoming signals are recorded at the level they are received. There is no opportunity, while recording, to apply gain or attenuation to the incoming signal within Cubase Sx. Setting the input level must be performed outside of Cubase Sx, and this is usually achieved via trim controls on a mixing desk, although some soundcards do have level adjustment features in their supplied software.

> ♪ **Note**
> You can rename input audio ports in the right-hand *Label* column of *VST Inputs* [F5].

To check an input level, activate the *Monitor* button for the Track. This switches the visual level indicator from showing the output (playback) level, to showing the input level.

Now adjust the level of the incoming source signal to an appropriate level for recording. It is important that the signal does not clip (that is, exceed 0dB FS). When this occurs the result is usually very audible, and very ugly. The only way you can safely check this is to check the numerical value above the fader in the *Track Mixer*. If this is negative, then you are clipping the input and you should reduce your input level for that channel. (See *Headroom* in the glossary (page 309) for more on this.)

Best practice, in general, is to get as strong an input signal to "tape" as possible. That said, it Is better to get a take that is useable than one that is not, so ensuring a safety margin of a few dB (say-3 to -6dB) is important when recording. (An engineer's worst nightmare is ruining a great take, so make maximum use of the dB you have available). On the other hand, be careful not to record too low a signal level, since when you later have to apply gain, you will raise the noise-floor with it, and you may introduce artefacts into the audio stream that are undesirable.

Recording Set-Up

The process of recording in Cubase Sx will create an audio file. The file will be placed in the *Audio* folder in the *Project Folder*; a Clip for the audio file will be placed in the Pool; and an Event for the Clip will be created on the Event Display.

The format of the recorded file is determined by settings in *Project/Project Set-up* [SHIFT+S] (Sample Rate, Record Format and Record File Type). Three file types are available: Broadcast Wave, Wave, and AIFF.

A note on Broadcast Wave Files

Broadcast Wave files contain embedded text information. The most useful of these is that the *Origin Time* is stored along with the audio. This information is extremely useful when moving files between different systems, and the precise start time is required. Along with *Origin Time*, the Date and Time of the recording is embedded. In addition text information can be embedded within each recording. These fields (Description, Author, and Reference) can be set-up in the *Preferences/Audio/Broadcast Wave* tab. These data can be viewed by clicking on the Info entry for an audio file in the Pool.

TrueTape

TrueTape

TrueTape applies distortion to the input signal, that *Steinberg* claim "emulates the behavior of a professional analog tape recorder". However, there aren't any alignment controls. Ain't marketing a beautiful thing?

TrueTape is an operation that can only be performed when you record. It is a little mystifying why this process can't be done later, but you can't, so you're committed to applying a input effect without the option to remove it later.

You switch it on via *Devices/TrueTape* [No Default], make sure your *Project Set-up* [SHIFT+S] is set to record 32-bit files, and then record as normal.

Recording a new Audio Track

This is a list of the minimum you need to do to record a new audio Track. You may well require an audio or MIDI guide-track if this is the first Track of the Project (or use the metronome, of course).

1. Add a new Track via *Project/Add Track/Audio* [No Default]
2. Choose mono or stereo for the Track
3. Assign the appropriate input port to the Track via the Inspector
4. Activate appropriate monitoring and check the input level
5. Record enable the Track
6. Position the Project Cursor ready for recording (with sufficient lead-in).
7. Start record via *Transport* [Pad *]
8. Press *Stop* [Space or Pad 0] when done

Recording onto a Track containing Audio Events

When you record on a Track that already contains audio Events, then any new Event, that coincides with existing Events, will be placed *on top* of the existing Event(s). Only the Event *on top* will be heard on playback. (If you have *Auto Fades* switched on for the Track, this can be a perfectly adequate, and simple, way of editing Track.) Note that when Events overlap, the overlapping area will be darker.

A stack of overlapping Events can be reordered by selecting an Event and using *Edit/(Move to) Front* [No Default] and *Edit/(Move to) Back* [No Default]. These images show an example of this.

♫   *Note*

If the *Preferences/Editing* tab option *Enable Record on Selected Track* is checked, then each Track will have *Record Enabled* activated when selected in the Track List.

Overlapping Events

Undoing Recording

When you undo a recording the following occurs: the Event is removed from the Event Display; the Clip is moved to the Trash in the Pool, but the audio file on disk is not deleted. You can, however, remove these files at any time via *Pool/Empty Trash* [No Default]. If these files are still available in the Trash when you close the Project (or Cubase Sχ) then you will be asked whether you wish to keep or to delete them. (A similar message will also be displayed during a *File/Project close* [CTRL+W] if you have imported audio files, and not saved the Project since their import.)

Punch-in and Punch-Out

A punch in, together with its opposite punch out, is the process of dropping in and out of record mode. This process is a fundamental process in analogue tape recording, and the same result can be achieved in other ways in the digital studio (e.g. record to another Track and edit the results). Nevertheless, punching in can still be useful and fast. Remember that when you record *on top* of an existing Event you are not overwriting the original Event, so you lose nothing by punching in.

The three buttons to the left of the Transport are, from left to right:

○ *Punch-in* [I]
○ *Cycle* [Pad /]
○ *Punch-out* [O]

The Punch-in button will initiate recording, on any armed Tracks, when the Cursor is in Play mode and crosses the *Left Locator*. The Punch-in button is automatically switched off when the Transport is stopped provided *Preferences/Transport* tab *Deactivate Punch-in on Stop* is checked.

The Punch-out button only has affect when in record mode. It will stop recording at the *Right Locator*. It will also stop playback at the *Right Locator* provided *Preferences/Transport* tab *Stop after Automatic Punch-out* is checked (any Post Roll value that has been set will still take place).

Since the Punch-in and Punch-out buttons work in situations where you are not strictly punching in, you might like to think of them as the "start recording from Left Locator" and "stop record at Right Locator" buttons. That said, for the former, you could always use *Transport/Start Record at Left Locator* [No Default] toggle to force this to happen whenever you hit record.

Punching In: Manually

For a detailed look at manual punching in, see later in this chapter, page 197.

To manually punch in:

1. Record enable the appropriate Track
2. Switch off the Punch-in button
3. If you wish, set the Punch-out button and Right Locator
4. Start playback before the desired punch-in point
5. Hit Record at the appropriate point

Punching In: Automatically

This is a hands-free punch operation and makes use of the Punch-in and Punch-out buttons.

○ Set the Left Locator to the punch-in point
○ Activate *Punch In* [I]
○ Start playback before the Left Locator.
○ When the Project Cursor reaches the Left Locator, recording is automatically activated.

Cycle Recording (and Playback)

For a variety of reasons, loop (or cycle) playback is an extremely useful and much-used feature of sequencers. For instance, looping playback is useful for repeatedly rehearsing a section of a song, while cycle recording is useful for capturing multiple takes of the same section for editing, capturing that perfect take, or building a cache of takes for comp'ing.

To loop playback:

1. Set the Left and Right Locators
2. Activate *Cycle* [Pad /]
3. Position the *Cursor at the Left Locator* [Pad 1]
4. Start *Playback* [SPACE or Pad 0]

To Record in Cycle mode, the process is essentially the same as for playback. However, note that you can start recording from anywhere before the Right Locator for the loop to have effect. When the Cursor reaches the Right Locator it will seamlessly reappear at the Left Locator and continue recording.

Results of Cycle Recording: Audio

Cycle recording in Cubase Sx is a powerful tool, and a big time saver, once you are conversant with it. Read on.

There are three modes available when recording with Cycle switched on, determined by *Preferences/Audio* tab *Cycle Record Mode*. The options are: (a) Create Regions, (b) Create Events, (c) Create Events and Regions.

Create Regions

In this mode, as you cycle record, a single continuous audio file is created on disk. While recording, the Event will show which cycle (or take) is currently being recorded.

Cycle recording

When playback stops, the last incomplete cycle is discarded as a Region (but can be accessed via the Clip, if required), and the last complete cycle recorded is placed in the Event on the Track.

If you examine the Clip in the Pool, you will see the Regions created for each cycle. Note the "extra bit" of audio in the Clip representing the last incomplete cycle. This portion invariably ends up containing the best ad libs of a session, so it's great that Cubase Sx keeps it available.

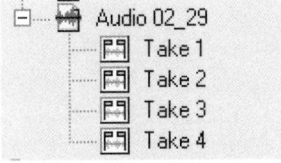
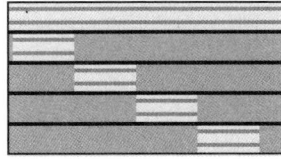

Regions in Browser

Using the Regions from Cycle Record

This next bit is quite clever,so pay attention, okay?

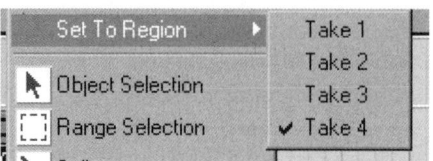

Selecting a Region for an
Event

If you now right-click on the Event, you will find, right at the top of the quick-menu, the *Set to Region* sub-menu, which allows you to select a Region for the Event. This gives you quick and easy access to all the takes right after recording.

> ✗   Tip
>
> Whenever an Event references a Clip with Regions, then the *Set To Region* sub-menu is available. It is not the exclusive preserve of Cycle Record. This opens up a lot of creative possibilities for using Regions.

Create Events

In exactly the same way as for Create Regions, when using Create Events during cycle record, a single continuous audio file is created on disk. While recording, the Event will show which cycle (or take) is currently being recorded.

When playback stops, you will find that all the completed cycles are stacked one on top of the other as a pile of Events, with the most recent cycle on top. If you examine the Clip in the Pool, you will see the simple single entry of the recorded audio file.

Using the Events from Cycle Record

If you right-click on the Event you will find a sub-menu allowing you to quickly select an Event and bring it to the front. This gives you quick access to all the takes after completing recording.

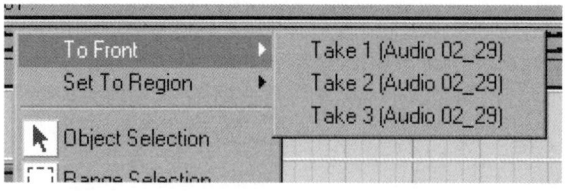

Moving an Event to the
Front

Create Events+Regions

As you would expect, you get both of the above. This is useful, since it allows you to immediately work on all the Events, which you may wish to do when combining them into a Part for comp'ing (see page 183), but it also allows you to recreate the original takes at a later date (from the Regions), should you need to.

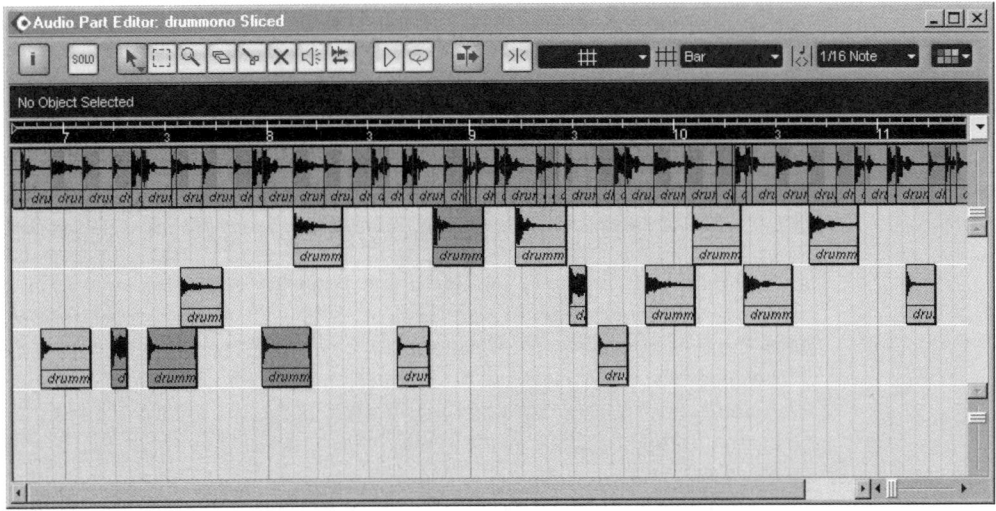

Fig. 14.1: The Audio Part Editor

The Audio Part Editor

Audio Parts are "containers" for audio Events. (The term Parts will be used for the remainder of this section, since the difference with MIDI Parts should be apparent.) A Part is a collection of Events. However, rather than simply being a collection of Events end-to-end (perhaps with crossfades in between) the Events can be managed in Lanes (where the bottommost Lane will always be the one heard for the Track).

Event manipulation available elsewhere in Cubase S$_X$, is also available in the Part Editor; double-clicking an Event will open the Sample Editor; right-clicking an Event will open the quick menu, etc. The Tools and controls are very similar to those available in the Event Display, although Glue and Draw tools are absent. Zooming, and Event selection are very similar to those in the Event Display.

You can open multiple Parts. The Parts can be on the same Track, or on different Tracks, or both. All Parts will appear in the same Part Editor window. In fact, even if there is an Event between two Parts, the Part Editor will recognize this, and leave a gap where the intervening Event lies. Clever stuff.

Not so clever, is the fact that each Event will retain its Lane from its Part. Thus, when opening Parts on multiple Tracks, you often end up with lot of Events all on one Lane. This may, or may not, affect you depending on how you work. (See page 183 for more on *Lanes*.)

The Part Editor has independent Auto-scroll, Snap, Snap mode, Quantize, and Ruler settings.

A major use of Parts is for comp'ing (most commonly vocals) when combined with Cycle Recording. There are features available to Parts that make them ideal for this purpose. See page 183 for more on *Comp'ing*.

These features make Parts extremely useful for manipulating and editing a potentially complex audio Track, or section of a Track.

Playback in the Part Editor

The Project Cursor is unaffected by the Play and Loop operations, which snaps back to its original location when play stops. If the Project Cursor is outside the bounds of the Part, then play will start at the beginning of the Part.

The Part Editor includes a Solo button to isolate playback to the Track on which the Part is located.

The Play button will playback selected Events (or Range Selection). If no Event (or Range Selection) is selected, then either the whole Part is played, or play starts from the position of the Project Cursor depending on the location of the Project Cursor.

The Speaker and Scrub tools can also be used for auditioning. (Speaker tool output is routed to the Master Bus.) The Speaker Tool plays the Event underneath it. It plays from the point selected, except when CTRL is held, when it plays from the start of the Event under the icon. Muted Events will play.

♪   *Note*

An audio Part can be quantized, just like a MIDI Part. Audio Events in the Part will be quantizes according to the settings in *MIDI/Quantize Set-up* [No Default] (see chapter 13, page 160).

Creating a Part

The simplest way to create a Part is to select one or more Events on a Track and perform *Audio/Events to Part* [No Default]. The Part will be selected after this action, so by hitting ENTER you will open the Part Editor.

You can also create a Part in the following ways:

○ Use the Draw tool on an audio Track
○ Use the Glue tool on two or more Events (or two Parts)
○ Double-click between the locators on an audio Track

Editing a Part

It is possible to slip the contents of a Part without opening the Part Editor (in the same way that you can slip the content of an audio Event). This is done by holding CTRL+ALT and dragging the contents of the Part on the Event Display. The Part will retain its location, and all Events in all Lanes will be shifted by the same amount. Snap, if active, is ignored.

   *Tip*

To merge two Parts, use the glue Tool.

The net result is a change to the *Offset* value in the Info Line. The Part's content can also be moved by editing this value. Note that offset for Audio Parts has a different meaning to offset for an Audio Event. In the case of Audio Parts, the offset value determines the start positions of the Events within the Part. Increasing the offset will move Events later in the Part, and vice versa.

This method can be used to precisely locate audio Events that have already been aligned with each other. This only applies to a single Track. You can slide multiple Parts, and Parts on different Tracks. Take care when making multiple selections, if you include an Event in the selection, then its *Snap Point* will be moved.

When slipping, it is permissible to slip Events right out of the Part; in which case they will no longer be audible and you will have to resize the Part to hear them.

Events can be added to a Part simply by dragging them into the Part Editor from the Pool (a shared copy is created), Browser or Event Display. Remove Events by selecting them and using DEL.

Lanes

One of the major benefits of using audio Parts is the Lanes feature. You create a new Lane by dragging an Event, or Range Selection, into the available empty space. Horizontal movement can be restricted when moving (or creating) an Event by holding CTRL, and a shared copy created by holding ALT. The *up* and *down* cursor keys will move a selected Event between Lanes while retaining its start position. The left and right cursor keys will move the selection between Events from *same* Part, although the order is not always obvious. The bottom-most Event has playback priority, irrespective of which Lane it is on. (If Events are stacked on top of each other in a Lane then the topmost Event has priority on that Lane.)

When a Part has multiple Lanes where Events overlap, it is likely that you will need to apply crossfades across Lanes. This can be achieved by using the *Auto Fades* (see page 196). However, once you have settled on a Part's final set-up, you may well wish to apply crossfades manually, and this can be achieved by selecting all Events requiring a crossfade and using *Audio/Crossfade* [X].

Comp'ing

Comp'ing is the process of compiling a section of audio from a number of takes. It is frequently used on vocal Tracks. This is often accomplished in tandem with cycle recording of the particular take, so that there are a number of versions of the-same-audio-but-different to work with. The intention is to create a composite take that is *better* than any of the individual takes. Let's not get into the artistic or creative merits of this, or indeed the issues regarding performance when applying this process. Here's how to go about comp'ing in Sx.

It is not a requirement to use Cycle Record for comp'ing, it is simply another tool in the armory that can be used to assist. The Part to be comp'd can be compiled from any audio Events. (It is technically possible to comp using Events stacked on top of each other, but this is quite fiddly; it is also easier to disturb the Events when left on the Event Display. By comp'ing within a Part, the Events are securely tucked away.)

When you record in Cycle mode you must make the choice between creating a Region, an Event, or both a Region and an Event for each completed cycle (or loop). This choice is set in *Preferences/Audio* tab *Cycle Record Mode*.

The result of Cycle recording will depend on the above selection. In all cases, however, a single Clip will be placed in the Pool.

- *Create Regions:* The Clip will contain one Region for each completed cycle. A single Event is placed on the Event Display. The Event will contain the last complete cycle recorded.
- *Create Events:* An Event is created for each cycle. The Events are stacked one on top of the other. The topmost Event will be the last complete cycle recorded.
- *Create Events + Regions:* An Event is created for each cycle. The Events are stacked one on top of the other. The topmost Event will be the last complete cycle recorded. The Clip will contain a Region for each completed cycle.

To create a Part from Cycle Record Events

After a Cycle Record that creates Events (including Events and Regions), you are presented with a stack of Events. Select the whole stack of Events with the Select tool by lassoing them. You will see the text *Multiple Objects Selected* in the Info Line. If you simply click on the Event, then only the top Event will be selected, so you must lasso them. Now select *Audio/Events to Part* [No Default] to create the Part. When you open the Part Editor, the Events will be neatly arranged in Lanes ready to be comp'd.

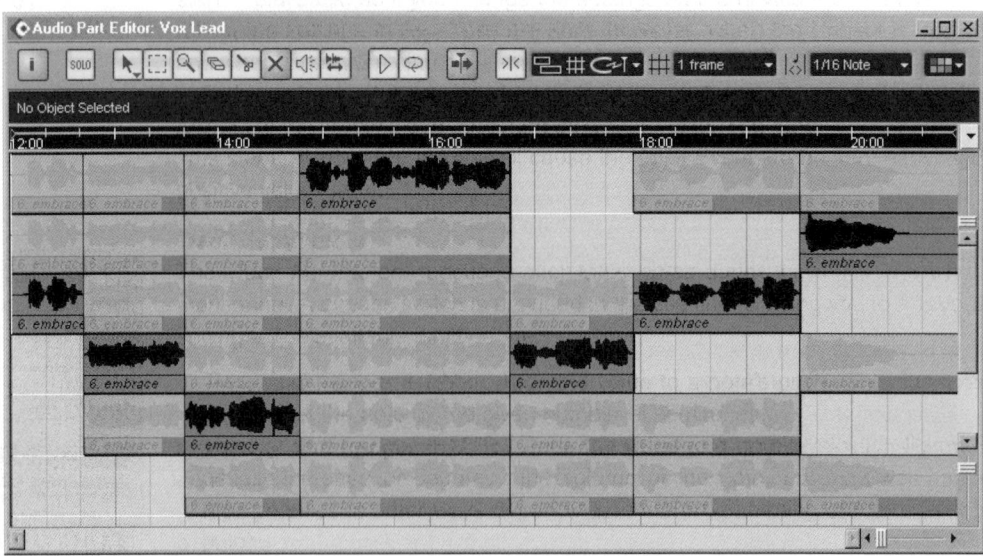

Fig. 14.2: A comp'd vocal Part

To create a Part from Cycle Record Regions

In this case, Cycle Record will create a single Event. So, select the Event and perform *Audio/Events to Part*. The window shown will open. If you click *Regions*, then for each Region, an Event is created in the new Part. If you click *No*, then a Part will be created for the single Event.

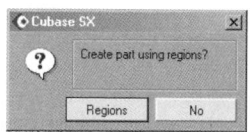

Create Part from Regions

It is well worth creating Regions during Cycle Record, as they can be used to recreate the cycles in the take long after you might have edited or deleted the related Events. Also, it is easy to create Events from the Regions (just drag them onto the Event Display), so you lose nothing by creating Regions.

Once you have brought the audio that you wish to comp into a Part, proceed by splitting all the Events at the same point in the timeline at the same time location. The choice of where you split will, clearly, be unique in each situation. There are two basic ways in which to perform the split, in both cases select all the Events first:

○ *Use the Scissors tool*
You can select Events with the Scissors tool providing you start lassoing in white space in the Part. The Scissors tool displays a faint vertical line to assist precise location of the split point.
○ *Use the Split Commands*
The most useful split command here is *Split at Cursor* [ALT+X], but *Split Loop* [No Default] and *Split Range* [SHIFT+X] should not be forgotten.

You will end up with a grid of Events in the Part, the bottom line of which will sound when played back. To make your selections, start by muting and unmuting individual Events until you find the perfect combination. You can either use the *Mute* tool (which works well here), or *Mute* [SHIFT+M] and *Unmute* [SHIFT+U], or *Mute toggle* [ALT+M]. You may wish to apply *Auto Fades* to the Track to smooth the transitions between Events; especially, but not exclusively, if you decide to extend the Events boundaries so that they overlap.

Using this feature of the Part editor provides for very rapid comp'ing.

The Sample Editor

The Sample Editor can be used for detailed editing at the waveform level, but also for larger scale editing (by selecting a Range) and for processing audio. The display is that of the audio waveform. As always you can reverse changes made due to the non-destructive nature of the edits.

The Sample Editor is opened by double clicking on an audio Event (or selecting an Event and pressing RETURN) in the Event Display. (You can also open it from the audio Part Editor, the Pool and the Browser.) In the Sample Editor you view audio as Clips. While you may open the editor via an Event, you will, nevertheless, be able to see the whole Clip, with the Event highlighted (unless the Sample Editor Event option has been switched off). A Ruler is provided that can be independently switched to your desired display format.

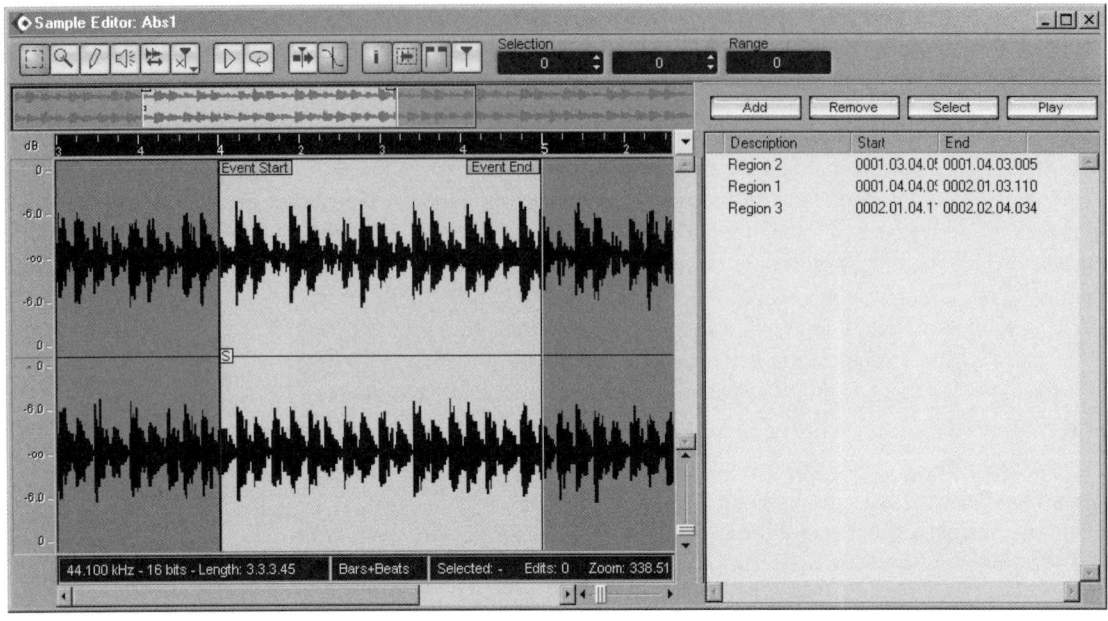

Fig. 14.3: the Sample Editor

Above the audio wave is a display of the whole Clip – the Thumbnail. Within this overview display is a blue box representing what can be seen in the main window. This box can be dragged to change the area of audio shown in the main window. It can also be resized by dragging either end (or clicking to the lower left or right outside the box). A new area can be selected by dragging the cursor over the require area in the upper half of the thumbnail.

Within the Sample Editor you can perform all the usual editing and processing functions and, in addition, you can draw directly onto the waveform. All actions are recorded in the *Off-line Process History* for the Clip (including drawing) and so can be reversed, if required.

Hit-point Processing is performed from the Sample Editor. This is covered in chapter 10, page 96.

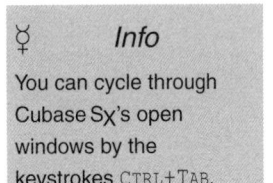

Info

You can cycle through Cubase Sx's open windows by the keystrokes CTRL+TAB.

Sample Editor detail

The contents of the Sample Editor window can be configured by selecting options from the *Elements* sub-menu item. This can be found on the Sample Editor's right-click quick-menu – it is right down the bottom. From here you can select the following options (some of which also have buttons to control them, as indicated):

○ *Audio Event* (button available): Switches on/off the display of Events in the waveform display. Events will only be shown if the editor is opened via an Event (i.e. not from a Clip).

○ *Regions* (button available): Switches the Region panel to the right of the waveform display on/off
○ *Info Line* (button available): Switches the Info line at the bottom of the editor on/off. The Info Line provides the following information on the Clip
  – Format (sample rate and bit depth)
  – Clip length (in Ruler format)
  – Display Format (as selected, can be changed from here)
  – Current selection range (in Ruler format)
  – Number of Edits made to the Clip
  – Current Zoom Level
○ *Level Scale*: Switches on/off the level scale on the left-hand side of the main window. This scale can be switched between dB and % via the button at the top of the scale. You can also switch Level Scale off here.
○ *Zero Axis*: Switches the zero axis on/off. This is a line added to the waveform display that indicates 0dB.
○ *Half Level Axis*: Switches on/off a line added to the waveform display that shows -6dB (or 50%).

The Toolbar provides access to the following tools:

○ Range Selection
○ Zoom
○ Draw (see below)
○ Play – This is useful for auditioning. Note that output is routed to the Master Bus; this is because a Clip has no associated Track/Channel.
○ Scrub
○ Hit-point edit

There are also Play and Loop buttons. Play will commence from the start of any selected area. In the absence of a range being selected, Play will start at the beginning of the Event. If no Event is present, then Play will start at the beginning of the Clip, unless the Cursor is showing in which case playback starts from the Cursor. (Note that the Region display (when switched on) provides its own Play button.) The Loop selection is the current Range Selection, Event or Clip by the same rules as above.

AutoScroll [F], and *Snap to Zero Crossing* buttons are also provided to toggle these functions. *Snap to Zero Crossing* ensures that all audio editing is performed at 0dB points in the waveform. This will reduce clicks due to amplitude differences between two audio segments. Finally, the current Cursor position and the current selection are shown in samples.

 Info

Snap to Zero Crossing is a local switch in the *Sample Editor.* The global switch is found in *Preferences/Audio* tab.

Zooming in the Sample Editor

The following commands are also available on the Sample Editor Zoom submenu:

Zoom In	H
Zoom Out	G
Zoom Full	SHIFT+F
Zoom to Selection	ALT+S
Zoom to Event	SHIFT+E
Zoom in Vertical	No default
Zoom in Horizontal	No default

You can also zoom with the thumbnail and the zoom sliders.

When you are getting close to a degree of magnification where individual samples can be seen, then the audio waveform being displayed will either appear in steps or as a curve, depending on the *Preferences/Event Display* tab *Interpolate Audio Images* setting (see chapter 5, page 37).

Sample Editor: making a Range Selection

♫   *Note*

Remember to set Snap to Zero Crossing as you require it.

The Range Selection tool is the most obvious starting point. Once you have made a selection, it is then possible to drag the left and right edges to resize the selection. You can also SHIFT+click to move either edge to that point. You can make sample level adjustment by using the spin buttons on the selection display fields. And, if you hold down ALT while clicking one of these fields, you will be able to make adjustments on a slider. Holding SHIFT will allow finer control of the slider.

The following commands are also available on the Select submenu:

Select All	CTRL+A
Select None	CTRL+SHIFT+A
In Loop (when appropriate)	No default
Select From Start to Cursor	No default
Select From Cursor to End	No default
Select Event	No default
Left Selection Side to Cursor	E
Right Selection Side to Cursor	D

♫   Note

To create a duplicate Clip, and audio file (although you will lose the Off-line Process History in the new Clip), perform a *Select All* [CTRL+A] in the Sample Editor and then select *Audio/Bounce Selection* [No Default].

Editing in the Sample Editor

There are two types of editing available to the Sample Editor:

○ *Copy, Cut and Paste Editing:*
 – *Copy* [CTRL+C]: Copies the selection to the Clipboard
 – *Cut* [CTRL+X]: Copies the selection to the Clipboard, removes the selection from the Clip. The gap is filled by shifting the audio that was to the right of the Cut, to the left.
 – *Delete* [DEL] or BACKSPACE: Removes the selection from the Clip. The gap is filled by shifting the audio to the right of the deletion, to the left.
 – *Paste* [CTRL+V]: The Clipboard contents replaces the current selection; expanding or shrinking the Clip as appropriate. If the selection length is zero, then the Clipboard contents will be inserted at the selection line and the audio shifted to the right, thus expanding the Clip. If the selection line is absent, then the Clipboard contents is appended to the righthand end of the Clip.
○ *Draw Editing (Sample Level):* Zoom in on the Clip until the Zoom reading in the Info Line is 1 or less. Select the *Draw* tool and start doodling.

> ☿   *Info*
>
> By holding CTRL and dragging a Sample Editor *Range selection* (cursor changes to a hand), you can drop an Event onto the Event Display.

♭   Warning

When editing a shared Clip, a warning is presented asking whether you wish the edits to apply to all instances of the Clip or to create a new copy. This option is not presented when you alter a Clip with Draw Editing.

Drawing in the Sample Editor

When drawing directly onto the waveform, it is necessary to Zoom-in to the audio waveform to a sufficiently detailed level. If you are not close enough and you select the Draw tool, you will get the message shown. So just keep zooming in until the zoom reading in the Info Line is 1 or less, and it will go away.

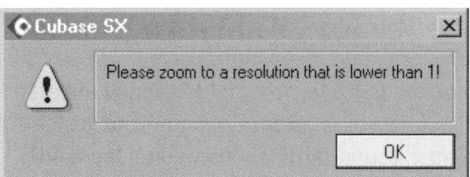

> ♪   *Note*
>
> CTRL will *not* restrict movement horizontally or vertically when drawing in the Sample Editor, so take care when moving the mouse.

So, why would you want to draw directly onto the waveform? Good question. It is possible, of course, to locate and then edit digital spikes, and other clicks, but this is serious audio editing and it can be very difficult to achieve seamless results, particularly if the audio is stereo. Replacing a section of the audio waveform via copy and paste can sometimes erase audible clicks, but again, this can be very hit and miss. In practice, a dedicated audio editor is a much better tool for this particular job. Recommended editors are *Wavelab, Sound*

Forge and *Cool Edit Pro*. In particular, since Cubase Sx cannot burn to CD, a complimentary tool that provides these functions should be seen as an essential companion to Cubase Sx.

Processing in the Sample Editor

Processing of plug-ins and the Cubase Sx Processes is performed in exactly the same way as for audio Events.

There is an additional *Edit/Range/Insert Silence* [No Default] function available in the Sample Editor. This will insert a section of silence into the Clip that is the same length of the current selection. The silence is inserted at the start of the selection and the contents of the Clip shifted to to the right by the same amount. To replace a selection with silence, use the *Audio/Process/Silence function* [No Default].

Example: moving a section of audio within a Clip

There are numerous other ways to achieve the same result. Outside of the *Sample Editor*, one method would be to create Events for the appropriate sections of the Clip and to crossfade these in the *Event Display*. When doing this, you can make use of CTRL+drag on a selection in the *Sample Editor* to create the appropriate Events. You might also choose to create Regions in the *Sample Editor*, and then arrange these on the *Event Display*. Yet another method would be to arrange Events in lanes in the *Part Editor*, maybe use *Auto Fades*. The choice is yours.

To achieve this result in the *Sample Editor*, start by double clicking the Event to be edited in the *Event Display*. Now make a selection with the *Range* tool. Drag the edges of the selection to the required positions. To help in this, you can make use of the *Select* commands. You might also want to set the audio to loop play, so that you can hear the effect of your edit changes. When you are happy with your selection, perform a *Cut*. Now simply select the intended insert position in the Event by a click with the mouse. For fine positioning of the selection line, zoom in, and use the spin buttons on the selection field (top right of the Sample Editor). Ensure that the selection length is zero, and then perform *Paste*.

Events in the Sample Editor

Show Events

As long as you open the Sample Editor from an Event (either by double-clicking or selecting the Event and pressing RETURN) and as long as the *Show Audio Event* button is active, then you can move the Event start and end points in the Sample Editor.

You can use the Loop audio trick here when adjusting the Event. Make sure that you don't make a selection in the waveform before starting Loop Playback, however. Once Loop Playback has started, you can move the Event flags and only the newly adjusted Event will Loop. This permits very accurate adjustment of the Event.

It is also possible to edit the Event's Snap Point in the Sample Editor

Regions in the Sample Editor

It's very easy to underestimate the usefulness of Regions when you have come
from one of the existing mainstream, sequencers. Most sequencers operate
in a similar manner to Events, which are clearly sufficient, but Regions can be
very effectively and creatively used.

Show Regions

    The Sample Editor is the main edit environment for manipulating Regions.
Ensure that the *Show Regions* button is active to enable the Region View. A new
Region can be created by making a selection on the Sample Editor's waveform
and pressing the Add button. The other functions are straightforward. You can
rename a Region by clicking the name field and editing it.

Add	Remove	Select	Play

Description	Start	End	
Region 2	0001.03.04.0!	0001.04.03.005	
Region 1	0001.04.04.0!	0002.01.03.110	

Regions in the
Sample Editor

There are two methods for editing the Region start and end points. First select
the Region from the list and then either:

o Drag the start and end handles in the waveform display.
o Edit the numerical values in the Region View.
    Note that these will be in the same format as that chosen for the Sample
    Editor's Ruler.

Selecting a Region from the list only highlights it in the display; to select it you
must click the Select button. You can also double-click a Region (its icon) in
the Pool; this will open the Region in a Sample Editor window with the Region
selected.
    Regions can be dragged onto the *Event Display* (either from the Pool or by
CTRL+dragging a Sample Editor selection) where an Event will be created .
Also available in the Pool are the *Pool/Insert into Project...* [No Default] commands, which will create an Event from the Region at the chosen destination.

✗   **Tip**

Pool/Insert into Project...At Cursor [No Default] can be used to replace an Event
with a Region. Select the Event and press *Locate Selection* [L]. Delete the
Event, then use the above command on the appropriate Region in the Pool.
You can also right-click and use *Set to Region*, if the same Clip is to be used.

Finally, you may wish to create a new Clip, or a new audio file, from a Region.
This is available via *Pool/Audio/Bounce Selection* [No Default]. This will create
a new audio file *and* a new Clip.

Fades, Crossfades and Auto-Fades

Fades come in two flavors: Fade in and Fade out. There are two types of fades in Cubase Sx:

1. Fades created and edited with *Event Fade Handles* (on the Event Display) (not available for audio Parts)
2. Fades created by processing the *Clip*.

Crossfades can be applied where two audio Events overlap. The earlier Event fades out, while the later Event fades in – hence the name *crossfade*.

Auto-fades are fade ins and fade outs that are *calculated during playback*. They are automatically applied to *all* Events on a Track when the Auto-fade option is active (by default it is off). Auto-fades can be switched on either for the whole Project, or on a Track-by-Track basis.

Fades

Event Volume and Fade Handles

♪   *Note*

The result of a fade is shown on an Event's waveform image. Use of the waveform zoom can often be useful for fine-tuning the fade (see page 58).

Every audio Event has three blue handles that are visible when the Event is selected. Before being edited, these are at the top and placed left, center and right of an Event. These are the volume (center) and fade handles. By dragging these handles you can create a fade in and a fade out, as well as adjust the overall volume of the Event. The important point to note here is that the fades are not applied to the Clip, but to the Event.

The *volume curves* for all Events will be visible in the Event Display providing *Preferences/Event Display/Audio* tab *Show Event Volume Curves Always* is checked. You will only see the curve (a thin blue line) when the curve has been edited.

The *volume handle* applies a gain adjustment to the Event. It performs the same function as changing the volume value in the Info Line. This value can be increased to a maximum of +6dB. The whole Event is affected.

By dragging the left-hand fade handle, you can create a linear fade in (similarly for the fade out handle). These movements are reflected in the *Fade In* and *Fade Out* fields in the Info Line. To change the shape of the fade, click above the fade line (once a fade has been created) to open the fade editor.

☿   *Info*

Multiple selected Events can have their Volume and Fade handles edited at the same time.

It is also possible to create fades with *Audio/Adjust Fades to Range* [A]. To do this, *Range Select* the appropriate section of the Event to which you wish to apply a fade. If you select the start of an Event, then only a fade in will be created. If you select the end of an Event, then a fade out will be created. If you select the center of an Event, then the fade handles will be moved to the edges of the range; any existing fade curve shapes will be retained.

These types of fades can be edited by dragging the fade handles; any existing fade curve shapes will be retained. To remove a fade, select the Event and perform *Audio/Remove Fades* [No Default], or simply drag the fade handles to the extreme end of the Event.

Fades created by processing

Process/Fade In and Out [No Default] (see page 227) can be used to apply a fade to a selected area. Like other S$_X$ processes, these functions edit the Clip. The editor is very similar to those described in the following section. You can later edit, or remove, a fade created in this way via *Modify* or *Remove*, respectively, in the Clip's *Off-line Process History*.

The Fade In and Out Editors

There are different Fade Editors for *Fade Handle*-type fades and for processed Fades (that edit the Clip). You need to be aware which you are using and why. Remember that processing the Clip has all the associated issues of editing a Clip in any other way, such as affecting other Events that use the Clip, or requiring the creation of a separate edit version.

The two types of editors provide identical functionality.

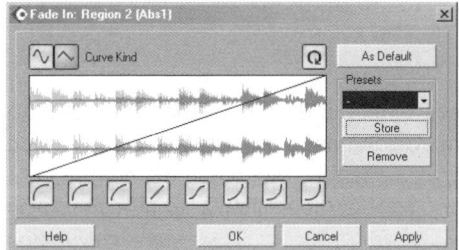

Fade In Editor

The Fade In and Fade Out editors are identical except for the obvious opposite slope. The Fade Editor can be opened by:

○ Clicking *above* the fade line on an Event (or Events)
○ Via *Audio/Open Fade Editor(s)* [No Default]
○ Via *Process/Fade In or Fade Out* [No Default] (for a processed fade)

The (handle) fade editor cannot be opened unless a fade has already been applied. If you try then you will be shown this rather confusing message:

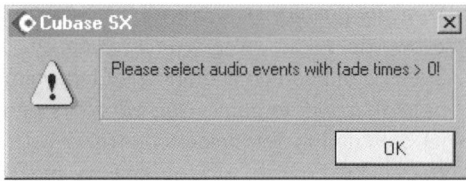

Fade to gray

You can select multiple Events when applying fades, and these will all have identical fades applied. If one of these Events does not yet have a fade applied, then it will not be affected by the Fade Editor.

In the Fade Editor you have a great deal of freedom to manipulate the fade curve as you wish, and a number of functions to assist. The *Curve Kind* buttons allow you to choose between a spline fade curve or a linear fade curve.

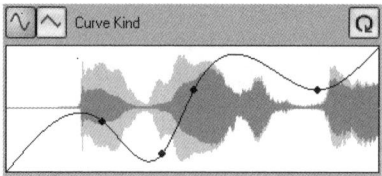 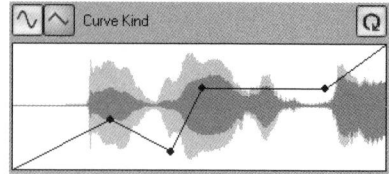

(Left) Spline Fade Curve
(Right)Linear Fade Curve

The buttons below the display give a few default, or starter, curves. You can add points directly onto the fade image by clicking, move existing points around by dragging them, or delete them by dragging them over the edge of the window. And, if you need to start again (handle fades only), then press the circular arrow, restore button.

You can also store and manage your own library of fade in and fade out preset curves, through the use of the Store, Remove and As Default buttons.

Crossfades

Creating and deleting a crossfade

You can apply a crossfade to overlapping Audio Events on the same Track, and on different Lanes in a Part. A crossfade is a simultaneous fade out of the earlier Event and fade in of the later Event. This process gives the best chance of a glitch-free transition from one Event to the next. Manipulation of the fade curves might be necessary to perfect the crossfade.

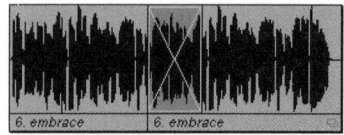

A crossfade.

♪   *Note*

If you hit **X**, then **X** again, you will apply a crossfade, then open the crossfade editor. This is true whenever a crossfade already exists.

♪   *Note*

The Clip description and file name are shown for both Events in the tile-bar of the *Crossfade Editor*.

To create a simple crossfade, select a single Event that overlaps another and apply *Audio/Crossfade* [X]. You can create more than one crossfade. simultaneously, by selecting further Events on the Track. The crossfade is created inside the area that overlaps. See below on how to edit the crossfade.

To remove a crossfade, select one of the Events and perform *Audio/Remove Fades* [No Default]. Or click on the crossfade and, holding down the mouse-button, drag the pointer over the edge of the Track.

If two Events *touch* (or are within 100ms of each other), but don't overlap, then a default crossfade will be created *as long as* the Events' Clips overlap. The crossfade is achieved by the Events being resized to accommodate the crossfade. If both Events can be resized, then the crossfade is applied equally to both (with appropriate resizing of both Events). If only one Event can be resized, then this is done and the crossfade is applied to either the start or end of the Event that cannot be resized. The size and shape of the default crossfade can be set with *As Default* in the Crossfade Editor.

Editing a crossfade: The Crossfade Editor

The quickest and easiest way to edit a crossfade is to grab an edge and resize. You can also move the whole crossfade (within the bounds of the underlying Clips) by dragging the whole crossfade to a new location.

To open the Crossfade Editor, double-click on the crossfade you wish to edit (or select an Event and use *Audio/Crossfades* [X]). The editor is very similar to the Fade Editor described above. First of all, note that this is a handle-type edit, and that separate curves are available for the fade in and the fade out. There are wet and dry preview options on this editor (that are sadly missing on the fade editor). When *Equal Power* is checked, the fade curves are adjusted to give constant energy (power) throughout the crossfade. When checked, only one edit point is available, but this can be moved around to produce differing results. (The other window will change to maintain the equal power output during editing.)

> ♪   *Note*
>
> Crossfades can be used across Lanes in the Part Editor.

> ♪   Note
>
> *Equal Power* is a useful feature that can allow you to take real liberties with certain material. Obviously, your ears must be your guide, but this little box can not only save a lot of time, but can also be used to produce excellent fades between material that would otherwise be quite tricky to mix together musically.

When *Equal Gain* is checked, the fade curves are adjusted so that the sum of the fade-in and fade-out amplitudes is the same throughout the crossfade. This can be useful on short crossfades where the two Events have similar levels. It is also useful when you have two or more crossfades very close to each other, or touching.

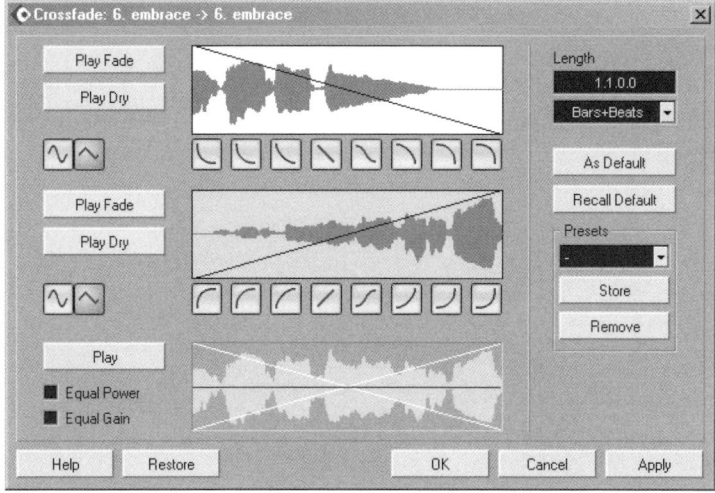

Fig. 14.4: The Crossfade Editor

Auto Fades and Auto Crossfades

What are auto fades? Well, the idea is that you can move seamlessly from one audio Event to another more easily when short fade ins and fade outs (and hence crossfades) are applied to the Events. To help out Cubase Sx provides you with the facilities for switching this on in the following ways:

1. Globally
2. On a Track-by-Track basis
3. Globally with Track-by-Track overrides

♪   **Note**

Auto Fades are calculated during playback (they are not saved as Clip edits), so computer power is required during playback to apply them.

Global Auto Fade settings

♪   *Note*

Equal Power and Equal Gain options are available for crossfades

By default Global and Track Auto Fades are switched off. Let's start by examining the Global Auto Fades options with *Project/Auto Fades Settings...* [No Default] (note the word Project in the title bar).

There are separate tabs for *Fades* and *Crossfades*. The checkboxes (upper right) allow you to select which fade options you wish to use for the *whole* Project (unless overridden Track-by-Track (see below)).

Fades and crossfades can be adjusted to your preferences in the same manner as ordinary fades and crossfades. The fade length is global and applies to both fades and crossfades. A time of approximately 30ms (from the available range of 1 to 500ms) is a good general start value.

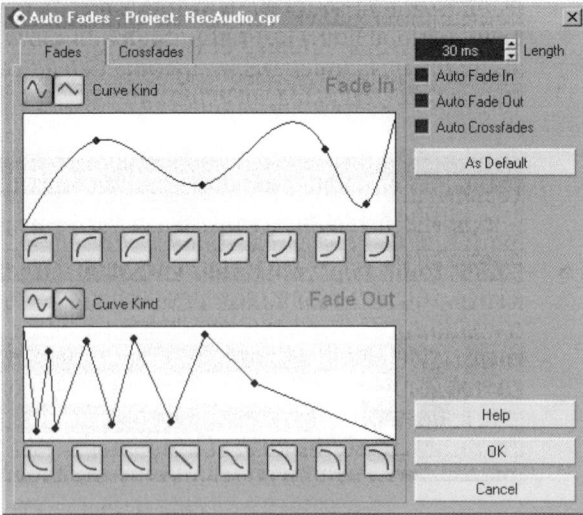

Fig. 14.5: Project Auto Fades Dialogue

♫   **Note**

The Default button will store the current settings for use with new Projects.

Auto Fade settings for an individual Tracks

The *Global Auto Fade* settings described above will be the default for *every* audio Track in the Project. So they will either be all on, or all off. However, the recommended way to use *Auto Fades* is to activate them on a track-by-track basis.

Open the *Track Auto Fades* dialog by right-clicking on the Track in the Track List and selecting *Auto Fades Settings...* (note the word Track in the title bar). The dialog can also be opened from the *Inspector*; the top-right button.

The options available are identical to the global options, with the exception of the *Use Project Setting*, which, by default, will be checked. To override the global setting, simply uncheck *Use Project Setting* and adjust your fade settings to taste. You can revert to the global settings at any time by re-checking this box.

Manual Punch-Ins

The Problem

The automated punch-in can be useful for certain operations, but in many studio situations it is very limited. Worse, trying to set it up and explain its use to the talent, who may be wanting to get right in and overdub an error on an otherwise perfect take, might blow the vibe that has been generated in a session. On top of that, the automated punch-in will only do one punch at a time. Frankly, in the real world, this doesn't cut it.

Let's take the example of a vocalist who has recorded a great take, from start to finish, with the exception of a few niggles here and there in the song. When recording on tape, one would simply playback the song and punch-in and punch-out where required, with the vocalist doing their thing. Once the take is done, you can check the playback and see whether it needs to be redone. This is committing stuff in the studio, but it's a very immediate thing and the session keeps going.

For a number of reasons, mostly due to restrictions in digital technology, and latency in particular, performing this operation in the digital world has proved difficult to perform. It has not been impossible, with the right tools, but it is certainly not ubiquitous.

One common workaround, that is certainly a valid working practice in its own right, is to record the vocalist a number of times singing the same thing and to comp' the vocal at a later date. There are pros and cons to working in this way, which I won't debate here. Suffice to say that some do and some don't. In fact, some vocalists now expect to be comp'd and are unfamiliar with punching in. It's a funny old world.

The essence of what we are trying to achieve is to insert a number of "snippets" of audio into an existing audio Track. Furthermore, we want these snippets to be seamless. (Note that doing this is a particular problem in the digital domain due to the audible glitches that occur when there is a large and/or inconsistent jump from one sample to the next.) Finally, we are placing a practical restriction on ourselves that this process must be immediate; we don't want to be messing around with fiddly bits of audio and messing with the progress of the session.

If we use Cubase Sx terminology, then we want to insert a number of audio Events into an existing audio Event with crossfades at all appropriate points. This process must be immediate.

The Solution – Manual Punch-Ins

Keeping it simply, the Project in front of us has guide drums, piano and an almost perfect vocal take. Our vocalist is in the booth, cans fitted and raring to go. What do you do? (Note that what follows can be applied to more than one Track simultaneously, if required.)

Monitoring Set-up

First, we need to determine the type of monitoring required and set this up (the talent usually has a preference). The vocalist will want to hear the Track being played back, through the cans, in preparation for the punch. At the point of the punch, the vocalist will want to hear her voice, and the song, continuing to play, but with the old vocal take muted. Whether she wants to hear herself in the mix prior to the punch is a decision for the vocalist; we will have to be prepared for both options.

One way to think of the options is to consider what is required in Stop, Play and Record modes. In this case we want playback of the whole Track to be continuous except when we drop in to record mode for the vocal punch. At that point, we only want to hear the new vocal take. Take a read through the above section on monitoring (page 171) if you are unfamiliar with the monitoring options available with Cubase Sx.

If the artist wants to hear herself throughout the take, and providing a mixer (software or hardware) is being used that can route directly to tape/disk, then the incoming signal can provide the monitoring signal throughout. In this case, simply remove the returned monitoring signal from the monitoring mix. Since we are not using Cubase Sx's monitoring features, the *Auto Monitoring* setting can be set to manual, if you wish. This might make applying effects (e.g. reverb) to the new vocal signal a bit tricky; it depends on the gear you have available.

Another neat trick is to duplicate the routing options for the Track in Cubase Sx (just use the Duplicate Track function and remove all the Events), and then switch on monitoring manually for the duplicated Track. In this way you can use the Cubase Sx controlled monitoring return. It is much simpler to add effects to this return.

If the artist does not want to hear herself throughout the take, but only during the punch-in, then remove the incoming signal from the monitoring mix and choose the preferred Auto Monitoring mode. The only appropriate choices being:

○ While Record Running
○ Tape Machine Style

The Cubase Sx controlled monitoring signal will now be routed (via ASIO Direct Monitoring, if available) and can be routed to the monitoring mix with or without effects.

Providing you have ASIO Direct Monitoring (ADM) available on your soundcard, then it is recommended that you use it, since it returns the input signal directly to the output without adding any latency.

There are many, many different routing options. Much is dependent on the gear you have available and what it can provide. As more and more powerful, zero latency software mixing options become available, monitor routing should become much simpler.

Applying the punches

At this point I will presume that you have you monitoring set-up in a fashion that works for you and the talent. Now let's apply the punches.

Record-enable the appropriate Track and start Cubase Sx in play mode. When you get to your first punch-in point, hit *Record* [Pad ∗]. This will drop Sx into record mode, and playback of any record enabled Tracks will stop. When you reach the punch-out point, hit the record button again. Easy, huh?

Assuming that everyone is happy with the result, there is one more problem. There will, inevitably, be audio glitches at the punch-in and out points. However, switching on *Auto Crossfades* for the Track easily rectifies this. Remember that there is a Project default for fade and crossfade settings.

One final point: *Auto Fades* are calculated during playback (they are not rendered and placed in the Fades folder), so you might want to merge the Track into something that avoids the crossfades. There are various ways of doing this. The most obvious would be to bounce the Track (*Audio/Bounce Selection* [No Default]), but this might be too permanent (though fast during session). Another way is to merge the Events into a Part (*Audio/Events to Part* [No Default]). Sx will do this in an intelligent way, but you can then drag the various Events into a single Track in the Part Editor and apply crossfades. This is slower, and not ideal during a session, but provides you with more editing options should further work be required; and, of course, it can all be backed out by using Undo.

That was a pretty lengthy trek through a task that is actually quite fast and easy, once you have been through it a few times. But it's a useful exercise in understanding a number of ways in which Cubase Sx can be used and exploited.

15 Audio: The Pool and Clips

The Pool [CTRL+P] is a file and Clip management system for all audio (and video) in a Project. For most folk, the Pool will become almost as familiar as the Project Window. The audio processing facilities of Cubase Sx are deep and flexible, and much of its power can be exploited here. All files that have been imported into the Project, or recorded, will be listed in the Pool. The Clips are displayed in a tree structure, and folders can be added in a hierarchical manner to help you organize the Clips in a manner best suited to your needs. Events are not listed, but Regions are shown. A count is displayed showing the number of Events using each Clip and a function is available (*Select in Project* [No Default]) to show the Events and Parts that reference a Clip in the Event Display.

The full range of file management functions is available, including import, deleting and renaming. Note that some operations performed from the Pool will affect the physical audio files on disk, while others will affect the Clip. (If you are unfamiliar with Clips, and how they interrelate to audio Events, then please see chapter 9, page 83 for an explanation.)

♫   **Note**

Many of the Pool key commands are found in the *Media* section of the *Key Commands Editor* [No Default].

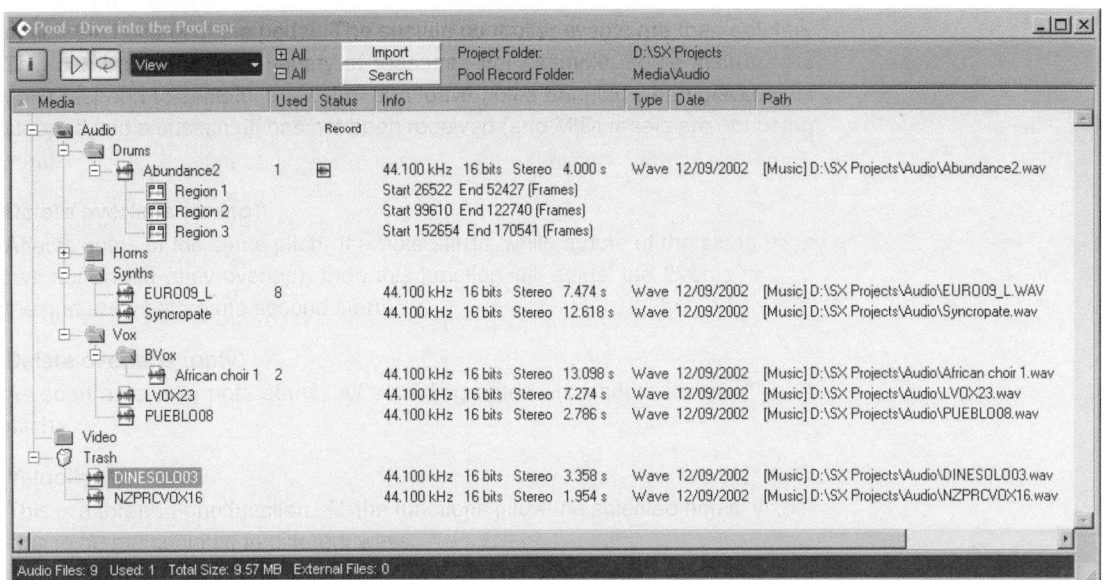

Fig. 15.1: The Audio Pool

The Audio Pool Window

Pool button

Pool folder structure

♪   *Note*

Right-click in *The Pool* to access the Pool's commands.

The *Project/Open Pool* [CTRL+P] can be opened from the Project Window by clicking the button shown in the Toolbar. Each Project has an associated Pool, and all Clips (including video) are listed there.

The Pool folder structure is displayed in the familiar tree format. On opening the Pool in a new Project, you will find three folders: *Audio, Video* and *Trash*. The names of these folders cannot be changed, nor can these folders be deleted.

You can create sub-folders in the structure by selecting an existing folder and then using *Pool/Create Folder* [No Default] (also available on the right-click sub-menu). You can rename the new folders by clicking on the name field and editing the field.

The Audio folder icon will, by default, be marked with a red icon that denotes it as the destination folder for any audio that you record in this Project. (If you also have the *Status* column showing in the display then it will have the word *Record* in the Audio folder's row.) You can change the location of the default record folder by using *Pool/Set Pool Record Folder* [No Default].

○ *The Audio folder* can contain sub-folders, audio Clips and Regions.
○ *The Video folder* can contain sub-folders and video Clips.
○ *The Trash folder* contains Clips moved to it by other Pool functions.

Clips are moved around the Pool by dragging and dropping.

The Pool Toolbar

The toolbar contains:

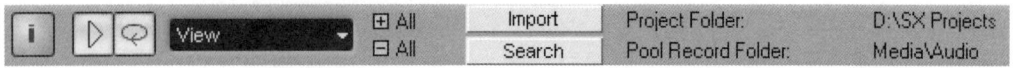

○ *Info Line button:* Displays a line at the bottom of the Pool showing:
  ▷ *Audio Files:* The number of *Clips* in the Pool that reference files that *are* within the *Project Folder* (usually in the *Audio* folder). The display says *Audio files* and not *Clips*, so even *Steinberg* get confused over the distinction between Clips and audio files.
  ▷ *Used:* The number of Clips with Events. (This number does not get refreshed when you add or remove Events. Toggle the *Info Line* button to refresh it.)
  ▷ *Total Size:* Total size of the audio files referenced by all of the Clips. This is *not* the size of the Project's *Audio* folder.
  ▷ The number of *Clips* (not files) in the Pool that reference files that are *not* within the *Project Folder*.
○ Play and loop buttons for the selected Clip.
  ▷ Note that you can also play a Clip by clicking on its image in the Pool. In this case, playback starts from the last point in the image that you click. If loop is on, then the Clip will loop from the end of the section you have

selected through until the end of the Clip. If you click a *Region*, then it will play in its entirety.

o View configuration dropdown (see below)
o Expand all and contract all folder tree buttons
o The Import audio file button (see *Pool/Import Medium* [No Default] below)
o The Search audio file button. Opens a handy audio file search window. Only Cubase Sx's supported file formats will be displayed. Use the *Import* button to bring up the *Import Options* dialog (see below). The Clip is included in the currently selected Folder.
o References to the Project Folder and Record Folder

The View Dropdown

The View dropdown in the toolbar allows you to configure the Pool display by adding and removing columns. The list can be sorted by clicking on some of the column headings. The column widths can be tidied-up quickly with *Optimize Width*.

The Media column is always shown far left, and lists:

Synths

Open folder

Vox

Closed folder

Abundance2

Audio lip

Region 3

Region

o Folders: Open and closed
o Audio Clips
o Video Clips
o Regions

The rest of the columns are optional:

o *Used:* The number of times a Clip is used by Events in the Project. This makes it easy to spot unused Clips.
o *Status:* Shows one of a number of icons, or nothing for an unprocessed, imported Clip. The icons are:
  ▷ *Record:* there is only one folder with Record status and it is always present. It indicates the current *Pool Record Folder*, where all newly recorded audio files will be placed. Change with *Pool/Set Record Folder* [No Default].
  ▷ This *Processed Clip* icon indicates that the Clip has been processed in some way. You can remind yourself of the processes applied by examining the Clip's *Audio/Off-line Process History* [No Default].

Processed Clip

  ▷ The *R* icon indicates that the Clip was recorded in this session of the Project. If you close and re-open the Project, then these indicators will be removed. They are not removed if you save the Project, only if you close it.

Recorded in session

  ▷ The question mark indicates a missing file. That is, a Clip references a file that it cannot find. Missing files are also brought to your attention when you load a Project, so while this is clearly an indicator to take notice of, by the time you see it you should be aware that a problem exists. You can remove this reference by using the *Pool/Remove Missing Files* [No Default], or point to a new audio file with the *Pool/Find Missing Files* [No Default].

?

External file

- ▷ The *X* icon indicates that the file is outside of the Project Folder. Note that creating folders in the Pool does not create folders on disk in the Audio folder hierarchy. However, you can create folders on disk in the Projects Folder and the files within them will be considered by Cubase SX to be in the Project Folder. So if you decide to rearrange your Project's audio files into a new folder structure in the Project Folder, Cubase SX will find them and adjust the Clips accordingly.
- *Info:* Shows different data depending on the data type:
  - ▷ *Audio:* Sample rate, sample depth, mono/stereo and length in seconds
  - ▷ *Region:* Start and end times in samples
  - ▷ Video: Frame rate, number of frames, length in seconds and display resolution.
- *Type:* The file type. E.g. Wave, Broadcast Wave, AIFF, etc.
- *Date:* The creation time stamp on the file.
- *Origin Time:* When a Clip is recorded, this field will show the start time in the Project. Some files types (e.g. Broadcast Wave) store this data in their headers. This allows audio to be moved between projects and other devices, and automatically have the audio placed at the precise time that it was originally recorded. If you are importing such a file, then use *Pool/Insert into Project/At Origin* [No Default] to achieve this. The *Origin* can also be updated to the current location of the Clip (in preparation for export, say), by using *Pool/Update Origin* [No Default].

> ♫ *Note*
>
> *Origin Time* is associated with a Clip. This is not the same as an Event's *Snap Point.* If you change a Clip's *Origin Time*, then the audio file on disk is immediately updated.

- *Image:* An image of the audio file or of a Region. You can click on this image to play the Clip. For a Region the whole Region is played. For a Clip, playback starts from where the mouse-button is released.
- *Path:* The location on disk of the audio file used by the Clip.

Audio After Recording

After a recording has been completed, for each record enabled audio Track, the following occurs:

- A new audio file is created in the Project's Audio folder
- An Clip is created for each audio file in the Pool
- An Audio Event, that plays the whole of the Clip, is inserted in the appropriate Track(s) in the Event Display
- Cubase SX then generates a waveform image for each Clip, which is displayed in both the Pool and in the Event. (File images can be created *during recoding* by checking *Create images during record* in *Preferences/Audio* tab.)

Forcing file formats to the Project defaults

Pool/Conform Files [No Default] forces all files *selected* in the Pool to be converted to the values set in *Project Set-up* [SHIFT+S].

For the files that need to be converted, a dialog opens giving you the option of keeping or overwriting the existing audio files. The original Clip references are always removed from the Pool, so this is simply a choice of whether you want to keep the original files or not.

Missing Files: Don't despair...yet!

If the following window appears when loading a Project, I can guarantee you that your heart will jump.

Resolve missing files

Quite simply, Cubase Sx has been unable to resolve the reference for a file, and is providing you with a number of options to help resolve the problem. Most often you will realize your have moved something that you probably shouldn't have and you will be able to locate the file using the Locate, Folder or Search options, which are quite straightforward to use.

However, if your heart is still pounding and you can't recall what has happened, then you might just get lucky when you select *Close* and examine the Pool. Cubase Sx is often able to reconstruct edit files, and this will be indicated by the word *reconstructible* in the status column for the Clip. If, instead, the field shows '?', then you are out of luck and will have to take appropriate action. Good luck.

To reconstruct the file, select it and perform *Pool/Reconstruct* [No Default]. Should you simply want to remove references to missing files, then either delete them or use *Pool/Remove Missing Files* [No Default].

Searching the Pool

Pool/Find in Pool [No Default] (*Media/Find* in key commands) is a powerful search utility for a Pool. Files can be filtered by name (part names work just fine), size, bit size, and mono/stereo. By checking the tick boxes, a *logical and* is performed on the selections, so you can use multiple criteria in your selection choice. The results are shown in the lower window after pressing the *Start* button. A handy feature is that you can then choose to have the Pool view show the highlighted Clip(s) by pressing the *Select in Pool* button. Unfortunately you cannot play the Clip(s) from the *Find in Pool* results list.

This feature is available from the Project Window. However, if the Pool is not open, then the *Select in Pool* button is unavailable, which somewhat limits its usefulness.

Importing and Exporting Pools

It can be useful to use the Pool of one Project in another. By using *Pool/Import Pool* [No Default] and *Pool/Export Pool* [No Default] (in the *File* section for Key Commands) you can facilitate the sharing of one Project's audio with another. The physical files are not moved, the Pool Export file will simply reference the files in the exporting Project. If you later wish to import the audio files that are used, then you can perform a *Pool/Prepare Archive* [No Default]. Be very careful not to erase any of the imported Pool's audio files that you might have moved to the Trash, when exiting the Project.

Note that the Project importing the Pool will have the references added to the existing Pool; it does not replace the existing Pool.

Templates containing Clips and Events

A Template can contain Clips and Events. If this is the case, then the Pool of a newly created Project based on the Template will "point" to the audio files in their original location. In other words, where they were located when the Template was created (or last saved). This is very unlikely to be what you require, since it will probably be a Project. However, if you immediately perform a *Pool/Prepare Archive* [No Default], then the audio files will be copied to the correct place in the new Project Folder.

Importing Audio (and other media) to the Pool

Import

Pressing the *Import* button on the Pool's toolbar will open the *Import Medium* dialogue window. (You can also use *File/Import/Audio File* [No Default].) This dialogue is used for importing files into the *Project Folder* and Clips into the Pool. The Clips are placed in any currently highlighted folder in the Pool. It is possible to audition files within the *Import Medium* dialogue.

♫ *Note*

Files that are not converted to the Project *Sample Rate* will play back at the wrong speed.

As well as using this dialogue, you can also drag and drop files directly into the Pool, and even directly onto the Event Display. If you are importing audio from a CD, then see the section below (page 208) for a description of the extended facilities available for importing from this medium.

If you attempt to import an audio file more than once, then you are given the option of creating a new Clip for the audio file.

Importing audio is affected by the *Preferences/Audio* tab option *On Import Audio File*. These options affect whether or not imported files are copied automatically to the Project Folder and, if so, in what way they are converted with respect to the settings in *Project Set-up* [SHIFT+S]. The options are:

○ *Do Nothing:* The Clips appear in the Pool, but the files are neither copied to the Project Audio Folder nor converted to match the Project Set-up settings.
○ *Open Options Dialog:* The *Options* dialog is always displayed when importing files. The content of the dialog depends on whether a single file or multiple files are being imported. Fields in the dialogs are disabled when unnecessary (i.e. if the Project is 16-bit and the files to be imported are 16-bit). These options allow you to select which import options you require at the time of import.

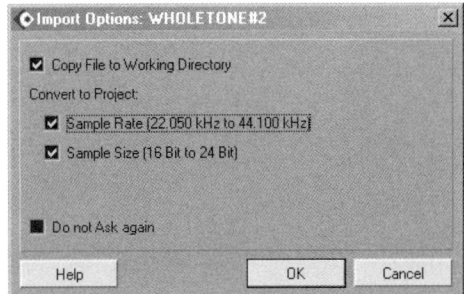
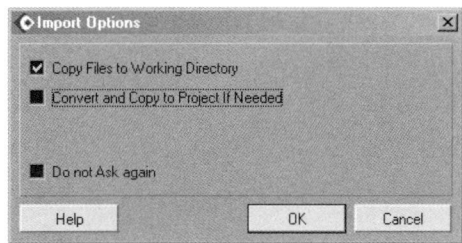

○ *Copy to Project Folder:* The Clips appear in the Pool and the files are copied to the Project Folder. If the file already exists in the Project Folder then a new *file* is created with a numbered suffix. The Clip also receives the numbered suffix.
○ *Copy and Convert:* As Copy to Project Folder with this addition: if any of the files have a different sample rate, or a lower sample depth, than the Project Set-up settings then they are converted to the Project settings.
○ *Convert if needed:* Clips for files that match the Project settings will appear in the Pool, but not be moved to the Project Audio folder. Files that don't match the Project settings effectively have a Copy and Convert applied to them.

Once you have selected a file for import, you may well be presented with a dialogue asking whether you wish to convert the file to match the *Sample Rate* and *Sample Size* in *Project Set-up* [SHIFT+S]. There is also an option as to whether you wish to copy the file to the Project Folder, which you will want to do in most cases.

As mentioned above, you will want to perform any necessary sample rate conversion (unless none is required for an effect). Sample rate conversion can also be performed later using *Pool/Convert Files* [No Default].

If you tick the *Do not Ask again* box, then these settings will be maintained for all Projects. What actually happens is that the *On Import Audio File* option in *Preferences/Audio* tab is updated to reflect the *Import Options* settings. The default (*Open Options Dialogue*) is the safest setting, but you may well wish to change it when bulk importing files.

Audio and video file import formats

Imported files can be stereo or mono; 8, 16, 24 bit or 32 bit float resolution; any sample rate (but if different to the Project *sample rate* will play back at the wrong speed). The following file formats are available for import:

○ WAV (Wave including Broadcast Wave files)
○ AIFF
○ AIFC (Compressed AIFF files)
○ REX and RX2 (Recycle files) – Import to a tempo-based audio Track. Audio is created as Events within a Part. (See below.)
○ MPEG, MP2 and MP3 (MPEG, MPEG Layer 2 and MPEG Layer 3 files)
○ OGG Ogg Vorbis
○ WMA Windows Media files
○ MPG (MPEG video files)
○ MOV and QT (Quicktime movie files)
○ AVI (AVI video files)

♫   *Note*

MPEG audio file imports are converted to the Project settings format and placed in the Pool.

Imported REX files are converted to a Part, with each *Recycle* slice being converted to an audio Event. Ideally, a REX file should be imported to a tempo-based audio Track. In this way, the tempo-based benefits of a native REX file can be maintained. The original tempo of the REX file is shown in the Pool's *Type* column.

If you want to edit the Events created from a REX import, you might prefer to have each Event on a separate Lane. To do this: First select the Part, then do *Audio/Dissolve Part* [No Default], immediately followed by *Audio/Events ro Part* [No Default]. You can create a macro for this if you think you'll be needing it frequently.

An alternative to the REX approach to slicing and dicing is to output the audio segments *and* MIDI file from *Recycle*. Next, load the audio into a soft sampler and fire the audio via the MIDI file. While, say, pure soft samplers such as *Native Instruments'* Kontakt is fine for this task, other tools, such as *Native Instruments'* Battery or *fxpansion's* DR-008 are ideal.

Importing audio from CD - Ripper!

The smart things about Cubase Sx's CD import is that it can grab *sections* of a CD Track, and that it contains a flexible audition facility.

Sʟ   *SL Info*

CD import is an Sx-only feature.

CD importing in Cubase Sx is a straightforward process performed by way of *Pool/Import Audio CD* [No Default]. This will display the window shown in Figure 15.2 allowing you to select your preferred CD device, the drive speed, and Tracks you wish to import into the Pool or Library (or another destination if you wish). Multiple Tracks are selected by holding down CTRL or SHIFT while making a selection with the mouse. You can import the audio files to any destination, the default being the Project Folder.

The Tracks can be named generically on import by typing a name in the *File Name* field. This entry affects all Tracks. These names can, of course, be

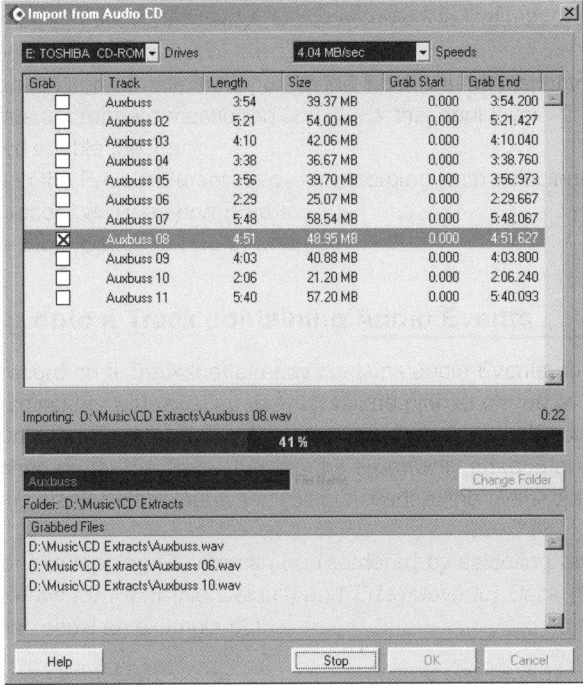

Fig. 15.2: Importing audio from a CD

changed later. Alternatively, Tracks can be named by typing directly into the individual Track name fields.

For an active Project, the first imported CD Track will be placed onto the selected Track, at the current Cursor position. Subsequent Tracks will share the Cursor position start point, but be placed in the audio Track below the first. New Tracks are created, if required.

To Play a Track, select its row and press play. You can select multiple Tracks and playback will take place for each, one after the other.

If you click anywhere in the white "ruler-like" timeline area then playback will immediately start from that point. You can stop playback at any time by pressing *Stop*. The numbers in the selector are *bars*, adjusted to the active tempo.

The small, black triangles at each end of the timeline can be dragged inward to create a selection for each audio Track to be imported. The upward and downward arrow buttons will play approximately 2 seconds of the start or end of the selection for a Track.

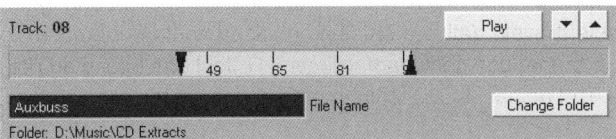

Select area to import

Other import file-types

Importing Options and File Types

Importing of files into Cubase Sx is performed via *File/Import* or by using the *Import* button in the Pool. Most file-types can also be dragged onto the Event Display. For some types you are given the option of creating a new Project from the file being imported, or simply including it in the current Project.

The *File/Import* option enables the following imports:

- Audio file – see page 208
- Audio CD – see page 208
- Video file – see page 208 and below
- Cubase song, arrangement, Part – see below
- MIDI file – see below

Video files

Cubase Sx recognizes the following video playback engines, file types and codecs:

Playback engine	File type	Codec
DirectShow	AVI (.avi), MPG (.mpg and .mpeg)	Cinepak, DV, Indeo, M-JPEG, MPEG
Video for Windows	AVI (.avi)	Cinepak, Indeo, M-JPEG
Quicktime	Quicktime (.mov and .qt) AVI (.avi), MPG (.mpg and .mpeg)	Cinepak, DV, Indeo, M-JPEG, MPEG

Video Events are placed on Video Tracks for playback (*Add Track/Video* [No Default]). Bizarrely, audio does not playback and so must be extracted in a tool outside of Cubase Sx, imported separately and aligned. Two, or more, Video Events on the same Track must be of the same type and format. Video Events are edited in the same way as other Events.

Playback set-up is made via *Devices/Device Set-up/Video Player* where you can select screen size and an appropriate playback engine (*Quicktime* will only be available if loaded on the computer – see the Cubase Sx CD). Playback can be viewed both on an external monitor (with appropriate drivers and codec), or within Sx via *Video* [F8]. There are also some settings in *Preferences/Event Display/Video* tab that can be used to changed playback behavior.

Cubase imports

Three type of files can be imported from old versions of *Cubase*:

- Cubase song files (.all) (Cubase version 5.0 or later.)
- Cubase arrangement files (.arr)
- Cubase Part files (.prt)

None of these files contains the audio itself, so the audio files that they reference must also be available for a successful import to be achieved.

A *song* with multiple arrangements can only be imported one arrangement at a time, as Cubase Sx does not support the arrangement concept. An *arrangement* is imported as a Cubase Sx Project.

There are quite severe limitations to these imports, which are detailed in the *Cubase Sx: Operations Manual* in the *File Handling* chapter (page 690 for Cubase Sx v1.03) and on the installation CD file *Importing Cubase 5 Songs*. These data may well be updated over time and will, no doubt, be described in the update documentation.

MIDI File

Cubase Sx will import and export Standard MIDI Files (SMF). Type 0 MIDI files will be imported onto a single MIDI Track with Channel set to Any. (Use *MIDI/Dissolve Part* [No Default] to create a single Track for each Channel.) Type 1 MIDI files will be imported as one Track per Channel present in the imported file. All tempo messages in the SMF are added to Sx's *Tempo Track* [CTRL+T].

Exporting files

MIDI File

Cubase Sx exports both Type 0 (all data on one track, but retaining channel information) and Type 1 (one Track per channel) MIDI files via *File/Export*. All MIDI data (including muted Tracks) are saved including: Master Tempo and Tempo changes. Note that initial Bank and Program values, and all other *Inspector* settings are not saved to the MIDI file. Some *Inspector* settings can be embedded into a MIDI Part by way of *MIDI/Merge MIDI in Loop* [No Default] (see page 128).

Audio Mixdown

This is covered in detail in chapter 17, page 246.

Clip Operations and Functions

Opening the Sample Editor

Double-clicking on a Clip, or a Region, icon will open the Sample Editor. Events cannot be manipulated from the Sample Editor when it is opened from the Pool. Double-clicking a Region will open the Sample Editor with the Region highlighted. Use *Zoom to Selection* [ALT+S] to zoom to the selected Region. (For more on the Sample Editor chapter 14, page 185.)

Renaming Clips

To rename a Clip, simply select it, click on the name and edit the text field. Note that this changes the name of the file on disk.

Copying Clips

To create a copy of a Clip, select it and apply *Pool/New Version* [No Default]. The new Clip is given the same name but with a version number appended in brackets.

> ♪   *Note*
>
> You can apply audio processing to a whole Clip.

The important thing to note, when copying a Clip, is that a new audio file is not created. Remember that a Clip is just a "pointer" to the audio file so multiple Clips can be created that reference the same file. These various Clips can, however, contain totally unrelated processing. Furthermore, the Clip created by *New Version* will have all processing applied to it that is present on the original Clip – and this cannot be removed. In other words the new Clip does not retain the original Clip's Off-line Process History (see chapter 16, page 219).

Deleting Clips and audio Files

When deleting Clips, Cubase Sx takes some care in determining whether or not you wish to delete the underlying audio file. While most delete operations can be undone, a physical file deletion cannot, so this is a good policy.

That said, the various messages that advise you on what is occurring are not very clearly worded, and it can be confusing. Hopefully the following will clarify things.

> ♪   *Note*
>
> An audio file can only be finally deleted by using *Empty Trash* [No Default]; and then only by choosing the *Erase* option.

To delete a Clip, select it in the Pool and pressing DEL or BACKSPACE. You can also drag an unreferenced Clip onto the *Trash* folder.

There are there are three cases to consider when deleting Clips:

○ The Clip is not used in the Project.
○ The Clip is used once or more.
○ The Clip has versions.

– The Clip is not used in the Project
Providing the Clip it doesn't have any versions (see below), then you will immediately be prompted with the *Remove from Pool or Trash* window, see next section.

– The Clip is used once or more

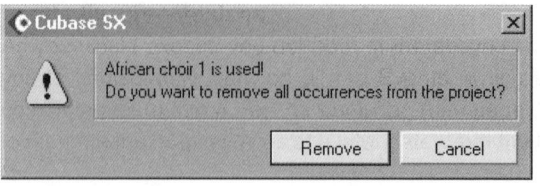

Remove *all* Events?

The message shown will be displayed. You are being asked whether you want to remove all Events that reference this Clip from the Project. If you choose to cancel then nothing happens at all. If you choose *Remove* then nothing yet happens to the Events or the Clip, but you are prompted with the *Remove from Pool or Trash* window, see next section.

– The Clip has more than one edit version
A new version of a Clip is created when, for example, you use the command *Pool/New Version* [No Default] on a Clip, or when you apply a process (such as an effect) to an Event that is not the only Event to reference that Clip, and then you choose *New Version* from the dialog that appears. (Although whether the dialog appears depends on the *On Processing Shared Clips* option in *Preferences/Audio*.)

   When performing this process, a new Clip is created in the Pool. This Clip references the same audio file as the Clip from which it is derived. In other words there will be one audio file, with two Clips (the original Clip and the processed Clip). Events can, of course, use either Clip, depending on what is required.

   So when you decide to delete one of the Clips, a message is displayed (below) to indicate that the Clip cannot be moved to the Trash folder since the underlying audio file is still in use.

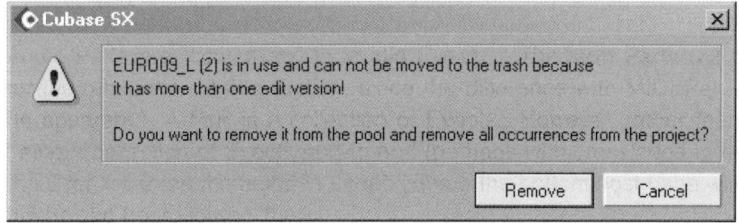

One file, two Clips

However, Sx will let you remove the Clip's Events and remove the Clip from the Project. If you press *Cancel* then no changes will be made. If you now press *Remove*, then all Events referencing the Clip will be removed from the Project and the Clip will be deleted. This is an important point to be clear about: *The Clip is removed, but the audio file is still available for reference.*

Remove from Pool or Trash window
This window (below) is only displayed when deleting a Clip from the Pool. If you press *Trash*, then the Clip is moved to the Trash folder from where it can later be deleted. Note that all edits stay intact when the Clip is in the Trash. If you press *Remove from Pool*, then the Clip is deleted, but the file remains on disk. Note that any edit files associated with the Clip are also retained.

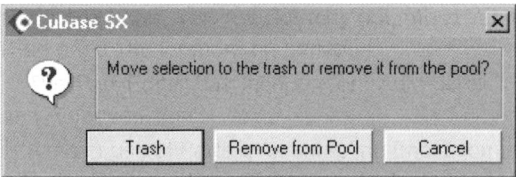

Remove or trash?

Emptying the Trash

↗   *Tip*

You can place all unused Clips in the Trash by using *Pool/Remove Unused Media* [No Default].

Clips in the Trash folder can be removed by using *Pool/Empty Trash command* [No Default]. If you press *Remove from Pool*, then all the Clips are deleted from the Trash folder, but the associated files remain on disk. Any edit files associated with the Clip are retained. If you press Erase then the Clips and the files are gone forever. Got that? *Gone forever.*

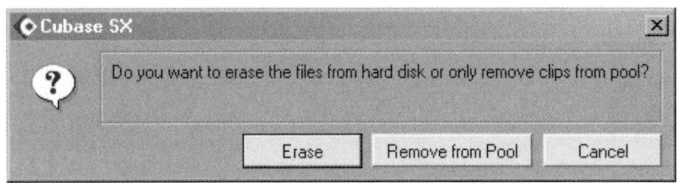

Erase or remove?

Replacing one Clip with another

From time to time you may wish to replace a Clip throughout a Project. It is not immediately apparent how to do this, but the process is quite straightforward.

Open *The Pool* [CTRL+B] and select the Clip you want to use. Drag the Clip from the Pool and place it over the Clip you wish to replace in the Project Window, ensuring that the start position is correctly aligned. Now press SHIFT and release the mouse-button. The window shown will appear:

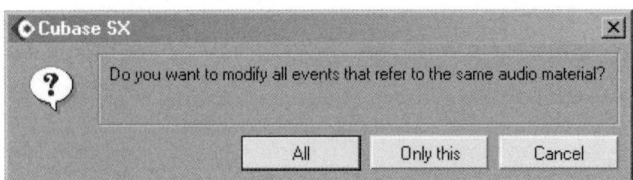

Replace a Clip

By pressing *All*, every Event will be updated to use the new Clip while retaining all other details associated with the Event.

Converting audio files into different formats

Although not strictly a Clip process, file conversion is handled in the Pool by *Pool/Convert Files* [No Default]. The dialogue shows that the range of options is comprehensive. This is a very flexible tool. Note that this function can operate on multiple files at one time. Also note that the last setting used becomes the default setting for the next use. It's easy to get caught out by that last fact.

Sample rate ranges from 8k-96k; Sample width: 16, 24, 32 float; Channels: mono and stereo-interleaved; File format: Wave, AIFF, Broadcast Wave.

The Options setting determines what happens to the resulting file, and its impact on the Pool:

○ *New Files:* A new file is created as per the settings and a Clip is added to the Pool. The original file and Clips are left untouched.

○ *Replace Files:* The original files are replaced with the new files. Clips are unchanged.
○ *New+Replace in Pool:* A new file is created and the original Clip references are moved to it. The original file remains on disk, but is removed from the Pool.

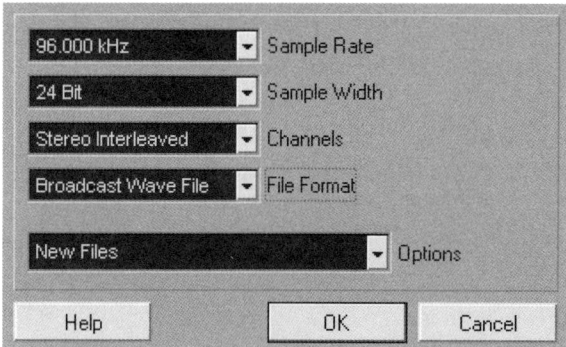

Convert Files

↗   Tip

Since you cannot mix mono and stereo file formats on a Cubase Sx Track, it is convenient to be able to quickly change the format when you need to add a Clip to a Track of a different format. You can't perform *Convert Files* on an Event or Range selection, but you can *Audio/Bounce Selection* [No Default] the Event and then perform *Convert Files* on the newly created Clip.

Clips and their Origin

There are a variety of reasons why you might want to relocate Events to their origin. This is easily achieved by *Audio (or Move To)/To Origin* [No Default].

You may also wish to update the Origin for a Clip with *Pool/Update Origin* [No Default]. The Origin is updated to the current Cursor position. One technique for achieving this is as follows:

○ Select the Event(s) containing the Clip to be updated
○ Do *Audio/Find Selected in Pool* [CTRL+F]
○ Select *Pool/Update Origin* [No Default]

Minimize File (for Clip maintenance)

↯   Warning

Very few commands in Cubase Sx alter the physical file on disk: *Minimize File* is one such command. In other words, *Minimize File* changes your file irretrievably. You have been warned.

Tip

Consider *File/Save Project to new folder* [No Default] as an alternative to *Minimize File*. This function has options to *Minimize Audio Files, Freeze Edits* and to *Remove Unused Files* and, effectively creates a backup by leaving the original Project untouched.

This function is used to reduce the amount of space that audio files take up on disk. It is performed on a Clip with *Pool/Minimize File* [No Default]. It works by taking only those sections of a Clip that have Events, and creating a single new audio file containing only the audio for the Events. *It then overwrites the original file*; so, a backup is in order before using it. The resulting Events and Clip appear unchanged in the Project, it is only the audio file that is edited. If you have applied any off-line processing, then these are frozen to the audio file too. Insert effects, etc. are not applied.

You can run into a problem when you have more than one Clip referencing the same audio file (e.g. if you have applied an off-line process with *New Version*). In this case, *Minimize File* will not be available in the menus.

For example, you may have a vocal take made from start to finish of a song. But the take only includes the verses as useful audio, with a lot of silence in between. Providing you have created Events for all the sections of the Clip you require, then performing a Minimize File will release the disk space for those parts that you don't want.

Minimize File

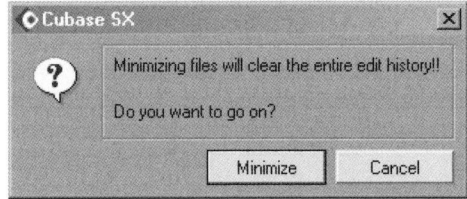

⚡ **Warning**

Be especially careful, since Minimize File clears the entire edit history. Not just the off-line process history for the Clip, but the whole *Edit History* page 220. And, once you press the *Minimize* button, the change is irreversible – the audio file has been changed.

Audio Processing Clips and Freeze Edit

♪ **Note**

The *Audio/Off-line process history* [No Default] for each Clip is also available from the Pool, allowing you to back-out the processing applied to Clips at anytime later.

Audio Processing is described in detail in chapter 16, page 219. While it is more common to process Events in the *Event Display*, there are times when it is convenient to do so in *The Pool*. The method is the same as for Events; simply select the Clip(s) that you wish to process and follow the preview and process method that Cubase S$_X$ uses.

Audio/Freeze Edits [No Default] gives you the option to either replace the existing file, or to create a new audio file with a file containing all of the processing applied to the Clip. Note that this process cannot be undone. (What happens is that the Edit file overwrites the original file in the Audio folder.) If a Clip has multiple versions, then the replace option is not available, and you will only be able to create a new file.

Pool Operations Involving Events

Adding Events to a Track from the Pool

Drag and drop
You can add Events to a Track by dragging and dropping a Clip (or Region) from the Pool onto the Track at the appropriate position. If active, then Snap will be applied. This creates a shared copy of the Event.

Insert into Project Command
You can also use *Pool/Insert into Project* [No Default]. When using this option to insert an Event, the Clip's *Snap Point* and the chosen insertion point will be aligned. By default, a Clip's *Snap Point* is positioned at the very start of a Clip, but this can be moved to a more useful or convenient point in the *Sample Editor*.

    If a audio Track is selected in the Track List, then the Clip is inserted on that Track. If an audio Track is not selected, then a new Track will be created at the bottom of the Project.

After you have selected a Clip (or Clips) and selected this command, you have three options:

- *At Cursor:* The Clip (or Clips) will be inserted where the Cursor is currently positioned.
- *At Origin:* The Clip (or Clips) will be inserted at the position shown in the *Origin Time* field for the Clip.
- *At Position: (Key Command only.)* Selecting this option will display a dialogue with a *Position* edit field. The format of *Position* will depend on the Ruler's *Display Format*. This value can be edited, and the Clip (or Clips) will be inserted at this point.

> ✗ **Tip**
>
> If you drag a Clip onto the empty space at the bottom of the Event Display, then a new Track will automatically be created when you release the mouse-button.

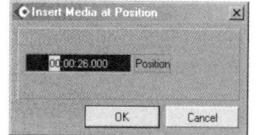

Insert at Position

Locating Events that reference a Clip

It can often be quite tricky to spot all occurrences of a frequently used Clip in the Event Display. *Pool/Select in Project* [No Default] highlights, by selection, all Events in the Project that are used by a Clip.

Finding a Clip in the Pool from an Event or Events

This is almost the reverse of the above. Select the relevant Events and then *Audio/Find Selected in Pool* [CTRL+F]. The Pool will open and the appropriate Clips will be highlighted.

Creating a Duplicate Clip from an Event (or Creating a non-shared Event)

If you want a unique copy of a shared Event (in other words, you want a duplicate Clip to be created), then apply *Edit/(Convert) To Real Copy* [No Default] to the copy of the Event for which you wish to create a new Clip.

Note that while a new Clip has been created, a new file has not. You can now process Events for each Clip independently of each other. This is, of course, a much more efficient use of file space than duplicating the file. If you need to create a new file, then use the *Audio/Freeze Edits* [No Default].

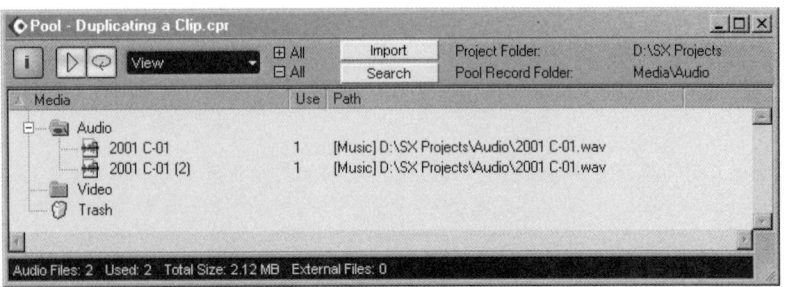

Duplicate Clip

Bounce Selection (New audio file and Clip)

Another method for creating a new file from an Event (Events or Regions) is to perform an *Audio/Bounce Selection* [No Default]. This will also work on a Range selection. You are given two options, as shown.

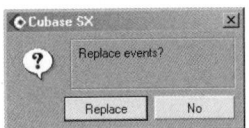

Bounce or replace?

Replace will create a new audio file and a new Clip, and the Event is altered to point to the new Clip. The original Clip remains in the Pool even if it is not now referenced. The *No* option will create a new file and a new Clip, but no changes are made to any Events.

When using *Bounce Selection* on an audio *Part*, the audio from all Events in the Part will be merged into a single audio file from which a new Clip is created. If you choose *Replace*, the Part will be replaced with a single Audio Event using the new Clip. The *No* option will just create the new file and new Clip.

Stop Press – Advanced Clip Tips

The term *shared*, when applied to audio Events, is a little dubious. The only thing that is shared is the underlying Clip. Every other property of the Event is unique to the Event. The only thing that the tiny graphic indicator tells you is that you will be asked to create a *New version* (a new Clip, in fact), if you process the Event. It would perhaps be better if Sx asked you this question, even if the Event were not "shared", since you might want to use the original Clip later. However, by then it might be too late, since you've already heavily processed the Clip.

The problem then is: How do I create a Clip, pointing to the original audio file, that doesn't contain any processing?

If you create *Pool/New Version*, then the new Clip contains the processing, but without the OPH. What you can do is re-import the audio file (the file itself is not copied, since it is already in the Pool). This will create a new Clip, without the processing. You will lose any Regions from the processed version, however.

16 Audio: Processing and Effects

Audio processing, and the ability to be able to back it out at any time later, is a key component of the sense of freedom you soon come to take for granted when using Cubase Sx. The unlimited, context-sensitive Undo feature is almost worth the price of entry alone. But it is the creative freedom that this one, seemingly small, function brings that is the main benefit. Undo, and its opposite Redo, are not simply about being able to back out mistakes and errors, handy though these are from time to time, they are also about the creative freedom that they bring. There is never any excuse not to experiment with your work when you know that you can retrieve everything that went before.

Undo, Edit History and the Off-line Process History

Cubase Sx has a very complete *Undo* [CTRL+Z] feature. Almost any sequence of actions, or processes, can be reversed. And Undo itself can be reversed by *Redo* [CTRL+SHIFT+Z]. Furthermore the Undo feature is context sensitive; meaning that when you have the Sample Editor open (and in focus) for an Event, then performing Undo will reverse the last action applied to that Event (providing there is one) and not another more recently performed action in the Project.

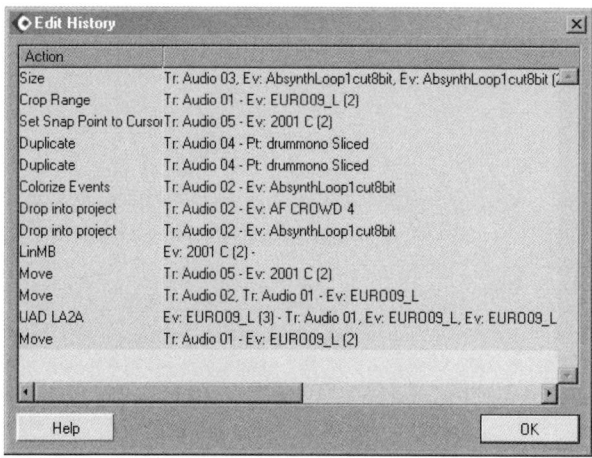

Fig. 16.1: The Project Level Edit History

The number of levels of Undo available can be changed from the infinite number default in *Preferences/User Interface* tab *Maximum Undo*.

The *Edit History* (the list of operations that can be undone by *Undo* can be viewed via *Edit/History* [No Default]. The last action is at the *top*. From here you can click on the list and undo multiple actions in a single step (you can drag the dividing line up and down also). In the diagram, the top, dark half shows a number of actions that have been undone. When you exit, the stack is still available via the key commands.

Take care when scrolling through the list if you have done any large off-line processes. These may take some time to action.

✗⁷   **Tip**

If you are unsure of the action that will be performed by Undo or Redo, then you can perform a quick check by clicking on the Edit menu. Next to the Undo and Redo entries, on the dropdown, are the actions that will be performed if selected. Alternatively assign a Key Command to *Edit/History* [No Default] and close with Esc.

Non-destructive audio processing

One of the reasons that Cubase Sx can provide such an extensive Undo feature is in the way that non-destructive editing has been implemented for audio. The way Cubase Sx manages changes to audio is by creating new sections of audio where processing occurs, leaving the original audio file untouched, and recording these changes in the Clip. On playback, Cubase Sx seamlessly places the new sections in the appropriate places. In fact, even if you process an entire Clip, the original audio file is still there on disk, unadulterated and ready for use in its original form.

Off-line Process History – for audio

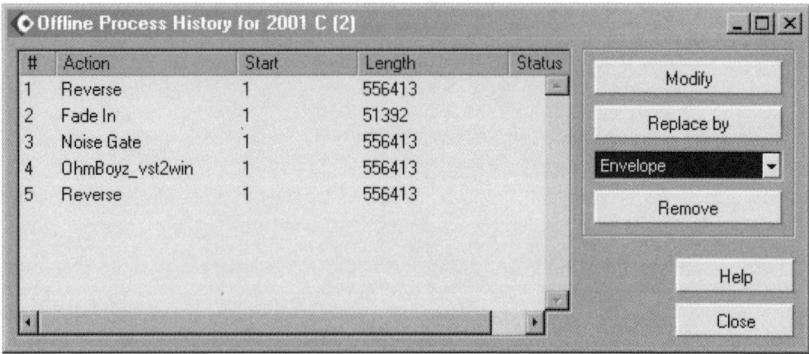

Off-line Process History

The *Audio/Open (Off-line) Process History* [No Default] (OPH) gives you access to all the processing applied to a Clip. This is an important point: when you select an *Event*, it is the OPH for the *Clip* that is shown, not the *Event*. There may well be processing listed in the OPH that is not applicable to the selected Event.

From the OPH dialog you can edit any of the processes that have already be applied to a Clip. They can be modified, removed, or replaced with another process. Furthermore you can replace processes anywhere in the Process History chain; although you need to start thinking about the implications of doing so. But "happy accidents" are all part of making music, right?

There are a couple of restrictions in what can be changed in the OPH.

○ Processes that have no parameters cannot be modified; they can only be removed (e.g. Reverse).
○ Where a process changes the length of a *Clip* (e.g. Time Stretch), then this process can only be removed. And it can only be removed when it is the last operation in the OPH list. There are icons in the Status column to indicate this, and by the function buttons being disabled (see image below).

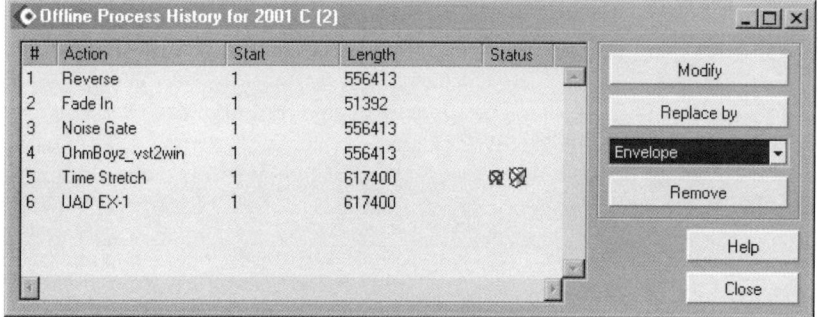

Remove only process

When you modify, or replace, a process in the OPH, what happens first is that the Clip is rebuilt to the point before the process being modified/removed takes place. Then all the processes are performed again. If the areas of the Clip being processed are large, and there has been a large amount of processing on it, then this could take some time.

The processing is applied to the Clip in a non-destructive way, but that might mean that a new Clip needs to be created when other Events share the Clip. When you do this, you will "lose" access to the original Clip's OPH, since the new Event will point to a new Clip. An example will hopefully make this clearer.

Example

Starting with a Clip that has not had any processing applied to it, we can create an Event and perform some processes on it. These will modify (non-destructively) the underlying Clip. Note that we can quite easily remove, modify or replace any of these processes from the dialog shown (over).

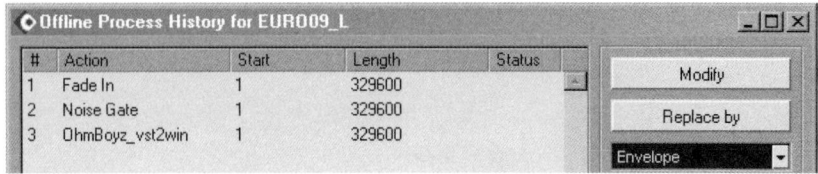

Example

Next, we create another Event that uses the same Clip. Using the Range Selection tool, we can now select a portion of the new Event and apply *Audio/Process... /Reverse*. We are then presented with the dialog that, in reality, is asking whether we want to create a new Clip (and thus make our Event unique to the new Clip) or process the existing shared Clip. If we choose *Continue*, then both Events will continue to be windows on the existing Clip, and both Events might well be affected by the change should they use the region that we have just reversed.

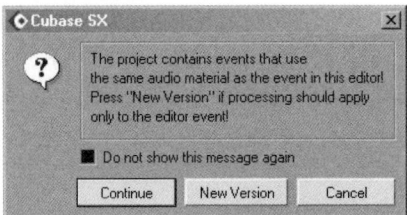

Create a new Clip?

If we click *New Version*, then a new Clip is created. But what does this new Clip contain? And what does its OPH look like?

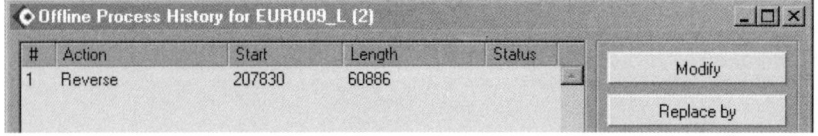

The Aftermath

Like that. Notice that the three processes applied to the original Clip are not present in the new OPH. However, the audio for the new Clip will indeed have had these processes applied, because the new Clip was created from the original Clip. That is the basis for the Clip, and even if we remove a process from the original Clip, it will not affect the new Clip. The new Clip is out there on its own, although it still "points to" the same audio file as the original Clip.

That example can be a bit confusing unless you have fully understood Clips, Events and audio files.

Freezing a Clip's OPH processes to an audio file

⚡   Warning

The results of this process are written to audio files. You can lose original files if you are not careful.

Audio/Freeze Edits [No Default] is used when you want to make the processes that appear in the Off-line Process History permanent for a Clip. It does this by *overwriting* the underlying audio file, or creating a new version of the audio file to which the new Clip will then be redirected.

When there is only a single Clip that references the underlying audio file, the window shown opens:

Replace audio file?

Replace **will overwrite the existing audio file. There is no Undo available after you click Replace.** *New File* will create a new version and the Clip will be altered to point to the new file. The original audio remains unchanged.

When more than one Clip refers to the same audio file you will get:

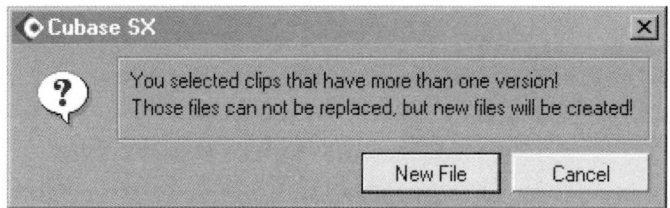

New file or nothing?

What this is trying to say is that the underlying audio file is used by more than one Clip. To freeze edits to this file will, most likely, lead to unexpected results. Therefore you only get the option to create a new audio file; to which the edits are frozen.

Audio plug-ins (Effects)

Managing plug-ins

Cubase Sx supports both VST and DirectX plug-in formats.

DirectX plug-ins
Each DirectX plug-in is supplied with its own installation process. Providing that this is successful, then the plug-in will be available to Cubase Sx. Steinberg recommends that DirectX plug-ins are not installed in the *vstplugins* folder.

VST plug-ins
There are two folder hierarchies available to Cubase Sx in which VST plug-ins can be installed: one will be under the directory in which you installed Cubase Sx; the other (the *Shared VST Plug-ins folder*) can be found, and changed, on

♪   *Note*

You can choose whether or not to pass keystrokes to a plug-in by setting *Preferences/Editing* tab *Plug-ins receive key commands*.

the *VST Plug-ins* tab on the *Devices/Plug-in Information* [No Default] window. Both usually have the name: *vstplugins*.

Cubase Sx should be the only program to use the *vstplugins* folder in the Cubase Sx hierarchy. Cubase Sx is supplied with plug-ins that cannot be used by other programs and so these should be kept separate to avoid errors in other applications. A list of the supplied plug-ins that can only be used with Cubase Sx is given in Appendix A, page 315.

Within either *vstplugins* folder, you can create sub folders named to reflect the use of the plug-ins they contain. The VST plug-ins (not the DirectX plug-ins that must remain where they were installed) can then be moved to these folders. The folders will appear in the selection menus.

Plug-in Information Window

Selecting *Devices/Plug-in Information* [No Default] opens the following information window:

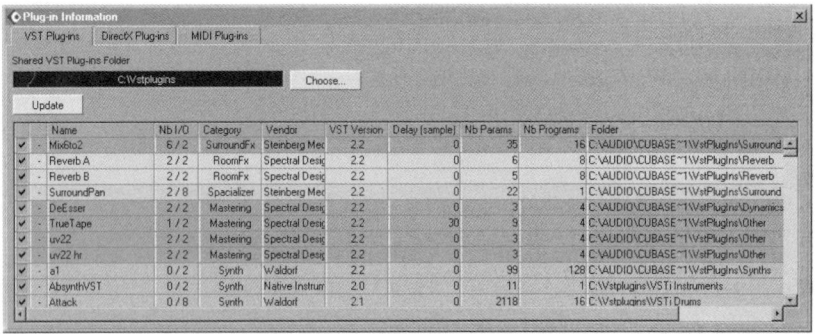

Plug-in Information Window

There are three tabs on this window: one for managing VST plug-ins; one for DirectX plug-ins; and another for MIDI plug-ins. Plug-ins can be removed from each of the selection lists by unchecking the tick-box in the left-hand column.

Columns of interest for VST plug-ins are:

○ *Nb I/O (Number of Inputs and Outputs)*
This is useful information should you not be sure whether a plug-in is mono or stereo

○ *VST Version*
Certain features (such as tempo sync and automation) only became available with particular versions, so this can confirm whether of not you can expect certain behavior from a plug-in.

○ *Delay (sample)* The delay, in samples, introduced, by the plug-in. It is very important to understand that delay compensation is applied for insert effects, but not for Send and Group effects. These delays can have significant impact on you audio. See chapter 20, page 281 for more on *Latency*.

Changing the shared plug-ins folder

In the unlikely event that you need to change your vstplugins folder, you can do so here. Cubase Sx will need to be restarted for the change to take affect.

♫   Note

The Delay figure shown for VST plug-ins should be updated when you require accurate figures (e.g. for latency calculations). The value is dependent on the soundcard buffer size and is not automatically recalculated every time you change the buffer size.

Bouncing a plug-in effect

Real-time effects for a Track, whether VST or DirectX, are loaded in *Channel Settings* or the *Inspector* (See chapter 17, page 231), and the parameters for these can be controlled via automation. From time-to-time you may wish to bounce an Event, Part or Track with the effect (or effects) that have been applied to it. One use for this is to release processing resources, but it is also good housekeeping. Certain processing you will want to retain until mixdown, but many effects can be applied prior to this. Remember that you can always remove the processing should you wish. So, while it might feel like you are making a permanent change, you're actually not doing so.

You can apply a plug-in to a Clip, or any number of audio Events and Parts. To do so:

1. Select the appropriate Events and Parts
2. Select a plug-in from Audio/Plug-ins (or the quick menu)
3. Preview and adjust the plug-in to taste
4. Press *Process*

See the section below (*Cubase Sx Processes*) for guidance on any further dialogue windows that require action.

There are a few configuration options available by pressing the *More* button.

o *Wet mix/Dry mix:* These allow you to make the usual wet/dry balance. They are reverse ganged, but can be moved independently by pressing ALT.
o *Tail:* Adds a tail (of 1 ms to 10 seconds) to the selection length to allow reverb tails, delay decays, etc. to be captured in the bounced result. It is active in Preview to permit auditioning.
o *Pre/Post Crossfade:* Creates crossfades (of 1ms to 10 seconds) for the effect level at the start and the end of the effect.

When you load a plug-in, in preparation for applying it to an Event, the settings of the plug-in will be those last used. If you you wish to reset the settings to the plug-in's default, then hold ALT when you load the plug-in.

SL   *SL Info*

Bouncing VST and DirectX effects, as described here, is not available in SL. SL users will have to use *File/Export/Audio Mixdown* [No Default] instead; in the same way that VSTi's must be bounced for both Sx and SL users.

↗   *Tip*

It is often useful to save the settings for an effect when you apply it.

Cubase S$_X$ Processes

⤢   *Tip*

To apply a *Process* to a
Region, select it as a
Range in the Sample
Editor.

The *Audio/Process* submenu contains fourteen audio processing functions. The functions can be applied to Clips, audio Events, or an audio Range Selection. Processes cannot be used in real-time, they can only be applied, or bounced, to the audio object in question.

When you Process an Event that shares a Clip (even if the two Events don't overlap), then the window shown will open, initiating a process that is important to understand.

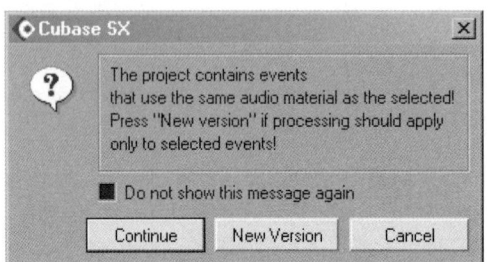

New version?

Okay, so the message is poorly worded, but what actually occurs is quite neat.

If you click *Continue*, then the underlying Clip is retained and so all Events that use it will be affected. Remember that an Event is just a window onto a Clip, so even if the audio being processed is not actually used by another Event, if you extend the Event's boundaries, then it could do so.

If you click *New Version*, then a new Clip is created in the Pool and the Event being processed will be changed to point to the new Clip. *It is important to note that the new Clip still points to the same audio file as before.*

The window discussed above is the window affected by the *Preferences/Audio* tab option *On Processing Shared Clips*. If you check the *Do not show this message again box*, then the value in *Preferences* will be changed to reflect the button you click for *all* future shared Clip messages. The default is to *Open Options Dialog*, and it is recommended that you leave this setting on this value.

Bouncing a Process

It couldn't be simpler. Select the Region, Event, or Clip to be processed and select the function you require from *Audio/Process...*

Some of the Processes will take place immediately (other than asking for the action to be taken for shared Clips – see above). These are:

○ Remove DC Offset
○ Reverse
○ Silence

The remaining eleven Processes will provide you with an options screen applicable to the process selected, but also with a number of general options. The window shown has had the *More* button clicked to show all the available options.

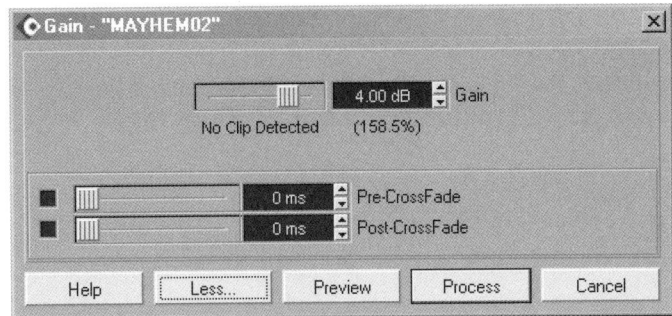

You want more?

o *Preview:* will just play the selection endlessly with the Process applied for evaluation purposes. Settings can be changed during Preview, and will apply on the next cycle.

o *Process:* will apply the selected Process.

o *Pre/Post Crossfade:* allow you to mix the Process in and out. The processing will be applied in a Dry to Wet manner over the duration of the Pre-Crossfade value. And the same in reverse: Wet to Dry, for the Post-Crossfade value. Clearly, the sum of the two values cannot be longer than the audio selected.

The Processes

There are fourteen audio process functions available in Cubase Sχ. You might find it easier to select these functions from the main menus, rather than the right-click quick-menus. Key commands can be set for all of the Processes. There is also the *Audio/Detect Silence* function that is not on this list, but which will be described below.

Envelope
Fade In
Fade Out
Gain
Merge Clipboard
Noise Gate
Normalize
Phase Reverse
Pitch Shift
Remove DC Offset
Reverse
Silence
Stereo Flip
Time Stretch

Envelope

Applies a level envelope to the selected audio. The envelope is highly configurable (much more so than the traditional ADSR (attack, decay, sustain, release) envelope. Presets can be stored.

Envelope can be used for detailed level manipulation, especially where it would be overly complex to achieve the same end by using automation.

Fade In and Fade Out

These processes are similar to *Envelope*, but with a few predefined curves available. Useful for rapidly applying fades. (Also see chapter 14, page 192.) Presets can be stored.

Gain

Applies gain and attenuation. Range is ∞dB to +20dB. There is a Clip indicator. To achieve 0dB maximum level in the selected audio, use the *Normalize* process with a 0dB maximum setting.

Merge Clipboard

This process merges audio placed in the Clipboard (copied or cut from the *Sample Editor*) into the selected audio. The dialog allows you to mix the relative levels of the two signals. The merge start point is the start point of both signals.

Noise Gate

A traditional noise gate where levels in the audio below the supplied threshold are replaced with silence. Attack, release and minimum opening time parameters are available for the gate.

Normalize

Normalize will raise (or lower) the maximum level in the selected audio *to* (rather than *by*) a chosen level. If you apply gain, then be aware that you are also raising the noise floor. Choose carefully whether you really need to "normalize" audio. If you later apply fader movements to the audio, then you will have processed your audio unnecessarily. It is much better to achieve the required levels when recording. *Normalize* should carry a government audio health warning.

Phase Reverse

Does exactly what it says on the tin. A nice touch is that you can reverse the left and right channels individually with a stereo Clip.

Pitch Shift

This is quite a complex pitch-shifting process (and has an interface designed to bamboozle). The idea is to adjust the pitch of the audio while retaining length. (The alternative being time-stretching, which retains pitch but changes length – see below). There are two independent processes here:

Single-pitch shift (Settings tab)

This process will transpose the audio by a given number of semitones (maximum 16 either up or down) and cents. You can also create "harmonies" or multiple pitch-shifts in a single pass from the source audio.

Envelope pitch-shift (Envelope tab)

Here the pitch offset (pitch-bend) is determined by drawing an envelope. The pitch range of the envelope can be adjusted.

In both cases there is formant preservation available, and there are a variety of quality settings. In most cases you will want to use the highest quality MPEX Algorithm when processing audio.

Overall, it is probably best to treat the Cubase S$_X$ *Pitch Shift* as a creative tool, rather than a retrieval tool. While it can produce interesting results, they are not the most accurate available.

Remove DC Offset

A DC offset occurs when the direct current component of an audio recording is too large. This results in the audio not being centered on 0dB. This will not affect the resulting sound from the audio, but it can affect audio manipulation processes, in particular, zero crossing detection. Because of this, you may wish to remove any DC offset occurring. When doing so, it is simplest to apply the process at the Clip level.

You can find the DC Offset for a selection of audio by using the *Audio/Statistics* [No Default] function.

If you frequently experience large DC offsets in your recordings, then you should investigate misalignments in your recording equipment, since this is the likely cause.

Reverse
Reverses the selected audio.

Silence
Replaces the selected audio with silence.

Stereo Flip
Works on Stereo audio only. This process allows you to:

- Swap left and right channels
- Copy the left channel to the right (or right to left)
- Merge (creates 2-channel mono)
- Subtracts the left channel from the right, and the right channel from the left, which results in any mono, centered sounds being removed from the audio.

Time Stretch
Time Stretch is a very useful, and effective, process that stretches while preserving pitch. You can easily change an audio snippet by known tempo to required tempo; from known sample length to required sample length; from known length in time to required length in time; and so on.

However, the most useful function is the *Set to Locators Range* button. If you have an audio Event that you wish to stretch (or shrink) to fill a section of a song:

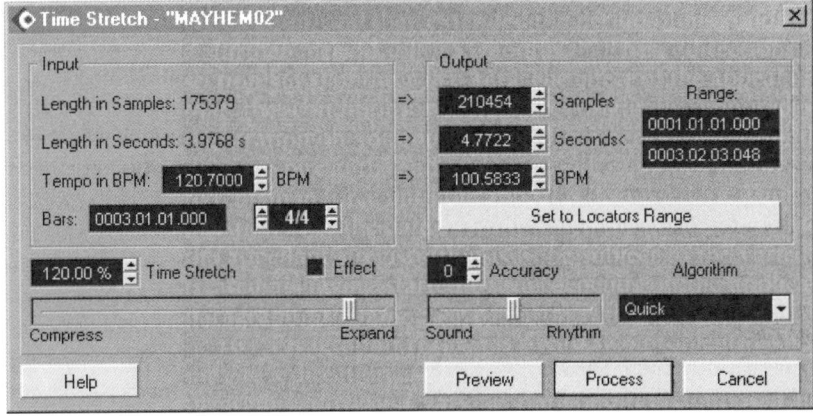

Fig. 16.2: Time Stretch

○ Select the Event
○ Open *Time Stretch*
○ Click *Set to Locators Range.*
   You may have to check the Effect box if the stretch is greater than 125% (or less than 75%)
○ Click *Process*
   Ensure that you select the appropriate Accuracy and Quality settings for your audio.
○ The Event will now fill the required time slot in the song.

Detect Silence

While not part of the Processing options *Audio/Detect Silence* [No Default] bears enough similarities to a *Process* to reside here. Detect Silence either creates discrete Events or Regions from the selected audio, discarding silence (which is defined by the parameter settings of the plug-in). It's an off-line gate, in effect.

When the audio is above the *Open Threshold* value, then this is considered non-silence. The audio must then drop below *Close Threshold* to be considered silence. These two values therefore will determine a resulting Event. *Min. Opening Time* sets the shortest length of a non-silent part. *Min. Closed Time* species the smallest gap (or silence) between Events.

Pre-roll will start the Event before the *Open Threshold* is met, so that you can preserve attacks. *Post-roll* is the same, but for the *Close Threshold*; it helps to preserve decay.

Preview the result by pressing *Compute* then *Preview*. An image of the result is drawn. One of *Add as Regions* or *Strip Silence* must be ticked.

> ✗   *Tip*
>
> *Detect Silence* can do great things with rhythmic loops, especially drums. The benefit is not necessarily apparent when the loop is played on its own, but really shines in the mix.

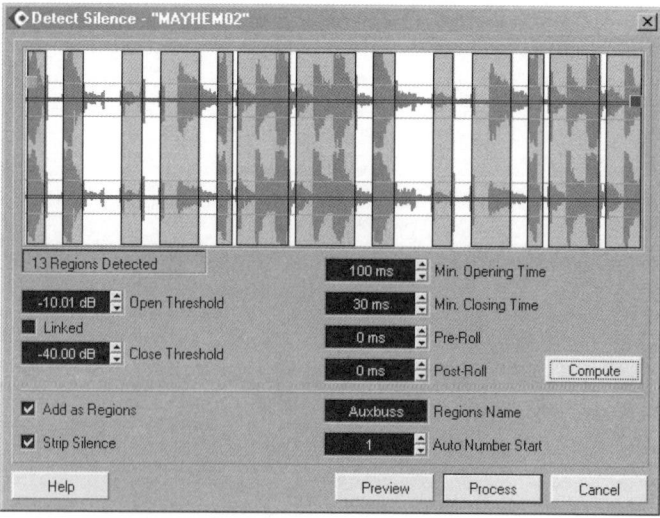

Fig. 16.3: Detect Silence

17 Mixing and Audio Control

Mixing is a subject of infinite complexity. The seemingly simple process of bringing all of the audio in a Project together and creating the final product is, in practice, a lot trickier than it appears. Voluminous tomes have been written on the subject, and much mystique and magic surrounds many of its techniques and protagonists. However, the *art* of mixing is not what we are about here. Cubase SX is but a tool in the process, albeit one that can smooth the path in all manner of ways.

Most folk will mix entirely within Cubase SX, producing a 2-Track master by way of the Audio Mixdown facility. However, with appropriate equipment, it is quite simple to mix externally, with Cubase SX acting as a digital "tape machine".

Routing Audio

To best use the tools available for mixing in Cubase SX it is necessary to understand the way that audio flows, or routes, through it from Track to output port. MIDI routing in considered separately (see chapter 13, page 151).

Main routing path

Here are the basic routings:

○ Each Track (audio, Group, Rewire or VSTi) is associated with a *Track Mixer* [F3] Channel .
○ Each Channel routes to a *VST Output Bus* [F4], or a *Group* Channel.
○ Each *Output Bus* connects to a physical port on a soundcard.

> ♫ **Note**
> MIDI sound sources (except VSTi's) are generally best recorded as audio if you wish to mix them.

One of the *Output Buses* is called the *Master Bus*. The *Master Bus* is fixed as the leftmost bus shown in the *VST Outputs* window, however it can be routed to any available physical output port. It is not a requirement to route anything through the *Master Bus* (but remember that many of Cubase SX's audition functions use the *Master Bus*). If you wish to mix externally, then you may well decide not to use the *Master Bus* for mixing. However, if you mix within Cubase SX, then it is the *Master Bus* that will be recorded when using *File/Export Audio Mixdown* [No Default].

As you can see, Cubase SX's basic routing is simple, yet effective. There is, however, a routing restriction that occurs in the *Track Mixer* worth noting: when routing a Group Channel to another Group Channel, it can only be routed to a Group Channel to its right (in the Track Mixer), or below it (in the Track List).

Channel effects routing

Each Channel can feed any of the eight *auxiliary buses*. Steinberg call these *Send Buses*, *Send Channels* or *Sends*, but this can be confusing since there are both *Send Buses* and *Send Effects*. I'll use the term *Send Bus* to distinguish it from an effect. By default the *Send Buses* are routed to the *Send Effects*, but they can be routed elsewhere. Each *Send Bus* can be routed to a:

♪   Note

To check the number of input and out buses for a plug-in effect, take a look in *Devices/Plug-in Information* [No Default].

○ *Send Effect:* This is a *mono* send only. Stereo channels are summed to mono before being sent. The return is stereo (so, for example, a mono source can be auto-panned).

○ *Group:* A Group channel is always stereo. You can send a stereo channel to a stereo Group, or a mono channel to a Group's left or right channel. (See below for more on *Groups*.)

○ *VST Output Bus:* A stereo channel will route to a (physical) stereo output bus, and a mono channel to either the left or right channel of a physical output bus. (See below for more on *VST Output buses*.)

○ *Left or Right Master Bus:* In these cases, a stereo channel will be summed to mono before being sent. A mono channel is routed unchanged.

Send Effect Bus routing

There are eight *VST Send Effects* [F6] slots available. These are available to *every* non-MIDI Channel in the Project. They are mono input and stereo output. Each Send Effect can be routed to a physical *Output Bus*. (A level control is available for each effect slot, and each effect can be individually defeated.)

Insert Effect Bus routing

S_L SL Info

Only five Insert slots are available in S_L.

Each Channel can route through up to eight *Insert Buses*. For stereo channels the Insert buses are stereo. If, however, the Insert effect has a *mono* input, then *only the left-hand channel* is passed to the effect for processing, and only the left-hand channel is returned. The right-hand channel is passed through unchanged.

    On mono channels the Insert bus is mono. For a mono input to stereo output plug-in (try the supplied *Autopan* plug-in), S_X will only take the left channel from the Insert effect's output; the right channel is discarded. For a stereo-to-stereo effect, both inputs are supplied equally, but only the left channel from the Insert effect's output is returned; the right channel is discarded.

S_L SL Info

Only four Master bus slots and one post-Master gain slot are available in S_L.

Master Bus Effects routing

The Master Bus has eight Insert effects slots; the first six are pre-fader, the last two post-fader.

Groups (or Group Channels)

Groups are created by *Add Track/Group Channel* [No Default] and appear in the *Track List* and *Track Mixer*. Groups are useful for sub-mixes and as *effects racks*. For example, if you have a number of vocal tracks that you wish to apply the same effects to (e.g. compression, EQ, reverb, etc.), then it is both simpler, and less processor intensive, to route all the appropriate vocal channels to a Group containing the effects. The balance of the sub-mix can still be changed from the original channels, but now it can be adjusted as one also.

If you *solo* a Track that is routed to a Group, then the Group is soloed also. This is not the case when a Track is *muted*. This makes sense, since other Tracks might be routed to the Group, and you want to listen to them. However, if you solo or mute a Group, then all Tracks routed to the Group are soloed and muted.

> ♫ **Note**
>
> A Group can be Muted and Soloed, but only from the *Inspector* [ALT+I] or *Track Mixer* [F3]; strangely the *Mute* [M] and *Solo* [S] key commands do not work from the Project Window.

Routing Send Channels to Groups

As an alternative to using *Send Effects*, consider placing each effect on a Group channel and using the *Send Buses* in the same manner as you would for *Send Effects*. In this set-up, the Group fader becomes, in effect, the wet/dry mix control.

Using Groups affords a greater degree of flexibility than using *Send Effects*. For one, you can route the Group to a further Group, and not just to a VST Output as with a *Send Effect*. You can also have multiple effects in the Group channel, creating a virtual effects rack.

> ♫ **Note**
>
> The *Mute* button on a Group Track's *Track List* entry is for muting automation.

Here are some of the benefits:

○ The most obvious advantage is that effects can be *chained* (as Insert effects) in a Group (This cannot be achieved with the current Send Effects routing in Cubase Sx.)
○ The Group fader, EQ, solo and mute switches can be used creatively.
○ The Group can be automated.
○ Send Effects are mono in only. Groups are stereo, and so are the Insert buses.

One final point: if you use this method, and Solo your Channel, then the Group will be muted. To circumvent this, remember to ALT+click the Group's Solo button to defeat solo.

> ☿ **Info**
>
> There will be latency associated with the Group Channel (the same as there is for the Send Channels, but not for Inserts) and you may need to take measures to tackle this (see chapter 20, page 281).

VST Output buses (F4)

Each *VST Output Bus* [F4] is associated with a physical output on your sound-card, and each can be adjusted individually for level. Stereo fader pairs can be unlocked (with the on/off toggle immediately above the faders), and left and right channels given different gain settings. This can also be done by holding ALT and moving a fader when the fader pair is locked.

The total number of output buses available is dependent on your soundcard. The *Master Bus* (far left) is always active, but the other outputs must be acti-vated for use with the on/off toggle at top of each bus. Default physical outputs are assigned to the buses, but these can be changed in the dropdown selector at the bottom of each channel strip. You cannot route two buses to the same physical output. *VST Outputs* are automated via the *Add Track/Master Automa-tion* [No Default] Track.

VST Outputs

The Track Mixer

The *Devices/Track Mixer* [F3] is the hub of the mixing world in Cubase Sx. This is where you can adjust levels, EQ, panning, apply effects, etc. Every audio, MIDI, and Group Track in the Project Window will have a channel strip that is uniquely associated with it in the *Track Mixer*. And for each loaded VSTi and Rewire application, a channel will be created for each active output. There is no practical limit to the number of audio channels available. Channels are always displayed in the Track Mixer in the following order: (a) Audio and MIDI (ordered as in the Track List, (b) Rewire, (c) VSTi's, (d) Groups.

There are, in fact, two Track Mixers available; the other is *Devices/Track Mixer 2* [No Default]. Since the Track Mixer is configurable, it is well-worth creating a key command for it. If you don't use *Devices/Video* [F8] very often then you might consider reassigning the [F8] key.

While the Track Mixer is an excellent place to manipulate channels, there are very few functions provided here that cannot be performed from the Inspector.

Figure 17.1 shows the basic *Track Mixer*. There are three distinct sections to the mixer.

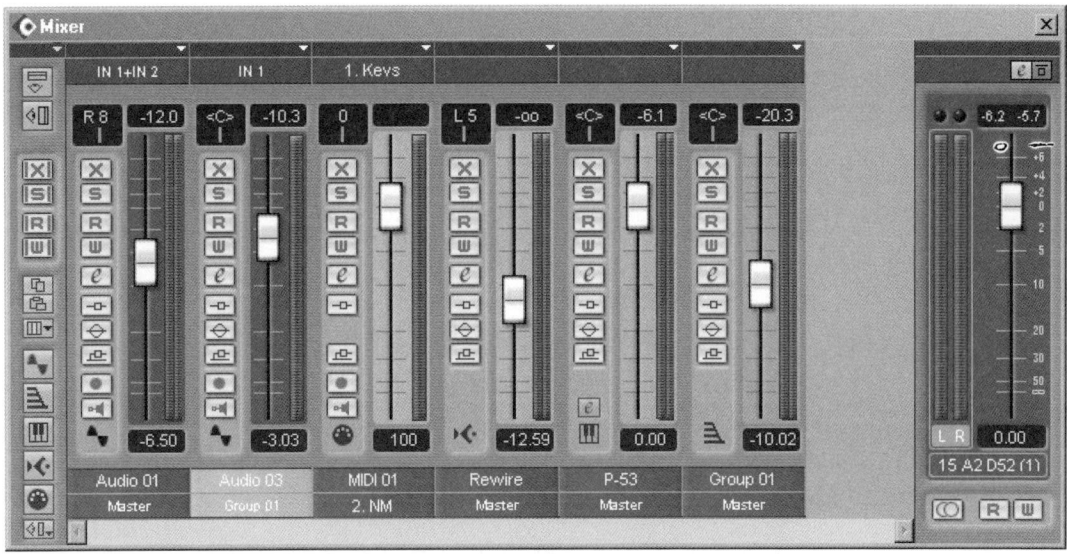

Fig. 17.1: The Track Mixer

- The *Common Panel* – the column of buttons far left
- The *Master Channel* – to the far right (activated in the *Common Panel*)
- The *Channel Strips* – with a single fader each

By clicking the top-left button in the *Common Panel* you can open the mixer's extended view. The extended view provides an additional strip of controls above each channel strip. Each channel can be individually configured to display either the insert, EQ (not MIDI) or send settings for each channel. Selection is made via the dropdown between the normal Track Mixer and the extended view.

Track Mixer configuration

As well as the extended view, noted above, there are a number of useful configuration features available to both Track Mixers. Some of these are described below in the *Common Panel* section.

The list shown in the margin is from the dropdown above the *Common Panel*. As well as being able to switch between normal and expanded views, it allows you to view all *visible* channels in their wide or narrow forms. This will permanently override the channel's own setting.

In the lower section are toggles than allow you to hide individual channel *types* (e.g. audio, MIDI, etc.) from view. These toggles are the same as the *Common Panel* buttons. The *hideable* option allows you to hide all channels set to *hideable* in their dropdown.

You can save *Channel View Sets* by clicking the button right at the bottom of the *Common Panel*. These sets save the narrow/wide, extended view and

Master Channel toggle

Extended view

S$_L$ *SL Info*

The extended view is not available in S$_L$.

Common Panel dropdown

hideable settings for each channel. Also saved are the hide/view channel type toggles and the Master Channel toggle. The sets are saved with the Project. (Try using *Channel View Sets* to view, say, used VSTi channels only. Perhaps save a default *View All (Wide)*.)

    If you right-click on the Track Mixer you will find that there are more options for saving mixer settings (including Insert, Sends and VSTi's). These are described later in this chapter (see page 244 onward).

Common Panel

Top to bottom, on the Common Panel we have:

- ○ *Extended view* toggle (see above)
- ○ *Master Channel* toggle (see page 236)
- ○ Mute: all off
- ○ Solo: all off
- ○ *Global automation switches* (see page 259)
- ○ Copy selected Channel's settings (see page 245)
- ○ Paste selected Channel's settings (see page 245)
- ○ Channel select dropdown
- ○ Channel-type toggles for audio, Group, VSTi, Rewire and MIDI (see above).
- ○ *Channel View Sets* dropdown (see above)

The main items of interest here (that are not covered elsewhere) are the global mute and solo buttons, and the Channel select. Switching off *all* muted or soloed Tracks can often be a lot quicker than doing so by hand; these are the buttons for those tasks. A quick [F3] and click does the job.

The Common Panel

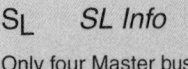

S_L *SL Info*

Only four Master bus slots, and one post Master gain slot, are available in S_L.

The Master Channel and Master Effects (F7)

The *Master Channel* controls the behavior of the Master bus. This bus is used for many Cubase S_X audition functions and is also the bus used for *File/Export Audio Mixdown* [No Default]. *Master effects* are muted when auditioning, but you can switch them back on manually, if you wish.

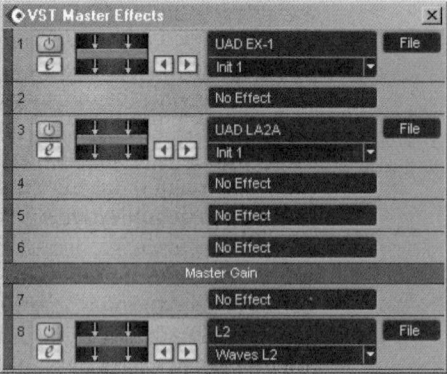

Master effects

There are eight *Master Channel Effects* [F7] slots – six are pre-Master Fader, and the final two are post-Master Fader. Take care when using mono input effects in the *Master Effects* chain, since no warning is given if you do this.

You can bypass all *Master Effects* using the switch at the top of the Master Channel in the Track Mixer. Each effect also has an on/off switch in the Master effects rack.

The *Master Channel* is displayed by activating the *Show Master Channel* button on the Track Mixer. If the *Mono/Stereo* button is colored orange, then all output on the Master bus will be mono.

The numbering on the Master fader applies to the fader only; it shows a maximum of 6dB gain. The numbers *do not* apply to the meter. The meters will peak at 0B FS. The same is true for the Channel meters.

> ↗   *Tip*
>
> Dithering should always be applied post (after the) master-fader.

> ♪   *Note*
>
> The Master bus fader and Master Effect levels can be automated on the *Master Automation* Track.

> ♪   **Note**
>
> It is important that you avoid lighting the Master Channel Clip Indicator (and all other VST Output buses). While there is generally no problem in lighting the Channel clip lights (due to the enormous headroom provided by the internal 32-bit FP summing bus), this is not the case with the VST Outputs. Clipping these buses will almost always result in audible clipping, and that is rarely a desirable occurrence.

Channel Strip

An example of each of the channel-types is shown in the *Track Mixer* figure above. The buttons are the same as those used in the *Track List* and *Inspector*, and were described in chapter 6, page 45 onward.

The Group, Rewire and VSTi Channels are very similar to the audio Channel Strip, but they lack the input bus and record controls. The VSTi Channel gains a button to open the VSTi for editing. Audio and MIDI Tracks can have their input channels selected here.

> ☿   *Info*
>
> In general, dragging a control with SHIFT held will allow you to move the control in smaller/finer increments.

The Fader and Pan Controls

All channel-types have *Level* and *Pan* controls. The manner in which the *Fader* operates is determined by *Preferences/User Interface/Controls* tab *Slider Mode* (see chapter 5, page 41). The precise value of the *Fader* control is shown in the field below the fader as changes are made (and similarly above the *Pan* control). To reset either the *Fader* to 0dB, or *Pan* to center, use CTRL+click. You can get fine control of both handles by dragging while holding SHIFT.

Pan and velocity will only work on MIDI instruments configured to receive these MIDI messages. Most modern devices will respond.

> ↗   *Tip*
>
> Use the mouse-wheel to adjust faders, knobs and other controls. This works well for *Pan*, in particular.

Pan Law

The finer points of Pan Law are outside the scope of this book. Nevertheless, let's tackle the outline, since the principle is important when mixing. When a sound source is panned across the stereo field, so that its location apparently moves from, say, left to right, what in fact occurs is an increase in the audio signal from the right-hand speaker and a decrease in the left-hand speaker. The rate at which these levels change, as the fader is moved, is determined by the *Stereo Pan Law*.

The *Stereo Pan Law* is set in *Project Set-up* [SHIFT+S]. The three Pan Laws available in Cubase Sx are: 0dB, -3dB and -6dB. The figure represents the attenuation in a stereo audio signal, at both speakers, when the sound is positioned dead center for each particular Pan Law. So, for a Stereo Pan Law of -3dB we have:

	Left Channel	Right Channel
Pan hard-left	0dB	∞dB
Pan dead center	−3dB	−3dB
Pan hard-right	∞dB	0dB

The attenuation curves, however, are not linear. The -3dB Pan Law is ideal for stereo, but a problem occurs when summed to mono, as the dead-center position will now be 3dB above the hard-left and right positions. This can be removed by using the -6dB Pan Law, but then there is a -3dB drop dead center when in stereo. Some systems do provide a -4.5dB setting by way of compromise, but this is not available in Cubase Sx. The 0dB Pan Law is used by some for music making.

Level Meters and Clipping

On playback, the Level Meter will show the output level, unless either the Record or Monitor buttons are active. In these cases, the meter will show the monitored input level (for MIDI this is velocity). The maximum reading on each meter is 0dB FS.

Peak levels are displayed above the level meter. The peak value is held until the fader for that channel is moved. This is odd, since one would expect it to follow the *Preferences/VST* tab *VU-meter peak hold-time*.

The meters have a couple of options available to them, accessed by right-clicking on the *Track Mixer*:

○ *VU-meter fast:* which increase the meter's response time.
○ *VU-meter hold:* which creates peak indicators on the level meters. These are held for the amount of time set in *Preferences/VST* tab *VU-meter peak hold-time*.

A Channel Strip

For input signals, if the value rises to, or above, 0dB, then you should attenuate your input signal to avoid clipping.

For output signals, a 0dB reading is not a problem (providing you are not routing any of the clipping buses outside Cubase Sx). This applies to the audio, Rewire, VSTi and Group channels only, not to the Master Channel. Clipping the Master Channel is a serious problem. The reason for there being no problem is the 32-bit floating point bus that Cubase Sx uses. This provides a very large amount of headroom for the 16 and 24-bit (and 32-bit FP) audio. MIDI outputs can't clip.

Solo

Multiple Tracks can be soloed simultaneously. You can force a single Track to be soloed by using CTRL+click on its Solo button. This is handy when you have many Tracks soloed, and quickly want to get back to a single soloed Track. You can also clear all soloed Tracks with the *Deactivate all Solos* button in the *Common Panel* of the Track Mixer. If a Channel is routed to a Group, then the Group will be soloed along with the Channel.

You can defeat Solo on any channel by ALT+click on its Solo button (in the Track Mixer and Track List). The Solo button will then remain active, even though no other channels are muted. The Channel will subsequently remain unmuted when another Channel is soloed. If Solo defeat is used on a Channel routed to a Group, then the Group will also need to be solo defeated for the Channel to sound when any other Track is soloed.

Selecting Channels

A Channel is *selected* by clicking its name field. The lower section becomes a lighter shade to indicate that it is selected. When selected the Channel will be visible in the *Channel Settings* window and active in the dropdown selection list on the Track Mixer. Multiple Channels can be selected by holding SHIFT.

The Channel associate with a Track selected in the Track List can be automatically selected in the Track Mixer by checking *Preferences/Editing* tab *Mixer Selection Follows Project*. This is actually a two-way thing; select a Track in the Track List, and it will be selected in the Track Mixer; select a Channel in the Track Mixer, and it will be selected in the Track List.

Channel Settings and effects

Clicking the *Edit* button in the Track Mixer, Track List or Inspector, opens the *Channel Settings* window. This is the same window that is available from the *Track List* and the *Inspector*. The *Channel Settings* for audio, Rewire, VSTi's and Groups are identical. For MIDI channels, *Channel Settings* shows the Channel Strip, and the Inserts and Sends. It is described in chapter 13, page 154.

Edit button

Fig. 17.2: Channel Settings

You can select another Channel from here via the *Selected Channel* drop-down, or by using the left and right cursor keys. To open another *Channel Settings* window, click another *Edit* button while holding ALT.

Virtually everything available on this window, and accessible from it (such as Insert and Send effects), can be controlled via automation. You can also copy one Channel's setting to another by using the Copy and Paste buttons on the Common Panel. A Channel reset can be found at the bottom left corner.

The *Channel Settings* window can be divided into five vertical divisions. These are (left to right):

○ Common Panel
○ Channel Strip
○ Channel Inserts
○ EQ
○ Aux buses (Channel Sends)

The Common Panel

All but one of the functions here are on the Track Mixer *Common Panel* (see above). The unique function being *Initialize Channel*, which is found in the bottom left corner. It is useful to remember that you can change the Channel being viewed with the *Selected Channel* dropdown. Alternatively, you can cycle through the Channels using the left and right cursor keys.

The Channel Strip

This is identical to the Track Mixer *Channel Strip*.

Channel Inserts

Each Channel can be routed through up to eight Insert Buses. Audio is routed through them from top to bottom. Inserts are pre-fader. Click on the name field, which by default reads: *No Effect*, to select a plug-in, which will be activated and its interface displayed.

   If you select an effect while holing CTRL, then that effect will be loaded into the same slot on all channels. Similarly, if you hold CTRL and switch an Insert on or off, then all Inserts in that slot for all channels will be similarly switched.

   The Edit button on an Insert slot will open an Insert effect's interface. If you hold CTRL+SHIFT while clicking the Edit button (or while loading an effect), then the standard control panel for the effect will be displayed, rather than any graphical interface. This function does not work with DirectX effects.

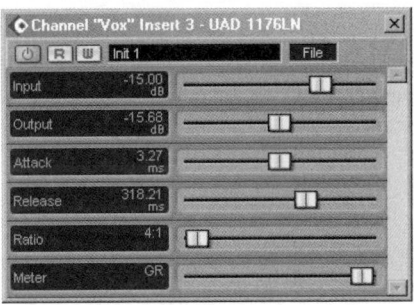

Wot, no graphics?

For stereo channels the Insert buses are stereo. If, however, the Insert effect has a *mono* input, then *only the left-hand channel* is passed to the effect for processing and only the left-hand channel is returned. The right-hand channel is passed through unchanged.

   On mono channels the Insert bus is mono. For a mono input to stereo output plug-in (try the supplied *Autopan* plug-in), Sχ will only take the left channel from the Insert effect's output; the right channel is discarded. For a stereo-to-stereo effect, both inputs are supplied equally, but only the left channel from the Insert effect's output is returned; the right channel is discarded.

   All Inserts for a Channel can be bypassed by clicking the *Bypass Inserts* button, not only here in Channel Setting, but also on the Track Mixer, Track List and Inspector.

EQ

There are four bands of EQ available.

○ Gain is ±24dB all bands
○ Frequency is 20Hz to 20kHz on all bands

○ Q is 0 to 12 (with additional Low Shelving and High Pass on the left-hand band, and High Shelving and Low Pass on the right-hand band).

You can activate a band by switching it on, or clicking and dragging in the graphic display. When a band is activated, a point (numbered 1 to 4) appears in the graphical representation of the EQ curve. You can use the knobs to adjust frequency, gain and Q (frequency and gain share the same knob). You can also click on a field and enter numeric values, and you can drag the points in the graph, where holding ALT changes frequency only; SHIFT changes Q only; and CTRL changes gain only.

There is a dropdown (bottom center) that allows you to select EQ presets. Presets can also be stored and deleted here. Rename by clicking on the name field and editing.

CTRL+click on any control will reset it to its default value. There is a reset all button to the left of the preset selector. Bypass from the channel strip.

Channel Sends and Effects (F6)

There are eight *Send Effects* [F6] slots and eight *Channel Sends* for each channel. It is important to understand that while the only way to route to the *Send Effects* is via the *Channel Sends*, the two are not permanently linked.

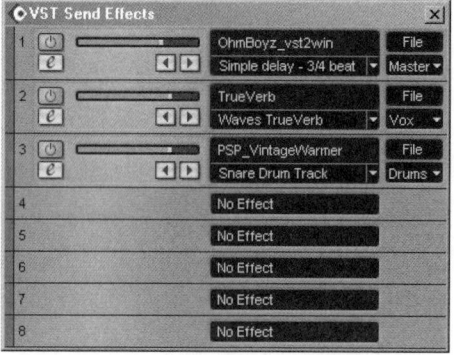

Channel Sends

The Channel Sends can be routed to:

1. any Group
2. any active *VST Outputs*
3. the left or right Master Channel
4. any of the active Send Effects.

To activate a *Send Effect* in *Devices/VST Send Effect* [F6], simply click on the dropdown for a slot and select the required plug-in. The effect is switched on by default, but can be switched off from here. The other controls allow you to route to an active output bus; to load a preset bank or effect into the plug-in; to open the effect's editor; and a slider to adjust the input level to the effect. You will also notice a text line beneath the name of the plug-in on an active *Send Effect* slot. This will contain the name of the current preset being used by that effect. The dropdown, also available on this line, will give you access to any further presets that are available. Presets can be also be loaded from the effects window, opened by pressing the *Edit* button (though sometimes a plug-in will manage its own presets and not use the VST method).

The *Send Effects* can only be routed to an active VST output bus. They are mono in and stereo out, so stereo sources are summed to mono before being passed to the effect. The *Channel Sends* are either stereo of mono depending on the Track.

Info

An effect's settings, or a bank of settings, can be saved, and loaded, from the effects edit window.

To use a *Channel Send*, click on the text field on one of the eight instances in *Channel Settings*, the *Extended view*, or in the *Inspector*, by default the setting will read *No Effect*. Now select the required routing destination from the list. By default, the *Channel Send* is activated. You will then need to set a send level with the knob or slider before anything can be heard. Set to taste.

The *Channel Sends* can be set pre-fader, by clicking the *Pre/Post Fader* button for the Send. This option allows you to route the signal from the Channel directly to the Send without being affected by any fader level or subsequent fader movement.

All *Channel Sends* can be bypassed in the usual way from the *Channel Strip*, or they can be switching off individually. *Send Effects* cannot be bypassed, only switched off from the *Send Effects* window.

Naming and saving Effects settings

Many plug-ins will load with a bank of default presets. These can be accessed from the dropdown at the top of the effect. Some plug-ins may not have a dropdown, in which case you can only load and save effects one at a time.

When you edit an effect (by using the controls), the settings are stored with the current Project without any action on your part.

You can edit effects, rename them, then save them either individually (*Save Effect*) or as a group/bank (*Save Bank*). The number of effects in a bank is determined by the plug-in. Many plug-in are supplied with a number of effects banks.

Some DirectX (and, indeed a few VST) plug-ins implement their own effects' bank and preset handling. Refer to your plug-in documentation if there is any confusion.

It is well worth saving effects settings in your own library (and perhaps with your Projects). One method is to store all effects banks and presets in a single folder hierarchy, with a folder for each plug-in. This ensures that effects can easily be located and provides a convenient location for storing new settings. See below for saving complete Channels with all effects' settings, and also saving all Track Mixer settings.

Tempo Sync for effects (VST effects and VSTi's)

The VST Plug-in specification makes it possible for plug-ins to receive MIDI messages from the host application. One of the most useful applications for this are automation data (see chapter 18, page 257) and for MIDI Clock (i.e. tempo) to be passed to a VST plug-in. Note that these features are not available for *DirectX* plug-ins.

Clock information is particularly useful in the case of temporal effects, such as delays, and also for the LFOs and delay effects in VSTi's. Many such plug-ins and VSTi's exist that make use of this feature (including a number of the plug-in supplied with Cubase Sx (e.g. Double Delay)). There are many older plug-ins that will not respond automatically to tempo, so check with your plug-in documentation if things are not working out as you expect.

In Cubase Sx, MIDI Timing information is automatically provided to any VST 2.0 (or greater) plug-in that requires it. No action is required y the user to make use of this feature.

Track Mixer Utilities

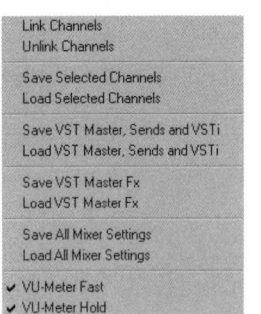

Track Mixer utilities

The Track Mixer has a number of useful functions available from its right-click, quick-menu. These functions are mainly for saving mixer settings in a variety of ways, but functions are also available to link channels, so that the linked channels can be changed in the same way simultaneously.

It can be useful to save the Track Mixer settings for a variety of reasons. For example, saving the Master effects settings will be of use if you frequently use the same plug-ins for processing your 2-Track mix. Rather than having to load each plug-in and adjust settings for each, you can simply load in what amounts to a preset of multiple effects. This technique might also prove useful for comparing one set of effects with another.

An obvious use is to use these functions as a back-up, or security aid, especially when mixing. It is not always convenient to restore a complete Project when trying alternative mixes, and these functions allow you to save all the relevant information without disturbing the audio, MIDI and automation data in the Project Window.

You can also save channels one at a time. This can be useful with VSTi's, in particular, when you can save an instrument setting and its associated Insert effects all in one place – a simple way of storing hybrid patches. Furthermore, if you discipline yourself to using Send slots for specific effects (e.g. Send 1 is always Reverb, etc.), then the Sends can be usefully saved also.

Linked Channels

Linking channels in the Track Mixer allows you to make changes on a number of channels in a single operation. Hold SHIFT to select multiple channels. You can defeat Channel linking by adjusting a control while holding ALT.

When linked, the connected items are:

○ Select
○ Faders (ganged, relative dB level is maintained)
○ Solo and Mute
○ Monitor and Record enable (providing input ports are different)
○ EQ (and bypass)
○ Send Effects (levels, on/off, pre-fader, bypass) (not MIDI)
○ Insert effect-bypass only (not MIDI)

The following are not connected:

○ Pan
○ Insert effects (excluding bypass)
○ Read and Write automation
○ Automation Events
○ Input and output buses
○ Time/tempo toggle

While you can add a Channel to a set of linked Channels, you cannot remove a single Channel. To Unlink a channel, select one of the set and ensure that all the Select buttons are lit; select Unlink Channels; now SHIFT+click the Channel to be removed and select Link Channels.

♪ **Note**

For the following functions, note that MIDI channels are *not* saved.

Loading Mixer Settings

The general point to note when loading channels is that they will need to exist in the Project prior to loading a saved setting. The act of loading will not create absent audio Tracks or Groups. If you need to use a particular Project set-up on a regular basis, then the best way is to use Templates (see chapter 5, page 34).

Save/Load Selected Channels

Only those channels selected in the Track Mixer will be saved. All parameters are saved, including any Send effects' settings, but the Send effect itself will not be saved (i.e. the actual loading of the Send plug-in into a Send slot), since this could obviously cause an existing Send effect to be overwritten.

The Track number, or position, is not saved. Thus if you save three Tracks, say Tracks 2, 4 and 8, then these will simply be saved as three Tracks, in the order that they appear in the Track Mixer from left to right.

When loading, the receiving Tracks must exist to receive the saved information. The channels changed are those selected in the Track Mixer. The Tracks

♪ *Note*

Remember that you can copy and paste channels settings from the *Common Panel* in both the *Track Mixer* and *Channel Settings* windows.

are changed in the same order that they are shown (left to right) in the Track Mixer. If you select more Channels than were present in the saved file, then the remainder of the Channels will be unchanged after the load.

Save/Load Master, Sends and VSTi

Saves the following:

○ All Master effects settings
○ All Send effects settings
○ All VSTi settings
○ Master set-up (e.g. level, bus, mono/stereo)
○ *VST Output bus* [F4] levels and active status

When loading, this behaves as you would expect: All Master, VSTi, Send effects and settings in the Project are overwritten by the contents of the file being loaded.

Save Master FX

All Master effects and their settings are saved. Note that the Master Set-up (e.g. level, bus, etc.) is not saved.

When loading, this behaves as you would expect: All Master effects in the Project are overwritten by the contents of the file being loaded.

Save All Mixer Settings

The effect of this option is the same as a combination of *Save Selected Channels* with all channels selected plus *Save Master and Sends*.

When loading, the effect is the same as applying *Load Selected Channels* for all channels plus *Load Master and Sends*. See above.

Audio Mixdown

Introduction

An audio mixdown is the final process in producing a Project's 2-Track master (or 6-Track for surround). A variety of file formats are available (see page 249) in which to save the mix (including Broadcast Wave and AIFF, as well as the Internet friendly MP3 and RealAudio). Resolution is available to 32-bit float and 96kHz, with all intermediate stages up to these dizzy heights (and resulting file sizes). Mixes can be saved with or without automation, and with or without effects.

In reality you will have a good idea of the required mix format before you start a Project. Most Projects are mixed to 16-bit/44.1kHz, in preparation for burning to CD. However, many folk prefer to master outside of Cubase Sx (for example in Wavelab, CoolEdit or Sound Forge). In this case you will want to produce an intermediate file (the output from mixdown) at the highest resolution that your mastering tool can accept. (If you are taking you mixes to a mastering house, then you will need to ask them which format they prefer, and take their guidance.)

♫ **Note**

You can use Audio Mixdown to create bounces of sections of your Project (very useful for VSTi's, for example). Any Tracks that are muted will not be included, so this method can be used to replicate entire sections of a Project in a complete or edited form. When doing this, it is recommended that you create a 32-bit float file.

Due to the effects of bit depth reduction, it is best, where possible, to output a 32-bit float mixdown from Cubase S$_X$, since this is the size of Cubase S$_X$'s internal bus. This will ensure that no bit depth reduction is performed within Cubase S$_X$.

If you do perform bit depth reduction from within Cubase S$_X$, then ensure that the Master Bus has a dithering stage as the absolutely final plug-in, post Master gain, on the Master Effects bus (see figure 17.3). This can either be one of the supplied dither plug-ins (i.e. UV22 (16-bit output only) or UV22HR), or a high-quality plug-in (such as Waves L2-Ultramaximizer, or similar).

S$_L$ *SL Info*

The UV22HR dither plug-in is not available in S$_L$.

While the internal mixdown process is extremely simple to use, it is not the only mixing method. Given Cubase S$_X$'s routing options, it is quite possible to route to external buses and mix using an external mixer. Indeed, for those with appropriate equipment, this is often the method of choice. See below (*Mixing Externally*, page 250) for further discussion on this topic.

Mixing Down within Cubase S$_X$

To mixdown a whole Project (audio Tracks and VSTi's with all effects and au-

♫   *Note*

MIDI Tracks (excluding VSTi's) must be bounced to audio if you wish to use them during an audio mixdown.

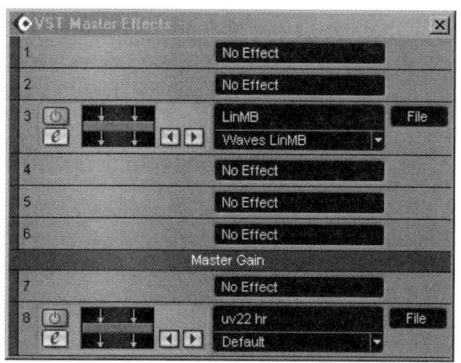

Fig. 17.3: Dithering post Master Gain

tomation), start by performing a *Select All* [CTRL+A] followed by *Locators To Selection* [P]. This will set the left and right locators to the very start and end of all Events and Parts in the Project.

You now need to ensure that the right locator is in an appropriate position to capture any decaying effects at the end of the project. Pay particular attention to reverb tails and other effects.

Note that muted Tracks will not be included in the mixdown. Essentially, the mix will contain precisely what you would hear if you played the Project from the left to the right locator.

To perform the mixdown, select *File/Export/Audio Mixdown* [No Default]. This window provides you with all the options available at mixdown.

There are three basic decisions to be made:

1. The file-type, name and destination of the resulting audio file.
2. Whether you require automation and/or effects to be included in the mix.
3. Whether to import the mix back into the Project, once it is completed.

The *Import To* section (available only for Broadcast Wave, Wave and AIFF file-types) allows you to choose whether to automatically import the mix into the Pool on completion, and whether to insert an Event for it on a new Track. This is very useful when using *Audio Mixdown* to bounce a section of the Project. The *Include* (all file-types) section gives you the choice of including or excluding automation and effects (i.e. Insert, Send and Master).

The serious business is in deciding the appropriate file type. The file type will determine what options you have available. For example, 6-channel Surround

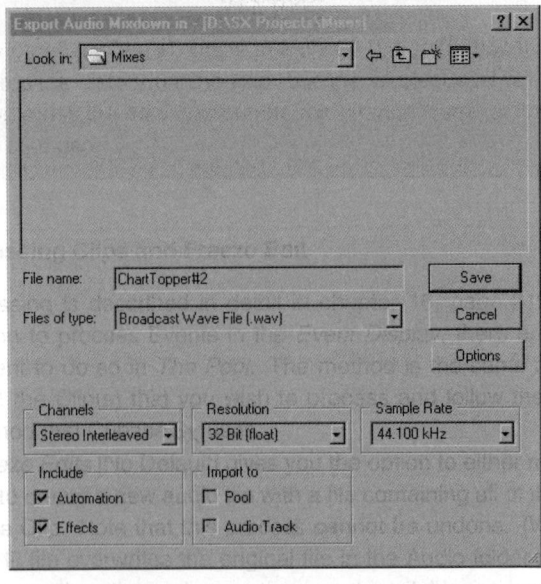

Fig. 17.4: Audio Mixdown dialog

mixes can only be achieved with Broadcast Wave, Wave and AIFF file-types. See the next section for a discussion on available file-types. These decisions having been made, click *Save* and let Cubase Sx do all the work.

Mixdown output file-types

The main mix files-types in Cubase Sx are: Wave, Broadcast Wave and AIFF. These are the only choices for 6-channel surround output or for 32-bit float output (usually required for mastering outside of Cubase Sx). The full range of sample rates, bit depths (word lengths) and encoding options are available for these types. All three share the following attributes:

- *Channels:* Mono, Stereo Split, Stereo Interleaved 6 channel split, 6 channel interleaved
- *Resolution (bits):* 8, 16, 24, 32 float
- *Sample Rate:* 8kHz through 96kHz

↗ **Tip**

Step through the available output *Files of type* to become familiar with options available.

Wave files have additional *Coding* options available, providing that the appropriate codecs are installed in Windows Audio Compression Manager (ACM). (See Windows Control Panel/Sounds and Multimedia/Hardware/Audio Codecs.) Options available will depend on the selected codec. The default coding is PCM/Uncompressed Waves, and it is recommended for normal use.

Broadcast Wave files are stamped with the information accessed via the *Options* button (the data portion can be preset in *Preferences/Audio/Broadcast Wave*). Note that the current date and time are stamped in the file. Also, most importantly, a Broadcast Wave file is stamped with an SMPTE timecode that would be shown as its *Origin Time* in the Pool, should it be imported into a Project. The default Timecode is that of the left locator at the time of export.

The other mix file-types available are all compressed file formats. None of these formats can be recommended over the formats above for their audio quality. However, they have uses for Internet distribution and streaming. The available formats are:

- *MP3 Layer 3:* Compression is via the *Fraunhofer* algorithm. Output is available from 8kbits/11kHz to 128kbits/44.1kHz at 3 quality depths. A dialog is available to add ID3 tag information to the output (e.g. title, artist, genre, etc.).
- *Ogg Vorbis:* Output is available with Sample Rates from 8kHz through 96kHz at 3 quality depths. A dialog is available to add ID3 tag information as with MP3 files.
- *RealAudio (V5 and G2):* Output is available from 5kbps voice to 80kbps stereo (V5) and 20kbps to 450kbps (G2). Internet download options are configurable. Track information can be embedded into the output.
- *WMA:* Output is available from 6.5 Voice to 128 CD Quality. A dialog is available to add title, author and copyright information.

SL **SL Info**

MP3 use is limited to 20 exports in SL. An upgrade for unlimited use is available (see the *Cubase Sx: Operations Manual*).

Mixing externally

Cubase Sx's *Audio Mixdown* will be sufficient for many folk wanting to produce a mix. Providing you have every piece of audio within the Project, then this is certainly the simplest and least error-prone method of producing a final 2-Track (or surround) mix. For a number of other folk, *Audio Mixdown* will be not be adequate. But fear not, mixing outside of Cubase Sx is simple, providing you have the appropriate equipment.

There are many reasons why someone may wish to mix outside of Cubase Sx. For example: real-time recording of a hardware MIDI device; the use of external effects, thus avoiding latency issues; ease of control via a hardware mixer; off-loading some of the computer's processing load (e.g. EQ) to a mixer; a preference for using an analogue mixer for the color that it imparts to the sound of the mix; and more.

The key to external mixing is the routing of the various Channels to appropriate outputs. These then converge on a mixing desk. This, clearly, presupposes that you have sufficient output ports on your soundcard, and sufficient D/A converters to support this activity, or more commonly nowadays, a digital mixing desk.

There is no fundamental difference in routing from Cubase Sx to either a digital mixing desk, or an analogue mixing desk. If you are mixing in analogue, however, you will need sufficient D/A converters to feed the mixing desk. A digital mixing desk is often supplied from ADAT outputs from the soundcard. For example an *RME Hammerfall* soundcard has 3 ADAT input and 3 ADAT output ports (plus an S/PDIF input/output that can also be set as AES/EBU). This makes available 24 channels of digital i/o. These can be connected directly to, say, a Spirit 328 digital mixing desk. If one wished to feed an analogue desk, then you would have to place D/A converters between the RME Hammerfall and the mixing desk, plus a whole bunch of analogue cables, of course.

VST Channels, Sends, Groups and VSTi's (and Rewire channels) can all be assigned VST output buses. The Master Bus, in effect, becomes redundant. But, since *Bus 1* is fixed to the Master, it is useful if you can route this to an output that won't be used; much depends on your routing options. If you do have to use the Master Bus, then take care over its fade setting and effects chain. Remember that Cubase Sx uses the Master Bus for auditioning, so you will probably want to route it somewhere that can be monitored.

When mixing externally, it is important not to clip the channels that are routed to VST output buses. While this is permissable when mixing within Cubase Sx (due the headroom afforded by the internal mix bus) this is not the case when routing the digital signals to output ports. Also remain aware of any bit-depth reductions conversion that might be occurring. If you are sending 24-bit audio from Cubase Sx to a 16-bit receiving device, then you will, in all probability, want to apply dither at some point in the conversion process.

Providing you have routed the channels successfully to your mixer, then you will undoubtedly want to record the output. Again there are many options, and the available equipment will dictate your choice. It is possible to route the mix directly back into Cubase Sx and record it there; some folk choose to do this on another computer. The choice is yours.

Mixing tips and tricks

Effects' routing example

This is a practical example of effects' routing that uses most of Cubase Sx's effects' routing options.

Let's say we have three vocal Tracks. We want to apply reverb to these track, but we also want to create a delayed version of the three tracks and apply reverb to that also.

We start with three audio Tracks and a reverb loaded in a Send slot. Next we link the channels. This is done in the Track Mixer, where we select the three audio Tracks by holding SHIFT while clicking on the three vox channels. Now, right-click on the Track Mixer and select *Link Channels*. Note that settings can later be made to an individual channel by holding ALT.

Now, adjust one of the vox channels to send a signal to the reverb. Since the channels are linked, all vox tracks will be equally affected.

We now add a Group Track and put the delay on its Insert path. Name it *Delay*. We also activate the reverb on the Group Track's Send path and open it up a little.

If we now open Channel Settings for one of the audio Tracks, we can route a Send to the newly created effects Group. To select the Group as a Send channel, click on the name field in the Channel Settings Sends block; a dropdown list will appear. Select the appropriate Group. We're done.

This is a powerful routing option and avoids endeavors to chain groups and other bus routing techniques. These can sometimes be found to be limiting when a change is required to the routing or another effect added. Nevertheless, remain aware of the latency issues of this chain (which have little consequence in this example).

Narrowing the stereo image

Cubase Sx does not have stereo pan controls that allow you to pan the left and right channels independently and narrow or widen a stereo signal. Thankfully, the excellent, and right-priced plug-in called *Stereo Pan* addresses this problem. It is available from
http://home.netcom.com/ jhewes/StereoPan.html

Re-leveling a bounced Track

It is often useful to bounce a Track that is consuming a lot of resources through its plug-ins, so that you can use the resources for other things. However, this leaves the problem of precisely matching its level against the existing Track.

The easiest way to do this is to place a phase reverse plug-in insert on the bounced Track. The plug-in mentioned above, *Stereo Pan*, will do this.

Now, solo the two tracks of interest and invert the phase of the plug-in. Also make sure that you set the pan of the bounced Track to match the original Track. Now start playback and adjust the bounced Track's fader, holding SHIFT where necessary, until the two Tracks cancel.

A byproduct of this process is that the new Track is free of automation, thus making level adjustment (trim) straightforward.

Recording audio at within Cubase S_X

It can be extremely useful to record audio from any point within S_X's audio path. Enter *Silverspike's Tapelt* plug-in. This plug-in will output to an audio file whatever is passing through during playback. The audio also passes through unchanged. Thus, you can record audio wherever you can place a plug-in.

The plug-in is available from
http://www.silverspike.com/PlugIns/Tapelt/tapeit.html

Audio analysis tools

Spectrum Analyzer

S_L   *SL Info*

The *Spectrum Analyzer* is not available in S_L.

The *Audio/Spectrum Analyzer* [No Default] (found under *Analyze* in the *Key Commands Editor*) is a graphical spectrum analyzer with a fair degree of flexibility. It computes and displays the average level of each frequency, within the specified range.

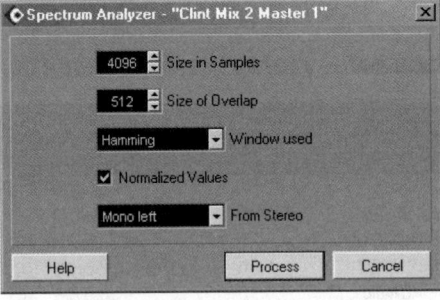

The Spectrum Analyzer

Note that the current selection (whether range, Event or Clip) is analyzed. If you analyze a Part, then a result window will open for each Event within the Part.

The *Size of Samples* value will dictate the frequency resolution of the graph; a higher value gives the highest resolution (approx 5Hz best to 350Hz lowest). For stereo audio, two lines will appear in the resulting graph (Left is white, Right is yellow). There are various display options on the results window that allow you to change the scaling and size of the two axes. The *Active* option, when

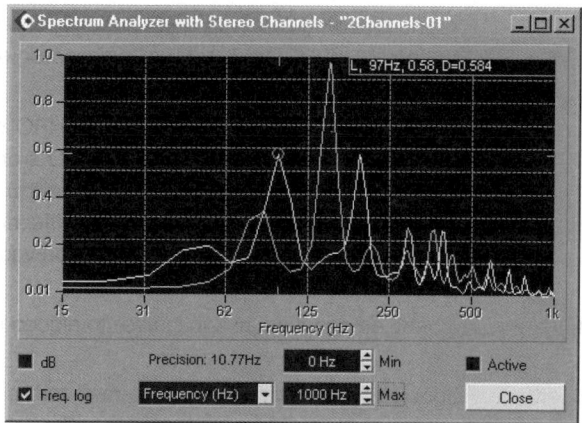

Fig. 17.5: Spectrum analyzer showing results

checked, allows you to reuse the current window for further analysis rather than open a new window.

By moving the mouse over the graph, a cursor will appear in the window, and the level and frequency of its position will be displayed. If the graph is stereo, the channel will also be displayed. To move between left and right channels, hold [Shift] and drag the cursor to the other line. The "D" value being displayed is a delta value. This allows you to find the difference in level between two frequencies. To reset the delta field, right-click on one of the frequencies of interest. As you move the cursor, the level difference between that frequency, and the one the cursor is over will be displayed.

The Audio Statistics function

Audio/Statistics [No Default] (found under *Analyze* in the *Key Commands Editor*) displays a whole bunch of data on the selected audio. The window is shown here, and what you see is what you get.

Most values displayed are self explanatory, but the *Estimated Resolution* seems a surprise, especially as Cubase S$_X$ *knows* the resolution of the audio. What in fact happens is that Cubase S$_X$ checks the smallest level difference between two samples and bases the *Estimated Resolution* on that value.

S$_L$ *SL Info*

No *Audio Statistics* for S$_L$ owners. Drag, huh?

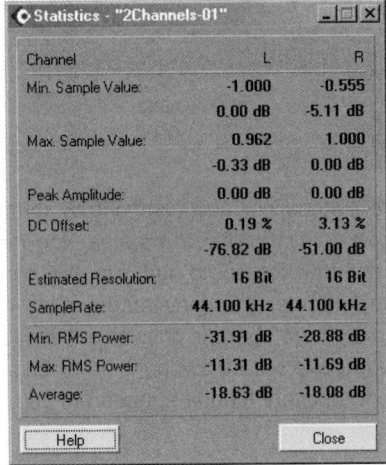

Audio Statistics

Surround Sound

This section is a simple background to *Surround Sound* and the features that Cubase Sx supports. You select a surround format via *Devices/VST Master Set-up* [No Default]. The detail on operation is covered in the *Cubase Sx: Operations Manual*. Even so, Surround Sound is a very large field in its own right, and anyone wishing to tackle it will, no doubt, be reading quite broadly before incurring the expense of a Surround Sound mixing set-up.

Surround Sound is a generic name given to a variety of ways in which audio can be mixed and played back, most frequently with more than two speakers (often up to eight). The extra speakers allow for the audio to be placed on a larger

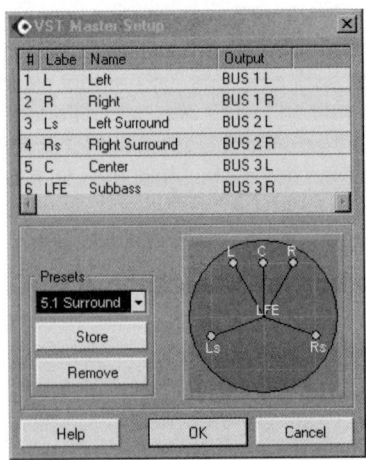

Fig. 17.6: VST Master Set-up

sound-stage than is possible with stereo, facilitating all manner of dramatic effects that lend themselves to cinema, in particular. Speakers will commonly be placed behind the listener, as well as in front.

Before contemplating experimentation with Surround Sound, you will need appropriate hardware. At a minimum you will need a soundcard with sufficient outputs to cater for the number of channels that you wish to mix. For a typical 5.1 Surround mix this will be 6 channels (Left, Right, Left Surround, Right Surround, Centre and Sub-Bass). You will also need a mixer (or other routing device) that supports the mixing of these channels. A standard mixer outputs on two channels, but can often be configured to handle a surround mix by using the auxiliary outputs. Nevertheless, you will still require extra amplification equipment and speakers.

> ♫   *Note*
>
> It is well worth experimenting with surround sound even if you only have limited equipment.

Surround Mixing with Cubase Sx

Setting up Surround mixing in Cubase Sx is surprisingly straightforward. The basic steps are:

1. Select a preset surround type from *Devices/VST Master Set-up* [No Default] (see figure17.6). The routing of a surround channel to an output is fixed. They are assigned, from top to bottom in the VST Master Set-up list, to the active *VST Output* [F4] slots.
2. In the VST Mixer, route each Track either to the *Surround Panner*, or directly to an output channel.
3. Position the audio for each channel in the surround field via the *Surround Pan* control (unless channel is routed to an output).
4. At mixdown, select appropriate output file settings. For example, 6 channel split or interleaved.

The main item of note is that all of the above are included with Cubase Sx. You can mix surround right out of the box. The only surround effects supplied with Cubase Sx, however, are the *Mix6to2* surround level mixer and the *UV22 HR* dither plug-in, so you will need to supply your own surround effects. The Surround Panner is available on Groups, but not Send channels.

Supported Surround Formats

The following surround formats have presets in Cubase Sx. It is not possible to edit these in any useful way, although naming labels can be edited.

Stereo	Standard stereo
Quadro	The original Quadraphonic music format. Designed to be used with 4 speakers, one in each corner of a room.
LRCS	LRCS = Left, Right, Center and Surround. This was the format used for Dolby Stereo in the cinema, and later as Dolby ProLogic in home cinemas.
Standard 3/2	As 5.1 but without the LFE channel.
5.1 Surround	6 speakers: a single center speaker (mainly for directional speech) and four surround speakers. An optional Low Frequency Emitter (LFE) sub-channel can be used for non-directional low frequency output. This is currently the most popular choice for both cinema and DVD. There are a various encoding implementations (e.g. DTS, Dolby Digital, and AC-3).
5.1 SMPTE/ITU and 5.1 Film Alternative	Versions of 5.1 Surround with different speakers orders.

18 Automation

In Cubase S$_X$, Automation is the automatic movement, during playback, of the Track mixer controls, MIDI Track controls, Inserts (audio and MIDI), Sends (audio and MIDI), Master effects, and VSTi parameters. The most fundamental of these being the movement of faders to control volume. Automation is intimately, although not exclusively, linked to mixing.

Automation Events can either be recorded during playback via an appropriate external device, or by movement of controls on the screen (e.g. moving a fader in the Track Mixer, or a slider on a VSTi), or by drawing them directly onto the Automation Tracks using the *Draw* tools. (This is called *static mode*.)

An additional benefit of automation is the instant recall of all settings at a particular moment within a song. These are often stored in objects called *snapshots* on other devices, but in Cubase S$_X$, automation data is updated when the Cursor is moved, so snapshots are unnecessary. That said, although not part of automation, it is possible to store mixer settings independently of a Project so that they can be used elsewhere (see page 244).

In Cubase S$_X$ automation is available for:

> ♪   *Note*
>
> *VSTi's* are automated via a separate automation Track called *VST Instrument Automation* in the Track List. Likewise, *Send effects* have their own *Effect Automation* Track. There is no automation available for a video Track.

- ○ The Master Track (*Master Automation* Track)
- ○ Each Audio Track
- ○ Each MIDI Track
- ○ Each *Rewire* Track
- ○ Each Group
- ○ Each VSTi Track and instrument (*VST Instrument Automation* Track)
- ○ Each effect plug-in
  - ○ Inserts including Master Effects (via their owning Track)
  - ○ Send (separate *Effect Automation* Track)
- ○ External hardware devices controllable via MIDI

While automation is, fundamentally, a mixing process, it can equally be used for creative control while writing. Indeed, for VSTi's and effects' plug-ins, automation has become an essential creative tool. In a creative context, automation provides us with a vast array of options to modulate the available parameters of an effect or instrument that might simply be impossible to achieve manually.

Furthermore, many external devices (e.g. synths and mixers) can be automated through the use of MIDI data. Most folk will be operating with hardware equipment outside of Cubase S$_X$ (and the computer on which it runs) and the

> ♪   *Note*
>
> As well as being available in the Project Window, automation data can also be viewed and edited from the Browser.

---

control of these external devices during playback may also be performed from Cubase Sx. In these cases it is usual to use the external device to generate the MIDI control data while recording to an appropriate MIDI Track in Cubase Sx (see chapter 19, page 267 for more on this).

As yet another tool in our creative armory, and a fundamental element of mixing, automation is an essential tool in modern music-making, and a very liberating one at that...once you've got your head around it.

Essential Automation

Automation Events are contained within dedicated automation Tracks that can be displayed in the Event Display. Each Track can have as many automation sub-Tracks as exist parameters to be automated. Each parameter (or control) resides on an automation sub-Track. Click the tiny + button at bottom left of a Track List entry to open the automation Track (repeat to open more sub-Tracks), or right-click and select *Show Automation*.

Automation will only take place during playback for those Tracks in automation *Read* mode; that is, where the green **R** automation button is lit for the Track.

The *Master Automation* Track is created via the *Add Track* menu. However, the *VST Instrument Automation* and *Effect Automation* Tracks are not created until write automation is activated in one of the instruments or effects, respectively. Indeed, for VSTi's, you get one automation Track for control of the instrument and one automation Track for *each* of the audio channels. You must activate write automation for each channel for it to appear in the list.

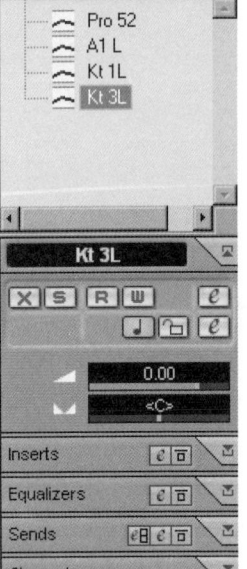

All VSTi channels and instruments.

There are some useful display commands available by right-click (or via *Project*). For a Track, *Show Automation* and *Hide Automation* are straightforward, although *Show used Automation* (which must surely get a toggle key command soon) is probably more useful than the former. The difference is that the *Show*

Automation display can have sub-Tracks added and removed, including sub-Tracks without any automation Events. However, this "separate" list will be destroyed if you use *Show used automation*. For the whole Project *Hide all automation* [No Default] and *Show used automation for all Tracks* [No Default] are also useful.

The best way to get to grips with automation is to get your hands dirty and try the effects described below. Please make sure that you read the section on *Audio Track Automation* if you are new to automation in Cubase S$_X$, because this section contains detail of operating techniques that apply to the other Track types.

The Global automation switches

Reading and writing of Automation Events can be switched on and off for the whole Project in the Track Mixer. The behavior of these buttons is twofold:

- ○ If *Read All* is off, then switching it on will activate automation reading across the whole Project (with the exception of the Master Track inserts, VSTi patch parameters, and Send effect parameters). Similarly, if *Write All* is off, then switching it on will activate automation writing across the whole Project with the same exceptions as above.
- ○ If *Read All* is lit, then it simply indicates that a Track with an audio channel is active (e.g. audio, VSTi, or Rewire). Switching it off will turn off all automation read-enabled Tracks with the exceptions noted above. The same is true for the *Write All* button, which will turn of all write-enabled Tracks.

If you have not created a *Master Automation* Track prior to pressing either the *Read All* or *Write All* buttons, then one will be created when you do so.

Global automation switches

Audio Track automation

Managing sub-Tracks

The automation Track for an audio Track contains both channel (Track Mixer) Events and Insert effect Events. (It also contains surround panner data where present. Not available in S$_L$.)

By default, an audio Track's automation Track is hidden. An audio Track can have many automation sub-Tracks to control both its channel settings and Insert effects. To display the first automation Track, click on the very small + (plus) button at the bottom left of the Track's *Track List* entry, or right-click in the *Track List* and select *Show Automation*. This will display the default automation Track: *Volume*. Note the horizontal line in the Event Display, which is called the *static line* (see page 263).

You can add further sub-Tracks to a Track in the same way. And you can close them by pressing the − (minus) buttons. Pressing the − (minus) button on the audio Track will close all the currently open sub-Tracks (or right-click and select *Hide Automation*).

The Buttons

The control buttons on all Automation sub-Tracks are:

Automation buttons

- ○ Read automation enable (all sub-Tracks are affected)
- ○ Write automation enable (all sub-Tracks are affected)
- ○ Mute automation (the current sub-Track value is held while muted)
- ○ Lock the automation Events on this sub-Track

> ♪   **Note**
>
> It's not uncommon to want to turn off the *Read* button to stop automation for a sub-Track. This will, of course, turn off *all* automation for the Track. To achieve the intended goal you must *mute* the sub-Track.

The Parameters

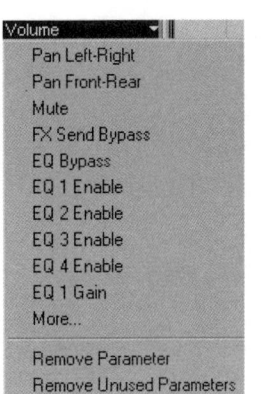

Automation parameters

The parameter field is changed by making a selection from the dropdown. This only contains ten parameters, the rest are accessed via the *More* option. *More* opens a list with *all* the available parameters. You can make multiple selections from this list and they will be added to the dropdown. The dropdown list can be expanded to fifteen entries in this way and is very useful for managing the parameters you need to appear in the dropdown for quick access. Parameters with Events, that don't have a sub-Track showing, get listed at the top of the dropdown and are marked with an asterisk.

Note that you can select freely from the list without fear of losing automation data. The act of selecting another parameter name from the dropdown does not delete the automation data of the parameter being replaced in the dropdown. In fact, one way of working is to keep a single automation Track open and select the automation Track, as required.

The method for editing the value field in the Track List depends on the type of field it is. For example, a binary parameter will simply swap values when clicked with either mouse-button. For numerical parameters, a left click will open a slider to set the value, and a right-click will allow a typed value to be entered.

> ♪   **Note**
>
> You can enter data at the current cursor position, with the Transport stopped, by holding SHIFT+ALT. This is great for accurately switching binary parameters.

If an audio channel is linked (to any other channel whether audio, Group or VSTi) it still requires an independent automation Track. This means that if, say, two audio channels are linked in the Track Mixer, then they will each need independent automation Tracks to control them. When writing data with linked controls, only the "touched" control has automation Events written.

The following items can be automated for audio and Group Tracks:

Volume	4 x EQ modules	8 x Send effect buses
Pan Left - Right	– EQ Enable	– Send Enable
Pan Front - Rear	– EQ Frequency	– Send Levels
Mute	– EQ Q (Resonance)	– Send Pre/Post switches
EQ Master Bypass	– EQ Gain	
FX Send Bypass		
Insert effect parameters (where present).		
These are prefixed by INSn in the list.		
Surround Panner Parameters (when used)		
These are prefixed by PANNER in the list.		

Group Track automation

A Group Track can only contain automation Events. Group automation is very similar to Audio Track automation. If a Group channel is linked (to any other channel whether audio, Group or VSTi) it may still have independent automation Track. The same items are available for a Group as an audio Track. See the audio Track section above for a list of available parameters that can be automated.

Master Channel Track automation

The Master Channel strip is displayed by pressing the *Show Master Channel* button, at top left of the VST mixer. It is labeled *Master Automation* in the Track List, and the sub-Track is labeled *VST Mixer*.

Master Channel toggle

A sub-Track can also be created for each Master Insert effect by write-enabling automation for each effect required. The read and write buttons for the Master Track Insert effects are not affected by the Global Automation switches.

If you have not created a Master Automation Track in the Project View prior to pressing either of the Master Read or Write buttons, then one will be created when you do.

All parameters can be automated for the Master Insert effects. The following items can be automated for the *VST Mixer* sub-Track:

- ○ Volume
- ○ Left *and* right Levels for all active output buses
- ○ Input levels for all 8 Send effect buses

Send Effects automation Track

The *Effect automation* Track controls the parameters of all Send effects. It is created by clicking an automation write button on a loaded Send effect. There is only one *Effect automation* Track, and it contains a sub-Track for each Send effect that has had automation write-enabled at some time. There are a maximum of eight Send effects available.

> ♪ *Note*
>
> Automation in Cubase Sx is very easy to use and very flexible in operation. It is certainly one of Sx's most powerful features, and a bottomless pit of creative potential. You gotta love it.

VSTi Mixer channel automation Track

The *VST Instrument automation* Track is created by either write-enabling a channel of a loaded VSTi in the *Track Mixer*, or write-enabling the VSTi from its interface .

To control a VSTi's parameters, such as a filter or delay time, you need to write-enable the VSTi from its interface. Doing so will create a sub-Track for the VSTi in the *VST Instrument automation* Track, and you can proceed, as normal, to select parameters for automation.

Note that many VSTi's have an extensive number of features available for automation and the current methods for selecting these is rather cumbersome.

For VSTi channel automation, note that the parameters for an Insert effect (or the surround panner) will also appear on the VSTi's automation Track, precisely as they do for an audio Track. There is nothing significantly different to automating a VSTi Track compared to an audio or Group channel, other than that the VSTi automation Tracks reside in the *VST Instrument automation* Track.

> ♪   *Note*
>
> The *Tip* on page 258 is worth referring to, in case you missed it. It's big. You can't miss it.

MIDI automation Track

You can automate pretty much everything that is present in the *Inspector* in the MIDI automation Track.

○ Volume, Pan, Mute
○ 4 x Send enables and 4 x Insert enables
○ *Track Parameters* on/off and all *Track Parameters*
○ Insert effect parameters (where present)
○ Send effect parameters (where present)

Track Mixer Automation

From the *Track Mixer* [F3], automation can be performed for all channels (i.e. audio, Groups, VSTi's, MIDI and Rewire) and the Master Track. You may wish to consider using a Remote Device to control the VSTi Mixer. (See chapter 19, page 270.)

The Track Mixer can be fully automated. Automation data is added by setting a channel's automation write button active and then moving the on-screen controls when in Play or Record modes. Automation data will *not* be recorded when in Stop mode unless SHIFT+ALT is being held. However, MIDI messages will be sent to the selected output ports, as usual. The automation Events are created in the corresponding channel's Automation Tracks and can be viewed and edited as the automation Events they are.

When you activate read or write for a channel in the Track Mixer, the correspond Track, and all associated automation sub-Tracks, will also be activated.

The Static Line

The Static Line. Not the most interesting picture.

An Automation Track for a parameter that doesn't have any automation Events will still have a "static" (or default) value. For example, a fader that is not automated will remain static throughout playback; the value at which it remains is its static value. When you first open an automation Track, this value is shown as the Static Line.

The Static Line will also be shown when there are automation Events for a sub-Track and the Read button is off. In this case the static value is used instead of the automation values.

You can adjust the value of the Static Line in the following ways:

o Grab it and drag
o Right-click the Track List value and type
o Left-click the Track List value and drag the slider

♪ **Note**

If you use the Draw tool on the Static Line, then the sub-Track's *Read* button will automatically activate and you will no longer be editing the Static line, but adding automation Events.

Automation Events

Adding automation Events

You can add automation Events in the following ways:

o Switch on the *Write* button for a channel and move the *Track Mixer* controls during playback (or the *Track List/Inspector* value slider). You can also add automation Events by controlling a parameter with a *Remote Device*. (See chapter 19, page 270.)
o Use the *Draw Tools* on the automation sub-Track to draw points, lines and curves. The *Select Tool* also works, providing the *Read* button is on. This can save on Tool switching. (You must click on the automation curve. Snap is applied when active.)
o Cut and paste from another automation Track

The drawing tools are very similar to those described for the *MIDI Editor's* CC display.

Draw tool
Unrestricted Event drawing tool. Disregards *Snap*.
Modifiers: None

⤢ *Tip*

When you move automation Events around, they will respond to the usual control functions. For example, if snap is on then this will be applied. Most usefully, holding CTRL will maintain the Event (or Events) either at its exact time position or value.

♪   **Note**

Modifiers can be applied one after the other. For example, it is quite possible to, say, draw a triangle wave, then shift its phase (CTRL), then increase its period (SHIFT), then move the whole curve (ALT+CTRL), then skew the curve into a saw wave (CTRL+SHIFT). Try it. You can have endless hours of fun.

Line

Snap on: Creates two Events to draw a line. The length is a multiple of the *Grid Selector* size. It will create a jump with any Event that exists at either of the end-points.

Snap off: Creates two Events to draw a line. The length is however long you draw the line.

Modifiers:

♪   *Note*

Becoming accomplished at adding and editing automation data is fundamental to creating the best possible mixes in Cubase Sx.

- ○ ALT+CTRL: Moves a drawn curve.

  Draw the required curve. Press ALT+CTRL. Drag the curve to the required spot. Release ALT+CTRL, then release the mouse-button. You can invert the curve before doing this. Snap (if active) for this operation is 1/4 of the *Grid Selector* value.

  Note that you can use this to move a curve vertically, as well as horizontally.

Parabola

Snap on: Creates a sequence of Events with start and end points determined by *Snap*.

Snap off: Creates a sequence of Events of the length drawn.

Modifiers:

♪   *Note*

Don't overlook the massive creative potential of automation, especially with effects and VSTi's.

- ○ CTRL: Inverts the curve (you have to move the cursor around a bit to force this to occur). You can achieve the same thing by drawing the parabola from right-to-left.

- ○ ALT+CTRL: Moves a drawn curve.

  Draw the required curve. Press ALT+CTRL. Drag the curve to the required spot. Release ALT+CTRL, then release the mouse-button. You can invert the curve before doing this. Snap for this operation is 1/4 of the *Grid Selector* value.

  Note that you can use this to move a curve vertically, as well as horizontally.

- ○ SHIFT: Alters the exponent (steepness) of the parabola.

  Draw the required curve length. Press SHIFT. Pull the curve-end back to the left. Release SHIFT. Return the curve-end to its intended endpoint. Release the mouse-button. The curve will have steepened. The further back you take the curve when holding SHIFT, the steeper the curve.

Sine, Triangle, Square

Snap on: Creates a sequence of Events with start and end points determined by *Snap*. The period of the curve is determined by the *Grid Selector* value.

Snap off: Creates a sequence of Events with start and end points as drawn.

The period of the curve is 2 seconds.

Modifiers:

- CTRL: Changes the phase of the curve.
  Draw the curve and, while still holding the mouse-button, press CTRL and drag the curve until the phase is as you require. Release CTRL and draw the required number of phases.
- SHIFT: Increases or decreases the period of the curve.
  Draw the curve and, while still holding the mouse-button, press SHIFT and drag the curve until you have the period length that you require. Release SHIFT and draw the required number of phases.
- ALT+CTRL: Moves a drawn curve (see above for explanation).
- CTRL+SHIFT: (Triangle and Square only.) Allows Triangle waves to be skewed toward a Saw shape in steps of $1/4$ of the *Grid Selector* value. Square waves can have their pulse width varied.

Automation modes

There are three modes available when recording automation Events. (See chapter 19, page 277 for more detail on these modes when using a *Remote Device*.)

S_L   *SL Info*

S_L only has *Touch Fader* automation mode.

- *Touch Fader:* Automation Events are written as soon as the control is clicked, and stops when released.
- *Auto-latch:* As *Touch Fader*, but all Events are overwritten until *Write* is de-activated (or the Transport stopped).
- *X-Over:* Short for *crossover*, this mode will allow writing of automation Events until an existing automation curve is crossed. This is not the same as reaching the first Event on a particular sub-Track, since the new automation curve could remain above or below the existing curve for an amount time.

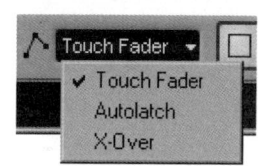

Automation modes

Reducing automation Events

Cubase Sx automatically reduces the number of automation Events added after they have been written. To be clear, some automation Events will, most likely, be *deleted* and you *do not* have the option to stop this. The reduction process occurs both after Write automation has been recorded, and after drawing curves manually. The degree to which automation Events are removed is determined by the *Automation Reduction Level* setting on the *Preferences/User Interface/Editing* tab.

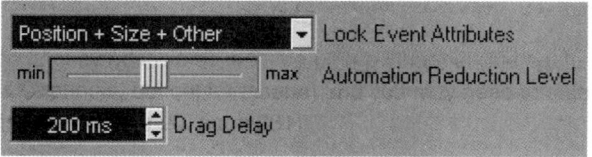

Reducing automation events

The further to the left the slider, the less reduction is performed. However, do note that this is not a "Reduction Off" setting. And, of course, the further to the right the slider, the more reduction is performed.

> ♪   **Warning**
>
> If you increase the reduction level, and then perform any automation Event editing on a sub-Track, then the whole sub-Track will have the increased reduction level applied. It is very easy to get caught out by this without realizing until much later. By which time, you might have lost important automation data. However, if you do realize immediately, the process can be reversed with *Undo*.

Editing automation Events

There are a number of methods for editing automation Events, and which you choose will depend on the degree of change required. Note that Events will turn red when selected. Use of the zoom controls becomes almost essential when manually editing automation Events, and it is highly recommended that you set up *Zoom In Vertical* [No Default] and *Zoom Out Vertical* [No Default] key commands to assist.

The methods you have available for editing are:

- Select and drag an Event (or Events) in the Event Display.
  (Use the CTRL key to maintain the Events' values as you drag.)
- The Info line (single Event only).
- The Browser.
- Rewrite a section of automation data while in playback with the *Track Mixer* controls (or the *Track List/Inspector* value slider, or from a remote controller). Ensure that *Write* is enabled for the appropriate sub-Tracks.
- Cut and Paste.
- Other Event editing functions (e.g. Nudge). Right-click on a selected Event to see the complete list.

All automation Events for a sub-Track can be selected by right-clicking on the sub-Track in the Track List and choosing Select All Events. This can be useful when copying automation Events. Also useful is *Edit/Select in Loop* [No Default] after *Transport/Locators to selection* [P] on the appropriate Event. Automation Events can be removed in all the usual ways (e.g. select and press DEL, using the Erase tool, etc.). Additionally, *Remove Parameter* (from the parameter dropdown) can be used to remove the sub-Track and all its automation data.

19 Synchronization and Remote Control

Cubase S𝗑 provides a number of pre-defined set-ups for devices that can remotely control features within Cubase S𝗑. In general, these devices allow you to remotely control the Track mixer functions, but some devices can have Cubase S𝗑 Key Commands assigned to them. There is also the Generic Remote facility that allows you to configure any external MIDI controller to control a vast array of Cubase S𝗑's functions.

Synchronization has always been critical in audio, but the digital audio era has raised its profile even higher. Simply having audio playback at a precise moment is not the only concern any longer. Indeed, the definition of "precise moment" is now much more critical.

Synchronization (or sync) is, most simply, the process of ensuring that all the audio streams and control information from different sources are precisely aligned. This is obviously desirable for audio playback, but becomes more complex due to the necessity of digital equipment having to remain synchronized to sample accuracy. For example, if you use a digital mixing desk, then you will need this to be synchronized to Cubase S𝗑.

There are three types of synchronization that we are concerned with:

- MIDI Clock (tempo-based, output only)
- Word Clock (sample rate based)
- Timecode (time based)

Cubase S𝗑 can also send and receive MIDI Machine Code (MMC). This is a method that enables control of a remote device's transport from within S𝗑.

☿   *Info*

The various synchronization options are managed from *Transport/Sync Set-up* [No Default]. Also accessed by holding CTRL+click on the Transport *Sync* button.

Synchronization

MIDI Clock

MIDI Clock is a tempo-based method of synchronization; 24 MIDI Clock signals are sent per quarter note. Additionally, MIDI messages called "song position pointers" can be sent to ensure that two devices stay aligned; these are often sent on Stop or Play, rather than during playback. There are many reasons why MIDI Clock is not a good source of timing information for a precision tool

---

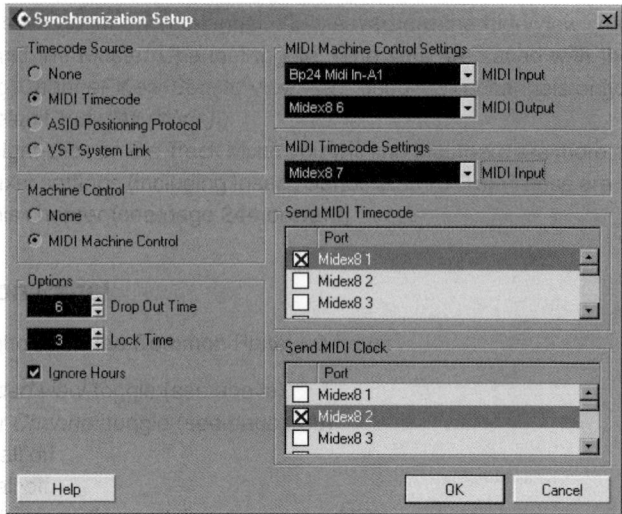

Fig. 19.1: Synchronization set-up

such as Cubase S$_X$ and subsequently Cubase S$_X$ does not slave to (or chase) MIDI Clock. However, Cubase S$_X$ will output MIDI Clock, allowing you to drive other devices that rely on MIDI Clock for tempo-based functions (e.g. delay times, synth LFO times, etc.). Tempo changes in a Project are replicated in the change in frequency of the generated MIDI Clock signals.

To send MIDI Clock from Cubase S$_X$, simply check the appropriate MIDI output in the Send MIDI Clock section of the *Synchronization Set-up* window. MIDI Clock is sent during playback and record only. If the MIDI port is being used in the Event Display, then the MIDI Clock messages will be merged with that data. Note that the MIDI Clock is a dense protocol on the MIDI wire (which is very low bandwidth by today's standards), and so it is possible that by sending it you can introduce timing errors in the music-based messages. This problem can be compounded by sending MIDI Clock to many different devices via the same MIDI interface.

Word Clock

For digital audio to be correctly transferred, processed and interpreted the devices involved must be locked to a well-defined sample frequency – termed "clock". If locking to clock is absent, then misinterpretation of the signal occurs which manifests as clicks, pops and other distortion.

Note that transfers made within you computer, or within Cubase S$_X$, are not subject to these sync issues. It is only when you want to input or output digital audio to, say, a digital mixing desk, ADAT or DAT that sync problems might occur.

Word Clock is a square wave with one leading edge per sample. The number of samples per second is the Sample Rate (typically 44.1kHz or 48kHz). When connecting you studio equipment, it is vital that everything is running at the same sample rate and that everything remains in sync. This is most often achieved by way of Word Clock. Word Clock runs over its own physical wire on BNC cables. There is one master clock source and everything else should slave to it. To sync to Work Clock you will need a device that produces it.

Some interconnection protocols are self-clocking. For example, S/PDIF, ADAT and AES/EBU, and will not, in theory, require a separate word clock connection. In practice, where available, it is safest to slave these device from a single word clock master.

The sample accurate synchronization of your soundcard and Cubase Sx should be achieved automatically. This is not always the case, and problems can occur for a variety of reasons. Do ensure that Cubase Sx is correctly operating with your soundcard before attaching other equipment.

Timecode

Timecode is a time-based method of synchronizing equipment. Timecode sync pre-dates the digital era and many timecode formats are analogue in nature.

Cubase Sx can receive and synchronize the following types of timecode:

o MIDI Time Code (MTC)
o ASIO Positioning Protocol

Various protocols are available. Your choice will be determined by the timecode available on your device and whether you wish Cubase Sx to be timecode master or slave. If you need to sync to an SMPTE audio Track, then you will need to use an SMPTE to MTC converter on the incoming signal.

It is recommended that you run Word Clock alongside any incoming timecode sync. If you do not do this then audio glitches are more likely. There is also a greater chance of timing drift with any MIDI Parts being played.

To accept incoming timecode, simply select the appropriate protocol in the Timecode Source section of *Transport/Synchronization Set-up* [No Default]. For MTC input, ensure that the incoming MIDI port is correct in the Synchronization Set-up window.

To commence playback when slaving to timecode, ensure that the *Sync* button (*Transport/Sync Online* [T]) on the Transport is lit, then start the timecode generating device. Cubase Sx should then commence playback. When sync has been achieved, the Off-line message will change to Lock *nn*, where *nn* is the frame rate of the incoming signal.

Cubase Sx can also send MIDI Timecode (MTC) during playback and record. To do this select the output ports on which you wish to send timecode from the Send MIDI Timecode section of *Synchronization Set-up*. The receiving device will respond, providing it has been set-up correctly. You don't need to activate the *Sync* button for this to occur. The frame rate sent is that chosen in *Project/Project Set-up* [SHIFT+S].

> ♪   *Note*
>
> If you need to stripe an external audio Track with SMPTE, then you can use the SMPTE Generator plug-in.

Sync button

Machine Control

Cubase Sx supports MIDI Machine Control (MMC) for the transport control of external devices. MMC is a protocol that runs over MIDI cables. It allows the transport features of a device to be controlled, and hence to mirror, what is happening within Cubase Sx. Example actions are: Play, Stop, Locate, etc. Note that it is quite possible for Cubase Sx to send a start command to an external device that, in turn, commences generation of MTC, to which Cubase Sx slaves.

Note that both input and output MIDI ports must be supplied for MMC to work correctly. Furthermore, in *Preferences/MIDI/Filter* tab, ensure that SYSEX is not filtered in the Thru section.

Remote Control of Cubase Sx

The Track Mixer, VST Effects (including Master effects) and the Transport can all be controlled by any MIDI device that can send control messages that Cubase Sx can interpret. Furthermore, Cubase Sx commands can also be issued using the same technique. The remote controller is called a *Generic Remote Device* in Cubase Sx and is described below. However, Sx also has a number of pre-defined Remote Devices. The list of devices will naturally be updated over time, but as at writing they are:

○ CM Automation Motor Mix
○ JL Cooper CS-10
○ JL Cooper MCS-3000
○ Mackie Control
○ Radikal SAC-2k
○ Roland MCR8
○ Steinberg Houston
○ Tascam US-428
○ Yamaha 01V
○ Yamaha DM2000

Once you have attached and configured your remote device, whether from the pre-defined list or via the Generic Remote, you will, no doubt, be itching to use it in full fury in Cubase Sx. Of course, automation is not the only use for a remote device; day to day vanilla operation of Cubase Sx can be made a lot more fun and flexible when freed from the constraints of the keyboard for every operation. Nevertheless, it is still early days in the development of the use of remote devices with sequencers, and it would be unrealistic to think that the manner in which current devices work is gong to free you entirely from the keyboard, certainly the mouse will remain an essential tool for many tasks.

Adding a Remote Device (inc. the Generic Remote Device)

To add a Remote Device so that it can be used:

o First connect the device as described in its documentation
o Open *Devices/Device Set-up* [No Default]
o Select the *Add/Remove tab*
o Highlight the appropriate device
o Click *Add*
o Select the *Set-up* tab
o Highlight the device in the Devices list
o The contents now shown on the right-hand Set-up panel will depend on the device selected
o Select the MIDI In and, if present, MIDI Out ports
o Close the dialogue by clicking on OK

Using a Predefined Remote Device

Essentially this is plug and play. It would be fruitless to describe the operation of each predefined device here. Needless to say, the remote device's faders will move the Cubase Sx Track Mixer faders, and so forth. Experimentation is the order of the day, as well as referring to the appropriate documentation that was supplied with the device.

Make sure you refer to the Set-up screen for the device you have added in *Device Set-up.* For some of the devices (the JLCooper MCS3000 set-up is shown in figure 19.2), this is where you can customize the configuration of the remote device. Take care when editing, as the change are applied immediately and *Cancel* does not rollback the changes.

The Generic Remote Device (GRD)

Before you start to change the values in he GRD set-up, you are well advised to Export the default set-up to some convenient location. The simplest thing to do

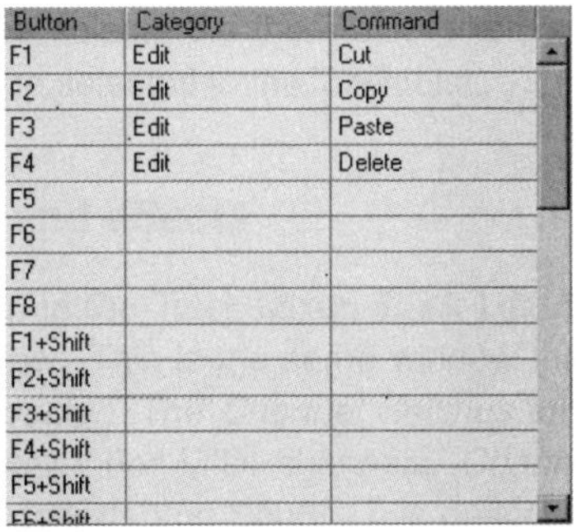

Button	Category	Command
F1	Edit	Cut
F2	Edit	Copy
F3	Edit	Paste
F4	Edit	Delete
F5		
F6		
F7		
F8		
F1+Shift		
F2+Shift		
F3+Shift		
F4+Shift		
F5+Shift		
F6+Shift		

Fig. 19.2: A remote device set-up dialogue

is to create a folder in the Cubase Sχ folder hierarchy and give it an appropriate name. This will make it easy to restore the default settings if you mess up. The GRD set-up process is not immediately intuitive, for most folk, so there is every possibility that this might happen.

The GRD is a very powerful alternative tool to the pre-defined devices available in Cubase Sχ, providing you have an appropriate MIDI device with knobs and/or sliders to use. Any MIDI device that outputs MIDI data can be used with the GRD, although the type of controller data output and the nature of the sending control itself (e.g. slider, toggle switch, etc.) may restrict the items in Cubase Sχ that you can control. After adding the GRD to Cubase Sχ (see above), the GRD can be configured in the *Set-up* tab of the *Devices/Device Set-up* dialogue.

♫　　**Note**

Before you can use the GRD, you must assign the appropriate MIDI ports in the GRD set-up screen.

GRD Status Window

It is not necessary to display the GRD Status window (*Devices/Generic Remote* [No Default]) to use the GRD, but when you do so, the small floating window shown will appear. This allows you to switch banks via the dropdown.

The Add and Delete buttons below the *Export* button are for adding and deleting lines to the top window (when you press *Add* you will have to scroll

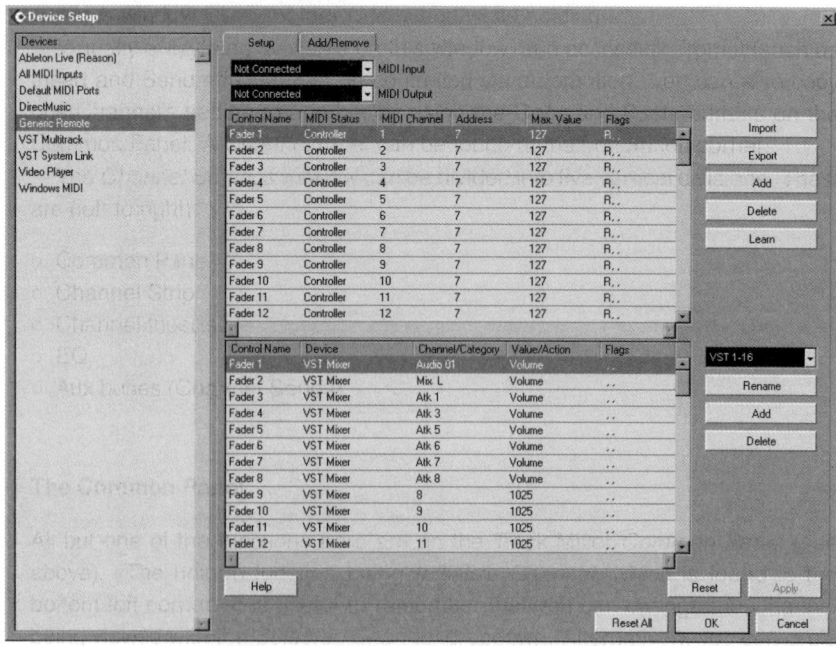

Fig. 19.3: The GRD (Generic Remote Device) dialogue

down to see the addition). The Add and Delete buttons below the *Rename* button are for creating and deleting Banks.

The fundamental building blocks of the GRD are:

○ Banks
○ Incoming MIDI control data (from your external device)
○ Assigning controls to Cubase Sx functions

Banks
Most MIDI devices only have a small number of controls. By using Banks, we can map the controller to as many Cubase Sx channels as we wish. For example, say our controller has 8 faders and 8 buttons. We can map these to, say: Bank 1, which controls audio channels 1 to 8 in Cubase Sx; Bank 2, which controls audio channels 9 to 16 in Cubase Sx; and so on. In this way we have an unlimited number of audio channels at our control.

Banks can also be used to re-map our MIDI controller to completely different functions in Cubase Sx. In the example above, we might well have mapped the 8 controller faders to Cubase Sx's VST Mixer faders, but we could easily set-up another bank that mapped them to, say, Send levels. This is explained below.

Banks are selected from the Remote Status window that appears when the GRD is activated (*Devices/Generic Remote* [No Default]).

Define MIDI Controller
On the GRD set-up page, the upper section is used to define the hardware MIDI controllers you wish to use; the physical sliders, knobs and buttons. As well as giving each individual control a name (the name is mirrored in the lower section and is the link between two panes), we need to tell Cubase Sx what type of control it will receive, and this is defined here also. There is a "learn" facility available that makes this straightforward. It is also possible to set things up so that Cubase Sx will send MIDI data when a VST Mixer control is moved. Be careful when using this feature that you don't accidentally set-up a MIDI loop.

Define Cubase Sx Controls
The lower section of the GRD set-up page is used to assign the external controllers, defined above, to specific Cubase Sx features. Almost every function and control within Cubase Sx can be assigned an external controller, and you are limited only by your own imagination as to how these may best be applied in your studio. See below for the full list of available functions.

Setting up the Generic Remote Device

The on-screen definition of the GRD is global. So when you make a change to this screen the change is immediate, and applies to all Projects. If you have not yet saved the current settings (by using the Export button), then you should do so before proceeding. Each time you load Cubase Sx, the GRD will load the last Imported or Exported definition, so make sure you save any changes if you want a new default definition.

> ♫ **Note**
>
> Export the GRD, then delete all the entries and build up a set of controls from the ground up. Try using any piece of kit that outputs MIDI. I frequently use a Line 6 POD as a controller.

Each GRD definition can use one or more external MIDI controllers. The incoming data is simply identified by its MIDI content. However, in most cases a single external controller will be used. A GRD definition is related to a device (or devices), so the upper window will not change between banks, only the lower changes.

Assigning external MIDI controllers

By way of an example, let's assign a volume fader and a mute button to the VST Mixer.

GRD MIDI ports

First, ensure that the device you are using is correctly attached to the appropriate MIDI port, and select that port from the MIDI Input dropdown.

Next, highlight the top line in the upper box of the GRD set-up window (by default this is labeled *Fader 1*). You can rename this field by double-clicking on it. (Note that the respective field in the lower window is not updated (or refreshed) until you click on the field in the lower window, or you close and re-open the GRD set-up window.) Unfortunately, when you move your external controller, there is no indication that the GRD set-up is receiving MIDI messages. However, if you now press the *Learn* button, the data in the highlighted line will change to reflect the incoming MIDI data just received. The content should be similar to that shown below. (You can change the order of the columns by dragging the column headings.)

Learn

Control Name	MIDI Status	MIDI Channel	Address	Max. Value	Flags
Fader 1	Controller	1	11	127	R,,

The fields have the following meaning and function, and can all be changed manually:

♪   *Note*

When using the *Learn* feature; first, move the controller, then press *Learn*

- ○ *Control Name*
  Name to reflect the function of your external control. This field uniquely links it to a single entry in the lower window.
- ○ *MIDI Status*
  This entry describes the type of MIDI data that the external controller is generating. This can take the following values:
  - – Controller (i.e. MIDI CC(Continuous Controller))
  - – Program Change
  - – After touch
  - – Poly Pressure
  - – Note On
  - – Note Off
  - – MMC
  - – Ctrl NRPN
  - – Ctrl RPN
  - – Ctrl JLCooper
  - – Ctrl Houston

o *MIDI Channel*

The MIDI channel of the sending device (value: 1-16)

o *Address*

Takes different values depending on the MIDI Status entry:

– Controller – MIDI CC Number

– Note On/Off – MIDI Note Number (Pitch)

– NRPN/RPN – MIDI CC Number

o *Max Value*

The maximum value that the controller transmits. This value is not part of the *Learn* feature and so must be input by hand if less than the default value. It allows Cubase Sx to scale the incoming values to the full range of the assigned Cubase Sx function.

o *Flags*

There are 3 flags and each one can be switched on or off. If all are off then, clearly, the controller is inactive.

– *Receive*

This signifies that Cubase Sx is to do something with the incoming MIDI message

– *Transmit*

The MIDI message defined in this entry will be transmitted on the GRD MIDI Out port when the related corresponding controller defined in the lower windows is moved/changed. (This does not work for all functions.)

– *Relative*

This flag denotes an endless dial controller that does not send absolute position values, but sends a value as it passes through some position as you turn it (often the 12 o'clock position).

> ♫ **Note**
>
> You can use the relative flag to enable a knob, or fader, to be used as a switch. E.g. to toggle mute or solo, etc.

Returning to our original aim, you should be able to see that the settings shown above are ideal for our fader

Let's move on to the Mute button. The process for making the details of the controller known to Cubase Sx is identical to that described for the fader. Usually a button controller only sends values of 0 and 1, but you should check this, either by reading the controllers documentation, or by recording some of its MIDI output and examining it in the Browser.

Mute 1	Controller	1	64	127	R..

Now that Cubase Sx has successfully identified our two external controllers, we can link them to the appropriate Cubase Sx functions. Before doing so, it might be wise to save (*Export*) your current GRD definition.

Return to the Project Window and create an empty Audio Track, then return to the GRD set-up window. Highlight Fader 1 (or whatever you might have renamed it to) in the lower window. Set the value to those shown below:

Control Name	Device	Channel/Category	Value/Action	Flags
Fader 1	VST Mixer	Audio 01	Volume	..

Now close the GRD set-up window, open the *Track Mixer* [F3] and move the external fader. All being well, the VST fader will move in unison with the external fader. Magic.

The settings for the mute button will be as below, but you may need to adjust the Flags setting to get the precise response required depending on the buttons on your controller. See below.

Mute 1	VST Mixer	Audio 01	Mute	P.T.

The fields in the lower window have the following meaning and function, and all but the Control Name can be changed manually.

Control Name
This field cannot be changed and simply serves as a reference to link it to the entry in the external MIDI controller definition in the top window.

Device
Options are:
- o *Not Assigned*
  Switches off all actions for the controller.
- o *Command*
  With this selected you can choose a Cubase Sx menu/key command from the next two columns. The selection list is very similar to the Key Commands list. Note that only the push button (P) option is available in the Flags column, which is a very regrettable restriction.
- o *VST Mixer, MIDI Mixer and Mixer*
  MIDI Mixer is restricted to MIDI channels; *VST Mixer* to all audio (including VSTi's and Rewire channels); while *Mixer* contains both.
  Three options in *Channel/Categoty* here (MIDI channels do not appear):
    - – *Device*
      This gives you access to level controls for all output buses, the Master Gain control and to the Send Effects input levels (from the [F6] window)
    - – *Selected*
      This will assign the control to the selected (i.e. highlighted) channel in the Track Mixer (single channel only). The Mixer control assigned is chosen from the Value/Action column.
    - – *A named Channel from the Track Mixer*
      This is the same as for Selected, but for the selected channel in the Track Mixer.
- o *Transport*
  At first sight this seems like a replication of some of the Command/Transport functions available above. However, two things to note:
  (1) The Time command is a very nifty way of moving through the project, much like the Position Slider, when assigned to a knob;
  (2) Toggle buttons are allowed.

Channel/Category
Options determined by Device. See above.

Note

If a controller is assigned to more than one function, then only one of the functions is affected.

Tip

The *Transport* categories contain some excellent functions that can be controlled by MIDI controller switches/buttons.

Value/Action
Options determined by Device. See above.

Flags
Options are:
o *P – Push Button*
Action only occurs when a value is received that crosses the mid-point of the Control Value. This allows you to get the functionality of a switch from a knob or slider, and many buttons. (Note: If the button toggles between a value of 1 and zero, then this button will only work in one direction, and then only once. Also, with some commands, the virtual switch toggles for every new MIDI message received.)
o *T – Toggle*
This will cause the parameter to toggle between its maximum and minimum values every time a MIDI message is received. (Note: This does overcome the potential problem noted in Push Button, but this option is not available for Commands.)
o *N – Not Automated*
Deactivates the action for this controller.

> ♫   **Note**
>
> Push Button and Toggle Flags can be used in combination, which may prove useful in certain situations.

> ↗   **Tip**
>
> The *Command* Device-type has a Category called *Remote*. This allows you to assign controllers to select the GRD bank. Assigning the functions can immediately quadruple the power of your controller. One word of advice: when assigning *Remote* functions to controllers, remember that you will need to assign them appropriately for each *Bank* you intend to use. It's kinda obvious, but I spent a good half-hour wondering what was broken. It was me.

Automation with a remote device

Once your Remote Device is attached and configured, you are ready to use it for automation. The process is a little different to automation via the VST Mixer. Clearly, on playback, the operation is identical; it is only the writing of automation data that differs.

The writing of Automation data can be performed for all channels (i.e. audio, groups and VSTi's), the Master Track and all effects; this is completely determined by how your remote device is configured (see above). Remote device generated automation data can be written in parallel (at the same time) as writing automation data generated by moving the Track Mixer (and other) controls, if you wish to do so.

As with the writing Track Mixer data, automation data is added by setting a channel's automation write button to on ('W' button is red) and then moving the appropriate control on the Remote Device when in Play or Record mode. Automation data will not be recorded when in Stop mode.

There is, however, a major difference in the way that writing automation data is performed when using a Remote Device, as opposed to doing it manually.

The difference when doing this manually, is that when you release the control (release the mouse-button) the remaining existing Events are retained; somewhat like an automated punch-out.

⚡   **Warning**

When automation data is written using a Remote Device, all Events that currently exist between the time that the control is first moved, until playback is stopped, are replaced.

S_L   *SL Info*

S_L only has *Touch Fader* automation mode.

The above warning describes how automation record operates in *Touch Fader* and *Auto-Latch* modes when using a remote device. To stop overwriting existing automation you must switch off a Track's write automation button. In *X-Over* mode, however, automation writing stops automatically for a Track when the first automation Event is reached by the Cursor. The "automation punch-out" point might well be at a different position for each Track.

⚡   **Warning**

The corollary to this is that for every automation sub-Track in *Touch Fader* and *Auto-Latch* modes, it is very important that you only move the controls for those Tracks on which you want to replace the automation data.

At first sight this does seem a little unreasonable, but the difference is that when performing an automation update manually, Cubase S_X "knows" that you still wish to write automation data because you are still holding down the mouse-button, even though you may not actually be moving the control. Clearly, this isn't the case for a control on a remote device that has no contact with Cubase S_X other than the data that is passed when the control is moved. The only way that Cubase S_X "knows" that you are done with a control is when you end playback

Since the market for remote devices is currently under rapid development, more devices may appear that offer equivalent functionality to indicate to Cubase S_X that automation data should only be recorded when the remote control is active. One such device that currently exists is the JLCooper MCS300. This device has faders that are touch-sensitive, so Cubase S_X can interpret the active state. Note that not all controls on this device can perform in this way.

When using a Remote Device, the automation Events are created in exactly the same way as described above for manual input, and Events can then be viewed and edited as expected. (See chapter 18, page 257)

Remember that when you activate the automation write button for a channel in the Track mixer (or any of the sub-Track automation buttons in the Track List), the corresponding Track, and all associated automation sub-Tracks, will also be

---

write enabled. Therefore, if you have remote device controls associated with the parameters for any of these sub-Tracks, then you must be careful to heed the warning above and avoid inadvertently destroying any exiting automation data.

VST System link

System Link is described in the *Cubase Sx: Operations Manual*.

System Link is a proprietary protocol (developed by Steinberg) that allows computers, that are running their products, to collaborate with each other and distribute the audio processing load. MIDI can also be distributed to a maximum 16 channels. Thus, one can run VSTi's and computer-based effects' racks on other computers, or even keep Tracks remote from your usual main machine.

The communication takes place over a variety of common digital protocols including S/PDIF, ADAT, TDIF, and AES/EBU, rather than the usual network protocols, such as Ethernet. A System Link network is "ring"-shaped, so that if there are, say, four computers in the network, then the data will always pass from the "master" computer to the the second, then to the third, the fourth and, finally, the results are returned to the first. It isn't a requirement that mixing is performed on a "master"computer, it is also possible to take the outputs from each computer and run them into a mixer in the usual way. Although, in this case, the latency issues would need be addressed carefully.

The minimum requirements for a System Link set-up would require two computers, each with an ASIO compatible audio interface with a matching digital input and output (and appropriate cabling between the two), and a copy on each machine of either Cubase Sx, *Nuendo* or certain versions of *Cubase VST*.

While latency is cumulative over a System Link network, the system runs to a common clock and so all data remains sample-locked. This is fine for recording (where the delay is automatically compensated for by Cubase Sx), but it presents difficulties for monitoring in a similar way to using a mixer.

This is early days for System Link, and it remains to be seen how well it operates in the outside world and whether users decide to take it up. It's certainly an interesting development.

20 Latency

This section is necessarily technical. So put your hard hat on and dig in.

It can be quite shocking to discover audio latency in a process that you never suspected was a problem, but it does happen. This will be a detailed chapter describing methods of measuring latency, and what to do with the results to ensure accurate recording and application of effects and dynamic processing.

Disk Latency

It is possible to have disk latency problems, although with modern disk drives this is unlikely, except in extreme cases. For those wishing to run very large Track counts, the best advice is to either ask for advice on the Cubase Sx boards, or to contact Steinberg directly. Technology changes so rapidly, that advice given here would be out of date before publication. Cubase Sx does have disk throughput tuning options in *Devices/Device Set-up/VST Multi-Track* tab where disk buffer size and number can be adjusted.

Latency is, probably, the most important issue facing a studio in the digital world. It is an unseen danger that lurks and bites. It can bite hard. It can have horrible consequences. It can cause music that seemed to ebb and flow, groove and swing, to die an ugly death. And it can leave the uninformed clueless to the cause of the problem, and hopelessly unequipped to fix it. Without a complete and thorough understanding of the various latencies in your studio, you are, even today, not getting close to the best result you can achieve from your equipment.

And don't think for a moment that Cubase Sx, or any other part of your studio is going to make it easy for you (although Cubase Sx does try). At this stage in the development of digital audio processing we are still on our own for the most part.

Bummer, eh? Well, the up-side is that if you think your music sounds good now, then it will sound a lot better once you know your way around what's really going on in your system. You will also have a fantastic story to tell dinner party guests that have outstayed their welcome.

Forget that sexy new piece of gear that's going to take you into the sonic stratosphere. Save the money, buy some tea-bags, put on a brew (or the coffee pot) and prepare to eradicate the monster that is...Latency

Latency? What latency?

Latency is the time it takes for an input signal to produce an output signal.

For example, the A/D conversion of an audio signal to a digital signal takes a finite amount of time (typically around 1ms), which can be measured (see below). This amount of time is the latency of the A/D conversion. Likewise when you playback audio there is latency in the D/A conversion. You can probably begin to see that when you are monitoring playback and recording simultaneously (how else would you record?), that there is both D/A and A/D latency in the chain. Similarly, when you hit a key on a MIDI keyboard there is a delay between you hitting the key and the sound being audible, since there is a finite time for a MIDI message to travel down the wire and open the synth's envelope. There will be yet more latency involved if the MIDI instrument is a VSTi. And even your trusty hardware synth takes a finite amount of time to start producing sound (in most cases). Latency is everywhere.

There is a tendency to talk about latency as a single entity. That somehow if we could just fix "the" latency then all our timing and synchronization problems would be solved. Unfortunately, things aren't that simple. Latency always refers to a delay, but there are subtle differences in the way some of these delays occur and can be compensated for. On the whole, every discrete cause of latency in the audio chain has to be treated individually.

Samples and milliseconds

Let's start by taking a look at the scale of latency. We need to keep in mind that sound travels through air at approximately one foot per millisecond (or $\approx 1/3$ metre per millisecond).

At a sample rate of 44.1KHz, 1ms represents 44 samples (ignoring the 0.1 of a sample). The maths is easy, but you can *see* this for yourself by zooming in on a piece of audio in Cubase Sx's Sample Editor. Figure 20.1 shows a 10ms region having been selected. The figure top-right is the sample at the end of the region. It reads 441, as expected. So, for our purposes:

1ms = 1ft (or 1/3m) = 44 samples

But what does that mean in real audio terms; when you actually listen to it? Now is the time to sit down in front of you monitors. Put on a drum loop (or something similar) and hear for yourself the effect of a 1ms delay. You really should do this if you never have. Continue to listen while you increase the delay in 1ms steps. You can do this with the Cubase Sx nudge function with the display format set to seconds and the snap value at 1ms. Another way is to use Inspector delay. Avoid using a delay effect in a Send since this may introduce other latencies (see below).

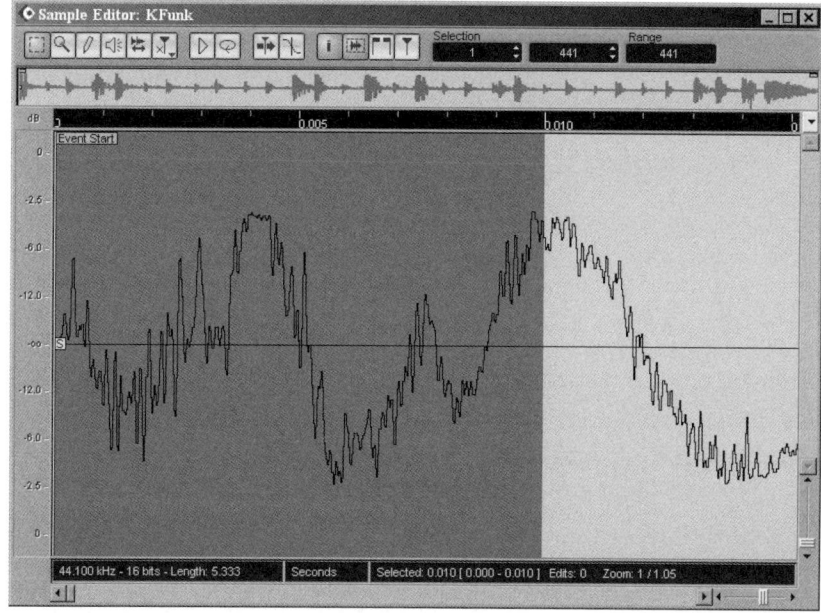

Fig. 20.1: 10ms = 441 samples of audio

Which latency?

The different types of latency

It make life easier to divide the types of latency into those that occur while recording and those that occur during playback and, sub-mixing and mixdown. There is overlap (e.g. your soundcard will be active in both record and play-back), but the practical issues are different. And, as well as developing under-standing, we are trying to help you find an appropriate modus operandi for your studio. Furthermore, we may well sub-mix an audio Track with VST effects, possibly with the use of Groups and Sends, between recording and mixdown, so we need to know whether there are any latency issues here, as well.

Recording latency.

Recording latency = A/D latency + Soundcard latency

This is the time it takes for Cubase Sx to record a sound. Cubase Sx can com-pensate for the soundcard latency, but it doesn't compensate for A/D latency. So, the digital waveform recorded in the Project will be "late" by the time of the A/D process in your studio. See below for more details on this topic.

Playback latency

Presuming a clean, effects free route through Cubase Sx, then playback latency will be:

Playback latency = Soundcard latency + D/A conversion latency.

Playback latency is only a major issue when monitoring through Cubase Sx (which is not recommended because of the delays introduced) and when playing VSTi's. When recording audio, Cubase Sx compensates for the soundcard latency, but it doesn't compensate for D/A latency. So, the digital waveform recorded in the Project will be "late" by the time of the D/A process plus the time of the A/D process. See below for more details on this topic.

Monitoring distance latency

We mentioned earlier that:

44 samples = 1 ms = 1 ft ($\approx 1/3$ m)

Therefore, if a musician is not wearing headphones for monitoring, then this will introduce an added delay in the recorded signal equivalent to 1 ms per foot (or ≈ 3 ms per metre).

Soundcard set-up

Every modern soundcard can have its buffer size adjusted (buffers are sized in samples not bits). These buffers are where digital audio is received from an audio application (like Cubase Sx) before being passed on down the digital chain. Only when the buffer is full does the soundcard pass the data on. The manufacturers usually supply a small program that allows you to adjust these buffers. The RME Hammerfall, for example, provides buffer settings between 64 and 8192 samples (namely: 64, 128, 256, 512, 1024, 2048. 4096 and 8192 samples).

Since the first sample into the buffer has to "wait" until the buffer is full before being sent on its way, you can see that this process introduces latency. You might ask why the samples are delayed. This is fair question. Let's not get into the gory details, but suffice to say that samples do not necessarily arrive from a DAW at the precise sample rate intervals required by digital hardware. To fix this, the soundcard buffers the digital audio until it has a decent size chunk, and then passes it on to the next process.

It should now be clear that the larger the buffer size, the larger the delay. Let's suppose we are working at a sample rate of 44.1kHz. So,

Latency = Buffer Size/Sample Rate

Therefore, for a buffer of 128 samples:

Latency $= 128/44100 = 0.0029$ sec (or 2.9 ms)

For a buffer of 8192 samples:

Latency $= 8192/44100 = 0.186$ sec (or 186 ms)

Keep in mind that this is *only* the delay for passing on the digital audio; there is no D/A conversion taking place.

Recording plus playback latency

Soundcard buffer latency is "known" to Cubase Sx, and so adjustments are made in the software to negate the effect. However, when recording and monitoring there is one more latency issue: the D/A and A/D conversion, and this is not compensated for, nor can it be automatically compensated for, in Cubase Sx.

Here's a simple test that you can perform (on any sequencer) to discover the D/A plus A/D time in your set-up:

○ Open a new Project
○ Turn on the metronome
○ Place a microphone right up next to your monitors (a finger width away, real close)
○ Record the metronome, then turn it off
○ Leaving the mic where it is, record the metronome audio Track to a new Track.
○ Now zoom right in and examine the two waveforms

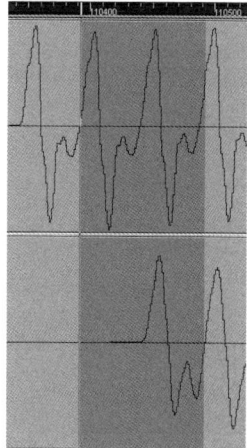

What you will see is something similar to that shown. In this case the difference between the two waveforms is 100 samples (just over 2ms @ 44.1 kHz). Cubase Sx has removed the soundcard latency, and what remains is the sum of the D/A and A/D.

If you are getting significantly worse results than 100 samples, then you need to investigate why this is happening as a matter of urgency.

In this example, it is known that the actual conversion figure is 92 samples (D/A plus A/D). System jitter can probably account for another 1 sample. This leaves 7 samples to account for, which will be the distance of the mic from the speaker.

This delay will be present on all recordings that you make; whether you need to adjust for it or not, is up to you. However, note that if you repeat the above process with the newly recorded audio file, then the "shift" will occur again; in this case we would be 200 samples from the original start-point. Put in the context of a song, this cumulative effect could be very noticeable and problematic.

Latency – a picture

As a final aside, if you are able, it is suggested that you perform the above test, but this time as a digital loop-back. In this case the offset should be no more than one sample.

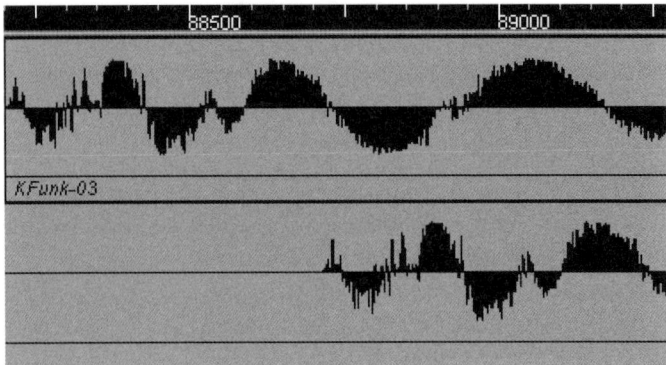

Fig. 20.2: Group Track Latency

Latency when using effects and buses

Some plug-ins may introduce a unwanted delay to the resulting audio. The amount of latency introduced by a VST plug-in can be found via Device/Plug-in Information. This figure is not provided for DirectX plug-ins (although is should be).

> ♪   **Note**
>
> Delay times vary with the ASIO (soundcard) buffer size; the larger the buffer, the higher the latency. However, the VST buffer ceiling is 1024 samples, even when the ASIO buffer is larger.

Insert, Send and Group Effects

Delay compensation is automatically applied by Cubase Sx to remove latency for Insert effects. Note, however, that this does not apply to Send effects or when routing audio via Groups, or VSTi's and Rewire channels that contain insert effects.

You can determine the sample delay introduced for each VST plug-in from the *Delay (Samples)* column on the *Devices/Plug-in Information* [No Default] window. Be aware that you might have to update the display to obtain accurate delay figures. The display requires updating after changing the soundcard's buffer size. Also be aware that not all figures are necessarily correctly reported. If you do have to shift audio Events by-hand, then it is essential to check the sample delay yourself (see below).

Take a look at figure 20.2. *Spektral Delay* was used in this example. It was listed as having a latency (sample delay) of 512 samples. The audio track (top) was routed to a Group Track with Spektral Delay as an insert effect on that Group

Track. The resulting Track (bottom) was created by performing an *Export/Audio Mixdown* [No Default]. As you can seen, the resulting mixdown is delayed, as expected, by exactly 512 sample (see image). Not pretty.

However, if we move the *Spektral Delay* plug-in to one of the audio Track's own inserts, the problem disappears. Try this yourself and confirm that the result is sample accurate by zooming down to sample level in the *Sample Editor*.

Also try the same thing with one or two DirectX plug-ins, both as an audio Track insert and as a Group insert. It is quite an eye-opener to *see* the effect. And a few plug-ins will, no doubt, surprise you.

Many folk get caught-out by, say, sending a number of vocal Tracks to a Group with a compressor Insert, and finding that the timing of the Project has gone askew. It is especially easy to go astray when using a Group as an effect rack, when routing a Send to a Group.

Delay compensation is not available on Send effects, nor on Group Tracks, VSTi channels nor Rewire channels. This is a very important point. Therefore any plug-in which imparts a delay will need to be considered individually. The delays are cumulative; the more effects you add, the more the delay.

Compensating for effect latency

One way to discover the latency figure of an effect chain is to bounce an Event. You can then compare the two audio waveforms by using the Range tool to read off the sample figure in the Info Line.

Depending on how you are routing your audio, you might be able to compensate by using the Track's Delay slider in the Inspector. Alternatively, you can nudge the audio Events itself into position.

It is not possible to compensate a Send bus directly, so they are best avoided in most cases. You might want to use Sends for some time based effects where phasing and precise synchronization is not an issue. As mentioned elsewhere, it is good practice to use Groups as Send effects racks, and this is another reason why.

One method for dealing with delay compensation is to route Tracks that do not require any adjustment to a common Group Track. Here you can insert a delay plug-in and then route the output to the appropriate bus. However, Tracks with differing delays will require different adjustments, so the whole thing can become very messy. If you are also sending Channels directly to output buses then things are complicated further.

Each Group needs to be considered on its own. Perhaps the most problematic plug-ins are compressors on Group Tracks. Since there is no time-based related effect associated with a compressor, the resulting delay tends to be obvious and unwanted. Sometimes, however, the delays are very small or insignificant on the material being processed. On other Tracks, even a small amount of delay may be unacceptable (drum Tracks, in particular), in which case you might have to consider bouncing the Track(s) and moving them into place as described above.

For PC users there is a small utility called *Sample Slide* (available from www.analogx.com) that allows you offset audio from 0 to 88100 samples, which may be of some help.

MIDI and VSTi Latency

MIDI Messages

It takes an amount of time for the MIDI Note On message to reach a MIDI device, whether hardware of software. So, whether recording or playing back, there will be latency inherent in the MIDI messages.

A MIDI Note on message takes approximately 1ms to be passed between one device and the next, purely because of the relatively low line speed that MIDI still uses. On top of this MIDI choke can occur when many messages are sent either to a device, or through a single device. And, of course, the sending and receiving devices have to interpret the messages, and the receiving device has to play a sound. All of these factors can throw a set of MIDI messages out of sync, at least temporarily, and there will always be delays present. Because of this, it is recommended that all MIDI audio is recorded and then treated like any other audio within Cubase Sx.

VSTi's

VSTi's are best recorded by using Audio Mixdown (solo the Track and go). The result is sample accurate, and it doesn't get better than that. Remember, however, that Insert effects' latency is not automatically compensated, so it is best to bounce the VSTi without effects, and then use the same effects on the resulting audio channel.

Real-time playback of VSTi's will be subject to the same latency issues as audio, with the additional overhead of a possible processing delay within the instrument itself. When playing a VSTi from a keyboard, MIDI message latency, soundcard latency and D/A latency will be added to the sum of the delays.

In fact real-time playback of VSTi's is subject to variations in latency (called latency jitter) due to the nature of buffering in ASIO. The latency of any particular sound will vary from one to two buffers.

LTB and the Midex8

Linear Time Base (LTB) is a Steinberg technology that aims to achieve improved MIDI timing. This technology has been included in Sx and their Midex MIDI interfaces. By sending MIDI messages to the interface early, they can be sent to their destination at precisely the right time, and simultaneously. This technology circumvents the serial nature of MIDI messages to multiple devices, and also guarantees timing accuracy that is not at the whim of the host computer.

21 Score: In Brief

The *Score Editor* is both a MIDI editor *and* a score print-formatter. It is a complex beast, and the size of the supplied manual *Cubase Sx: Score Layout and Printing Manual* reflects this. No book on Cubase Sx would be complete without some mention of *Score*, but what to cover? Folk seem to sit in two camps: one lot use *Score* as an essential tool, and so are happy to dig deep into the manual, experiment and become expert at its use; the other lot *never* use it. This chapter caters for the latter. Hopefully, a brief introduction to the basic functions will arm them with a set of editing tools that they might not otherwise use, and may, in some cases, be easier, or more intuitive, to use than via the other MIDI editors. We will focus on editing, but with a respectful eye toward the display and printing of scores, which is, after all, the ultimate purpose of the *Score Editor*.

♫   *Note*

Notes on a score are affectionately called *dots*. We'll use this term throughout, since it makes it easier to distinguish between Sx MIDI Events and dots on the page.

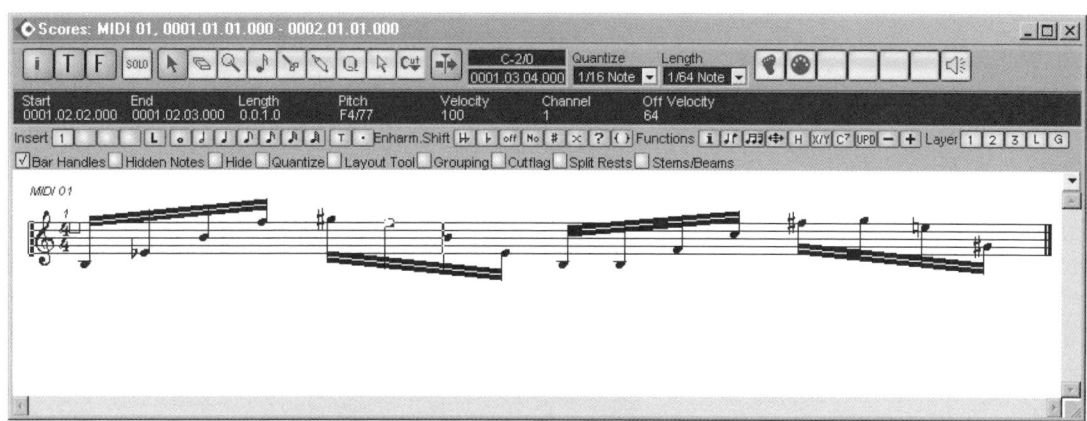

Fig. 21.1: A one bar Score

Score: A practical 101

♪   *Note*

As with all Cubase S$_X$
MIDI editors, when *Score*
opens, the associated
Track automatically
becomes record enabled.

S$_L$ *SL Info*

S$_L$ has quite a limited
version of *Score*. The text
covers the S$_X$ version.

♪   *Note*

You can make *Score* your
default editor in
*Preferences/Event
Display/MIDI*.

Start by creating a MIDI Track and a one bar Part. Set *Quantize* to 1/16th and fill the one bar Part with 1/16th notes of various pitches in the *Key Editor* [No Default]. Try to keep the notes in the approximate range **C3** thru **C5**. This will ensure that the dots appear nicely centered on the default *treble clef* in *Score*. Now, select the Part and do *Edit/Open Score Editor* [CTRL+R].

You will see something that looks like figure 21.1: one *staff*, treble *clef*, 4/4 *time signature*. Each dot represents a MIDI Note Event. In the figure, a note has been selected, using the *Select* tool (either click or lasso), and its MIDI Event data are shown in the *Info Line*. Try it for yourself. You can change MIDI Event date in the *Info Line*, as with other editors. Usefully, the start and end bar locations are shown in the window title.

In the toolbar, switch off the three buttons on the far left. That looks better. These buttons are for the familiar *Info Line*; the *Tool Bar*; and the *Filter*. Don't worry about the last two for now (but make sure that you leave *Bar Handles* active in the *Filter* line). The toolbar is very similar to that of the *Key Editor*, and you might want to take a look at the section in chapter 12 on page 133. Also useful is the section *Editing MIDI notes from a keyboard* on page 144.

To select a dot, you can use the left and right cursor keys (or click on a dot). Hold SHIFT to select multiples (or lasso), and SHIFT double-click to select all notes to the end of the staff. To deselect everything, click in the whitespace.

Moving dots is the main objective right now, and to do so just select and drag. You can restrict movement to the horizontal and vertical axes by holding CTRL, as usual. If you want to hear the note as you move it, then switch on the speaker icon in the toolbar. Dots snap to the quantize value, so change *Quantize* to 1/32 in the toolbar and try moving a dot.

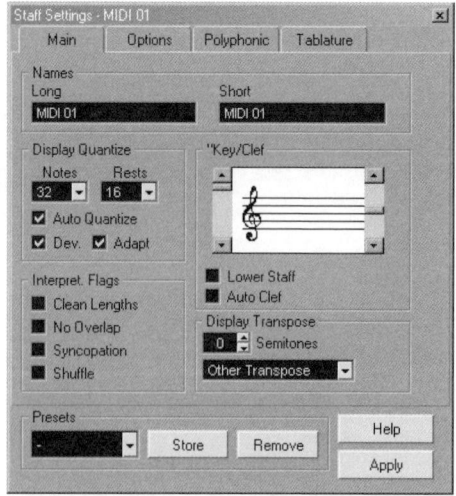

Fig. 21.2: Staff settings

But what's this? As you drag a dot left or right, you can see it snapping to 1/32 but, as soon as you release the mouse-button, it snaps to 1/16. We have stumbled onto an important feature of *Score*: *Display Quantize*. Double-click to the *left* of the staff to open *Scores/Staff set-up* [No Default]. *Notes* sets the shortest displayable note and position size on the staff.

In the *Display Quantize* section, change the *Notes* dropdown from 16 to 32. Click *Apply* and close the window. You can now drag your dots in steps that match the *Quantize* value.

The important point to take away from this is that there are two operations going on in *Score*: First we have the *editing* of MIDI Events for playback; second, we have the *formatting* of the score for display and, ultimately, printing.

One thing you probably noticed: there is no *Ruler*. But don't panic, if you click *in front* of a dot, or double-click in most places, the Cursor will align itself with the *Quantize* setting. If you run the Transport, then you can click in *Score* and the Cursor will immediately jump to that point.

♩   Note

Right-clicking in the *Score* toolbar gives access to most of the items in the MIDI and Score menus.

The next step

Moving notes

The above section was a very simple and, hopefully, straightforward introduction to the absolute basics of *Score*. Let's move things along a little.

Dragging dots around the screen is a little imprecise, so why not use key commands? Usefully, *Nudge/Left* [No Default] and *Nudge/Right* [No Default] work just fine. These will nudge the MIDI Events by the *Quantize* setting, but what will be displayed will be determined by the *Display Quantize* setting, as shown above.

To nudge the note up or down a semitone at a time, you can use *Nudge/Top* [No Default] and *Nudge/Bottom* [No Default]. Delete notes in the usual way with DEL, etc. You can also move all selected notes up or down an octave by using SHIFT+up and SHIFT+down.

Okay, we're starting to get into the useful stuff. It's already easy to see how, after setting a loop going, we could nudge notes around to create a groove on a drum or bass part, or even something more complex. But, to make this practical, we need to be able to create new notes.

↗   Tip

For *Nudge Left/Right/Bottom/Top* consider CTRL+SHIFT+ *Left/Right/Down/Up.*

↗   Tip

For rapid input of notes, assign the key commands for the *MIDI Quantize* functions. Assigning *Select Next Quantize* and *Select Previous Quantize*, then setting *Length* to *Linked to quantize* is a speedy way to create a melody.

New notes

It's a shame, but *Edit/Duplicate* [CTRL+D] doesn't work in *Score*. To duplicate a note you must ALT+drag. *Duplicate* would allow us to create new notes on the fly, and nudge them into place. It's still possible in the *Key Editor*, of course.

New notes are created with the *Note* tool. As with the *Key Editor*, length is determined by the *Length* field in the toolbar (although you can also make a selection on the *Tool Bar*), and the notes' start positions are constrained by *Quantize*. Remember that the display quantize will determine what you see, so

Note tool

it's a good idea to set this to one of the higher resolutions (e.g. 32 or 64) when adding notes.

Create an empty Part of one bar to experiment with here, and route the channel to something with a fast attack and moderate decay, like a piano patch. *Set locators* [P] and let it loop in playback. Open *Score*, set the *Display Quantize* to 32 and both *Quantize* and *Length* to 1/8th (or *Length* to *Linked to quantize*, if you prefer). Select the *Note Tool* and add away. Try creating two note chords in a couple of places. Nudge the notes into place. Missing *Duplicate* yet?

Changing a note's length

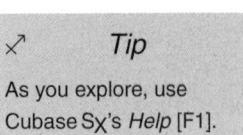

The simple way to change a note's length is to select the *Length* required and click on the note with the *Note* tool. This doesn't present a problem in the current example, where note lengths being displayed are the actual note lengths, but the material being edited and the *Display Quantize* settings may mean that this isn't the case, so the act of changing a note's length may not *appear* to give the expected result in some cases.

Tied notes can be *cut* with the *Scissors* tool into two separately sounding notes. Similarly, clicking a note with the *glue* tool will either merge, or tie, it to the next note of the same pitch on the staff.

Tied notes

More display set-up info

We already had a brief look at *Display Quantize* in *Scores/Staff set-up* [No Default], and we'll return to it in a second. First, double-click on the *treble clef* and explore the clefs available. Note the drum and tab clefs right at the end of the list. Now, double-click on the *time signature*. Hit [F1] for a detailed explanation, but note that changing the time signature here will insert a time signature change in the time signature track and thus will affect *all* Tracks.

Also note the editable text above the clef; this is the *Staff Name*. This is also found in *Scores/Staff set-up* [No Default] as the *Long Name* and is very useful when you start editing multiple Parts.

Multiple parts

Duplicate [CTRL+D] the one bar Part that we created at the start of *Score: A practical 101* (no need to glue them). Next duplicate the whole Track (right-click the *Track List* and use *Duplicate Track*). Now transpose the duplicate Part down an octave in whichever way you prefer. Finally, select *all* the Parts and do *Edit/Open Score Editor* [CTRL+R]. You should have something similar to figure 21.3.

If the staff names are the same, then rename one so that they are differentiated. The obvious problem here is that the notes on the lower staff are not really on it. No problem, just double-click the clef symbol and pick the *bass clef*.

You can edit in the same way as above, but with the addition that the *up* and *down* cursors move between staffs. Unfortunately, when doing so, the point of selection returns to the start of the score. The *active staff* is indicated by a

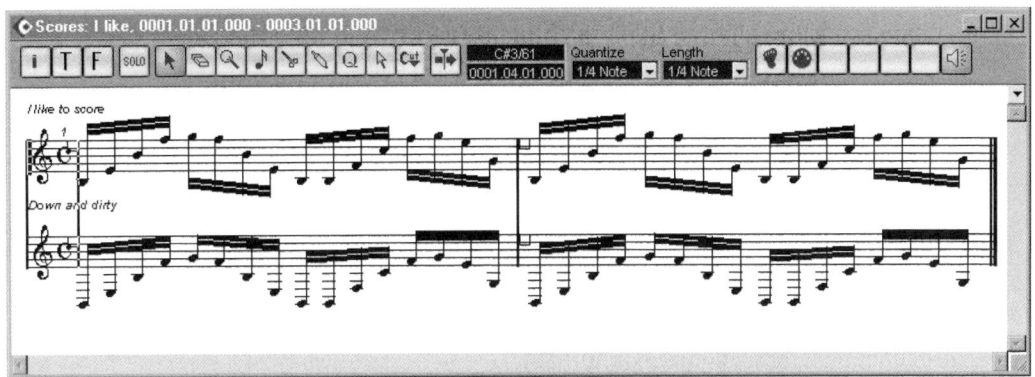

Fig. 21.3: A two bar, two part Score

small vertical bar to the left of the clef. It is this staff/Track that will be record enabled. This same process works for as many Tracks as you wish. The maximum number of bars shown horizontally is four, but can be changed in *Preferences/Scores*.

Immediately above and to the right of the *time signature*, between the two top lines of the staff, is a small box; this is the *Bar Handle*. If you click this, then the bar will be selected. You are now in bar-editing mode, so you can't edit notes. You can, however, select more bars in the usual way with SHIFT and the cursor keys.

By grabbing the *bar handle*, you can drag the bar to another location. By holding ALT, a copy is taken. (Unlike other Cubase SX editors, you must press ALT *before* clicking the *Bar Handle*, otherwise a move is performed.) The notes are not added to the receiving bar, the receiving bar is *overwritten*. This operation opens the *Bar Copy* dialog, from which you can select the item, and the number of repeats, that you wish to copy/move.

> ♪ **Note**
>
> Each staff has its own settings. So, for example, *Scores/Staff set-up* [No Default] is unique for each staff.

Tidying an existing part

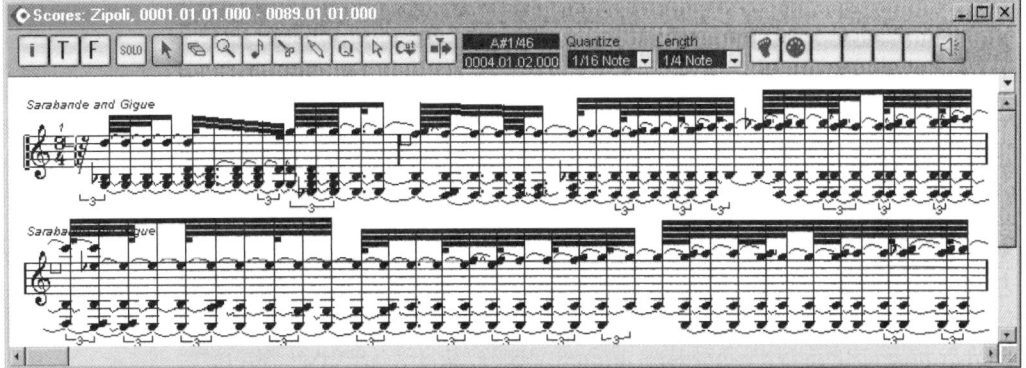

A common requirement of *Score* is to take a piece recorded in realtime (with all those non-quantized, human timings) and transcribe this for use by others. Here we'll do this by example, and keep it simple. There is a huge amount of power under the hook within *Score*, and we can only scratch the surface here. Note that we will only adjust *display* options, we are not altering the MIDI Events in any way. However, at the end of the section, we'll look at how to create a MIDI version of the displayed score.

The example shown above is a piano piece, so the first step is to split the staff into treble and bass clefs. You do this from the *Polyphonic* tab of *Scores/Staff set-up* [No Default]. Select *Split* from the *Staff Mode* dropdown and click *Apply*. Providing you have sufficient screen real estate, then keep the dialog open

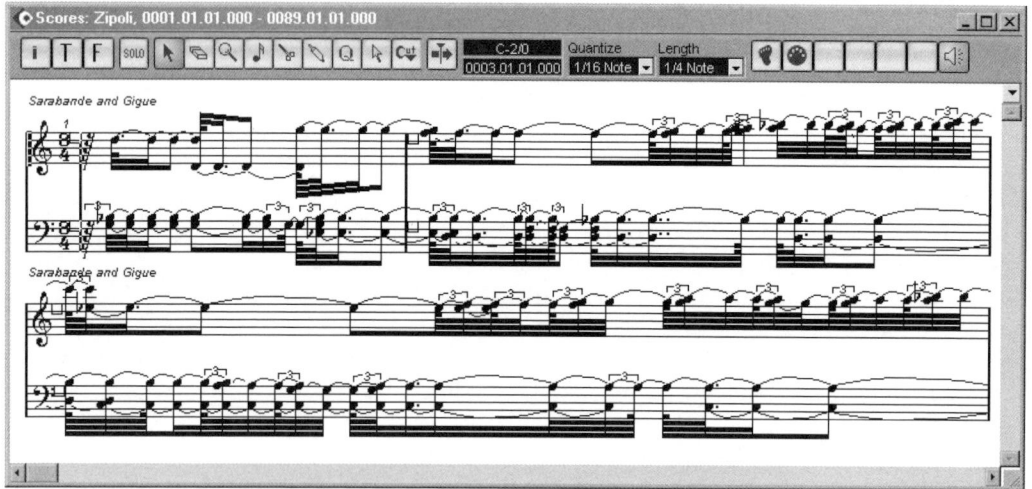

Clearly the *rest* at the start is not intended, and the 64th notes are questionable, so let's go back to the *Main* tab on *Staff set-up* and adjust the *Display Quantize* entries for *Notes* and *Rests*. There are clearly 32nd notes here, so we'll set *Notes* to 32nds. But *Rests* is only used as a *recommendation* to *Score* (*Score* will override this value if it needs to), so we will be brutal and set it to 4. We also note a couple of flats in the score, so we will also adjust *Key/Clef* to have two flats.

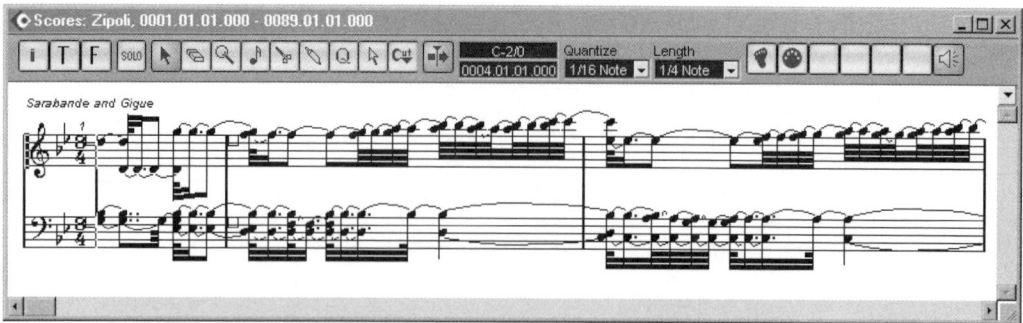

That looks a lot better, but a piano player would still feel a bit queazy glacing at it. However, by checking *No overlap* in the *Interpret Flags* section of *Staff set-up's Main* tab, we get the following:

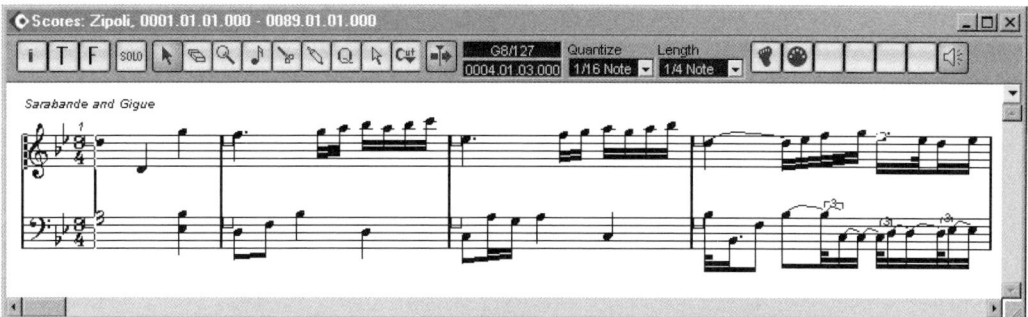

However, those 32nd notes don't look so important on this section and those triplets may not be triplets at all. So, let's change *Display Quantize Notes* to 16 and uncheck *Auto Quantize*.

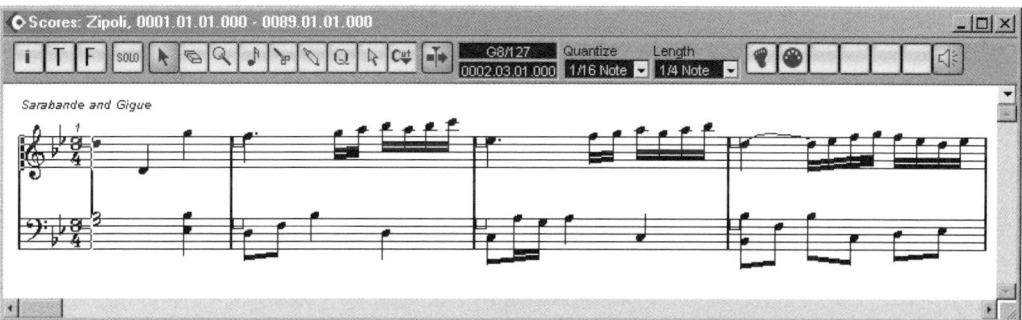

And the finished score above proves to be quite different to the original below.

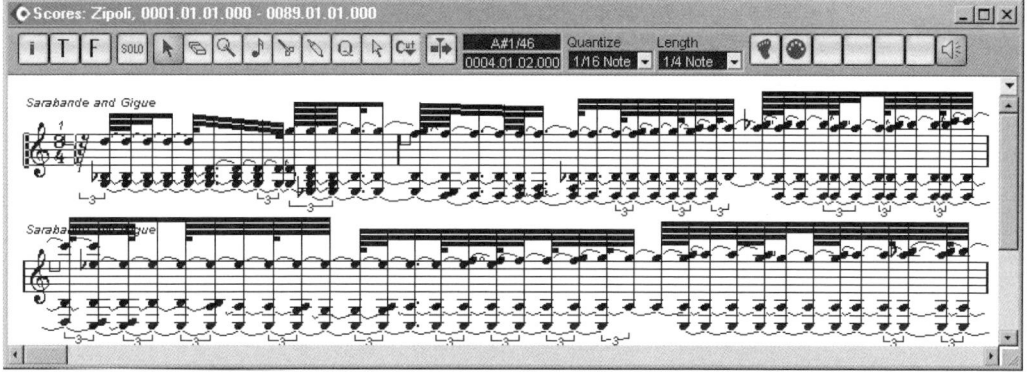

So now you have the *perfect* score of you part, you might like to create a MIDI version of the displayed score (since all your edits are for display only). Before issuing the function to do this, make sure you create a new copy of the Part or Track that you will be converting. The easiest way to do this is to use *Duplicate Track*, as this will bring across all the *Score* settings. Open the Part in *Score* and select *Score Functions/Scores notes to MIDI* [No Default] (which is *Scores/Global Functions/Scores notes to MIDI* in the menus). Now playback and compare the two examples.

In this example, global settings were made to the staff to help it display our intended end result. But there is a awful lot more to this feature. The **Q** tool allows you to inserts changes to the *Staff set-up* at any point along the staff, so you can make changes to the score for a few bars, or just a few notes. And, if you are viewing polyphonically (i.e. two staffs for a Track), then you can change each voice individually. Check-out the chapter *Transcribing MIDI recordings* in the *Cubase Sx: Score Layout and Printing Manual* for much more detail on this topic.

Some Preferences

Full explanations of all *Preferences/Scores* and *Preferences/Scores/Event Layer* tabs are given in the help system. You are strongly encouraged to read through the list, since there are some excellent features and subtle changes to the interface available that might be just what you are looking for.

For example, a selection:

○ *Edit all Parts on Track:* Saving you from selecting all Parts before entering *Score*.
○ *Keep moved notes within key*
○ *Tied notes selected as single units:* Select either note of a tied-pair and both are selected.
○ *"Apply" closes Property windows*
○ *Show note info by the mouse:* For a dragged or inserted note, displays the position, pitch and note number.

Scoring Drum Tracks

Drum and percussion tracks can be given special treatment in *Score*. There are two main ways in which you can change how *Score* displays a drum Track. First, you can replace the usual black blob of the note on the staff with a different *note-head* (e.g. an **X**, a square or a triangle). These symbols are freely assignable, so you can choose which *note-head* symbol is assigned to which drum sound. Secondly, you can display the drum staff as a single line. If you create your drum tracks as a single MIDI Track in Sx, then this could make the score quite cluttered, but if you keep drum sounds on separate Tracks (or only related sounds, such as high hats, on the same Track), then the score will be more useful.

You can create many sets of *note-heads* symbols. Each set is related to a *Drum Map* (see page 120). There is also a *default note-head* set that is used when a *Drum Map* has not been assigned.

Let's look at an example.

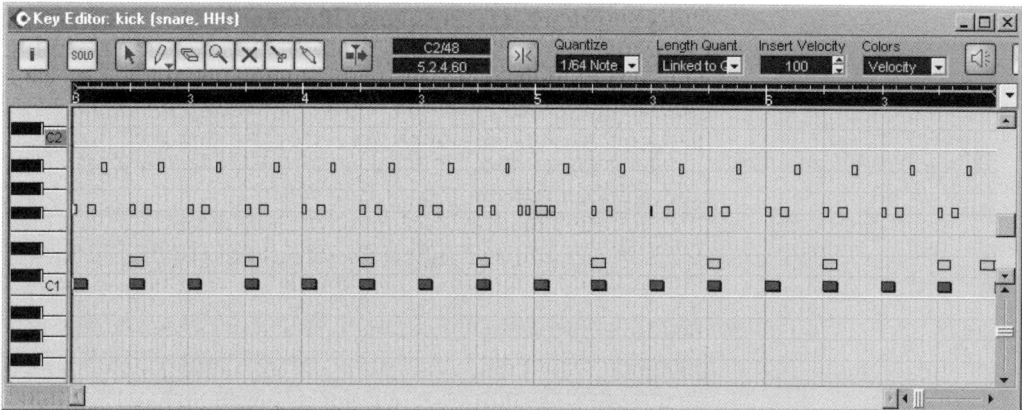

Here is a simple 4-bar drum pattern, containing three Tracks: Kick; Snare and high-hats (HHs). And here it is in *Score* (bar 4 is not shown).

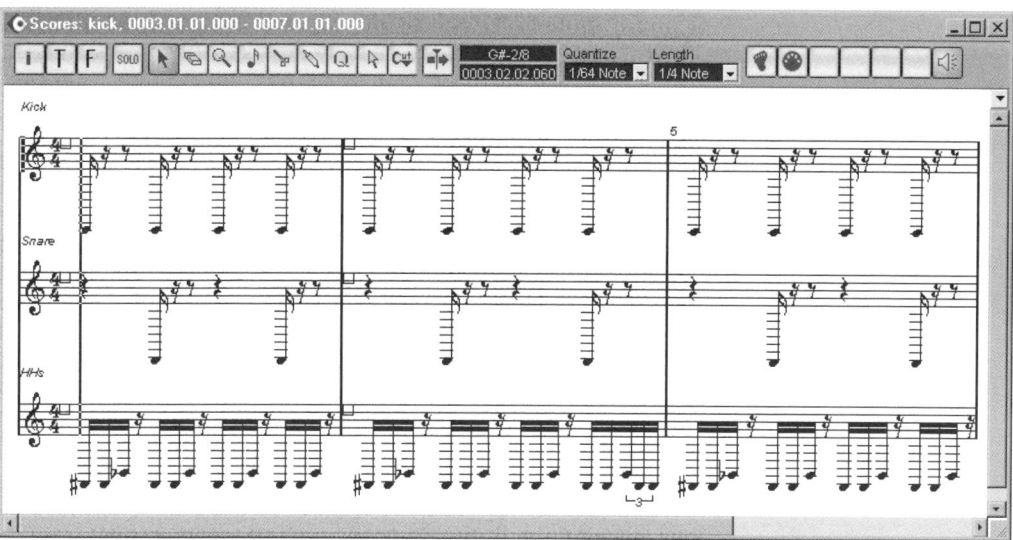

We will not assign a *Drum Map* to any of the Tracks, but it is simple to do so if we wished. In this case we will use the default *note-heads*.

We start by changing the *treble clefs* to *drum clefs*: double-click on each and select the appropriate clef. Now, open *Scores/Staff set-up* [No Default] for one of the staffs. Remember that each staff has its own settings, so we must change each one individually. Go to the *Options* tab and check *Use Score Drum Map* from *Score Drum Map*. We get the following:

If you are the least bit familiar with dots (and even if you only learned recorder at school), this probably conveys quite a lot of information to you. Observe that the HHs have new *note-heads*, and that the Open HH has a different note-head to the Closed HH. This is the effect of the default *note-head map* mentioned above. You can view this map via *Scores/Global Settings/Drum Map* (*Scores/Drum Map* [No Default]). When you click a dot on the score, the *Score Drum Map* will locate to that sound. Check help for more information on what can be edited here. If we had used a *Drum Map*, then the *Score Drum Map* would be unique for the chosen *Drum Map*. In that case, the *Score Drum Map* would be created with the same symbol for all pitches, so you would have to assign a symbol for each pitch (if you wanted anything other than the default). Just for the heck of it, let's change the symbols for the kick and snare.

> ♪   **Note**
>
> *Score Functions/Tools:*
> *Flip* [No Default] will flip
> the stems on selected
> notes. There is also a
> button on the *Tool Bar* to
> fulfill the same function.

Let's keep tweaking. The *Kick* and *Snare* staves are not representative of those sounds. Quarter notes (crotchets) would look better, so we simply change *Notes* in *Display Quantize* to 4. this gives us:

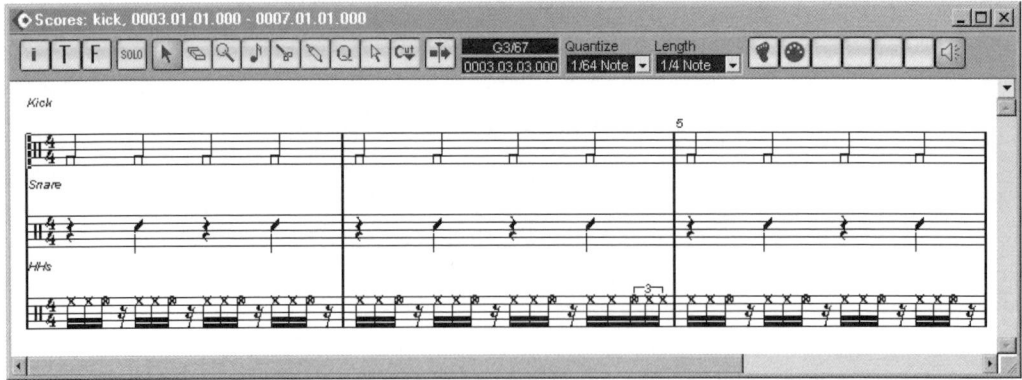

As a final embellishment, we'll set each drum sound on a single line. Do this in *Staff Settings*, by checking *Single Line Drum Staff* in *Score Drum Map* on the *Options* tab. With some other minor adjustments, this leads us to our final result; this time showing all 4 bars.

When using dots on a single line, you have the option of placing them either

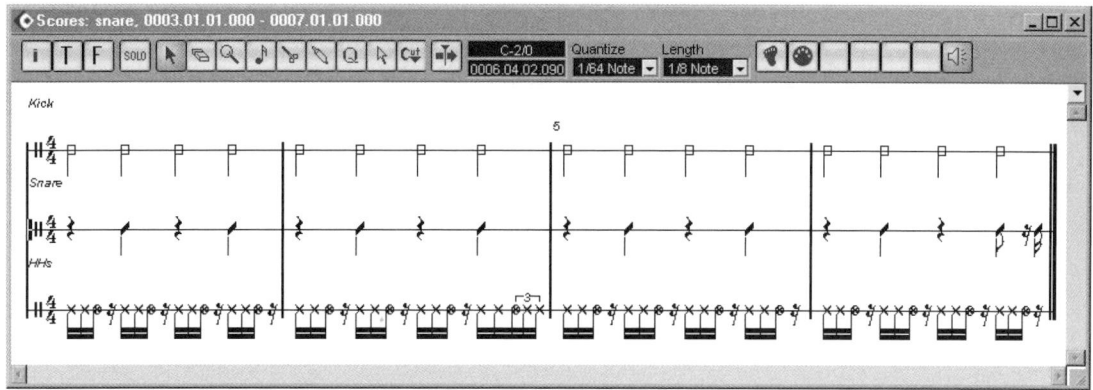

Fig. 21.4: The completed drum score.

on, above or below the line, depending on their pitch. We could have done this with the HHs, for example. But if you take a look at the *Display* column in the default *Score Drum Map*, you will find that the HHs are adjusted to *display* (not sound) at the same pitch. When you create your own drum maps, this is one of the finer points to consider.

Scoring Guitar Tracks

In this section we'll add chord figures to a score, but rather than doing this directly, we'll first convert the score to tablature (tab). In the process, this will introduce a few more of *Score's* common functions. We start with a score.

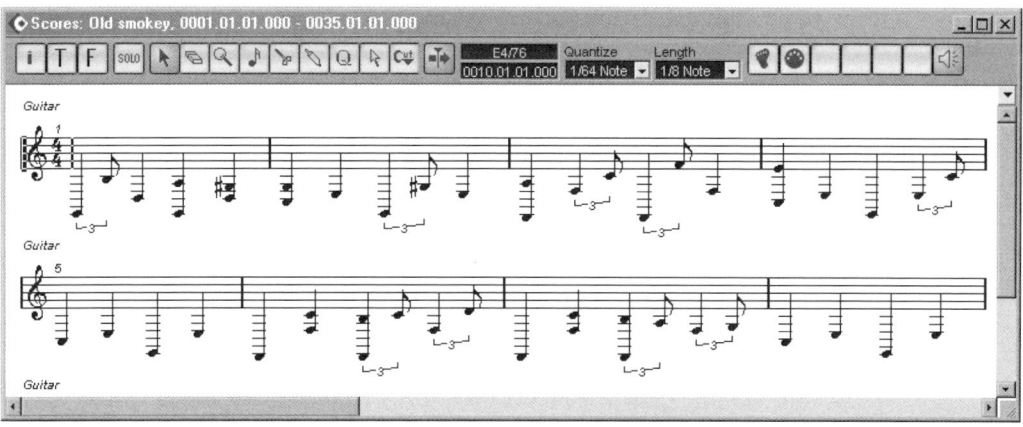

To convert this to a guitar tab, open our old friend *Staff Settings* and select the *Tablature* tab. The default settings are fine for our needs, so check *Tablature Mode* then *Apply*. Voilà, instant tablature (fig. 21.5). Almost. There are a few steps we need to take to tidy things up.

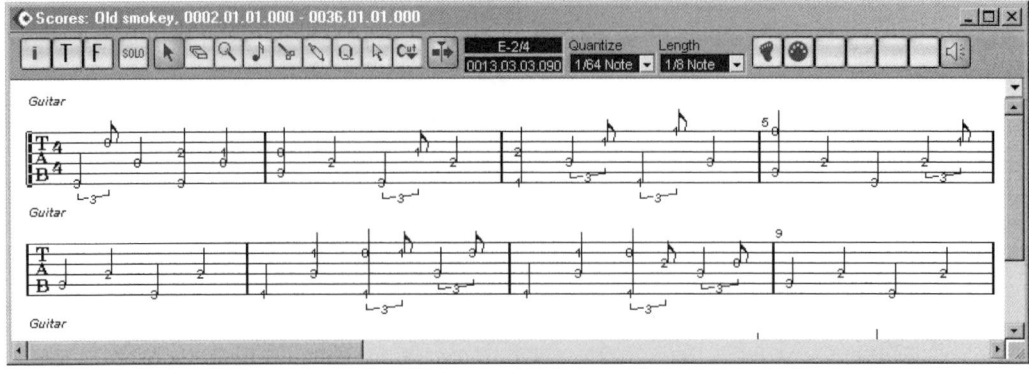

Fig. 21.5: A tabulated score

First, change the clef to one of the two tab options. Back in the, now exhausted, *Staff Settings*, select the *Options* tab and, in *System Sizes* increase both *System Lines* and *Add Space* by one (to 6 and 1, respectively) and *Apply*.

If you find the tablature numbers a little small in the default setting, open *Scores/Global Settings/Text* and select *Tablature* in the *Font For* dropdown, and adjust to taste.

Should you wish to edit some of the notes, perhaps by bracketing or removing a stem, double-click the note to open *Note Info*. One trick is to *Select All* [CTRL+A] then open *Note Info* and set *all* the stem in the direction your prefer.

Adding Chords

To add guitar chord diagrams to a score, we have to use one of *Score's* symbol palettes. Open *Scores/Symbol Palettes/Other* and click on the guitar chord symbol (above the keyboard symbol). When you move the mouse cursor over the score, you will find that the cursor has become a pencil. Click on the score where you want to place the symbol. You can drag it freely later, so don't worry about precise placement. This action will open the *Guitar Symbol* window, from which you can design a chord.

This method works just fine, but if you open *Scores/Global Settings/Guitar Library* you can create a repository of named chord-shapes. Each entry can then be selected from the *Library* dropdown in the *Guitar Symbol* window.

To create a chord diagram in the *Guitar Library* click *New*, then double-click the image in the *Guitar* column. Design your chord, then click *Exit*. The chord will automatically be named. If the name is not to your liking, then you can edit it by double-clicking the existing name in the *Chord* column.

You can now select the new symbols from the *Guitar Symbol* window. You will need to close and re-open the *Guitar Symbol* window for the new names to appear in the *Library* dropdown. You can also right-click the symbol on the score and make a selection.

To finish tidying up the score, we need to add the chord names under the chord diagrams and align the text and diagrams. Text entries are created in the same way as chord diagrams, by selecting the *Text* symbol from the palette and

♫   *Note*

You can only have a single *Guitar Library* loaded at one time. Make sure you save your changes.

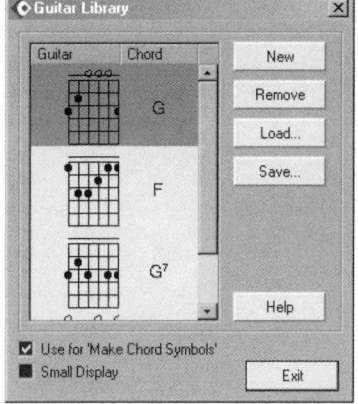

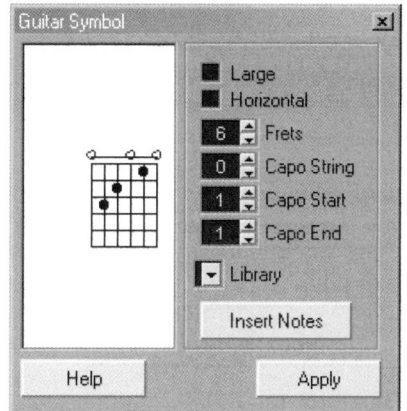

clicking on the score. To align items, first select them, then use *Scores/Align Elements/....*

In the final version, a tempo indicator has been added. To do this you must change to Score's *Scores/Page Mode*. This is the mode that one uses to prepare the score for printing. You can do everything in *Page Mode* as you can in *Edit Mode* (the mode in which we have been working), but *Page Mode* provides a vast array of addition print-related functions. To add the tempo indicator, open *Scores/Symbol Palettes/Layout* and pick the *Tempo as number* symbol, then drop it on the score. The symbol will use the current tempo as its number part, and you can right-click the symbol to select the appropriate note-type.

> ♫   *Note*
>
> If you have an open palette, then you can right-click it to select any other palette. (*Global* and *Layout* only operate in *Page Mode*.)

End-piece

As you have, no doubt, come to realize, *Score* is a deep and complex beast. However, it can be tamed. The aim of this chapter has been to guide you into the basic features of *Score* in a way that, hopefully, you will find of practical use and, at the same time, raise your interest in what *Score* can do for you.

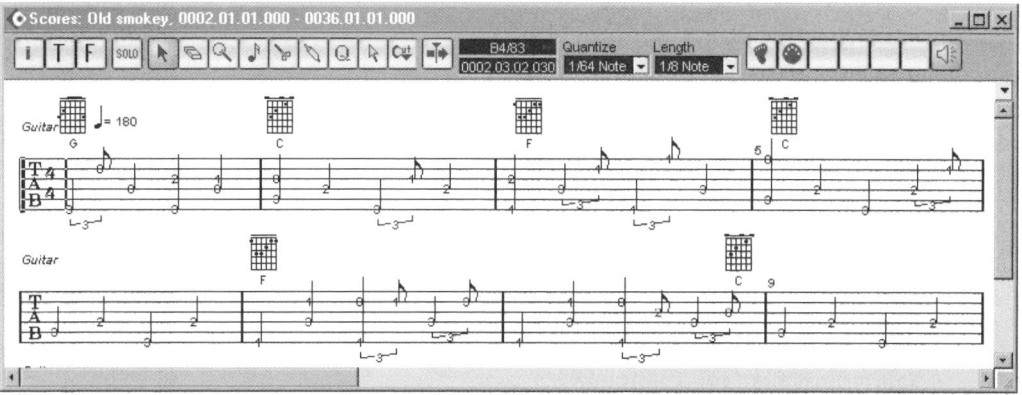

Fig. 21.6: The completed guitar score.

22 Project Maintenance and Archiving

Project Maintenance may appear to be about as interesting as watching paint dry (and let's face it, the process is not a whole lot more exciting), but it is an essential element of music production. Ensuring that our work is safely archived for future retrieval is something we must do as a matter of course, both for ourselves and for our clients.

Cubase Sx makes the process of archival and archival preparation quite simple with a number of functions specifically designed for the job.

We are not going to discuss the basics of backing up data onto alternative media, since this should be done automatically by anyone who values their work. There are many tools available to assist with incremental back-ups, and the like, and many devices appropriate for long-term file archival. Selecting the most appropriate and cost-effective solution is outside the scope of this book. But do it, okay.

And one really important tip: Be Paranoid. While writing this book I would save my work every evening to another disk on the same machine. I would then copy the whole directory structure to another machine. Then once a week I would write the whole lot to a rewritable CD and give it to a friend. Paranoid? You bet. But I never lost a thing, and I slept soundly.

> ♪ **Note**
>
> The golden rule is to test the copied Project thoroughly.

Copying a Project

Cubase Sx provides a special function that automates the process of copying a Project to a new location, *Save Project to new folder* [No Default]. However, it doesn't come without its dangers. Options are provided in the dialog to apply *Audio/Minimize File* [No Default] (see page 215) and *Audio/Freeze Edits* [No Default] (see page 222), and both of these functions change audio file irretrievably, so be absolutely clear about what you are doing when selecting these options. A third option, *Remove Unused Files* is also available that, on the surface, seems a sensible option. However, if you are using a VSTi sampler, for example, Sx will not necessarily know about the files that it uses and these might not be copied to the new location/archive, depending on how you work. Furthermore, you may want to keep unreferenced audio file in the archive, so again, be clear about what you are doing before deleting anything. The golden rule is to test the copied Project thoroughly.

Moving a Project

In most cases, you can move a Project Folder to another location without a hitch. Providing the Project folder structure remains unchanged, then Cubase Sχ is smart enough to work things out and let you continue working.

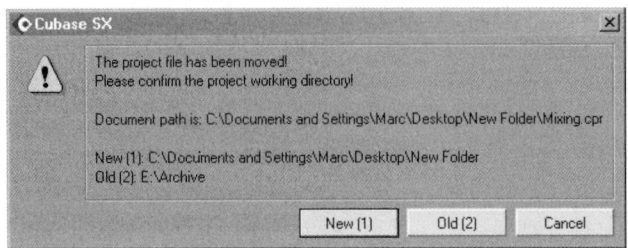

Moving a Project

Where you might have problems is if you simply take the Cubase Sχ .cpr file to another location. In this case Cubase Sχ will ask you to confirm whether you wish to continue to use the original Project Folder or start working from the new location. If you choose the new location, you will have to resolve any missing files. If you locate files outside the *Project Folder* then they will not be copied into it.

It is strongly recommended that you only move *Project Folders* as a single entity, and then perform further actions once safely relocated.

Preparing an Archive

Step 1

> ♪   *Note*
>
> The golden rule is to test the copied Project thoroughly.

Before archiving a Project you will wish to ensure that all the require data are available. This is most easily confirmed by reopening the Project, since any errors will be reported. However, there is the possibility that some data used was not imported into the *Project Folder* and Cubase Sχ provides a command to pull everything into the Project Folder in preparation for archiving.

The *Pool/Prepare Archive* [No Default] command does the following:

○ Copies any files that are located outside the *Project Folder* structure into it.
○ For any Clips that have been processed, the option will be given to *Freeze Edits* on these Clips.

You should consider carefully how and whether to apply the freeze edits option. While it is a committing action to permanently apply processing to your audio files (which is not necessarily a bad thing), it might be just as risky to not apply freeze edits since, for example, a plug-in that you use today, might either be unavailable, or have changed significantly when you return to the Project. The safest option is to preserve the original audio in a separate folder with zero usage, and to apply the freeze edits to copies. In this way you maintain the final sound files for the Track, and maintain the originals should you wish to change the processing at a later date.

Step 2

Now that we have everything we need in the *Project Folder*, let's get rid of the stuff we don't need. Hopefully alarm bells are ringing loudly in your head at this point. Good. This next step involves deleting files from disk permanently, so if you get it wrong, you have a problem.

Prior to this, and subsequent steps, you are strongly urged to secure your entire *Project Folder* until you are 100% happy that your archived version is completely intact. Remember: Be paranoid.

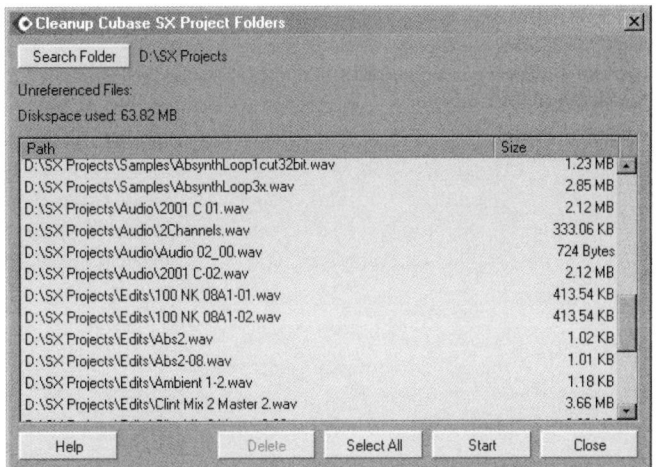

Clean-up. Are you sure that you want to delete all of these files?

The function that identifies unused audio files and facilitates their deletion is *File/Cleanup* [No default]. You can only use *Cleanup* when all Projects are closed. On selecting the command, you will be presented with a window that requires you to navigate to a *Project Folder* or simply perform a *Cleanup* on all partitions on all disks. If you do select a *Project Folder*, then any audio files not used in any Project files in that *Project Folder* hierarchy will be made available for deletion.

It is at this point that you need to be absolutely sure that you have your files in the correct places. As long as you have a backup, then you are protected in any case.

For a Project that has been:
○ managed entirely by Cubase Sx from start to finish
○ and where a folder has not been renamed
○ and where the Project files have not been shared by another Project

you should be safe to delete the files listed by the result of the *Cleanup* operation. Nevertheless, read the list carefully and make a conscious decision that it is okay to delete each and every file.

Here are a few examples of things to watch out for. It would not be unusual to use a tool, such as Native Instrument's *Battery*, and store the `.kit` file in the *Project Folder*, and its related samples in a folder within the *Project Folder*. These samples would not be "known" to Cubase Sx and *Cleanup* would present them for deletion. This is not what you would want to do. Likewise, you may have stored some master audio files for the project in a folder in the *Project Folder* hierarchy. Unless you used these exact same audio files (i.e. imported into Cubase Sx without conversion), then *Cleanup* would present them for deletion.

One solution to this potential problem is to organize your *Project Folder* structure in such a way that the Cubase Sx Project files and folders are in a completely independent hierarchy, but also part of a general Project hierarchy of folders. There are many ways to achieve the same goal, but you should take time to find a method that is going to allow you to fully exploit the features, functions and, indeed, limitations, of Cubase Sx, as well as the way that you work.

Step 3

♫   *Note*

The golden rule is to test the copied Project thoroughly.

Having tidied up your Project as far as you can, you should now reload it to ensure that there are no problems. If there are, then use you back-up to restore missing files or, at worst, start again. All being well, you can archive the Project to your preferred destination.

23 Recommended Reading and Web-sites

The Internet is a vast resource of information. One needs to take care over advice offered and what you read, since there is a lot of misinformation out there. In general, it is probably wise to locate a reliable source of information via one of the many Web communities and take pointers from there, rather than trawl the Web for information.

Usenet

RAP: rec.audio.pro
4-Track: alt.music.4-Track

Web-sites

Cubase Sx forums: forum.cubase.net
Steinberg main site   www.steinberg.net

Communities

Yahoo Groups: groups.yahoo.com

Background Reference

Studio Covers
www.studiocovers.com/articles.htm
Digital Domain
www.digido.com
ProRec
www.prorec.com
Others
www.prosoundweb.com/recpit
www.phys.tue.nl/people/etimmerman/RecordingFAQ.html

General

All Music Guide (reference)   www.allmusic.com
Sound on Sound (magazine)   www.sospubs.co.uk

Books

Digital Audio
Principles of Digital Audio, Ken Pohlmann (Howard Sams, 1985)

Mic Technique
Microphone Manual, David Miles Huber (Howard Sams, 1988)

MIDI
Midi for The Professional, Paul Lehrman and Tim Tully (Amsco, 1993)
The MIDI Files (2nd Ed.), Rob Young (Prentice Hall, 2001)
Handbook of MIDI Sequencing, Dave Clackett (PC Publishing, 1996)

Music in Film
Music in Film & Video Productions, Dan Carlin (Focal Press, 1991)

Mixing
The Mixing Engineer's Handbook, Bobby Owsinski (MIX Books, 1999)

Production
The Audio Pro Home Recording Course (Volumes I, II and III), Bill Gibson (MIX Books, 1999)
Recording Techniques for Small Studios, David Mellor (PC Publishing, 1993)
Practical Recording Techniques (2nd Ed.), Bruce and Jenny Bartlett (Focal Press, 1998)
The Art of Recording, William Moylan (Van Nostrand Reinhold, 1992)
How to become a Record Producer, David Mellor (PC Publishing, 1998)

Glossary

ADAT Optical
8 channel optical unidirectional interface for interconnecting digital audio devices with fibre-optic cable.

ADC (Analogue to Digital Converter)
An electronic device that converts an analogue input signal to a digital output signal. (See DAC.)

AES (Audio Engineering Society)
International organization that manages the audio industry's standards

AES/EBU
A type of digital-to-digital interface that usually runs over XLR terminated cables. (See S/PDIF).

AIFF
Digital audio file format used mainly on the Mac.

Aliasing
Aliasing is a form of distortion occurring in a digital waveform. It results from conversion anomalies in the higher frequencies when the signal was converted from analogue to digital. These frequencies are usually removed by using an anti-aliasing filter in the ADC.

Amplitude
The "quantity" of a signal; usually the level or volume of an audio signal.

Analogue
An electronic signal whose waveform resembles that of the original sound.

ASIO (Audio Stream Input Output)
Steinberg's proprietary soundcard driver format (more correctly ASIO is the API and drivers are written to this API). Most hardware manufacturers support ASIO on their soundcards. An ASIO driver allows direct communication between an audio program and the audio card, with little interaction with the the operating system. As a result, these drivers can provide lower latency times. The ASIO specification also provides facilities for hardware manufacturers to exploit other functionality that can be useful in an audio environment (e.g. ASIO Direct Monitoring and sample accurate synchronization).

Asynchronous
An engineering term indicating that a data stream that there is only one-way communication between two devices. Hence, there is no acknowledgement made by the receiving device that it has received the information sent to it. The result of this is that data can go missing without an error being indicated. MIDI is an example of an asynchronous protocol.

Attenuation
Reduction in level of a signal measured in dB.

Bit
A single binary digit that can only represent 1 or zero.

Bit Depth, Bit resolution, Word Length, Sample Resolution
The number of bits used to record each digital sample. (See Dynamic Range and Sample Rate.) Typical bit depths are 16-bit and 24-bit.

Bouncing
Mixing two or more Tracks into one, or permanently adding effects to a Track.

BPM (Beat per Minute)
An expression of musical tempo.

Buffer
An intermediate storage area for digital data. In general, the data is only passed on when the buffer is full. Buffer sizes can often have their size changed, making them smaller or larger. The effect of making them smaller speeds the data flow, but might result in problems downstream if the receiving device cannot cope with the increased amount of data being received.

Clipping
Distortion (often digital) caused by overloading a signal.

Comp'ing (Compiling)
Building a good take or Track from several others. Frequently used on vocals.

Crossfade
Fading out one signal and gradually fading in another to replace it.

Cycle
A periodic quantity.

DAC (Digital to Analogue Converter)
An electronic device that converts a digital input signal to an analogue output signal. (See ADC.) Essential for audio playback from a DAW such as Cubase S$_X$.

DAT (Digital Audio Tape)
The digital equivalent of the cassette. Format is 16-bit and 44.1kHz or 48kHz.

DAW (Digital Audio Workstation)

A program such as Cubase Sx or Pro Tools used for recording, mixing and playback of digital audio.

DC Offset

This can be viewed in an editor by the waveform being off-center. It is caused by a direct current being added to the signal at some point in the audio chain.

Decibel (dB)

A measure of relative intensity. An important point to note is that doubling of the amplitude of an audio signal is represented by a gain of 6dB. Subsequently, each additional bit in the bit-depth of a digital signal represents a 6dB increase in the dynamic range of that digital signal. Hence, an 8-bit digital audio will have a theoretical dynamic range of 8 * 6 = 48dB; 16-bit 16 * 6 = 96dB; 24-bit 24 * 6 = 144dB. Note: In practice, these figures are not attainable for a variety of reasons (e.g. dither, conversion imperfections).

Digital

A method of manipulating audio signals as sets of numbers. (See Analogue.) Its advantage is low noise and low distortion, and instantaneous access.

Dither

The addition of low-level noise in order to reduce quantization distortion in a digital signal. Quantization distortion occurs when a digital signal is reduced in bit-depth, say, from 24-bits to 16-bits. The distortion appears as a number of unwanted harmonics in the signal. The addition of dither, prior to truncation, removes quantization distortion and, while it raises the noise-floor by a small amount, nevertheless retains audible information below the noise-floor.

Driver

A driver is a piece of software that provides a communication link between a piece of hardware and a piece of software, usually the operating system. The loading of the driver will often boot (or initialize) the hardware device.

Duplex

Full duplex is the simultaneous input and output of signals to and from a device. Frequently used to describe a soundcard's operation. Half duplex describes a device or driver that can only perform one of these operations at a time.

Dynamic Range

The range within which volume can fluctuate measured in decibels.

EBU (European Broadcasting Union)

Organization that manages the audio and broadcasting industry's standards in Europe.

EQ (Equalizer)

An audio manipulation tool that enables alterations to the frequency balance of a sound.

Full Duplex
Simultaneous 2-way communication between two devices. Often ascribed to a soundcard's ability to record and playback at the same time. This is an essential requirement for using a DAW, such as Cubase Sx.

Gain
For audio: the increase in level of a signal in dB. (In the analogue world, gain is the ratio of the output load power and the input load power. It can equally be applied elsewhere.)

Harmonic
A frequency that is an integer multiple of the fundamental frequency.

Headroom
The difference between an audio signal's level and the maximum level available. In digital audio there is an absolute maximum level ceiling; this is called 0dB FS (Full Scale). When an incoming audio signal is at too high a level it will reach this limit and information will be lost; a process called clipping. In an analogue environment, headroom is the amount that a signal can be increased above the current level before overload distortion occurs.

Hertz (Hz) or Cycles/Second
The unit of measurement for frequency. Most often used in relation to the pitch of a sound. The higher the frequency, the higher the pitch. Human hearing has a range of approximately 20Hz to 20kHz.

I/O
Shorthand for input/output.

Impedance
Measurement of the restriction of flow of an alternating current.

Latency
The delay between generating a sound and its output, whether audible or recorded.

MIDI (Musical Instrument Digital Interface)
A standard serial, asynchronous communication protocol defined in the MIDI Specification that is used to exchange musical information, such as: note pitch and velocity, tempo, etc.

MIDI Clock
A tempo-based MIDI Message. MIDI Clock messages are sent at the rate of 24 per 1/4-note. Used to synchronize devices to a song's tempo. Note that VSTi's now (since v2.0) receive MIDI Clock automatically.

MIDI Controller (or CC - Continuous Controllers)
A type of MIDI message that has a predefined role, such as adjusting Pan, Volume or Pitch-bend. A complete list is given in Appendix 5: MIDI Controllers List.

MIDI Event
A recorded MIDI message.

MIDI Interface
A piece of hardware that plugs into a computer with a number of MIDI inputs and outputs allowing MIDI messages to be routed between the external devices and the computer. The interface usually connects to a USB, serial or parallel port on the computer.

MMC (MIDI Machine Control)
MIDI messages that allow the transports of external devices (such as ADATs or hard disk recorders) to be controlled from a DAW.

MIDI Message
Formatted data that is passed from one MIDI device to another. For example: MIDI Clock, Note On, Note Off, Program Change.

MTC (MIDI Time Code)
A time-based synchronization protocol that functions over MIDI. It is analogous to SMPTE (timecode), and converters exist from one to the other.

Phase Shift
The displacement of a wave in time. When two signals with similar content are mixed and one is phase shifted, then cancelation can occur.

Plug-ins
Software audio effects.

Punch In
A technique for overwriting a small section of an audio take. Often used to correct a small error or fault in a take.

Quantize
A process whereby MIDI events (and sometimes audio events) are aligned in a defined manner. Most simply, events would be aligned on some fraction of a bar (i.e. 1/4 beat, 1/16th, etc.). It can be use both for "correcting" a section of MIDI or creatively to generate movement, or other effects.

Root Mean Square (RMS)
The square root of the mean value of the squares of the instantaneous values of a varying quantity over some period of time (often over one period of a periodic function).

Routing
The path a signal takes through devices or components.

Sample Rate
The number of times per second that samples are taken when converting an analogue signal to digital. Typically this would be at rates of 44.1kHz or 48kHz.

If the recorded audio is played back at a different sample rate than when recorded, then it will be both pitch-shifted and of a different duration.

Serial (communication protocol)

The sending device only sends one message at a time. The alternative is a parallel protocol, where multiple messages are sent at the same time. MIDI, for example, is a serial protocol. Thus, even if you have two MIDI notes with the same start position going to the same MIDI port, they will nevertheless be sent to the receiving device at different times, one after the other.

Signal to Noise Ratio (SNR)

The ratio of the magnitude of the audio signal level to the noise floor measured in decibels (dB). Hence, a larger SNR indicates less noise. There are a variety of SNR's (e.g. measured instantaneously or over time).

SMF (Standard MIDI File)

Files of a standard format (there are in fact a variety of formats) that enable streams of MIDI events to be move from one software application or piece of hardware to another.

SMPTE (Society of Motion Picture and TV Engineers)

[pron: simpty] 1. US-based film and audio standards organization. 2. A format of timecode that is audio-based.

S/PDIF (Sony/Philips Digital Interface)

A type of digital-to-digital interface that usually runs over RCA terminated cables. (See AES/EBU).

SYSEX (System Exclusive)

MIDI message type that enables almost free format communication between MIDI devices. Typically a device will send SYSEX, which is recorded for later playback to the same device. An example of use would be the dumping of a device's patch information to a DAW, so that the DAW could automatically load the patch at playback. As digital storage and memory has become larger, faster and cheaper, the need for SYSEX has declined.

Timecode

A time-based synchronization reference signal either recorded as audio (e.g. SMPTE), or sent as messages (e.g. MTC). A timecode message is formatted as follows: Hours : Minutes : Seconds : Frames : Sub-Frames The number of frames is varied for different timecode formats (between 24 and 30). There are 80 sub-frames to a frame.

USB (Universal Serial Bus)

Computer interface for external devices (e.g. MIDI Interface).

Word Clock

Sample rate frequency synchronization signal for digital devices. A high quality master word clock is an essential item in a digital studio.

Appendix A

Cubase Sx's Plug-ins and VSTi's

Out of the box, Cubase Sx comes with a large number of VST audio effects plug-ins and seven VSTi's. As well as these audio plug-ins, fourteen MIDI effects plug-ins are provided.

The MIDI Effects are described in the chapter *MIDI realtime parameters and effects* of the *Cubase Sx: Operations Manual*. The audio plug-ins are described in detail in a number of PDF manuals provided with Cubase Sx which follow:

1. *Cubase5 Instruments*
2. *Cubase5 Plug-Ins*
3. *Earlier Plug-Ins*
4. *Effects Parameters*
5. *Cubase Sx: Operations Manual*

These numbers will be used in the tables below to indicate in which manual you can find the appropriate detailed description.

The plug-ins are listed here by type with a brief subjective view on their suitability for their intended task.

A list of all the plug-ins and VSTi's available to Cubase Sx, along with a variety of information about them. This can be viewed by opening the *Devices/ Plug-in Information* window (see figure A.1).

Of particular interest are the columns showing:

○ Number of inputs and outputs
○ VST version (tempo sync requires v2.0 and greater)
○ Delay in samples (which is compensated for automatically on Insert channels, but not on Groups or Sends)

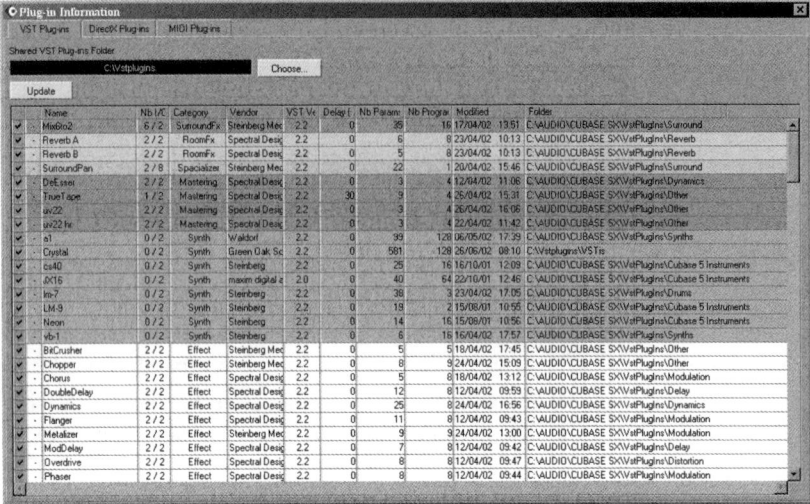

Fig. A.1: Plug-in Information

Sharing Cubase Sx Plug-ins

Below is a list of all of the plug-ins supplied with Cubase Sx with an indication of whether they can be shared with other applications or not. As you can see, very few of your plug-ins can be used elsewhere.

Sharable plug-ins	Sx only VSTi's	Sharable VSTi's
Autopan (3)	A1 (5, ch. 9)	LM-9 (1)
Choirus (3)	CS40 (1)	Neon (1)
Choirus2 (3)	JX16 (1)	VB-1 (1)
Espacial (3)	LM-7 (1)	
Fuzz Box (3)		
Grunelizer (4)		
Karlette (2)		
Scopion (3)		
Stereo Echo (3)		
Stereo Wizard (3)		
Wunderverb3 (3)		

	Cubase Sx only plug-ins	
Autopole (2)	MIDI Gate (4)	Rotary (4)
BitCrusher (4)	Mix6to2 (4)	SMPTE Generator (4)
Chopper (4)	ModDelay (4)	Step Filter (4)
Chopper2 (2)	Mysterizer (2)	subBass (2)
Chorus (4)	Overdrive (4)	Surround Panner
Da Tube (4)	Phaser (4)	Symphonic (4)
DeEsser (4)	PhatSync (2)	Tranceformer (4)
Distortion (2)	Quadrafuzz (4)	Tranceformer2 (2)
Double Delay (4)	Reverb (2)	TrueTape (5, ch. 2)
Dynamics (4)	Reverb32 (2)	UV22 (5, ch. 8)
Flanger (4)	Reverb A (4)	UV22HR (5, ch. 8)
Metalizer (4)	Reverb B (4)	Vocoder (4)
Metalizer2 (2)	Ring Mod (2)	VST Dynamics (4)
MIDIComb (2)	Ring Modulator (4)	VST DX (n/a)

Supplied Audio Effects Plug-ins

Delay
DoubleDelay	Flexible and useful dual delay with tempo sync
Karlette	4-tap delay with tempo sync
ModDelay	Simple delay with pitch modulation and tempo sync
Stereo Echo	Separate left and right channel delays

Distortion
Datube	Tube amp simulator
Distortion	Versatile distortion with selective LP filter
Fuzz Box	Aggressive distortion pedal
Overdrive	Guitar amp simulation
Quadrafuzz	Excellent multi-band distortion. Drums, drums,...

Dither
UV22 HR	8, 16, 20 and 24-bit dither
UV22	16-bit only dither

Dynamics and Pan
Autopan	Simple auto-pan without tempo sync
DeEsser	Sibilance reducer
Dynamics	Gate compressor and limiter
MIDI Gate	MIDI activated gate
Stereo Wizard	Stereo width enhancer
VST Dynamics	Gate compressor and limiter with auto-level and soft-clip

Filter

Autopole	Dual Filter (LP, HP, BP and Notch) with LFO tempo sync
PhatSync	Pattern controlled filter (LP, BP, HP) with tempo sync
StepFilter	Pattern controlled filter (LP, BP, HP) with tempo sync

Modulation

Choirus	Chorus plus flanger (updated by Choirus2)
Choirus2	Chorus plus flanger
Chorus	Standard chorus
Flanger	Standard flanger with tempo sync
Metalizer/2	BP filter with variable frequency and width with tempo sync
MIDIComb	MIDI activated comb filter
Phaser	Standard phaser with tempo sync
Ring Mod	Standard Ring Mod
Ringmodulator	Ring Mod with LFO tempo sync
Rotary	Classic Leslie effect with MIDI control of speed
Symphonic	Auto-pan, chorus/flange, and stereo enhance in one
Tranceformer	Dual oscillator ring mod with tempo sync
Tranceformer2	Dual oscillator ring mod with tempo sync

Other

Bitcrusher	Distortion by bit reduction. Decimate your sound.
Chopper	Combined tremolo and auto-pan with tempo sync
Chopper2	Combined tremolo and auto-pan with tempo sync
Grungelizer	Lo-fi noise and static generator
Mysterizer	Interactive multi-effect
subBass	Pitch-tracking low freq generator
TrueTape	Tape emulation (for use during recording only)
Vocoder	Flexible vocoder with optional MIDI control of internal carrier

Reverb

Espacial	Reverb effect
Reverb	Simple reverb
Reverb32	Simple reverb with LP and HP filters
Reverb A	Simple reverb with LP and HP filters
Reverb B	Simple reverb
Wunderverb3	Cheap and cheerful reverb

Surround

Mix6To2	6 channel to 2 channel surround mixer
Surround Panner	Surround positioning panner

Tools

Scopion	Single channel oscilloscope
SMPTE Generator	Sends SMPTE time code to audio output

Supplied VSTi's

A1	Dual osc synth with FM and PWM, single sync'd LFO, filter (4 types), chorus/flanger
CS40	Dual osc synth,single sync'd LFO, and LP filter
JX16	Dual osc synth with PWM, single sync'd LFO, filter (LP, BP, HP) and chorus
LM-7	Simple 12 sound drum machine
LM-9	Simple 9 sound drum machine
Neon	I'm sure someone loves it!
VB-1	Virtual bass, based on physical modelling

Supplied MIDI Effects

The MIDI Effects are described in chapter *MIDI realtime parameters and effects* of the *Cubase Sx: Operations Manual*. (See appendix D, page 339 for a complete list of MIDI Controllers CC). The use of MIDI effects, along with more detailed descriptions, can be found in chapter 13, page 151.

MIDI Effects

Arpache	Straightforward MIDI arpeggiator
AutoPan	An LFO for MIDI controllers
Chorder	1. Assign any chord to any single note
	2. Assign one chord and the note transposes it
Compress	Compressor-like control of MIDI velocities
Control	Slider control of up to 8 MIDI controllers
Density	Randomly reduces or adds new notes. Effective.
Micro Tuner	Use alternative tunings
MIDI Echo	Flexible MIDI echo with pitch variation, quantize, length and rate control
Notes to CC	MIDI Controller generator from notes
Quantizer	Does exactly what it says on the tin
Step Designer	Pattern sequencer (does not use MIDI input)
Track Controls	GS and XG control panel
Track FX	Duplicates Track Parameters with added functions
Transformer	Real-time version of the Logical Editor (see page 164)

Appendix B

Key Commands

Below is a full list of Cubase Sx's default Key Commands. The *Process Plug-in* section is not included, since this will differ for each user. Remember that you can assign a Key Command for any plug-in, since this can be a big time-saver. The Key Commands for *Score* are provided in a second list that follows the main list. These lists are handy references, so please feel free to photocopy and use as you wish.

One way to keep your Key Commands selection handy is take a photo-copy then cover the paper in clear plastic film and anchor it under your keyboard. Another suggestion is to skim through the list once a month, just to remind yourself of the available Key Commands.

Where a Key Command is used in a lot of places, such as *Devices/Set-up*, then the term *Many* has been used. Common operating commands, such as Cut and Paste, are labeled *Common*.

Nudge top and bottom can be used to assign additional keys to the up and down cursors.

Command	Key	Page
Add Track		
Audio		48
Folder		48
Group Channel		48
MIDI		48
Marker		48
Master Automation		48
Multiple		48
Video		48
Analyze		
Spectrum Analyzer		252
Statistics		252
Audio		
Adjust Fades to Range	A	192
Bounce		218
Close Gaps		99

Command	Key	Page
Create Regions		100
Crossfade	X	194
Detect Silence		230
Dissolve Part		85
Event as Region		86
Events from Regions		86
Events to Part		85
Find Selected in Pool	Ctrl+F	217
Freeze Edits		222
Minimize File		215
Open Fade Editors		193
Open Process History		220
Remove Fades		192
Snap Point To Cursor		109
To Origin		215
Devices		
Generic Remote		272
MIDI Device Manager		117
Plug-in Information		224
Set-up		Many
Show Panel		65
Time Display		65
Track Mixer	F3	234
Track Mixer 2		234
TrueTape		176
VST Inputs	F5	175
VST Instruments	F11	124
VST Master Effects	F7	236
VST Master Set-up		254
VST Outputs	F4	234
VST Performance	F12	64
VST Send Effects	F6	232
Video	F8	210
Edit		
Auto-scroll	F	101
Back (Move to)		104
Copy	Ctrl+C	Common
Crop Range		111
Cursor (Move to)	Ctrl+L	104
Cut	Ctrl+X	Common
Cut Time	Ctrl+Shift+X	111
Delete	Del/Back	Common
Delete Time	Shift+Back	111

Command	Key	Page
Duplicate	Ctrl+D	104
Fill Loop		104
Front (Move to)		104
History		220
Insert Silence (Range)	Ctrl+Shift+E	190
Left Selection Side to Cursor	E	188
Lock	Ctrl+Shift+L	106
Move Insert Cursor To Part Start		144
Mute	M	106
Mute Events	Shift+M	106
Mute/Unmute Objects	Alt+M	106
Open (Editor)	Ctrl+E	38
Open Drum Editor		137
Open Key Editor		135
Open List Editor	Ctrl+G	138
Open Scores	Ctrl+R	290
Open/Close Editor	Return	Many
Paste	Ctrl+V	Common
Paste Time	Ctrl+Shift+V	143
Paste Time at Origin		111
Paste at Origin	Alt+V	104
Record Enable	R	20
Redo	Ctrl+Shift+Z	219
Repeat	Ctrl+K	104
Right Selection Side to Cursor	D	188
Select All	Ctrl+A	102
Select All on Tracks		102
Select Event		101
Select None	Ctrl+Shift+A	102
Select from Cursor to End		102
Select from Start to Cursor		102
Select in Loop		102
Snap On/Off	J	108
Solo	S	20
Split Loop		106
Split Range	Shift+X	185
Split At Cursor	Alt+X	105
To Real Copy		217
Undo	Ctrl+Z	219
Unlock	Ctrl+Shift+U	106
Unmute Objects	Shift+U	106

Command	Key	Page
Editors		
Show/Hide Infoview	Ctrl+I	61
Show/Hide Inspector	Alt+I	45
Show/Hide Overview	Alt+O	47
File		
Cleanup		305
Close	Ctrl+W	Common
Export Audio Mixdown		246
Export MIDI File		211
Export Pool		206
Import Audio file		206
Import Audio from Video		Bug
Import Cubase Arrangement		210
Import Cubase Part		210
Import Cubase Song		210
Import MIDI File		211
Import Pool		206
Import Video file		210
Import from Audio CD		208
Key Commands		31
New	Ctrl+N	28
Open	Ctrl+O	Common
Page Set-up		Common
Preferences		34
Print		Common
Quit	Ctrl+Q	Common
Revert		27
Save	Ctrl+S	27
Save As	Ctrl+Shift+S	27
Save New Version	Ctrl+Alt+S	27
Save Project to New Folder		303
Save As Template		34
Hitpoints		
Calculate		98
Create Audio Slices		99
Create Groove Quantize		162
Divide Audio Events		100
Media		
Conform Files		204
Convert Files		214
Create Folder		202
Empty Trash		214
Find		205

Command	Key	Page
Find Missing Files		203
Import Medium		206
Insert into Project at Origin		217
Insert into Project at Cursor		217
Insert into Project at Timecode		217
New Version		212
Prepare Archive		304
Reconstruct		205
Remove Missing Files		205
Remove Unused Media		214
Select In Project		217
Set Record Folder		202
Update Origin		215
MIDI		
Delete Controllers		168
Delete Doubles		168
Delete Notes		168
Delete Overlaps (mono)		169
Delete Overlaps (poly)		169
Dissolve Part		127
Drum Map Set-up		120
Fixed Lengths		168
Fixed Velocity		170
Freeze Quantize		159
Iterative Quantize		159
Legato		168
Logical Editor		164
Merge Midi in Loop		128
O-Note Conversion		124
Pedals To Note Length		169
Quantize	Q	159
Quantize Ends		159
Quantize Lengths		159
Quantize Set-up		160
Reset		114
Restrict Polyphony		169
Reverse		170
Toggle MIDI Input		144
Toggle Step Input	0	144
Transpose		168
Undo Quantize		158
Velocity		169

Command	Key	Page
MIDI Quantize		
Auto Quantize On/Off		129
Set Quantize to 1th		291
Set Quantize to 2th		291
Set Quantize to 4th		291
Set Quantize to 8th		291
Set Quantize to 16th		291
Set Quantize to 32th		291
Set Quantize to 64th		291
Set Quantize to 128th		291
Toggle Quantize Triplet		291
Toggle Quantize Dotted		291
Select Next Quantize		291
Select Previous Quantize		291
Navigate		
Left	Left Cursor	Common
Right	Right Cursor	Common
Up	Up Cursor	Common
Down	Down Cursor	Common
Add Left	Shift+Left Cursor	Common
Add Right	Shift+Right Cursor	Common
Add Up	Shift+Up Cursor	Common
Add Down	Shift+Down Cursor	Common
Nudge		
Start Left	Ctrl+Left Cursor	105
Start Right	Ctrl+Right Cursor	105
End Left	Alt+Left Cursor	105
End Right	Alt+Right Cursor	105
Left		104
Right		104
Top		See note.
Bottom		See note.
Graphical Left		Score
Graphical Right		Score
Graphical Top		Score
Graphical Bottom		Score
Process		
Envelope		227
Fade In		227
Fade Out		227
Gain		227
Merge Clipboard		227
Noise Gate		227

Command	Key	Page
Normalize		227
Phase Reverse		227
Pitch Shift		227
Remove DC Offset		227
Reverse		227
Silence		230
Stereo Flip		227
Time Stretch		229

Process Plug-ins

All VST & DirectX plug-ins can be assigned key commands.

Project

Auto Fades Settings		196
Beat Calculator		94
Bring To Front		45
Hide All Automation		258
Notepad		65
Open Browser	Ctrl+B	79
Open Markers	Ctrl+M	73
Open Master/Tempo Track	Ctrl+T	73
Open Pool	Ctrl+P	201
Remove Track		48
Set-up	Shift+S	62
Show Used Automation		258

Score

Available Key Commands follow in a separate list.

Set Insert Length

1/1		134
1/2		134
1/4		134
1/8		134
1/16		134
1/32		134
1/64		134
1/128		134
Toggle Dotted		134
Toggle Triple		134

Tool

Next Tool	F10	54
Previous Tool	F9	54
Select Tool	1	54
Range Tool	2	54
Split Tool	3	54
Glue Tool	4	54

Command	Key	Page
Delete Tool	5	54
Zoom Tool	6	54
Mute Tool	7	54
Draw Tool	8	54
Play Tool	9	54
Drumstick Tool		142
Hitpoint Tool		99
Scrub Tool		54
Tool 1		54
Tool 2		54
Tool 3		54
Tool 4		54
Tool 5		54
Tool 6		54
Tool 7		54
Tool 8		54
Tool 9		54
Tool 10		54
Transport		
Panel	F2	67
Start	Enter	61
Stop	Pad 0	61
Start/Stop	Space	61
Record	Pad *	177
Rewind	Pad −	68
Forward	Pad +	68
Cycle	Pad /	70
Loop Selection	Shift+G	72
Locate Selection	L	72
Locators to Selection	P	75
Return to Zero	Pad . (point) , (comma)	20
Goto End		76
Restart		39
Play to Next Marker		76
Play from Selection Start		72
Play from Selection End		72
Play to Selection Start		72
Play to Selection End		72
Play Selection Range	Alt+Space	72
Nudge Up	Ctrl+Pad +	69
Nudge Down	Ctrl+Pad −	69
To Left Locator	Pad 1/Shift+1	76

Command	Key	Page
To Right Locator	Pad 2/Shift+2	76
To Marker 3	Pad 3/Shift+3	76
To Marker 4	Pad 4/Shift+4	76
To Marker 5	Pad 5/Shift+5	76
To Marker 6	Pad 6/Shift+6	76
To Marker 7	Pad 7/Shift+7	76
To Marker 8	Pad 8/Shift+8	76
To Marker 9	Pad 9/Shift+9	76
Locate Next Event	N	72
Locate Previous Event	B	72
Locate Next Marker	Shift+N	76
Locate Previous Marker	Shift+B	76
Set Left Locator	Ctrl+Pad 1/Ctrl+1	74
Set Right Locator	Ctrl+Pad 2/Ctrl+2	74
Set Marker 3	Ctrl+Pad 3/Ctrl+3	74
Set Marker 4	Ctrl+Pad 4/Ctrl+4	74
Set Marker 5	Ctrl+Pad 5/Ctrl+5	74
Set Marker 6	Ctrl+Pad 6/Ctrl+6	74
Set Marker 7	Ctrl+Pad 7/Ctrl+7	74
Set Marker 8	Ctrl+Pad 8/Ctrl+8	74
Set Marker 9	Ctrl+Pad 9/Ctrl+9	74
Insert Marker	Insert	74
Input Position	Shift+P	69
Input Left Locator	Shift+L	75
Input Right Locator	Shift+R	75
AutoPunch In	I	70
AutoPunch Out	O	70
Metronome Set-up		71
Metronome On	C	71
Sync Online	T	269
Sync Set-up		269
Mastertrack On/Off		72
Start Record at Left Locator		178
Use Pre/Post-Roll		70
StartStop Preview		Bug?
Window Layout		
New	Ctrl+Pad0	43
Recapture	Alt+Pad0	43
Organize	W	43
Layout 1	Alt+Pad1	43
Layout 2	Alt+Pad2	43
Layout 3	Alt+Pad3	43
Layout 4	Alt+Pad4	43

Command	Key	Page
Layout 5	Alt+Pad5	43
Layout 6	Alt+Pad6	43
Layout 7	Alt+Pad7	43
Layout 8	Alt+Pad8	43
Layout 9	Alt+Pad9	43
Zoom		
Zoom In	H	57
Zoom Out	G	57
Zoom to Selection	Alt+S	57
Zoom to Event	Shift+E	57
Zoom Full	Shift+F	57
Zoom Preset 2		57
Zoom Preset 3		57
Zoom Preset 4		57
Zoom Preset 5		57
Zoom In Vertical		57
Zoom Out Vertical		57
Zoom In Tracks	Alt+Down Cursor	57
Zoom Out Tracks	Alt+Up Cursor	57
	Ctrl+Up Cursor	
Zoom Tracks Exclusive	Z	57
	Ctrl+Down Cursor	

Command	Key

Score Align Elements
  Bottom
  Center Horizontal
  Center Vertical
  Dynamics
  Left
  Right
  Top

Score Functions
  Auto-group Notes
  Build N-tuplet
  Build Trill
  Clean-up Layout
  Enharm Shift #
  Enharm Shift ##
  Enharm Shift ()
  Enharm Shift ?
  Enharm Shift b
  Enharm Shift bb
  Enharm Shift no
  Enharm Shift off
  Explode
  Export Scores
  Extract voices
  Grace Note
  Hide Empty Staves
  Insert Slur
  Make Guitar Symbols
  Marker Track to Form
  Merge All Staves
  Move All Bars
  Move All Staves
  Move Bars
  Move Staves
  Multi Insert
  Number of Bars
  Optimize All
  Paste Note Attributes
  Score Notes to MIDI
  Select Range
  Show
  Show Marker Track
  Spacer and Hidden to Layout

Command	Key
Spread all Pages	
Spread Page	
String 1	
String 2	
String 3	
String 4	
String 5	
String 6	
Tools: + (1 up)	
Tools: + (1 down)	
Tools: Auto-layout	
Tools: Flip	
Tools: Force Update	
Tools: Get Info	
Tools: Group	
Tools: Hide	
Tools: Make Chord	
Tools: Position Panel	
Voice 1	
Voice 2	
Voice 3	
Voice 4	
Voice 5	
Voice 6	
Voice 7	
Voice 8	

Score Meter Scale

Command	Key
Zoom 50%	
Zoom 75%	
Zoom 100%	
Zoom 120%	
Zoom 200%	
Zoom 300%	
Zoom 400%	
Zoom 600%	
Edit Mode 50%	
Edit Mode 80%	
Edit Mode 100%	
Fit Page	
Fit Width	
Hide Unused	
Ruler Off	
Ruler cm	

Command	Key

Ruler inches
Ruler pt
Score Symbol Palettes
Clef, etc.
Custom
Dynamics
Global Symbols
Graphics
Layouts
Line/Trill
Note Symbols
Others
Words
Scores
Accidentals
Chord Symbols
Drum Map
Edit/Page Mode
Export
Find and Replace
Guitar Library
Import
Move to Next Page
Move to Previous Page
Notation Style
Set Font
Set-up Layout
Show Layout List
Spacings
Staff Set-up
Text
Scores Status-bar
Toggle Filter Bar Handles
Toggle Filter Cut Flag
Toggle Filter Grouping
Toggle Filter Hidden Notes
Toggle Filter Hide
Toggle Filter Layout Tool
Toggle Filter Quantize
Toggle Filter Split Rests
Toggle Filter Stems/Beams

Appendix C

Preferences

Below is a full list of Cubase Sx's default Preferences.

Option	Page
Audio	
Create images during record	35
On processing shared clips	35, 213, 226
Snap to zero crossing	35
On import audio files	35, 206, 207
Cycle record mode	179
Use additional level scan for hit-point detection	35
Audio/Time Stretch Tool	
Algorithm	35
Rhythm	35
Accuracy	35
Always use drum mode for close gaps	99
Audio/Broadcast Waves	
Description	176
Author	176
Reference	176
Editing	
Enable record on selected track	177
Mixer selection follows project	239
Auto select events under cursor	102
Plug-ins receive key commands	223
Delete overlaps	36
Link editors	36, 135
Lock event attributes	107
Automation reduction level	36
Drag delay	36
Editing/Tool Modifiers	
Drag & drop – Constrain direction/Copy/Shared copy	36
Erase tool – Delete later events	36
Mute tool – Rubberband mute and unmute	36

Option	Page
Select tool – Slip event	36
Size object –Disable snapping	36
Split tool – Split repeated	36
Event Display	
Colorize background	34
Quick zoom	37
Transparent events	37
Show data on small track heights	37
Show event names	102
Event Display/Audio	
Interpolate audio images	37
Wave image style	37
Show event volume curves always	38
Event Display/MIDI	
Default edit action	38
Part data mode	38
Show controllers	38
Edit as drum when drum map assigned	38
Note name style	38
Event Display/Video	
Show video thumbnails	38
Video cache size	38
MIDI	
Snap record parts to bars	38
MIDI thru active	115
Reset on record end	114
Reset on part end	114
Reset on stop	114
Note On priority	147
Length correction	147
Solo record in editors	147
Record catch range in ms	147
MIDI/Function parameters	
Legato overlap	148
Split MIDI events	148
MIDI/Chase events filter	
Selection of seven MIDI data types	148
MIDI/Filter Filter	
Record and Thru of seven MIDI data types by channel	149
Scores	
Thirteen on/off options	n/a
Number of bars per staff	293

Option	Page

Scores/Event Layer
Assignment of fourteen score objects to one of three layers

Transport

Stationary cursors	76
Locate when clicked in empty space	77
Zoom while locating in time scale	77
Cursor width	77
Return to start position on stop	77
Deactivate Punch In on stop	77
Stop after automatic Punch Out	77
Always use MIDI clock start	77
Show timecode sub-frames	78

User Interface

Auto-save	39
Auto-save interval	39
Show tips	9
Maximum undo	220
On start-up (Project selection)	40
Language	39

User Interface/Controls

Knob mode	41
Slider mode	41
Value box/Time control mod	41

VST

Scrub response speed	42
Auto monitoring	42
VU-meter peak hold time	42, 238
Pre-load Waves plug-ins on start-up	42

Appendix D

MIDI Controllers List

A complete list of all MIDI Controllers.

0	Bank Select MSB	32	Bank Select LSB
1	Modulation wheel	33	Modulation LSB
2	Breath controller	34	Breath LSB
3	—	35	—
4	Foot controller	36	Foot LSB
5	Portamento time	37	Porta LSB
6	Data Entry MSB	38	Data Entry LSB
7	Main Volume MSB	39	Main Volume LSB
8	Balance	40	Balance LSB
9	—	41	—
10	Pan	42	Pan LSB
11	Expression	43	Expression LSB
12	Effect Type Selector 1	44	Effect Type Selector 1 LSB
13	Effect Type Selector 2	45	Effect Type Selector 2 LSB
14	—	46	—
15	—	47	—
16	General Purpose 1	48	General Pur pose 1 L SB
17	General Purpose 2	49	General Pur pose 2 L SB
18	General Purpose 3	50	General Pur pose 3 L SB
19	General Purpose 4	51	General Pur pose 4 L SB
20	—	52	—
21	—	53	—
22	—	54	—
23	—	55	—
24	—	56	—
25	—	57	—
26	—	58	—
27	—	59	—
28	—	60	—
29	—	61	—
30	—	62	—
31	—	63	—

64	Damper/Sustain Pedal	96	Data Increment
65	Portamento On/Off	97	Data Decrement
66	Sostenuto Pedal	98	NRPN LSB
67	Soft Pedal	99	NRPN MSB
68	Legato Pedal	100	RPN LSB
69	Hold 2	101	RPN MSB
70	Sound Variation/Exciter	102	—
71	Harmonic Content/Compressor	103	—
72	Release Time/Distortion	104	—
73	Attack Time/EQ	105	—
74	Brightness/Expander/Gate	106	—
75	–/Reverb	107	—
76	–/Delay	108	—
77	–/Pitch Transposer	109	—
78	–/Flange and Chorus	110	—
79	–/Special FX	111	—
80	General Purpose 5	112	—
81	General Purpose 6	113	—
82	General Purpose 7	114	—
83	General Purpose 8	115	—
84	Portamento Control	116	—
85	—	117	—
86	—	118	—
87	—	119	—
88	—	120	All Sound Off
89	—	121	Reset All Controllers
90	—	122	Local Control
91	FX1 Reverb Depth	123	All Notes Off
92	FX2 Tremelo Depth	124	Omni Mode Off
93	FX3 Chorus Depth	125	Omni Mode On
94	FX4 Celeste Depth (detune)	126	Mono Mode On
95	FX5 Phaser Depth	127	Poly Mode On

Index
